THE SCOTTISH MOUNTAINEERING CLUB JOURNAL

| Vol. XLII | 2012 | No. 203 |

FJORDLAND ICE

By Martin Moran

TO WRITE OF matters Norwegian in these pages admits the guilt of disloyalty to the home country. Scottish winter climbing is absorbing, varied and competitive, and punches far above its weight on the world stage, but the difficulty comes with ice. Even in a great winter like 2010 Scotland simply doesn't produce enough. My defections over the North Sea began in 2005 in the waning days of wrist loops and Russian ice screws. The masses were flocking to Rjukan courtesy of Ryanair, but the true ice domain lies around the western fjords. The hour flight from Aberdeen to Bergen enables the world's biggest icefalls to be reached in less time than it takes to get to the CIC Hut. Seven years of homage have barely dented my excitement. First up was Hydnefossen, the jewel of the eastern valleys and rite of passage to the realm of Norwegian grade VI.

Hideous Hydnefossen

Height is not the issue here. A plunge of 160m is modest by fjordland standards, but this fall is almost twice as wide. Hydnefossen sits at 1000m altitude in the eastern cleft of Veslehødn and exudes its menace over the forested flats of Hemsedal. The top is rimmed by cornices, the approach couloir an avalanche trap. The first ascent is credited to Cubby Cuthbertson and Marius Morstad back in 1980. I'd give a penny for Cubby's inner thoughts on squaring up to this monster. The Ben's Psychedelic Wall is a sideshow by comparison.

Plan A was to grab my best clients and guide it, but the Hyd casts a wicked spell. On the approach we veered off the avalanche track and David got tangled in a birch-clad buttress. As he screamed for a rescue a pony-tailed veteran Italian guide passed with his client. After one blood-sapping pitch under bombardments of powder sloughs and Italian ice

Vettisfossen – 'the highest single-plunge waterfall in Northern Europe.' Photo: Martin Moran.

lumps I called the retreat. We abseiled off and watched our victors inching their way through the cauliflowered walls above.

Plan B saved the rematch for my next day off. With twin support of 17 year old son Alex and Scotland's own aging hippy, Andy Nisbet, we got to the central line first. Here a 20m snow cone gives an enticing start and a tiny cave offers sanctuary under the bulging crux. Nisbet was hampered by a rack of rusting Snargs and recent memories of a fractured femur on *Poachers Fall* so declined the lead. Alex was an inquisitive observer. A narrow 80° ramp led to a maze of broccoli heads choked with powder. A long and lonely diagonal line on precarious axe hooks led towards a tiny pulpit above roofs. Loop-trapped forearms slowly drained of all strength and feeling. Left eight metres short with just two ice screws left I faced a dilemma: save the screws for the stance and risk a massive swing into space for either father or son, or put in one now for protection and risk the inadequate belay? I opted for the swing, but neither Alex nor Andy obliged. They arrived intact but duly impressed.

A tussle with terror took me back right across vertical shields and into a soaring corner. Smoother ice brought solid placements and a sense of control was regained when a flurry of chipping excavated a snug belay cave. After another 20m the angle eased off to 70°, 15m under the cornice loom. It seemed enough and as darkness gathered we spun to ground in three huge abseils. I was sure that flickers of Aurora Borealis glowed over the northward ranges or was I just adrenalin-drunk? Lessons were learnt. This was a whole new game. Leashless climbing, monopoints and a 16 strong rack of Turbo Express screws were requisite on all future adventures. Scottish VII, 7 hardly tells the tale.

The Might of Thor

Take the lonely drive from Hemsedal over the drifted plateaux, steer down the hairpins into the trench of Lærdal and behold the promised land. Hydnefossen stands alone but in Lærdal every bend of the E16 brings astonishing lines of ice into view. Oblivious, the truckers rumble through the sombre walls by day and night on the Oslo-Bergen run. The side valley of Råsdalen holds the greatest wonders, a series of 1000m canyons or *gjeli*, so steep that one cannot give glaciers the credit for their creation. Mighty Thorfossen plunges down Klypegjeli, 500m tall with a lower fall attractively offset from a stupendous upper plunge. The upper fall rarely touches down but Guy Lacelle got in from the side on the likely first ascent. Will Gadd came in 2005 and dry tooled the gap, placing six bolts for protection.

Extreme guiding ratios were required on this occasion. Irishman Dave Hollinger bolstered the professional contingent to make the odds 1:2.

Martin Moran starting out on Hydnefossen (VI, WI 5+/6), Hemsedal.

The lucky client was Russ Chapman, a burly heating engineer who drove a van to work with livery proclaiming the size of his tool. He seemed just the sort of man we needed for the task. A grind up the lower gulch reached the lower fall. This monster of verticality soared a full 60m to stretch both ropes and credulity. With this despatched, easier ice steps took us into the central basin, which we quitted on the right side by icy grooves. Deep powder snow smothered the 50° terrace that led us back left for 100m to gain the upper fall above the missing icicle. Now Dave led a 60m pitch of unyielding blue ice to a hanging belay. Russ seconded with trademark ferocity, yelling 'Gerr in there!' with each swing of his Quarks. I could barely keep up.

A little midday sunshine crept reluctantly into our canyon and the improbability of our situation became evident. We gazed giddily down the 800m canyon to our car parked by the raspberry canes of Råsdalen's summer orchards. A series of convex snow-caked mountain bulwarks framed either side of Lærdal, each the size of Ben Nevis. Above them, white clouds and blowing spindrift shrouded the high plateaux. I imagined the vast volume of water that would plunge down here with uninterrupted fury on a wet summer's day. Only my pocketful of wine gums gave comfort and succour.

The fall briefly relented at a snow apron under the final 80 metre curtain. Dave continued up perpendicular grooves and pillars to gain a tiny cave. I claimed the finale, which bridged over a bulge into a tight funnel. The ice became increasingly wet and colonnaded as I reached the terminal umbrella where winds had drawn the icicles into outward-pointing spears. Suddenly, the fall ended at a measly spring of water surrounded by moss, with nought but scattered birch trees and a grey sky above. Our altitude was 1150m.

A thread of old rope through a jammed rock flake gave a sure start for descent. The five ice thread abseils included a dramatic swing off the huge stalactite that hung 20m over the bottom tier. This was Russ's fourth year of Norwegian ice and he knew the game was up. He would never do a greater climb than this and so he never came back.

Ardalstangen's Double Whammy

The Sognefjord is the greatest glacial trench in Europe, its waters dropping to 1000m in depth and its enclosing walls soaring to 1500m in a dizzy sweep of vertical birch wood and overhanging rock scars. At its head the smelting towns of Ardalstangen and Øvre Ardal make a grim industrial landscape. Fort William seems like Elysium by comparison. Ardal's winter fumes are eternally trapped in the sunless valley floor, but its ice production is also conducted on an industrial scale.

During a scouting mission in 2009 Martin Welch and I spotted astounding double pillars of ice in the forests above the Ardalstangen. Although just 300m above the valley they were invisible from the main

Double Whammy (350m V, WI6) – Martin Moran starting on the 1st pitch of the upper pillar.
Photo: Martin Welch.

road, and there was every chance that these slender pencils had never been climbed. We stood abreast of the first pencil at dawn. The angle was unbroken at 85° and we guessed its vertical height at 100m – later revised to 120m! We led through on three pitches of 45m, 50m and 45m at an unyielding WI5 standard. We clambered into a miniature rock amphitheatre to be confronted with the upper pencil, which was both higher and steeper with a free-standing pillar near its exit. We needed to raise our game to get up this in the four remaining hours of daylight.

The first wall proved twice as high as expected. I attacked with intent placing no ice screws until 15m up where the ice broke up into cauliflower formations. Leaving straightforward wall-ice I now had to bridge and jink my way from cavity to cavity pulling gingerly on hooks over the flowers and placing ice screws wherever a solid runnel materialised. I stretched the rope to a solid belay. The pillar looked close and as Martin led through I condescended, 'Thirty metres of grade 4 and we'll be at the icicle.' An hour later and with just three metres of rope left Martin made a belay, still 20m under the crux pillar. I seconded in mute humility. Now it was dark, the orange glow from the smelting factories offering the best available light until we switched to torches. I hurried under the icicle which was guarded by a triple-layer of giant sundew formations. Each was four metres high and formidably overhung, so I skirted round to a cave refuge to the left and behind the ice pillar.

We had to face work the next day. The barren night frost had clamped on dampened clothes, gloves and ropes; descent would take at least three hours. There were reasons enough to retreat, without considering the hollow screen of glass ice that formed the pillar, and yet we would never be here again, on the cusp of glory. So I left the cave, placed an axe in the screen and swung out on to the front face, my heels pivoting above a 150m free-fall into the shadowed gulch. Above was a fragile assemblage of organ pipes. I squeezed and bridged between the pipes, then placed a screw which produced alarming creaking from the ice. For a moment I regretted my folly. There was no way back and no hope of an early rescue if this went wrong. I squirmed upwards for another eight metres until I found solid blue ice, which offered better protection and positive progress. After another ten metres I reached an easement. We were still 40m from the top of the pillar but the angle was considerably less. By the time Martin joined me the first Abalakov thread was already in place. At seven full pitches this had been a medium length route by local standards. How on earth do they do the really big ones in a day?

Hall of the Mountain King

At 275m vertical height the Vettisfossen is claimed as the highest single-plunge waterfall in Northern Europe and is the most famous of all Norway's falls. Due to its relatively low altitude (400–700m) and the high volume of its feeder river Vettisfossen very rarely freezes completely. The three month freeze of 2010 coupled with relatively dry autumn produced the necessary conditions for an ascent. The Vettisfossen was first climbed in 1977 by Americans 'Hot' Henry Barber and Rob Taylor in one of the most astounding feats of ice climbing of all time, given the equipment of the day. It remains a certain grade VI and had only been repeated 12 or 13 times, the last-known being in 2006. If there is one ice climb you want to do before you die the Vettisfossen has to be it. The downside is that it may be the last ice climb you do before you die given its multitude of hanging ice fangs.

Despite potential negatives I had more than a sneaking interest in this frozen colossus. Vettisfossen is well-hidden 6km up-valley from the roadhead in Utladalen; so I took a walk to check out the conditions. There was no indication of the coming drama as I wandered through the birch woods past Vetti farm, but quite suddenly a remarkable rock canyon opened in the east flank of the valley, revealing vertical rock walls split by a silver plunge. My guess was right – Vettisfossen was in! The base of the canyon was peppered with the debris of fallen icicles. A base cone 90m high reached up to the lip of a cavern where the tendrils of ice from above dropped over to make a delicate curtain. An ominous and persistent splash was audible to the side of the joining curtain where the residual water flow still drained through. The 'kark, kark, kark' of the resident raven echoed round the enclosing walls. Otherwise, there was a terrifying silence. Truly, this is the hall of the mountain king.

I reckoned that the curtain looked thick and dry enough to enable a direct ascent and had no difficulty in co-opting Martin Welch to the plan. Five days later we drove round the Sognefjord and through Øvre Ardal to reach the gate of Hjelle in Utladalen at 4.45 a.m. The parking lot was empty so we would be alone. At first light we scrambled into the amphitheatre over the swathe of fallen ice blocks and prepared to tackle the initial cone. I peered up to the overhang through the morning murk and realised that my crucial curtain and its linking icicle had disappeared in the intervening days since my last visit. Presumably, we were now standing in the debris of the collapse. I was completely spooked. I had been sure that the ice curtain was solid and would only grow with time.

Thankfully Martin got the bit between his teeth. We soloed 30m up the cone and I belayed under the shelter of an ice umbrella while Martin forged quickly upwards to escape the imminent threat from the daggers that were still stuck to the overhang. His lead took us into a massive cavern behind the cone. The upward view was sobering. The water poured from two circular drainage chutes which looked like the thruster cones of a space rocket. Perhaps the growing pressure of blocked water had caused the curtain to collapse. There was not the slightest hope of a climb there, but there was a chance that we could by-pass the overhang using ledges on the rock walls to its right side. A long ramp of glass ice led to a point level with the roof. Above the roof a series of snow-covered ramps and ledges led 30m back to regain the ice. If only we'd brought some rock protection gear!

Martin stepped into the breach and led a hair-raising pitch across the rock wall, linking blobs of snow-ice with very limited protection. Amazingly, the pitch was little more than Scottish grade III in technical standard, but definitely the most stupendous of its grade I've done. Now the climb was back on track. I led a long pitch of WI5 to gain a cave on the right edge of the fall: a gigantic claw of ice that hung overhead. This appendage was attached to the icefall by a slender horizontal arm and had no right to be where it was. I lengthened my belay rope and planned a desperate dive to the back of the cave if the claw snapped. With the passing hours a sense of resignation to such eventualities took root, and was replaced by cautious enjoyment of our remarkable situation.

Martin now led leftward up ramps and through a squeeze-box behind an icicle to gain the centre of the upper fall, where the ice narrowed and steepened into an 80m series of columns and grooves, split here and there by overhangs. This was where 'Hot' Henry reputedly hand-jammed up the icicles with his leather gloves on the first ascent. Martin's arrival at his belay was greeted by an alarming cracking sound that reverberated down to my stance. His stance had a hanging *bosse* of ice fangs as a

Martin Welch on the big traverse on pitch 4 of Vettisfossen (VI, WI6). Photo: Martin Moran.

canopy and sported a glass window, through which he could see the water flowing down the central drainpipe of the fall. He seemed anxious to continue leading through the roofs! Having spent two hours standing under my own 'claw of death' I was more than eager to get out in front myself.

The pitch above overhung about three metres but sported grooves and lips which allowed for funky bridging. Any ice splinters that I kicked off now fell uninterrupted for 150m to hit the bottom cone. The Vetti raven wheeled overhead then settled on a pine tree at the lip of the fall to watch the outcome. After 25m I reached a tight standing stance, wound in three screws to the hilt and relieved Martin of his miseries under the fangs.

With 70m to go the objective threat was steadily diminishing. I could relax and even enjoy the plunge of the abyss beneath and the wider views over to Stølsmaradalen and the Hurrungane range. I contentedly hummed my tune of the day, which inappropriately was Dougie Maclean's 'Solid Ground'. Martin's pitch sported a 10m wall that overhung gently and wrung much of the strength from my upper arms as every move required a lock-off. Martin was on fire today. Perhaps his new diet of Maximuscle protein supplement and malt whisky was working. Previously he had survived on malt whisky alone.

The light was fading as I took to the final pillar on the left of the icefall. The angle stayed vertical but the ice was solid. The drain on muscular resources was unyielding. Each six-metre run-out between protection points became a psychological trial. I drew level with the fringe of trees crowning the canyon and pulled into balance at the very lip of the fall. There was a brief pang of reluctance to leave. Over many years Vettisfossen had become an obsession and now the dream was all but over. I stepped on to the level river bed and lashed myself to the biggest birch within reach.

The thought of abseiling the icefall induced renewed panic. However long it took we would walk down. Within a few hundred metres we struck the trail back to Vetti farm and skipped down its zigzags, floating in the euphoria of relief. Neither the 4km return walk back to the base of the fall to retrieve our sacks nor the 5km slog back to Hjelle dented my energies. For those brief hours in the night I felt boundlessly strong and indestructible. We got back to the car by 9.30 p.m. and at the next dawn two very different characters staggered out of bed to start another day's work![1]

Voldemort is Slain

As a base for the southern side of the Sognefjord Aurland is by far the most congenial spot, for here the sun may shine from early February. Any ice climber who stays at Aurland town will notice the evil eye of Voldafossen winking from the clefted face of the 1211m Voldenosi mountain. The waterfall makes two giant leaps of two hundred metres then funnels its might over a roofed amphitheatre to plunge a further 60m into a hidden lower canyon. This was a big ice baby – beautiful, massive and alluring in equal measure. We dared to believe that it was a winter virgin. Voldafossen is a truly rare bird. Tim Blakemore had inspected the lower pillar in 2010, but it was not formed despite the prolonged freeze. Winter of 2011 had started with extreme cold but a fortnight of thaw in early February had been catastrophic to many ice lines. We saw that the upper tiers of ice were fat but did not expect the icicle to have survived. This could be proved only by hiking up to its base or signing on for the Gudvangen-Aurland boat trip. I took the latter option and my 250 Krone proved well-spent. As we motored up Aurlandsfjord the full line of Voldafossen hove into view including a very plump bottom pillar.

Having invested serious money in the project I laid claim to lead the pillar, provided we could muster some energy on our day off from work. Martin Welch had to suffer the agony of seeing Tim and I set off at 6 a.m. while he packed for his flight home. We had gained barely two hours' sleep due to the drunken revelling of music night at the pub adjoining our cabins, but soon perked to a nose-twitching air temperature of minus

1 We thought our ascent was the first by a British party. Messrs Clothier and Hawthorn followed on our heels a fortnight later, taming Vettisfossen in a weekend hit from Scotland.

The 500m cascade of Voldafossen from Aurlandsfjorden. Photo: Martin Moran.

6°C. After a steady climb on hard névé snow up the wide lower canyon we scrambled through a Tolkienesque maze of chimneys, caves and wooded ribs to reach the side canyon where Voldafossen touches down. In the twilight the pillar was a magical lingam of white ice. Tucking Tim in a cleft on its right, I tackled the frontal face, but was continually deflected rightwards where the ice was steeper but more solid. Every lump I knocked off fell straight into his lap. He withdrew under a curtain of icicles as I reached an obvious crux where the pillar had become detached during the thaw and now presented a horizontal break overhung by febrile flutings of fresh glass ice. Trickles of water added to the discomforts but a rib of bottle-bottom blue ice lay to the right. After clearance of decorative coving I swung over and pulled through the bulge.

The canyon twisted right to the second tier, which was promised to Tim. A 50m pitch of WI4+ barely touched its defences and we were pinned in a cave under a massive stalactite when the sunrise flashed green light through roofs of shattered glasshouses. Tim traversed tenuously for 10 metres to avoid the dripping panes then attacked a drier pillar in the middle of the fall. The verticality of the next 20m necessitated a sequence of lock-offs and extracted a matching series of grunts and gasps from both protagonists. The angle then eased to WI3+/4 and we simul-climbed 80m of calorie-sapping, bullet-proof ice to the top of the tier.

Already it was 2 p.m. as we sweated up the snows to the final and biggest tier. The scenery was majestic. Below us the deep fjord snaked up to Flåm, backed by the vastness of the snow-caked plateaux. Lofty gabbro pinnacles topped by Scots Pines towered on either side. A distant sea eagle flew against an azure sky and another gigantic plug of gleaming ice soared overhead. Here the sun-softened ice became harrowingly insecure to climb. Progressively, we became wet and stressed as Tim led 50m, I led 60 and Tim another 50, all at WI4+ and 5. The sun sank and accumulated moisture in gloves and clothing froze in minutes. Instantly, I felt the dread cold attack and willed myself to follow Tim's last long lead wearing both belay jacket and overmittens. With fear of the cold came fear of the long stressful abseil descent that we must undertake in darkness, for there was no way out at the top save an all-night trek over 1500m summits.

A last pitch gave an easier romp to a final 10m vertical wall. No sooner had Tim joined me than he conjured an exceptional display of Abalakov ice threading and had us lashed to 6mm threads within a couple of minutes. Against the neon strings of Aurland's streets 800m below we threaded the fall in eight 60m abseils. Our swooping descent was accompanied by the terrifying whiplash of flying rope-ends as we cleared each abseil. At 9.30 p.m. we tripped back down the lower gully to the sea shore and were able to send the triumphant text to Martin that 'Voldemort is slain'.

— . —

New routes, big classics – had we done it all? The answer lies through the road tunnels west of Aurland, and is firmly in the negative. Emerge at the Gudvangen garage and prepare to be blown out of complacency. Six hundred metres above the coffee and hot-dog stop, the Kjellfossen suspends a thousand tons of blue ice over the abyss. The 20km trench of Næroydalen from Gudvangen to Stalheim offers an ice climbing Yosemite with a multitude of prodigious lines, some of them close to 1000m in length. Remarkably, no climbing was recorded here until the last decade. Pride of place goes to the Fossilimonster, which cascades eight hundred metres over a rock face to within a stone's throw of the

Tim Blakemore on the first ascent of Hungryfossen (WI6), one of several beautiful climbs discovered in Flåmdal in 2011. Photo: Martin Welch.

main road. Robert Jasper's ascent in 2009 was badly marred by the placement of 15 bolts for belays and protection where the ice was thin, and caused ethical outrage among Norwegian climbers. If Næroydalen is found too oppressive for aesthetic tastes there's Flåmdal, Fortunsdal, Jostedal and a host of other ice realms ringing the Sognefjord to quicken the pulse.

A lifetime is much too short, but that's no reason not to try.

NEIL'S FALL

By Roger Webb

SOMETIMES YOU find yourself in a bad place, you didn't consciously make a wrong decision or even make a wrong decision you were just unlucky. This wasn't one of those occasions. We were in a bad place because we'd pushed our luck and a little foresight would have saved a deal of grief.

I was belayed at the end of the chimney pitch, at the top of the final tower on Orion Face, where the guide book tells you to trend right towards the plateau. I had spent a long time building that belay. My inspiration was the fear that had filled me as I had struggled from the end of the chimney to the nearest available rock. The beautiful ice and névé we had climbed until that point had still been there, but now were covered by nearly a foot of crusty slab that came away in great chunks if touched. From the end of the ice I had chopped and cut that layer away, aware of the fall beneath, digging a trench and burying my axes in the sanctuary of the hard snow below until, having spent longer in that struggle than climbing the pitch, I had gained rock. More time had passed chopping, clearing and trying and testing in typically blank Ben Nevis andesite. I had done my best, but best wasn't much, a tied-off knife blade, a number two rock that seemed half exposed, two ice screws in rubbish, axes shafts in and a sling over a nubbin. To my right a snow slope continued to easier-looking rocky ground, above me was steep rime-encrusted rock but everywhere I looked the ground was loaded with slab that looked like death. I had stamped a stance, wedged my back against a fin of rock and brought Neil up. It was dusk and he was querulous about the delay but sobered by the fear with which I greeted him. We discussed the options, considered retreat but considered the belay and eventually decided 'stick to the rock'.

Neil set off but, to my dismay, not straight up, but trending rightwards as the guidebook says, across the top of the loaded slope. Later I realised that it was now dark, he hadn't seen what I had seen or experienced the terror I had felt before. His interpretation of 'stick to the rock' was keep to the rocky edge, not climb it. On this miscommunication our lives unravelled.

In helpless dread I fed out rope, halfway passed and we were still alive, ten metres and hope edged out dread, five and we were home, the rope hung runnerless but Neil was surely there. I craned my neck to see his dark shadow above, then, a hesitation, a ripple in the white beneath him, fear and terror drove out hope. I braced my back and feet as he accelerated toward me. Hitting something unseen he spun out airborne, a shade in the night, a glint of his face and he was gone but the ropes hissed past still. I remember the feeling well, resignation and regret, he was dead and I was too, I waited for the jerk of the hundred-metre fall to pull me helplessly on, but when it came it was no jerk but irresistible force. My stance collapsed, the ice screws whipped past my face, the peg failed and I was dragged down to eyeball the nut and watch in horror as it squeezed down its crack. The movement stopped.

Time slowed and my reactions improved. Neil's full body weight was hanging on me, I was hanging on a half-in nut whose movement had stopped and the afterthought sling perched on its nubbin. If the nut failed the small swing might take the sling off its perch, if the sling failed the nut would go leaving us both hanging from two axe shafts for an instant before we fell. Without conscious thought I brought my feet up, knees bent, and slammed them into the slope. Fuelled by adrenalin I straightened my legs and got my back against the fin of rock once more. Imminent death was staved off, but what now?

Neil's body hung on the rope; I could detect no movement. I shouted into the night, 'Neil!, Neil! Are you OK?' There was no response, for a lifetime I called but was met by silence. My legs began to quiver from the strain, and then, from beyond the grave, 'I'm alright!' Blessed relief crushed by the killer afterthought, 'I've broken my leg though.'

Whirling thoughts, how bad is this? 'Is it your femur?' 'My leg!' More miscommunication, on that answer I assumed a lower leg, bad but not

Neil high up on the Orion Face, two decades later, approaching the exit chimney. Photo: Al Todd.

awful. In fact his femur was shattered. Coming to a halt, most unexpectedly he considered, he had thought his leg was gone but found it wrapped behind him and had paused to retrieve it by hooking an axe through his crampon before replying to my shouts.

He was in space but on the line of the last pitch and requested a lower to our last belay. I obliged. With a good application of grit he was able to gain it and get some gear in. I tied him off and enjoyed for the moment the absence of his body weight.

A discussion ensued. It was dark, we were in cloud and couldn't see the hut. Neil had a broken leg and I was probably about eighty metres from the top. We could retreat, but would really be in trouble if Neil lost consciousness. We could stay and hope the cloud would clear and try to attract help from the hut, or I could leave to get that help. We decided on the last course. I untied myself and contemplated the problem above.

Below, Neil suffered.

I gave the windslab a miss and set off up the rock above, which was probably harder than anything I'd done all day but somehow it didn't seem so. I remember thinking I should be scared, but I wasn't. I'd gone through fear and come out the other side. I was in control, these days it's called 'the zone', I just knew I wouldn't fall. A pull-through placement put paid to that and I whimpered to the plateau where reality hit me in the face. Now I was on the summit of Ben Nevis in the dark in the cloud and my map and compass were in Neil's rucksack, 'Oh ****!'

Memory, I've got Orion face at my back, keep the cornice in sight, turn right and the summit trig pillar should show up on the left. It did. Walk in a straight line from the pillar to the shelter, keep going for a further 50 double paces. Turn right through a right angle, turn a bit more, remember where the wind is, walk on and you should find your way off the hill. Keeping the wind on my left cheek I passed through an all-white world. I passed an igloo (I swear it!) but no one was in. There were footprints but they went all ways. The ground fell to my left so I trended right, the footprints coalesced and I put my trust in them. About an hour after topping out I dropped out of the cloud, on the tourist track, not far above the halfway lochan.

Meanwhile, Neil was bleeding out internally.

When I left the cloud I had left the snow and now I broke into a jog. Inspired by the lights of Fort William I missed the turn for the Youth Hostel, it was a black night, and arrived in anxiety at Achintee Farm. What marvellous people: the police were called, soup appeared, and undeserved sympathy was given.

Neil by now had found just how useless a bivvy bag is if you can't get in and was freezing as well as bleeding to death in a freshly ripped Gore-Tex blanket. On the plus side, he'd been able to tie his legs together to ease the pain.

The police came, in efficient mode, questioning: Who was I? Was I competent? Could my assessments be trusted? Donald Watt the Lochaber MRT leader came and questioned me further until, satisfied that he knew exactly where Neil was, he decided on an immediate call out. Men pulled from their Saturday night trooped in. I felt guilty but then thought of Neil and got over it. I offered to help, but a wiser head than mine noticed I was cold, wet, stressed and exhausted. The offer was turned down. Instead, I was told I could assist by going in the radio van. 'Why a radio van?' I asked. 'So that the man being lowered can communicate with the men doing the lowering,' was the reply. It was then that I fully realised what this rescue entailed. There was no visibility, it was night, there wasn't going to be a helicopter flyby, it was going to be a man on a very long rope being lowered down Orion Face, picking up Neil and them both then being lowered to the bottom to be picked up by more team members. I wondered at the trust that the man on the rope was placing in his friends and at his confidence. He was called Mick Tighe and he had questions about what he could expect from Neil. I told him that Neil was half Caithness sheep farmer and half German. He thought Neil sounded hardy, I told him that was an underestimate. He asked about injuries, with misplaced confidence I told him 'broken lower leg' and he set off with the wrong splint.

On the hill, Neil kept up the suffering, but the sky had cleared a bit and he had glimpses of view.

I was placed in the capable hands of Kevin Byrne and away we went to take post somewhere near Corpach with lines of sight to the summit and the face. The RAF arrived and were able to lift the team onto the hill. By now it was midnight or past and Neil had broken his leg about seven hours ago. Kevin was occupied with the radio and there was nothing I could do. I had been quite rightly parked where I was accessible in case of need, but unlikely to get into further trouble. With the loss of useful function I found myself damp, depressed and spent; Kevin gave me some coffee. Revived I listened in, Mick was going over the edge and we heard his commentary.

Neil had revived a bit too; he had heard the helicopter and seen lights streaming up from the CIC but still was expecting nothing until morning.

Time passed, all we heard were muttered instructions and curses from Mick. I began to wonder if I'd correctly described Neil's location and my doubts about his survival grew, this futile reverie was interrupted by Mick reporting he could see a light.

Sometimes news is so good you cry, that was my reaction when Mick announced that he had located Neil and he was alive. Kevin chose not to notice and gave me more coffee. We waited while Mick, having dosed Neil with morphine, dealt with the problem I'd given him, and manufactured a splint for a femur. It took him half an hour or so before he was ready to continue the lower. Kevin relayed the news to the summit and then became fully engaged as Mick tried to keep control, warning

Neil and Mick land at the bottom of the Orion Face after their 1000ft lower. Photo: LMRT.

the team above as overhangs came up, or pleading for more or less speed when hanging free.

It sounded like cold misery for all.

A thousand-foot lower, in the dark, in the spindrift, with an injured man trying not show his agony, while you try to sound collected and ignore your own pain as the harness cuts in, all whilst communicating with the people lowering through a third party. On the summit when you should be in bed, sorting out a thousand feet of rope in the snow, lowering one man and then two, their lives in your hands. Waiting at the bottom in the spindrift, stretcher ready, to start the backbreaking carry to where a helicopter can land. Being lowered, down an enormous cliff, in the dark, in the snow, by strangers, while hypothermic and hurting, more trauma in an already traumatic day.

It was bad enough listening and imagining, I'm glad I missed the reality.

At dawn the lower was completed and an hour or so later Neil was in the helicopter. Not bad, accident to hospital in about fourteen hours.

Back at the police station I was briefed and debriefed, then given a lift back to the car. The helicopter flew past taking Neil to Inverness after a stop at the Belford to top him up with blood.

The day was over, but the ripples spread through our lives for years.

Neil finished the route two decades later.

COUNTERING WISDOM
and the art of the designer-epic in 12 easy steps

By Ian Rowe & John Spencer

A MOUNTAINEER of worth has probably survived an epic or two, and values the credibility it may provide in good craic. It is certain that a real epic cannot be planned. But in these days of the commodification of adventure, it is apparent that the sub-epic can be designed. To the unknowing it may resemble a real epic, and that will suffice as reward for the most part. To the knowing, it is simply safer. Some may be under the belief that adventure is a matter of pushing physical and mental boundaries, but when time is getting shorter and abilities are dropping, the designer epic provides an option for the indolent and wise. The primary vector is a selective amnesia which simply ignores the wisdom of the years. No tedious training or pedantic preparation is required. Step by step, the adventure is preserved. Piecemeal ignorance ensures success. The left side of the brain can be subdued if not entirely shut down.

1. No alpine season needed
Yes, we all read the books and how they worked up to the North Faces carrying snowballs and sacs full of rocks. Well, the Engineer's daughter was getting married in the meadow and there was no time for that. There was a huge and fabulous party, the tribes had gathered; old friends were here and we two were, as usual, anxious to confirm that the bodies still worked. The dancing was over; there was a day to spare before everyone dispersed; the time was ripe, and we could surely make it back down before the Brother's barbecue.

2. Pick a route but don't make it a research project
Rumour had it that Tim Auger's *Homage to the Spider* on Mount Louis in the Banff Rockies was a sandbag at 5.8. Well, since most routes in Dougherty's book[1] have been accused of this, there seemed very little point in worrying about it. No point in searching for the beta on the Internet, where it was all documented in gory detail. There's the route, in the one-minute window above the Banff highway. Looks good, the Engineer having been there back in 19-dot – we should make it.

3. Set off late
Take a nephew novice along, since three can (probably) climb as quickly as two. But wisdom momentarily breaks out of its confinement and said 'No', so waste the benefits of the dawn start by meandering over to his digs to explain.

Mount Louis.

On the way, since this is the National Park, take the scenic route, stop for some photos of a roadside grizzly, break for a second breakfast of coffee and bagels, and use the wrong (lower) car park – after all, it was forty years since you were last there. In the same category, overshoot the turn-off on the trail and back up for a few minutes as the sun begins to think about coffee break. Oh, the sweat was good, with the fullish packs. We could still walk up a trail.

4. Ignore progress

At last, the start. A hard-scrabble approach over friable slabs requiring some pitching leads to the fabulous corner. Pause for a sandwich or two, it's lunchtime after all, we like our meals regular. This is the real departure point. The dedicated practitioner may experience at this stage a certain osmosis of wisdom through the membrane of judgment which

Pitch 2
5.8 (sandbag)
5.10a (actual).

may be hard to ignore. One of us may actually know we are too late and already looking at a bivvy. But there are devices to overcome this potential failure; for example, a wee look at the first pitch – we might as well since we've come this far. Up goes the Prof, well done laddie. Then no hesitation to the second and third…he's climbing fast as the skies darken and the sun leaves us for the glum afternoon. Three pitches of sustained climbing – a stretch of off-width here, some jamming there, and ouch, some wide bridging too…we look at each other. Bloody hell, this is harder than 5.8. We have to go home now if we are going to make the barbecue. But then, would we ever be able to do this again? Could we not just make it? Surely the wives and family down below would understand if we were just a little bit late?

A crux then. But simply too easy to give up and make the right decision. The wrong decision was needed, and made with courage; on we went; there's the art, and here comes the epic.

5. Eschew helpful technology 1

A watch can be useful, though longitude is not required. Having forgotten to bring one, and in the absence of a sun and shadows, the only option was to check the time stamp on photographs, and to subtract the required number of hours to compensate for time-zone differences, the camera having been purchased in Australia and never recalibrated. How many hours is Melbourne behind, or is it ahead? Gosh, time's flying. Rain threatens.

6. Get off route and climb above the point of no return

Getting off route is a given. Fortunately in the Rockies this is very easy to do. The Prof duly goes off route, led astray by a renegade peg. Rock features were easily contorted to fit the route description. Onward and upward. Even the obvious no-one-goes-this-way indicators (loose rock, pointless meandering) were rationalised for a while. The much awaited whispers of panic were suppressed, deliciously. Game on. Then precarious reversal and retreat. Back on route.

The Prof was going well. Actually both were. Alpine climbing, trying to hurry, making bold moves and pulling them off. Yarding up cracks and grooves, thrutching over a roof. Until 'returning were as tedious as go o'er.'[2] It was spitting now. If we could just get to the summit, descent would be fine. We just might make it…might even get back for the barbecue. The attainment of self-delusion is a valuable metric here. This is a successful sub-epic.

And then the light ran out – no real surprise, and no need to consult photo time stamp for confirmation. No point in feigning surprise except for the irony. The Class 4 scramble to the summit was not appealing in the wet, in the dark. Or the dogleg rappels, best enjoyed in the morning. Or the sloping rubble ledge on which we now hunkered down. But ah, that nostalgic and familiar thrill of settling down for the night; had forgotten that one. The sweet lights of Banff and the highway flickering in the gloom. Where the people and families lived, clustered around the barbecue…

7. Eschew helpful technology 2
…in full swing by now, we imagined. Wouldn't it be nice to be able to find out how things were going? Perhaps, more importantly, to be able inform anxious friends and family that all was well up on Louis' shoulder. A cell phone in the end might not have been much use, on account of lack of a signal, but the fact is that ours were sitting on the table back at the ranch…next to the watch. At least they weren't getting wet.

8. Drop your food
It was now drizzling. Worse weather had been forecast, but obviously having the ability to update the information would be moot. Here's hoping it holds off.

'I've found a neat little alcove for stuff in the rocks over here' announced the Engineer. That it turned out to be a bottomless alcove meant that one half of our food supplies went a-tumbling into the abyss. So, no caribou steak sandwich, culled from the wedding feast, now returned to the wild. And we're down to two small beef patties, an

The bivouac.

orange, some raisins and a couple of pieces of chocolate. Guerrilla warfare followed, as FARCs of Colombian ground squirrels forayed out of their holes to steal our food. As conversation lapsed, bouts of uncontrollable shivering blended with gentle snoring. Occasionally we awoke and briefly renewed the chatter. Time lengthens, again and again. Fortunately no watch to torment us. The heavy rain holds off.

9. Assume it's all over when you top out

Here is a potential hazard. The protagonists can be overcome with self-deluding relief that the epic is over. There can be awkward tendencies to apologize or invoke awkward bonding gestures. This should be avoided; after all, this is design, not random experience.

10. Screw up the rappels

No, don't do this. Enjoy them in the warming sunny day. Fabulous.

11. Avoid rescue

Now the planned unplanned epic should probably not include rescue as this, if rules were set, would be a disqualification. But the almost-rescue is the pinnacle of the art. It takes a long time (years and years) to plan. For example, it helps to have a partner accustomed to spousal benightment

It's all over?

so that this becomes normal. In this way, the fears of the wedding party will be allayed. In addition the partner will be able to pitch the concern at the correct level when reporting to the Park dispatcher in Banff. The Engineer's reputation as a gnarly old Brit does not hurt. 'Just leave them up there, we'll get them in the morning, they like spending nights out etc., etc.' was the reported response. Have one of the Park Rangers live in your house for a year or so, and when you hear the 'whack whack' of the helicopter as you reach tree line, you may declare 'About bloody time!' and pretend this was arranged.

And sure enough, the chopper lands in the meadow a couple of hundred feet below. Now we wouldn't claim that Ranger B said 'Taxi for Mr R?' or anything like that. But since they were going our way they could offer a lift. And we could see the possibility of accepting. It would assist with their training routine and so would be churlish to decline. Our knees would be grateful to be spared the hammer down. Perhaps we could just fly past the route and take a few snaps on the way?

Certainly not rescued.

12. Be prepared for domestic opprobrium and accept it with good grace

This is one area which requires no planning and is possibly the easiest component to achieve. In some cases it can be achieved without leaving home.

Postscript; oh, the irony

This could negate all that went before. Might it be that this route is forever doomed to sandbag? A wee story, learned from the bear himself at the Calgary Mountain Club reunion:

Tim Auger (the first ascentionist, did we mention?) and Urs Kallen went back the next year to re-equip the route. They spent the night out. This is a rare case of auto-sandbagging. If this was a case of un-wisdoming it certainly beats our own.

— . —

References
1 S. Dougherty, *Selected Alpine climbs in the Canadian Rockies*, Rocky Mountain Books, Calgary, 1991.
2 William Shakespeare, *Macbeth*, III. iv.

The route: *Homage to the Spider*, Mount Louis, 1000+ft, 5.10a, FA T Auger & R Bunyan, August 1987.
<http://www.summitpost.org/homage-to-the-spider-iii-5-10a/426448>

Step 10.

THE DE'IL LEADS BLACK MAMBA

By Iain Smart

THE EVENTS I would like to tell you about now began at the summit of the Capel Mounth, the broad pass that crosses the eastern Grampians from the head of Glen Clova to Glen Muick in Deeside. I left the road end at Braedownie in the late evening and trudged up the track through the deserted glen. The path climbs quickly through the woods into the freedom of the upper air. I reached the summit about the midnight hour and settled down beside the track to relax awhile and enjoy the serene ambience of space and soft colours that hang in the half-light between dusk and dawn on the night of the summer solstice. I had just got nicely tuned in when a man approached. He must have been following ten minutes behind me, yet I hadn't noticed him when I looked back. He had, I suppose, as much right to be there as I had, perhaps even more; he looked somehow as if he belonged. Nevertheless I was enjoying the solitude and felt a little miffed at the intrusion.

'A fine night,' he remarked.

'It is that.'

'Mind if I join you?'

'It's a free country,' I said, without enthusiasm.

He sat down facing me looking south silhouetted against the brightest part of the northern sky. He lent, or rather reclined, against a boulder with his arms behind his head. His face, therefore, was in shadow framed by two triangles of bright light between his bent arms. I made him out to be strong-featured and athletic. He seemed to be relaxed about his intrusion and in a leisurely mood. The last thing I wanted at that moment was a dominant intruder getting between me and the approaching magic of the midnight hour. I radiated displeasure. He didn't seem to notice. Indeed I could feel he had his antennae out. He was registering whatever it is that sensitive people are able to register about other people even when they have retreated into their shells.

He was dressed in tweeds of a distinctive pattern of subdued blues, greens and browns, like a summer hillside. I noticed his waistcoat was uncompromisingly black.

He remained silent for a while, obviously sizing me up, as I was him. Eventually he said, 'I noticed how you trudged so slowly up the glen just now.'

I glared at him.

Then after a pause, as if to let this sink in, he added, matter-of-factly, 'As it happens I have power. I could give you back the elasticity of your youth. I could restore the lengthy stride o'er moorland wide that you took for granted not so long ago.'

I have had plenty of encounters with delusional people in my time and

I wasn't going to put up with this destruction of my tranquillity.

'Man,' I said, with my birse getting up, 'haven't you anything better to do than wander around lonely hillsides thrusting your fantasies on people who would rather be left alone? Why don't you just b***** off? I suppose you think you're Mephistopheles?'

Blandly he replied, 'No, I'm not Mephistopheles. As it happens I'm his boss. I am His Satanic Majesty Himself.'

'The de'il you are,' I exclaimed without thinking.

'At your service,' he answered.

He spoke in a pleasant voice of a Scots provenance with good clear consonants and pure vowels. None of the latter went back up his nose to emerge as triphthongs in the Southron manner. This was no ordinary loony; he had a 'presence'. There was an odd sincerity about him. I had no alternative but to humour him.

'Your Majesty,' I said, wearily, 'I know all about your offer. I have read the story, been to the opera, seen the film, know the ending. Can't you think up anything more original?'

'I obviously underestimated you,' he replied in a friendly tone. 'My offer may not be original but it has a perennial appeal to mortals when their physical powers start to fade. I'll try again later, more subtly the next time. But for tonight let's call a truce. You've no idea how refreshing it is to meet someone experienced enough to see through my ploys. Let's relax and enjoy each other's company.'

Then, giving me a look of appraisal, he said, 'You don't seem too far gone physically to do a climb with me. Let's go over to the Dubh Loch. I have a rope in my sack and I've led a few climbs in my time.'

'Well, what the hell,' I thought, without realising the appropriateness of the expression. 'Why not go for it?' I have spent a large part of my life in the company of eccentrics. I could surely handle this one.

'Okay, my friend,' I replied, 'as it happens I have a lang spoon with me, so I should be safe enough.'

This amused him greatly and we set off together heading westwards over the moorlands wide in the luminous dimness of a midsummer midnight.

'Why are you wasting your time with a run-of-the-mill sinner like me?' I asked. 'I would have thought you were too busy with bankers and multinational wheeler-dealers. Global crime I believe is growing exponentially.'

'Oh, these cattle are well on the way to the everlasting bonfire without my help. After I give them the initial push I leave them to it. I would much rather pass my time in the company of someone like you who can put up some intellectual resistance. It's better for me; keeps me on my toes.'

We walked in companionable silence. I seemed to cover the ground with a lighter step than usual and we made rapid progress towards the

Broad Cairn. However, it's not often you get a chance to have the De'il all to yourself, so I thought I had better make the most of it and get him on his 'subject'.

'Tell me about Predestination?' I asked.

He looked bored, but acquiesced. 'Your brain has two conflicting processing systems,' he began. 'A large part is devoted to ensuring your long and short term survival, at almost any cost and in any situation; your "hard-wired core processing systems" take their task seriously. Therein lies Predestination. You are predestined to make the best attempt you can to survive.'

He went on about this at some length. Eventually he said, 'I'm fed up talking shop. Have you no sense of aesthetics? This is as fine a midsummer's night as I can remember. The air is still; the acoustics are perfect. Let's rest for a while and amplify the ambience with a little music. As it happens I have my fiddle in my sack here.' By now we had covered a couple of miles of moorland wide in less than an hour. This man seemed to have bestowed on me the lengthy stride of yesteryear. He swung down his knapsack, took out a fiddle case and withdrew a venerable, well-cared-for instrument and spent a moment tuning it. I sat down while he played a set of tunes. Some I recognised; others were unfamiliar – wild and strangely beautiful, all played in the eastern style. Gow and Skinner and a hundred others down the ages would have recognised the deep roots from which their inspiration had sprung.

After this unexpected recital, we sat for a moment in silence while the emotional harmonics died away into a deep tranquillity.

After some minutes he seemed to recover his old self.

'Now I suppose you are going to ask me about Free Will?'

'Yes, I would like to know.' Old Nick back on his subject would be worth hearing.

'It lies in the superabundant information processing networks of the human brain.'

I must have looked baffled because he sighed again, as if unnecessarily pointing out the obvious.

'You humans are endowed with surplus brain power – far too much of it, in fact. The evolution of the human cerebral cortex was a big mistake. It has landed you with a prodigious ability to process information and modify the behaviour of your core program for good or ill; therein lies "Freewill" or less grandiosely the wobbliness of your emotions. The conflict between what you call good and evil is deciding how these intermeshed systems will control each other.'

He paused.

'Now that's enough practical theology, let's get on with enjoying the here and now.'

In the here and now we were in the wild land east of the Broad Cairn. As we started our descent towards the Central Gully we became aware of the sound of bagpipes. In the improving light we could make out a small tent about half a mile away on the slopes above us where a man was playing a salute to the dawn. I recognized that most soaring of all pibrochs, *The Old Men of the Shells*. The notes spread over the plateau lands and soared over the dark trench of the Dubh Loch adding an aural dimension to space-time. The tenor and bass drones seemed unusually sonorous in the still air, forming a three-threaded background tapestry to the singing of the chanter.

We stood for a moment while land, light and music interwove in a sett of harmonious sensory impressions – music deeply rooted in the land and its history. All the ambient resonances were in phase. Deep in our surplus brainpower an awareness of ancient days generated itself. I suppose it was what is sometimes referred to as 'folk memory'.

The music followed us as we wandered off to Central Gully. In the improving light we picked our way to the foot of the cliff and traversed right until we arrived at a likely-looking crack. 'This will do,' he said taking a rope of scarlet, silky material from his sack.

'I'll lead of course.'

'Of course,' I agreed. 'This is all your idea.'

'I wouldn't be too sure of that,' he replied.

We climbed the cracks, corners and overhang with, on my part, unfamiliar competence. The cliff was bathed in the glow of the coming sunrise; it was all very exhilarating.

At the terrace we sat down to give me a rest.

'What did you mean by inferring this might be my idea?' I asked him.

'Because I am a construct of your own brain. I reside in your superabundant circuitry. Everything that has happened this morning was already in the model of the world, already created in your own neural networks – in your mind if you wish to call it that. Since you don't want to get involved with me in any serious way, at present I am just functioning as your quality control system. For example, will you claim to have climbed Black Mamba?'

That, as it happened, was the climb we were on.

'Many years ago,' I replied, 'I got up this far, behind the gifted Allan Pettit and the Good Professor Slesser; then it started to rain and we had to traverse off – so it wouldn't be a complete lie; this far anyway.'

'Well the next bit will be. We are off to finish the upper crag.'

We couldn't find the route in the dimness and finished up somehow at the top of the rocks on the edge of the broad plateau just as the sun was rising. The piper on the slope to the west was now playing the *Desperate Battle of the Birds*.

'That last bit we climbed might be a new route,' said my companion. 'I think we were off the line of Blue Max. If it is, what would you like to call it? You choose.'

'How about "The Exciseman"?' I suggested.

This amused him no end – he had a weakness for feeble jokes.

'Very good,' he said.

'Well I must go now. I think I'll have a word with yon fellow piper. I'm going to ask him to play Neil Munro's *Lost Pibroch*, and if you know anything about that I would advise you to get out of earshot before he starts.'

We shook hands – that was real enough. As he walked away towards Cairn Bannoch, he turned and said, 'By the way, I left my Aston Martin in the car park at Braedownie. I don't need it anymore. You can have it with my compliments. The keys are in the ignition and the registration documents in the glove compartment.'

So that was that. The supposed figment of my imagination walked off with his back to the dawn.

It was never my intention to return through Braedownie; the offer of the Aston Martin must have been his last Parthian shaft of temptation. I continued north on my original errand to visit friends near Logie Coldstone on the other side of Muir of Dinnet.

A couple of days later, however, I read in the Dundee Courier that a search had been mounted for someone who had left a customised Aston Martin DB5 in the Braedownie Car Park with the doors unlocked and the key in the ignition. I suppose someone claimed it because the story went dead.

A full transcript of my conversation with this entertaining character (who may actually have been who he said he was) may be had as an e-mail attachment by sending a request to ihms7x7x@btinternet.com

DAS GULLY

By Mark Litterick

I CAME TO Germany a few years ago mainly for work reasons – our engineering consultancy had a requirement and Munich had the possibilities of a nice change. I'm still here. It's not just that Munich is a world-class city and that the Bavarian and Austrian Alps are on the doorstep, but also I quickly discovered that the locals are both friendly and familiar. They have a genuine sense of humour verging on dry Scottish sarcasm and an equally genuine need to party – Oktoberfest (in September), Frühlingsfest (in spring), Starkbierfest (strong beer, during Lent – and why not?), etc. Oh, and of course they have great beer (not on its own a reason for living in a country, surely) and better weather than back home. Much better.

Within a few hours' drive of Munich we have almost all the Austrian ski areas, unbounded ski mountaineering possibilities and spectacular ice climbing. I say spectacular because many of the routes are indeed impressive columns of near-vertical ice threading up the forested valley sides for six or more pitches. It is not hard to find quality routes that provide more actual ice than *Point Five* or *Zero* but you need to keep your skills polished and your screws sharp since most of the pure ice climbing here is steeper and more sustained than back home.

But let's face it; spectacular as they are, these frozen waterfalls are not a patch on the classic ice of Ben Nevis. More ice, steeper, sustained and exciting – yes. The real McCoy – no. *Point Five*, *Zero*, *Orion*, even *Green* and *Comb* – these are world-class mountaineering routes in epic situations which demote the impressive frozen waterfalls in the Alps to cragging status. That is one of the two things I miss most about the mountains of Scotland – the other being the genuine wilderness which simply does not exist in the European Alps.

In the early days I discovered a thin section in my guidebook describing Jochberg, an unassuming little peak in Loisachtal between Munich and Garmisch. The key thing that caught my eye was a reference to 'schottische' style routes with names like 'Linkes Gully', 'Mittleres Gully' and 'Rechtes Gully'. Unimaginative names maybe, but with explicit references to Scotland because they saw fit to borrow our 'gully' word. (Actually 'der Gully' does exist in German but it refers merely to a drain, in this context 'das Gully' has been borrowed to put the route character in context.) There were other interesting things I understood right from the start too – these routes were long, all between 400m and 500m, and the dictionary told me the 'Nordwand' was threatened with falling stones, ice and avalanches. Too late, my appetite was whetted.

With great anticipation I went with a work friend one November day to check out the approach and have a look at the face by way of reconnoitre.

The view south from Jochberg. Photo: Mark Litterick.

The first hurdle as ever was the language – my foetal German at the time was telling me to park the car at the 'third-last hairpin', which makes about as much sense as having 'Oktoberfest' in September. After driving around a bit, observing that all hairpin bends in fact had parking possibilities, we set off and found ourselves on the wrong side of a subsidiary ridge in the forest below Jochberg. Nonetheless, when we crested the ridge we were afforded enough of a view of the impressive face for my resolve to harden.

Later that season I set off with a local ex-pat American climbing friend, Justin, under typically marginal Scottish conditions to have a go. I had of course overestimated the similarity of the routes to real Scottish gullies – yes they climbed gully-like features, but alas I was reminded that it is Scotland's famously variable and dramatic weather fluctuations that bind everything in place with a glorious freeze-thaw cycle. Here on the mainland we don't get that. We did however get reconfirmation of the stonefall and avalanche dangers of such a big face in poor climbing condition. We left for some conciliatory waterfall cragging in the woods with a plan to sit and wait for ideal conditions before we went back to the Jochberg.

Several years later we had a tremendous period of cold clear weather before the big snows of the season arrived. The most recent snowfall was a month old and the ski resorts were suffering – icy pistes polished to a sheen by incompetent side-slipping snow-boarders and dotted with accidents by incompetent over-speeding skiers. Justin and I on the other hand were on our way back to Jochberg. Anticipating crowds, we embarked on a Scottish, if not Alpine, start. In the event we were first at the car park and miles ahead of the nearest followers even at the foot of the face. In our excitement we went right to the middle of the face to consider one of the options. To our disappointment these routes looked

'Das Gully', Pitch 2.

Photo: Mark Litterick.

very lean indeed and the poor quality rock was much in evidence. However on the right was a huge gully with a big fat icefall oozing out the bottom – the obvious choice.

The first three pitches were easy climbing and certainly afforded a nice warm-up – a gentle cascade of continuous ice with steps of not much more than Scottish III, after which a short walking section led us into an awesome amphitheatre. This route was meant to be WI4 and we were now standing speechless below towering icefalls all of which looked vertical and just a little bit scary. Now a peculiar aspect of the German language is that they tend to call a spade a spade (for example a kettle is simply a 'Wasserkocher' or water cooker). However, they have a multitude of phrases for wimp, many of which could be applied in a scenario such as this; for example the descriptive 'Weichei' (soft egg), the mocking 'Schattenparker' (one who parks their vehicle in the shade)

*A climber solos 'Das Gully'
(Via Classica, WI4),
Nordwand, Jochberg.*

Photo: Mark Litterick.

or the ultimate 'Frauen Versteher' (a woman understanderer!). So here I was, not a quarter of the way up this huge face, filled with awe, overwhelmed by choice and on the cusp of understanding women, when some bloke appears and mutters 'Servus' (an informal greeting) and then proceeds to solo the biggest of the icefalls in the amphitheatre.

Our guidebook had no individual pitch descriptions, but the appearance of the solo climber settled the choice, diminished the awe, and destroyed my chances of ever understanding women. After allowing the soloist time to clear the top of the pitch I took a deep breath and set off, immediately enjoying the exciting exposure of a spectacular ice pitch on a real mountainside and not tucked away deep in a wooded valley. This was what we came here for – the Nordwand of Jochberg was emulating the North Face of Ben Nevis. The pitch was hard enough – certainly harder than WI4, more like Scottish VI – but good ice nonetheless.

After several more straightforward pitches we arrived at what we later found out was meant to be the technical crux of the route – a free-standing pillar of vertical ice. However, this was dispatched with no more complications than, say, the icicle pitch of *Smith's*. Around about this point we were tiring and slowing down. Another pair of climbers arrived with smiles and greetings and we all agreed this was a superb day in great conditions. From these mountain comrades we also found out we were only about halfway up the route! What they failed to tell us (or more likely what we failed to understand from the German conversation) was that the remaining pitches were mostly straightforward and time-wise we were well on our way to success. After the main ice pitches on The Ben one gets to flash up bomber névé to the summit crags and waiting sunset, here we were treated to a continuous ribbon of water-ice of about the same 50° angle. Believe my calves when they tell you several hundred metres of 50° hard water-ice is grounds for tears. Only the last section offered snow to release the tension and soon we were lying on the summit slopes sucking in the glorious view over reflective lakes and jaggy peaks to the south with contrasting flat plains towards Munich in the north.

With over 12 ice pitches and some walking sections the 'Das Gully'(aka *Via Classica* WI4) on the Jochberg's Nordwand had delivered even more than we expected. We packed our stuff and headed off into the sunset. An epic descent down an icy path ensued but after the whole day on front points we refused to torture ourselves further and left the crampons off, instead choosing the age-old technique of cursing as protection against the innumerable slips. As we clumped wearily down the final section of the road in the dark the guidebook instructions finally became clear. There was the car exactly where we'd left it many hours earlier, at the third-last hairpin.

SKI TOURING IN THE FRENCH PRE-ALPS

By Peter Stewart

OK SO I KNOW that Scotland enjoyed two of its best winters for a couple of decades with ski touring opportunities to rival the Alps (I read of Roger and Finlay Wild's trans Scotland trip with a degree of envy as this was always a major ambition when I lived in Scotland – conditions and opportunity unfortunately never coinciding). However, this last winter seems to have seen a return to normal.

The Alps of course provide an almost infinite number of options for ski touring from the classic Haute Route between Chamonix and Zermatt to multi day tours on the high mountains of the Bernese Oberland and Monte Rosa, to the Vanoise and Haute Maurienne to mention just a few.

However, maybe the Aravis and Chablais regions of France could provide an interesting alternative for those wishing to mix some ski touring with a bit of piste bashing or even combining with a family holiday. Situated conveniently between Geneva and Chamonix the northern pre-Alps offer numerous summits suitable for ski touring typically between 2000 and 3000m. In the majority of cases these can be comfortably done in a day from a valley base.

Of course, when we think of the French Alps, Chamonix is usually at the top of most climbers and skiers lists of prime destinations, and while not disputing its undeniable attractions for the skier and climber, the areas either side of the A40 Autoroute en route to 'climbing Mecca' have many attractions of their own. For years I took climbing holidays based in the Chamonix valley and drove with blinkers on through this area, not realizing on my way to the Big mountains what a wealth of options it offers.

Geneva of course boasts an international airport and good rail links to the rest of Europe with direct flights from Edinburgh, and economy airlines providing routes via Luton and Gatwick. There is a good choice of catered and self-catering accommodation in the area during the ski season to service the downhill ski areas of the Grand Massif (Samoens/ Flaine etc.) and Portes du Soleil (Les Gets/Morzine /Avoriaz) and all within an hour's drive from Geneva.

The area has much to offer in terms of climbing and general mountaineering, the Cirque du Fer a Cheval in the upper Giffre valley, for instance, offers a large selection of ice routes and is a French National Heritage site and the numerous limestone faces throughout the Aravis and Chablais host multi-pitch and single pitch routes of all grades. The Chaîne Franco-Suisse running from Lac Léman (Lake Geneva) to the Col des Montets and pioneered by the Englishman Alfred Wills offers extensive mountaineering possibilities and is accessible from the upper

Têtes des Lindars ridge and Tête du Colonney, Grande Massif. Photo: Peter Stewart.

Giffre valley. However, the intention here is to give a flavour of some of the ski tours that are available in the area.

Since moving to the Giffre valley from Scotland eight years ago, I have been able to spend many enjoyable days skiing the local hills with a variety of companions ranging from Locals to visiting SMC members and what follows are just some examples of what is on offer.

The 2406m summit of Tête de Bossetan is situated to the north of the Val du Giffre and is accessible from either the south (Samoens) or the north (Morzine) sides. It provides one of the classic ski tours of the area and is often in condition when snow conditions on other summits may be less sure. The approach is via the Col de Golese at the eastern end. There is a refuge here but not open in winter. Early season or when snow conditions at lower levels are marginal, the best approach is usually from the Morzine side. The long broad ridge connecting the eastern top of L'Avouille and the main summit gives fine views of the neighbouring summits including the Dents Blanches, the western summit of which provides an excellent tour from the Samoens side. The ski down is normally by the route of ascent (PD) but if conditions permit, the confident can opt for the grand couloir, first descended on skis by Anselme Baud in 1970, on the impressive north side of the mountain which is graded D and has some 'barres rocheuses' to negotiate. For my first ascent of the Bossetan I accompanied a local who with

Skiing off Tête du Colonney, Grande Massif. Photo: Peter Stewart.

uncharacteristic chauvinism assured me it would be an easy day as his girlfriend would be coming with us. Being used to long days and big sacks on the Scottish hills I smugly assumed a leisurely outing. How wrong I was, toiling at the rear trying to maintain visual contact with the two receding figures in the distance. It was a similar story on the descent, this time due to deficient technique as much as lack of fitness. The guidebook suggests a time of around six hours and approximately 1200m of ascent. Other worthwhile summits in this area are Pointe Rousse des Chambres and Les Avoudrues both of which can be done via the Folly

refuge which while not guarded in winter offers a comfortable, if somewhat cold, winter room equipped with blankets and a gas cooking ring.

Another local classic is the Pointe de Chalune in the western sector of the Chablais. This group of hills despite being close to the relatively small ski areas of Praz des Lys and Sommand provides a number of shorter tours with easy access and views of lake Geneva to the north and the Mont Blanc massif to the south. The normal start point is Bonnavaz on the south east side, with the route of ascent via the Col de Foron. In good conditions the grade is PD+ with 930m of ascent. Other recommended shorter tours in this area are Pointe D'Uble, Haute Pointe, and Pointe de Chavasse with its sporting ski off the summit ridge if snow conditions allow. The South faces of Roc d'Enfer and Pointe du Replan provide more challenging descents.

On the other side of the Arve valley, the summits of the Aravis offer many opportunities for memorable ski tours. The classic in this sector is probably the Pointe d'Areu, preferably making the traverse from Romme to Sallanches by descending the large couloir above the refuge de Doran. The Pointe de Bella Cha and the Pointe de la Carmelite at around AD standard also give good days out. For the more adventurous and technically competent, Point Percee (it can't have escaped your notice on the drive down from Chamonix) would make a challenging objective. At a grade of TD and involving a 30m rappel its one to save for good conditions. All of these summits give magnificent views of the Mont Blanc massif.

Mont Buet at 3100m, and overlooking the head of the Giffre valley, makes a fine objective and gives a challenging day out. It can be accomplished on skis from the Giffre side approaching via the impressive Cirque des Fonts but the normal and easier approach is from the east, starting from the hamlet of Le Buet close to Vallorcine on the Chamonix side. With a grade of PD S3/S4 the technical difficulties are reasonable but with a vertical ascent of 1800m it should not be under estimated.

This is just a small selection of what the area offers. In most years it is possible to ski from about mid-December to mid-April although January to mid-March usually give more reliable snow conditions. A number of worthwhile tours are accessible from the pistes. In particular, Point D'Anterne and Tete du Colonny from the Grand Massif area and the Pointe de Vorlaz above Avoriaz are to be recommended.

Further information can be found in the following guidebooks:

1. François Labande, *Ski de Randonnée Haute-Savoie, Mont-Blanc*, Guide Olizane Sport, Olizane, 2007. (A good selective guide but in French.)

2. Ruedi Meier, *Guide Chaîne franco-suisse – Du col des Montets au lac Léman*, Club Alpin Suisse, Bern, 2003.

3. Philippe Batoux, François Damilano & Ludovic Seifert, *Cascades de Glace du Mont Blanc au Léman* (Vol 2 covers the Giffre Valley and Chablais), JMEditions, Chamonix, 2007. (A photo-topo guide in French and English.)

MOUNT CAMEROON (4040m)

By Steve Chadwick

Saturday 31 Jan 2004

IT IS A SIGN of our times that we were more concerned about the journey to, rather than the climb up, Mount Cameroon. Nevertheless it was four intrepid hashers[1], as ever, that met at Cemal's house in Intels Camp, Port Harcourt, early on a fine Nigerian dry-season morning. For Cemal Dervish-Uman and Ton van Dijk it was their final crazy fling to 'do something' before leaving Nigeria. Third member was Andrew Woodrow; he was doing the grand tour and was due to climb Mount Kilimanjaro next month so this would be just a warm up. As for me, an old fart that still harboured memories of past climbing glories – in his own mind – I just wanted to see the view, having been thwarted on my last ascent in April 2000 by thick hill cloud. This time we were going overland and sea, after all the country of Cameroon was only next door, so it couldn't be that difficult to get there could it?

Apprehensive not so much because armed robbers frequent the route but more by the thought of Nigerian Police roadblocks, read extortion traps, we loaded ourselves in three vehicles with an armed Mopol guard in each one. The Nigerian Mopol is a seriously heavy unit that is a cross between the Police and Army, with a reputation for not taking prisoners. They can be hired, at a price, to act as your personal bodyguard, and the Police do not stop vehicles guarded by Mopol with automatic weapons.

We left Port Harcourt on schedule at 07.00 and sped along the Elema PH express towards Eket. The good road gave way to a country road which is much improved since its notorious pothole days, when robbers would wait for cars to negotiate the huge road cavities, which in places could make a car disappear before it began to climb out the other side. I dozed in the back, to the sleep-inducing background rhythm of Ton telling me tales of his days in the Dutch army. I glanced up at one point to see a burnt out petrol tanker and car by the side of the road. The tarmac across the road had been burnt and seriously reduced by the inferno and we could only imagine the horrific engulfing fire that had consumed both vehicles.

On through ten police roadblocks without hindrance with the Mopol guards waving to the Police, some of whom glowered back at the thought of three vehicles of whites going by without a chance to try and get a dash – bribe – to get through the road block.

We arrived at the coastal town of Oron at 09.40, as it was from here we planned to hire a fast skiff to Idenao in Cameroon. The crowd of would-

---

1   Members of Hash House Harriers, an international group of non-competitive running/social clubs. Sometimes called 'running clubs with a drinking problem', or 'drinking clubs with a running problem'…

Boat-hire bargaining.

be boat hirers gathered, and bargaining began. No fools these people, and they quickly established who among them was going to take us, thus no chance for a Dutch auction. The first call was 70,000 Naira for a fast twin-75hp-outboard skiff. The journey in the two-engined skiff would take about three-and-a-half hours, whereas a one-engined skiff could take up to six hours with no speed to evade the Bakassi peninsula pirates that frequent the area.

Bakassi is a peninsula of disputed land between Nigeria and Cameroon. In 2000 the International Court in The Hague awarded the area to Cameroon, but in the meantime the locals, not having a government whilst both sides awaited the outcome, had developed their own lawless autonomous society. We had dismissed reports of the piracy dangers of the boat trip as being exaggerated, but the boatmen told us otherwise. Well, we had come this far so negotiations continued, finishing at an agreed price of 60,000, about £240, for the one way trip.

Cemal argued, in his inimitable 'let's get on with it' style, that we should jump in and go. Andrew and I argued to get our passports stamped at immigration, which we found to reside in a hot, doorless, faded-yellow plastered building just along from the boats. We spent over an hour in the hot room whilst in turn three people did exactly the same thing to our passports, wrote down a raft of details and asked us each in turn exactly the same questions that their partners sitting next to them had asked

One of our Mopol guards, with Andrew and locals during boat-hire bargaining.

minutes before. Meanwhile we sat patiently in the hot airless room and melted.

Anyone who has travelled in out-of-the-way places will tell you that patience is a virtue. Chat nicely to authority, ask how their national football team is doing, be interested even if you're not. Be constantly polite and do exactly as they ask. All the papers were in order so nothing to fear. At last we were free to go and we trooped out only to be called back this time by customs that asked the same questions and wrote the same details down again. They were actually all nice people with a bureaucratic job to do. Everything was in order so we had to pay no dash.

Leaving our drivers and Mopol guards in Oron to await our hopeful return we at last loaded the skiff along with a stowaway that we had somehow picked up and set off from Oron at around 11.30, only to be immediately called back to shore by the police on duty in a moored boat by the foreshore, they were pointing guns, so stopping seemed a good idea. 'What were we doing trying to leave without seeing them?' Diplomacy kicks in again, be nice, smile say sorry no harm meant, we hadn't seen them, hand over passports, talk football, and sing a little song in your head. Eventually their glowering warms to a smile. 'OK, everything in order, you can go.'

Smuggling hard drugs, tobacco and other commodities between Cameroon and Nigeria is big business, so we expected to be stopped, but we were surprised at being stopped a further three times as we made our way out of the estuary by officials in moored boats carrying automatic weapons. All checked our papers and I was glad Andy and I had insisted on getting our passports stamped. The last stop, before open sea beckoned, was by navy police in a large dugout canoe powered by an outboard. Automatic weapons were lying casually around, one of which lay on the side of the dugout and was pointing directly at me.

'Where are you going?'

'Cameroon.'

'You must pay us tax.'

'Oh yes, what tax is that?'

'What are you doing?'

'Well, tourists really, going to climb Mount Cameroon.'

'You each pay us 1,000 Naira tourist tax.'

'You give us receipt for this tourist tax.'

'No, just pay us.'

Relaxed diplomacy kicks in again. It would have been easier just to pay them off, but after a while the sheer scale of corruption here begins to wear you down and you get sick of it. We bided our time and refused to pay. You could say this wasn't too bright, after all they had the guns. There is one thing on your side, they are afraid of killing white men due to the official trouble it will bring. However given the situation of being alone in the middle of nowhere with no chance of recriminations, you could be shot by a policeman or robber for your clothes or anything you carry. The days of being white and travelling without hindrance are long gone. I am a liaison officer for the British High Commission and we regularly get search requests asking if any of us has seen/can keep an eye open for so-and-so who was travelling alone from say Chad to Nigeria. One guy was videoing the route of the explorer Mungo Park and disappeared somewhere near the Chad/Nigerian border – just vanished. His camcorder would be reason enough to kill him.

I digress, our documents were all correct, so we sat it out while the water around the boats lapped and gurgled and the sun beat down. At last they gave in, and with a very grumpy look at us they sped off saying we should follow. We feigned misunderstanding and our two 75hp motors roared at full power, the bow rose to a disconcertingly high angle and we set off the other way soon outdistancing them. We would have to return in a few days, but for now we were at last speeding jumping from one low wave to another towards Cameroon. We carried a GPS and tracked our speed at between 40–50 km per hour. We were seriously moving.

We left the estuary and took to the open sea rounding the Bakassi peninsula, with the boatmen watching out for any fast coastal pirate boats. One man would handle the outboards and steer, whilst the second man would stand up hanging onto a thick hemp rope looking out for obstacles in the way. Floating logs from palm trees were a favourite; also drums and fishing nets were a hazard. There was total reliance on the lookout, as due to the high angle of the skiff, the tiller man couldn't see a damn thing. The lookout would raise his arm one way or another and the skiff would turn accordingly. We passed dozens of fishing dugouts, each manned by two smiling waving fisherman paying out or hauling in long nets that hung from floats on the surface. Each net had to be avoided though on occasion our boatmen seemed to take a chance and speed directly between two net floats.

The land slowly disappeared as we headed across the Bight of Bonny, cutting off the huge bay of Rio-del-Rey. Out at sea we slowed to one engine due to the serious danger of completely flipping the skiff by going too fast hitting a wave.

Out at sea with no sight of land in a twenty-foot open boat manned by two guys and a stowaway we had never seen before. Thoughts of collusion with pirates came uneasily to mind, but this was unfounded and they turned out to be really good guys who knew their trade, and they were making a killing anyway for ferrying white men at a good price. We headed out to the Gulf of Guinea whilst the sun beat mercilessly down on these four experienced travellers who had all forgotten to bring sun cream! Don't tell anyone please. We covered our bare arms and heads with spare clothes as best we could, whilst I at least had a sun hat and felt vaguely smug at getting something right.

Land hove to as we neared the coast of Cameroon and the flank of Mount Cameroon became visible. The shore had changed from sandy yellow to black lava pumice sand. Viewed from anywhere the scale of Mount Cameroon is impressive, with its sheer bulk and spread dominating everything. As we neared Idenao the proverbial boatload of officials had to be passed. These were nice guys decked with umbrellas to keep off the sun and with no guns in sight. They checked out our passports and waved us cheerily on. Landing at the little creek of Idenao brought more serious officials. One step off the boat and we had to open all our bags. I'm not sure what we could have smuggled for a profit, but there must have been possibilities that they were looking for. We were directed to the small immigration office where once again officials took copies of the same data, but at least here they only did it twice. More strange was the little jail just next door to the little immigration room. It was complete with a solid steel door which had a large letterbox opening near its top. Out of this slot peered a hapless miscreant no doubt jailed for some smuggling or paperwork problem. We knew ours was OK, well we hoped it was but can you ever be sure? The jail looked pretty bad, a hot hell. The prisoner would put out an arm now and again, but said nothing. He was pleading I guess for water or sustenance of some kind. I felt compassion but had nagging doubts of the advisability of giving something to a prisoner in a country in which we had only just landed, and this thought overrode my feelings. So once our papers were stamped we uncomfortably left immigration and the prison with its single arm held out of the letterbox in pleading supplication.

Next was the bargaining for the taxi fare from Idenau to Buea, a journey of about an hour and a half. We fell into some natural role-playing here – good guy, bad guy. Cemal would be the hard-nosed 'We're not paying that' role, whilst I would be the more reasonable 'Well perhaps that's too much' friendly approach. This does reflect our real characters so our roles came about quite naturally. Bargaining went on for some time with Cemal getting more and more irate, culminating at a final outburst 'I don't care if you're the only taxis, we're not paying that!'

Cemal was putting his foot down so the other three of us looked uncomfortably down at our own feet and nervously stirred the sand with them. Cemal wasn't the biggest man size-wise on the planet, but no one messed with him when he was aroused!

All of a sudden there was complete capitulation by Cemal, we were gobsmacked and I pulled him to one side. He smiled his wry little smile and said, 'I know when I'm beaten.' The outburst had just been a last ditch, failed ploy.

We piled ourselves plus rucksacks into a pair of taxis and left Idenao heading for Buea, stopping off for a minor detour. One of the last major eruptions on Mount Cameroon, which is an active volcano, was in 1999. The lava flow had reached the coast, just, and a section of road some 30m long now had a slight detour round the snout of lava that was the outpouring of mother earth. There was a sign pointing left saying New Evans Hotel. The old hotel was to the right under the lava field! The road climbed up from the coast to finally reach Buea, which sits at just under 1000m. We found our hotel pre-booked for us by the Buea Mount Cameroon agency, all done by the wonders of e-mail.

We decamped to our various rooms, mine being on the ground floor with a romantic view of a concrete wall and the gravity water tank that was leaking in a steady noisy flow just past the window. It would do for one night; and at least there is a shower with the immersion heater light on. I turned the hot tap on but cold water came out. I checked out the cold tap, you get used to them being the wrong way round when you travel to more esoteric places in the world. But no luck, that too was cold. Ah well, the rusty-coloured water flowed which was a plus.

We met at the upstairs bar for a beer, and then headed for the deserted restaurant for a meal. Deserted eating places are deserted for a reason and always make you nervous. What does every local know that we did not? One thing we did know, there was no cook! One was roused from somewhere by the management and upon being asked she confirmed she did have soup.

'What else is on the menu?'

'Chicken and rice.'

'Anything else?'

'No.'

So soup, chicken and rice it was then – hey, we just needed food. After a long wait the chicken and rice came.

'Where is the soup?'

'We don't have any soup.'

'But…never mind.'

So chicken and rice it was, and it was fine, filling enough and preparing the body with reserves for tomorrow. After another beer we then retired to our rooms to try and be sensible, and get a good sleep before our climb. The walls were a bit thin; I found this out when I heard the guy next door open his newspaper. The whole place carried sound from outside and in, and all the water pipes talked to each other in a disconcerting unrhythmical gurgling rattle. Well, at least we were too high in altitude for mosquitoes. Wrong, I tried to drift off but heard the high-pitched drone of the homing female mosquito. Why is it that the female of most species is predatory and needs blood to survive? It was not a good night.

Sunday 1 Feb 2004

A restless night culminated in my lying awake waiting for dawn. It came accompanied by a chorus off birds and cockerels doing their thing helped by dozens of barking dogs. I went upstairs to wake the others to find Andrew and Ton already awake but Cemal was sleeping like a baby. I was seriously jealous!

Breakfast was ready because the previous evening we had really laid it on that we needed it on time. So by eight we were away in a local taxi for the short ride to the Buea Mount Cameroon Ecotourism office where the pretty girl who had been my e-mail contact through the preceding weeks was ready and introduced us to our guide and porters. Local law allows no one on the mountain without a guide, and the porters carry your equipment up the hill. Kind of decadent, but hell, at my age I'll take all the help I can get. The guide and porters were collecting their food, which was a mixture of rice and meat wrapped in banana leaves. I tried a bit and choked with tears in my eyes, it was spicy hot. The porters were also carrying 24 large plastic bottles of water – we would need them all.

By around nine we were finally on our way up the hill. For the first two hours the climb winds its way up through the fields of the prison farm, with the workers shouting in a friendly banter 'You never go make it.' Then on through the rich thick jungle where we met several descending runners, who were training for the Mount Cameroon race that was to take place in a few weeks. Later we heard that the winner had gone up and back in 4hrs 50mins, outrageous. We stopped for a good rest at Hut 1, refuelled and set off again for the short trek through the remaining jungle, coming out onto the open savannah flank of the

The Magic Tree rest stop, halfway between Hut 1 and Hut 2.

mountain which marks the start of the climb to Hut 2, the steepest part of the climb.

The eruption hundreds of years ago that formed the gradient of the climb from Hut 1 to Hut 2 must have been colossal. The crater itself in those days must have been kilometres across. The surface on this section is treacherous being the steepest whilst being covered with loose lava stones and chips overlaying the lava rock underneath. Some way up at a brief respite in a slight easing of the gradient, workmen were busy building a midway hut, a sort of Hut 1b. This was also to be used during the race as the main medical post. It is these slopes descending from Hut 2 to Hut 1 that see the most casualties during the race, with contestants leaping down and often loosing their footing on the loose stones, then tumbling on down, scraping and breaking limbs as they go. On up, with our guide in front and the porters coming on behind. The next rest stop is called the Magic Tree, so called as this lone tree seems to get no nearer no matter how hard you struggle to reach it. Eventually it is reached though, and we all sat down for a rest by this solitary tree atop a small outcrop of lava boulders.

We took off our sacks and carefully placed them in a secure position. Andrew decided to move and in doing so inadvertently kicked his sack. The sack took exception to this and decided to leap off down the mountain, followed for a few steps by a concerned Andrew. We all shouted that he should let it go, rather than himself risk a fall down the

Cemal at Hut 2, with the top way beyond.

jagged lava slope. We watched in morbid fascination as it leaped, tumbled and fell down the slope, eventually coming to rest after 200m of freedom. A crestfallen Andrew looked down appalled not so much at his own mistake, but at the thought of the ribbing he knew he would get from the other three members of the team. Would we slag him off? Most certainly, such chances are not to be missed!

A porter volunteered to go back down while we rested, and in what seemed minutes was back with the errant rucksack. I should say at this point that all the porter's feet are clad in flip-flops. Nevertheless they displayed a degree of agility that far outweighed our own high-tech booted footwork. But then this was their livelihood.

Off again and ever upwards though soon the angle eased back as we gained the old rim just beyond which was the perch of Hut 2. It was here that I had to take off my old trekking boots as the poor old soles had collapsed. This could have spelt the end of my trip but Andrew had a pair of trainers in his sack. They were a bit on the tight side but they enabled me to continue – thanks Andrew.

Serious rest time, rehydrate and try to persuade the guide and porters to go on to Hut 3. It is normal to stop at Hut 2 and wait until early next morning before going on to Hut 3 and the summit. But we were determined to be atop for the sunrise, which meant going on to Hut 3 to spend the night. One reason for the reluctance by the guide and porters to sleep at Hut 3 was the considerable drop in temperature between the two

At about 3,500m – below Hut 3 – with fumaroles visible just below the summit.

huts, so they took some persuading, but with the offer of another few thousand West African Francs, the deal was struck. The initial climb between Huts 2 and 3 is not as steep as the preceding section but it is relentless, and the altitude gained with its associated lack of oxygen was making itself felt. We all slowed down, resting repeatedly, myself more than the others. Some way up Ton had a bad attack of cramps and I feared for his ascent, but it passed and he went on up. After a few hours of unremitting twenty steps up, rest, twenty more steps, the ground eased off once more prior to the last few hundred metres to Hut 3.

The will to make it returned and with some relief I joined Ton, Cemal, Andrew, the guide and porters in the top hut which sits on an easing of the lava at just on 3800m. Priorities asserted themselves and I rolled out my karrimat and the sleeping bag I had hired from the Mount Cameroon Ecotourism office, and lay down. The other three considerately took turns in passing hot soup and other foodstuffs to the old man. More alarming were our pulse rates. We were all pretty fit, with very low resting pulse rates varying from 50 to 60. Our bodies were struggling even at rest to supply oxygen at this attitude to our unacclimatised tired bodies. My pulse even after an hour's rest only came down to 80, though eventually came down to 70.

As we settled down for the night it became apparent that our porters did not have enough warm equipment, so I passed to one shivering porter my outer waterproof and another my nylon-shelled thick fleece, and

Steve, Cemal and Andrew on the summit just as dawn is breaking.

tried to get some sleep, which did not come too easily. I moved around trying to get comfortable whilst realising that my hired sleeping bag was not up to the job. I was cold, but could hardly ask for my fleece back from the porter who was in a worse state than I was. I redressed in my trousers and socks, and tried again, this time with more success and in snatches passed away the rest of the night.

Monday 2 Feb 2004

Around five I lit a candle and we began to rouse ourselves. Cemal, whose ability to sleep anywhere under any circumstances verges on the uncanny, was the only one who required a nudge. By 05.45 along with the guide and porter we set off for the remaining few hundred metres to the summit in blessedly clear, if dark and cold, weather. Last time here with no guide, they had rebelled and stayed in Hut 2 whilst we had pressed on to Hut 3. I had led our four-man team to the top in the dark, thick hill mist – why mention it, because I was very chuffed at the time to have done it. We passed several fumaroles giving off hot steam as we plodded our way up, feeling however much better for a night's rest. The track weaved its way round contorted lava flows and a final easing led to the last steeper ascent to the summit rim.

It was 06.15 and the dawn was cracking the horizon way away to the east. The view was spectacular as the sun woke up and climbed above the still sleeping lowlands. Night turned to day in changing colours whilst we busily took photos of the lovely scene. At least this time we could see how the crater rim had been destroyed by what must have been a huge volcanic explosion. The north and west rim had totally collapsed leaving the high point on the south-east side alone and proud. We were all hashers and as we began the decent back to Hut 3 one of us said it was the biggest checkback he had ever experienced in his life.

I was in front at this point, possibly for the only time on the trip, and reached Hut 3 ahead of the others. In true mountain tradition I lit up the stove and put a brew on. We stoked up on liquid, noodles and Nita's home-made carrot cake, repacked our bags and set off down the hill to Hut 2, where we were reunited with the porters who had remained there.

The tight trainers were starting to pinch and hurt my big toes and ahead we still had the steep descent to Hut 1. The guide cut a strong staff for me to use for support and balance, and thus equipped I set on down with Ton. The descent is tricky with small lava chips overlaying the steep lava rock. Nowhere is there enough scree to allow scree running, and to trust it is to skid and come down on the sharp lava. We were all counting our falls, and soon had cuts on our hands to prove it. Nevertheless the angle gradually eased off and we eventually reached the tree line which marks the short walk on to Hut 1.

Another short stop then on down the forest trail with no sign of wild life. Apparently the other quieter side of the mountain supports a count of over 500 elephants, but most on this side had been shot for bush meat.

On the descent between Huts 1 and 2.

These smaller North African jungle elephants are notoriously more belligerent than their larger South African cousins, so maybe that was a good thing.

My toes by now were in agony at each placement and I used the staff to try to take the pressure off them. Had they been mine the trainer ends would have been cut long ago to release the pressure. The going got slower as the pain increased. Just before reaching the outskirts of Buea, the others overtook me, and soon we collapsed by the roadside where we hailed a taxi to take us back to our minus-one-star hotel. We paid up our bribe money to the guide and porters who had stretched the rules and gone on up to Hut 3 with us to spend the night. I gave out a few bits of kit which had seen better days, but which porters were very happy to receive. The taxi deposited the four of us outside our hotel, and I hobbled to my room having agreed to meet for a beer in half an hour.

It was with a feeling of bliss that I took off the one-size-too-small trainers, and dumped my smelly dirty clothes in the corner.

I turned on the shower taps and stepped in, only to jump smartly out again – they had fixed the hot water whilst I had been away and I received a scalding shock. Back in with the hot turned off I washed away two days of volcanic dust that had seemed to get everywhere, and I mean everywhere. I donned clean clothes and non-pinching open-toed sandals that made me feel somewhat more human and I was the first to the bar so I set up a round of celebratory beers for the other three.

Andrew had to leave for Douala as he was flying direct back to the UK, whilst the remaining three set off to meet Chris, our pretty Ecotourism Officer, and a porter for a meal. After which the three of us set out for a tour of the bars of Buea. I stopped after two beers whilst Cemal and Ton drank on into the night. I had this amusing voyeuristic evening of watching my two friends getting slowly paralytic as the alcohol speedily reached the brain of their dehydrated bodies. Someone had to stay sober to get us all back.

We stumbled back to the hotel around 23.00 and crashed into bed. I was dead tired so managed to ignore the whine of female mosquitoes looking for a blood supper, groaning water pipes and barking conversational dogs.

Tuesday 3 Feb 2004

The body-clock alarm woke me around 06.00 and I checked for bites but found only two, a good night. I checked the others and delighted in waking Cemal from his usual comatose state. Around 08.45 the three of us packed our sacs and ourselves into the taxi and set off for Idenao. With about half an hour of journey to go, the car's overheating water light came on. A quick check showed a water pipe connection had frayed and broken. Out came my Leatherman tool. I untwisted the wire clamps, cut the pipe, reset and clamped the pipe in place. Real backwoods Boy Scout stuff and egotistically good to do, then we were back on the road.

Ton, Cemal and Steve celebrate.

This time emigration and boat securing proved tougher. At one point I refused point blank to pay the exorbitant boat fee they were demanding and walked off in a feigned huff, hoping they would give in and call me back. Thank goodness they did, or I might have been forced to climb down. They deferred with some respect to the oldest of our party – me – and bade me sit down again and poured me a glass of water. In the end we settled on the same price as the outward journey and we climbed aboard for the fast ride back to Oron.

We sped over the sparkling water and on past the Bakassi peninsula. A couple of times we spotted fast boats approaching, once from the shore and once from out to sea. Each time our boatmen veered away and had the power to outrun them. Once I lifted my head to check the pursuing boat and my sun hat was off in an instant, flying through the air to splash down some way back in our wake. We did not go back to pick it up. Luckily we did not come across the boatload of armed Navy Police and we made it into Oron without too much water-borne authority hassle. Immigration grilled us as usual and customs took our details but no bag searching this time. Our drivers and guards were waiting and we sped back past the roadblocks to Port Harcourt where we stopped off at the Igben Gardens, a hash bar of note, where it seemed fitting to have a beer and toast a successful trip and ascent.

THE COMEBACK

By Jack Hastie

THE OLD MAN had been flattered by the invitation to lend his vast experience to a climbing expedition in Glen Coe, though, admittedly, he had had to offer to finance it before being included in the team. The organiser was a former SAS officer, a Ranulph Fiennes figure whose military exploits in troubled parts of the world were still concealed by the Official Secrets Act. The rest of the group was to consist of several young women. The Old Man rubbed his palms together.

'Yes,' he enthused, 'John will certainly need somebody of my experience to help shepherd these impressionable and inexperienced young ladies round the gullies, buttresses and ridges that defend Bidean nam Bian.' Then, not without some difficulty, he dug out his Ordnance Survey map of the area, dusted off the cobwebs and spread it out before him.

'Hmmm,' he mused, 'I see Magnetic North was 9° west in 1962, decreasing by ½° every six years. That means,' he did some nimble mental arithmetic, 'it should be about 5° west today, if the change has been constant. But what if it hasn't? Could be a problem in thick mist.'

The Old Man remembered a friend who had inadvertently tried to descend the wrong side of the Bidean ridge in a white-out and had fallen three hundred feet. Unfortunately he couldn't quite recall which had been the wrong side.

'Need to look out the compass.'

The Old Man's compass was his pride and joy. It was a liquid-filled prismatic, something you could have used to direct artillery fire and greatly superior to these new Silva things he'd heard about that were only good for finding your way around forests in Finland. Locating the instrument was at first a problem, but at last he unearthed it in its elegant khaki case under an old copy of Climber Magazine in which was reported the first British ascent of the north face of the Eiger.

Alas, when he opened the compass he found that a large bubble had invaded the face and rendered the instrument useless unless you tried to read it upside down. Fortunately his grandson came to the rescue with a compass the size of a 50 pence piece with a picture of Denis the Menace on the back.

The rest of his gear was easier to locate. He discarded his four-and-a half-foot-long, wooden-shafted Aschenbrenner ice axe as probably unnecessary in October, and then re-instated it as likely to demonstrate his technical competence to the SAS man and, more importantly, certain to impress the young ladies. His Bergen rucksack, Black's Standard anorak and Tricouni nailed boots completed his outfit.

'Never did trust these new vibram rubber soles,' he muttered to himself. 'Unreliable on wet rock and useless on ice.'

At last the day of the expedition dawned. The Old Man reckoned he cut a dashing figure, although he'd been unable to get into his climbing breeches because the waistband had inexplicably shrunk and his boots were so bone hard that he couldn't get them on and had to settle for his wellies instead. As a final precaution he draped around his person 100 foot of kinky hemp rope.

'Probably won't need it, but the birds might be a bit scared on the headwall of the Lost Valley. Or I might show them a trick of two on the Problem Boulder.'

The SAS man was to do the driving. Not that the Old Man couldn't have handled it himself, for he still drove regularly to his local library and once or twice recently had taken his Morris Minor to the summit of the Cathkin Braes.

'High time they improved the lochside road,' he thought to himself. 'That and a bridge at Ballachulish is what we climbers really need.'

They set off. The Old Man, despite the close proximity of the girls sitting beside him, soon settled into a quiet doze. After all he'd had to be up unusually early for the nine o'clock Alpine start the SAS man had insisted on. When he did open his eyes he stared in disbelief. On his right, certainly, there was a loch. It had to be Loch Lomond, because unmistakeably, to the north-east reared The Ben. But in front of him, instead of the old twisting lochside road there stretched a super highway.

'I'm dreaming,' he muttered and banged his head against the side of the car to wake himself up.

'You all right?' purred girl number one protectively.

The Old Man realised instantly that it would not enhance his standing in her eyes if he admitted confusion. 'Yes. Of course. Always a good idea to get a bit of sleep before tackling a big climb. Climbing can be dangerous.'

'Oh, we'll be all right,' crooned girl number two. 'John will look after us.'

Jealousy, green-eyed, flashed across the Old Man's mind, but as always, he was equal to the occasion. 'Can't always rely on young squaddies,' he warned. 'They're trained to carry out certain routines. Ask them to do something on their own initiative, like work out the best route up a mountain, and they're lost. I remember once when we used to climb in Skye – it really is time they built a bridge to the island – there was a big route called Waterpipe Gully. The rock was gabbro, a coarse plutonic crystalline lava, but there were dykes of basalt and dolerite, extrusive igneous rocks, the crystals of which are much smaller, running across it…' He broke off and glanced at girl number three to assess the level of admiration in her eyes. But unfortunately she too had been lulled to sleep, undoubtedly by the motion of the car.

They all wakened up in Glen Coe. The SAS man parked the car. Everybody got out. They straggled down across the bridge over the River Coe at Three Waters, beneath the beetling brows of the Three Sisters. Then they were on the track that led to the Problem Boulder at the mouth of the Lost Valley, where generations of aspiring young rock climbers had honed their skills. That was where the pace began to tell on the Old Man.

'I'll bring up the rear,' he puffed to the SAS man. 'Strongest member of the party should always come last. I'll take care of the stragglers. If you've any problems with route finding, just give me a shout.'

He then set a sensible pace as recommended in the first edition of the Scottish Mountain Leadership Manual. The SAS man and the girls attacked the track with reckless speed. The Old Man sweated and swore.

'Silly bugger. Doesn't have a clue. Set a pace like that and the girls'll be burned out in no time.' Then, as they diminished into the distance, 'Far too f*****g fast!'

The advance guard – that is everybody except the Old Man – reached the Boulder and, burned-out or not, sat down to wait for him. In their full, and leisured, view he peched and plodded, sweated and swore.

'Far too fast,' he repeated, glaring at the SAS man. 'Just because you're in the Commandos doesn't mean you know how to climb mountains.'

It was perhaps just as well that that military man had once been part of a peace-keeping force, but before he could respond girl number one intervened sweetly. 'Just you sit down and get your breath back. When I did my Duke of Edinburgh's gold I was trained to look after elderly people who become distressed.'

That did it. Stung to the quick the Old Man attempted an acrobatic leap to his feet from a nearly prone position. Old muscles stiffen quickly and elderly eyes take a wee while to focus; so it was that, as he placed his right wellie on an innocent looking lump of rock, it rotated treacherously under him, his ankle twisted with an excruciating crunch and he landed on his bottom in a trackside puddle. Independent to the last, he resisted the attempts of the girls to help him to his feet and tried to get up himself. He rolled over on to his knees and then gingerly transferred the weight to his feet. Instantly a stab of pain shot up his right leg and he tumbled back into the puddle.

The position was now clear. For the Old Man an epic retreat was in prospect. Still heroically refusing all offers of help, he considered his locomotor options and settled on a kind of hirpling crawl modelled on something he'd seen a baby orangutang execute in a foreign zoo. But progress was painful and slow and he soon had to give up.

'Death from exposure in high places,' he reflected, 'would not be a dishonourable way to go.' The climbing literature was full of such stuff. Mallory and Irvine, for example. Or that Italian bloke whose body had hung on the north face of the Eiger for years. To these would now be added the story of his own martyrdom on Bidean. 'I'm just going out. I may be some time,' he announced dramatically, momentarily confusing Mallory with Captain Oates of South Pole fame.

The Old Man was just beginning to enjoy, in anticipation, his posthumous heroic status when his reverie was rudely cut short by the Commando. 'Never thought we'd need a hundred foot of bloody rope just to get into the Lost Valley. But you never know.'

It transpired that, in training for some desperate mission behind enemy lines, he had learned how to make an improvised stretcher out of a hundred foot of rope. After about twenty minutes the device was complete and the Old Man was loaded on to it. Thus he found himself being carried by three impressionable and inexperienced young women off the hill, en route for the bridge, the road, the car.

Cheated of his martyrdom, he re-assessed his situation. His injury, he reasoned, had to be massive in order to justify his present undignified predicament. In which case he ought to be in extreme pain.

He contorted his face in a silent grimace.

Nobody noticed.

When a series of low moans also failed to elicit a sympathetic response he adopted an operatic approach. 'Wahooa!' he howled. 'Just keep going. I can handle the pain.'

'No need for that,' said the SAS man, deftly unzipping his first aid kit.

It further transpired that, while preparing for another undercover expedition in darkest somewhere he had been trained to administer morphine. Which he now did.

It was, therefore, a nearly comatose Old Man who was decanted from the rope stretcher on to the back seat of the car, but he brightened up considerably when the SAS man announced, 'Right. That's Bidean out for the day. Might as well cut our losses and head for the Kingshouse for some refreshment. You girls have certainly earned it.'

Before long the Old Man was ensconced in front of a roaring fire in the inn with a glorious view of the Buachaille through a picture window. He was beginning to revel in his 'casualty – lucky to be alive – status' and was already anticipating that he would shortly be asked to narrate the story of his accident and desperate struggle to survive against fearful odds. As the SAS man was asking the girls of the stretcher party what they would like to drink –what the hell were vodka blasts and Baccardi breezers? – he felt free to indicate that he thought he might manage a small single malt, only to be told in no uncertain terms, 'Not bloody likely! With that dose of morphine in you, strictly no alcohol.'

PLATEAU TALES

By Bob Reid

One

BE HONEST. How many of us own one of those fancy yellow gizmos called an 'eTrex' but have left it sitting in a drawer? Or perhaps you carry it religiously around the hills but secretly pray you won't have to use it? Does such a confession invoke a degree of apprehension, of fear even? Are you like me – unwilling to admit to a degree of technophobia? Do you find that even the English sections of 'manuals' appear to be written in a foreign language?

If I am being hyper-analytical (and I realise I am straying into 'who cares' territory here…but bear with me) it isn't these fears I need to own up to but an emerging laziness born of the fact that I've been around long enough not to have to resort to intensive learning any more. My education is complete. My head is replete. If that sounds too uncomfortable a notion, then you'll probably feel easier with that old adage, 'my character is built'.

So what on earth possessed or motivated me to sign up to a Mountaineering Council of Scotland Global Positioning Satellite course. If I am really honest, I have succumbed to a bout of acute embarrassment. Some of my contemporaries seem to have mastered this technology, to have tamed the 'yellow thingummy'. Oh my God, he can actually use it and he's hardly any younger than me. Can it be easier than I thought? Let's stick that idea to the wall for a moment and consider.

I remind myself that I am a good navigator. Having been lost a few times, I have learned from my mistakes. My brain also reminds me that you cannot rely on something that's driven by batteries, built in Taiwan and dependent upon (that greatest of all oxymorons) American Military Intelligence. Combine those attributes with my own capacity to make mistakes (especially with gadgets) and there's enough room for error – disaster even – to keep many a mountain rescue team busy.

You'll have gathered that I am sceptical, though not cynical about electronic navigation devices – or GPS. They first entered my reckoning when I heard someone from a mountain rescue team extol their virtues on the radio when recounting being landed in remote parts by helicopter in the dark. 'Where are we…was always difficult to confirm until GPS came along.' Let the yellow bird whirr away and switch on the yellow gadget [what is it about yellow?]. A near instantaneous confirmation of grid reference is given.

So that is why I religiously carry mine around in my pack, on all my hillwalking and climbing trips. When the weather is bad or the light runs out, in theory I can check where I am. I know that sounds slightly surreal, but it really is a terrific advance. Though not very often used, and probably as a consequence, poorly understood, I felt it was about time that I immersed myself in the technology a little more.

Two

The last time I had attended a course at the Lodge I was acting (being the operative word) as an observer on a Winter Skills Course. As a so-called 'skilled' mountaineer I suppose I was fair game as demonstration fodder.

'Bob will now show you how to slide on your back, head first downhill, right yourself, perform self-arrest using classic axe brake…and come to a stop before you go over the cliff at the bottom of this slope.'

'Erm, thanks, but no thanks,' I replied. But the young instructor's point had been well made. Practice must be perfect.

Would the same happen to me today, I wondered, even though the death potential admittedly looked considerably smaller. Perhaps pride was more at stake.

Fellow SMC member Heather Morning's breezy smile welcomed all the GPS noviciates to the 'New' Glenmore Lodge, as we settled into one of the teaching rooms. The scene was slightly surreal as a dozen or so folk (average age close to mine and most with reading specs) peered expectantly at their GPS devices. I swear I could hear cogs whirring, producing a collective, Homer Simpsonesque, 'Duh!' hanging over the assembled heads.

'What edition is yours?'

'Is yours 3.1 or 3.2? What year's model?'

'Does this really display the actual maps?'

'Sit down Bob, join in,' Heather's northern lilt was as welcoming as her smile. Heather's invocation to 'join in' on the other hand was a little more alarming. As the technophobe within began to gain the upper hand, the anxiety attack I was experiencing was almost enough to have me make a bolt for the door.

This was the first MCofS GPS course. Heather announced it was four times oversubscribed, confirming a theory I have that most folk buy a GPS device without any underlying comprehension of how they work or how to work them. The truth was at hand though, as we were all to introduce ourselves to each other and explain why we had signed up. The words 'ritual humiliation' suddenly conjured themselves in my head, but among strangers I thought it better to suppress the bad jokes. They'd only reveal my nervousness.

Caroline lived in Cairo, but was a Munro Compleater. There were no maps in Egypt so GPS, now covering more than 90% of the globe, was the only alternative. David, another Compleater, told a tale of biking into Glen Affric in the dark. Another David was retired but had been motivated by comments made by a Rescue Team Leader in the national press that very few folk could use a GPS. Linda wanted to know how to 'track-back' (whoaaa!! jargon already). Helen was retired but was now a volunteer leader. Clair had done all the Munros, Corbetts and Grahams (obviously a very experienced hillgoer) but also needed help in learning how to do track-back. And so on; Alan, Bob, Colin, Mike, Andrew…and me? My motivation…to help with ski touring navigation, of course. Well, it sounded plausible enough at the time.

No one was young, well, really young. There was a thirty something. Most of the novices were in their forties, fifties or were pensioners. Confirms my second theory that the PC gaming generation of cyber nerds either don't go climbing or have Cobol Basic hard-wired into their genetic make-up. My own teenage children just switch on the GPS device and play with the buttons. Requests to, 'Don't play with the buttons, please,' simply elicit eyeball rolling and faintly patronising responses like, 'Whatever.'

My musings ended abruptly as Heather and Graeme helped each of us to 'lay-in a course'. Aha! 'Trekkie' talk at last. Everyone could obviously map read, that much was clear. Hackneyed acronyms betrayed the knowledge that had seen most of these hillgoers into seniority. We patiently read the grid references and painstakingly punched them into our GPS devices – not easy.

David was clearly struggling with eyesight, finding difficulty reading

On a GPS course. Photo: Heather Morning.

the screen and with the dexterity of the 'page up/down' and enter functions. 'I'm with you David,' I thought. It is abundantly clear to me that the designers of GPS Devices had never thought about sitting with ordinary hillgoers in the non-geek world to see exactly what they would require and what they were capable of dealing with. No amount of rational explanation will alter my view on this. My determination nevertheless grew as I realised that unless I could master the basics, this fancy bit of kit was still master-of-me and luxury, chocolate teapot in my hands. If I were honest, I was really struggling.

Clair graciously came to my rescue. She had obviously run the ordeal-by-fire of working with the GPS device manual and even spoke some of the jargon. Impressive. Its Americanisms had irked me plenty, leaving me with the unnerving thought that the reason folk across the pond might be more GPS proficient than I owed much to us being separated by a common language.

Turns out where I was going wrong, was in not quite 'conceptualising' my GPS device correctly. In spite of my Luddite tendencies I do pride myself on being fairly PC adept, so Clair suggested I see my GPS device as, yes, 'a mouse'. Readers pondering the amount of single malt available at the Lodge should suspend their incredulity just a little while longer. As a mouse? Old hat by now, I realise, but a learning model I could at least understand. Though just to confound matters my teenage son has just shown me a cordless, button-less mouse. However the penny actually dropped. The 'page up/down' functions were just like left and right mouse, and 'enter' was carriage-return, to borrow a century-old bit of jargon.

Our first set of inputs were then tested outside in the immediate environs of the Lodge. Looking like Captain Kirk and his away team playing with 'Tricorders' we followed where the arrow pointed. I realise with hindsight this was an essential part, not so much of the learning process, more of the mindset shift, if you will, of the leap of faith required to trust the arrow in the yellow gizmo. Two more exercises, each in turn more complex, taking the novices into forests and then onto the hills, were not designed to impart just the knowledge, but equally to instil the faith.

There are times when it is hard enough to trust the compass in your hand. I always carry two now. So trusting a technological gizmo does require acquired confidence. Most readers will have heard tell of the 'wobble' introduced into the original satellite signal that needed de-coding to make it useful. The US military allegedly thought we'd all make cruise missile guidance systems with our GPS devices and our childrens' playstations. We also hear bothie banter about two-metre or five-metre accuracy, normally followed by a list of known summit cairns sitting jaw-droppingly close to serious verticality. Beinn Alligin is my own favourite example and once my own near nemesis. Heather and

Graeme studiously continued to emphasise all day that the GPS should be used as an adjunct to your map and compass and not a substitute.

After a day's immersion in GPS (perhaps two days would have been better), the real revelation was not in having a little more faith, or in feeling satisfied that you could at last read the manual, but in the eye-opening presentation about digital mapping. What you could do with a GPS device if you worked it in conjunction with a digital mapping facility on your computer is quite frankly astonishing. The possibilities are extraordinary and probably should form the basis of future Lodge courses to help us cope with technology in the mountains. They could just have significant impacts on the cohort 'skills levels' of mountaineers and mountaineering in Scotland.

Scorpion (V, 5).

Hamish Irvine emerges from the subterranean crack.

Photo: Alec Keith.

Three

'How do you do that?'

I was about 10m up the first pitch of Scorpion on Càrn Etchachan. Tom's question drifting up from the belay threw me slightly. He was a far better climber than I, especially on rock. Here was steep, hand over hand climbing, clutching the granite jugs, best done with axes dangling from their wrist loops. Not exactly contempt born of familiarity, just a confidence over that sort of ground. I don't think I answered Tom at the time, absorbed with the task in hand.

It was late season and conditions were lean. As a consequence the unusual opportunity arose to climb the somewhat esoteric subterranean 'through-route' on pitch two. Allen Fyffe later suggested this was rarely

Hamish Irvine leads the final corner of Scorpion (V, 5).

Photo: Alec Keith

done. Usually the snow filled up the chimney tunnel, which squeezes behind a cyclopean granite shield. My first ever Gore-Tex cagoule was scarred irreparably by the jagged quartz crystals pressing onto my chest, as I thrutched awkwardly upward. Recompense came as pitch after pitch of near perfect snow and ice followed. I eventually watched Tom's wiry frame dispatch the 'sting-in-the-tail', final corner without much ado. I recall I found it hard.

Strangely, 20 years later, little of this resonates with any real force. Yet in stark contrast I remember the events that subsequently unfolded every time I have to resort to use of a compass. We'd started late on Scorpion and by the time we'd finished, it was practically dark. The weather had also deteriorated considerably and it was snowing heavily, two pence piece size flakes blowing in strongly from the north – in truth, a snowstorm. Strong gusts caught me as I took out map and searched for compass having put my headtorch on. I conferred with Tom. He had no compass and, if I recall correctly, no map either. No pressure then and a mental note to check in future before setting off from the car park.

The way off Càrn Etchachan flirts with no fewer than three huge, re-entrant gullies, Castlegates Gully being the aptly name first. To avoid them, at least a kilometre of westward leeway was needed. The snowstorm had deteriorated to full white-out and so an added sense of urgency weighed upon us both. We knew we had to 'box' the head of Glen Avon. The third leg of that box was the really awkward one. The plateau between the precipices of the Northern Corries on one side and Hell's Lum and Stag Rocks on the other tilts and twists, its aspect continually varying. Plateau is probably a misnomer, it's most devious characteristic being the way it narrows between Coire an t-Sneachda and Coire Raibeirt above Loch Avon to not much more than half a kilometre's width.

An hour and a half had passed since we'd topped-out and I concentrated on counting paces, two kilometres' worth so far. This wasn't easy in ever deepening snow, stumbling into drifts, tripping through sastrugi. Conversation was impossible. I signalled to Tom that we'd veer 90°, resetting my bearing for the third time, this time in a north-easterly direction.

'Are you sure, Bob?' Tom shouted. 'As sure as I can be,' I replied, any hint of certainty drifting off in the wind. A five percent error on three successive bearings – where would that lead us? Over which precipice would we stumble?

An hour later in pitch-dark, full-blizzard white-out, Tom asked again. There was the strongest temptation to remark upon there being only one map and compass, but I bit my lip. With hindsight, I am not sure that two would have made much difference. It would just have altered the balance of dependency, with fewer questions asked.

This third leg of the box was nearly three kilometres, but counting

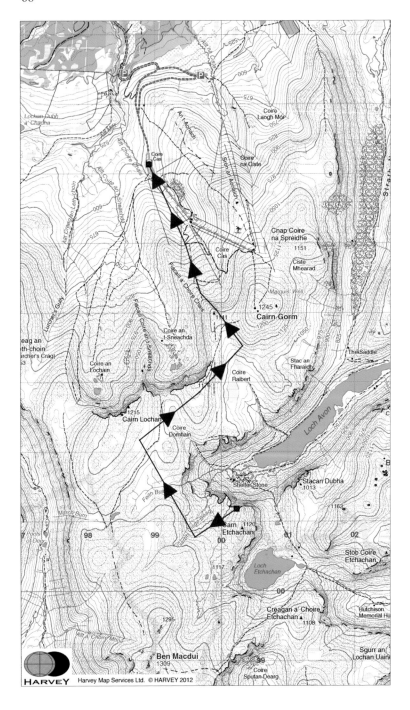

paces had become virtually impossible, we were stumbling so much in the deep soft snow. I'm not sure how many times Tom checked with me, three times, perhaps four, at increasing frequency. It fed my doubts and anxieties. If only I could have been sure where we were. The only geographic reality worth clinging onto was the solid frozen ground buried in snow beneath our feet.

Five kilometres into a descent route, most of which was uphill, and the snow was now falling thicker and faster, the hour getting ever later. After a pre-6 a.m. start, we'd been on the go nearly seventeen hours. Tiredness was affecting us physically and mentally just as the most crucial judgements were needed. If it were at all possible, the ground began to further steepen uphill. Something had changed. The realisation slowly dawned that we'd reached the summit pyramid, the nunatak if you will, of Cairn Gorm itself. We traversed northwesterly along the contours, remembering to veer northward into Coire Cas, avoiding its headwall.

There's a cliché about relief being palpable. I think we were too tired to be relieved. We knew the remainder of our day was downhill, if somewhat surreal, drifting past the paraphernalia of the deserted ski centre. I recalled Jim Perrin's comment in *Cold Climbs*, on climbing Scorpion. He suggested 'he'd been taxed as much as he cared to be taxed'. I mused that the sting-in-the-tail of Scorpion will so often be the 'descent' across the plateau.

Four

With a GPS we could have pre-programmed in the grid reference for the top of a route or crag, and also the key navigational waypoints on a descent where changes of direction would be required. Counting paces would only have been back-up for the GPS device. And on a digital map you can check at the click of a button that the 'descent' would entail:

7km in length
reaching a maximum height of 1,177m
descending to 617m
with a height ascended of 346m; and
an estimated time of 2hrs and 11mins based on Naismith's rule.

The six hours we took is understandable and was more than we spent on Scorpion itself. A GPS device would have seriously eased our anxiety levels but more importantly increased our safety margins. On many subsequent ski traverses over the intervening years, from the Ski Car Park to Ben Macdui, you soon realise that the plateau can be a fickle friend. Easy and amenable when skiing on good snow and with clear visibility. Another story completely the moment visibility has gone.

BURN BIG GRAY HILL, BURN

By Phil Gribbon

IT WAS THE traditional Easter club meet on the weekend after Easter and the early spring weather at Torridon was exceptional and showing no sign of drifting away. The skies spanned our world, dancing blue and infinitely carefree, the rocks were sun-kissed and our fingertips itched to stroke their crystalline curves. Every southern hillside was soaking in the long hours of sunshine, crinkling up the shaved strips of old deer grass, prying up loose mats of dried moss, luring out lizards on to flat hotplates, and wafting up insects in search of their fleeting pleasures.

We were wandering across the hillside and sampling the little outcrops pushing out of the ridge. When viewed earlier from across Loch Torridon their silvery slabs had poked out of the dry ground like the blunt snouts of a pod of killer whales scanning a sea for their prey. We had succumbed to the attraction of these polished roche moutonées pushed up from their ancient basal gneiss foundations and standing close to the massive Torridonian sandstone layers making up the northern flank of Beinn Shieldaig. We had sneaked across and were indulging in happy frolics on their rough flanks. It was a convenient place to go with the road a few hundred feet below and it suited those who were forced to indulge themselves in gentle outings. It had quick access, single pitches, good for ledge lounging and vista viewing, all quite ideal. Just the thing before dinnertime at the Kinlochewe Hotel.

I followed up his route until there was nowhere else to go. That was the way it was nowadays. Let someone else do all the work and I'd take the role of holding the rope at the bottom and passing encouraging remarks. I looked across the loch to the rocky features that fringed the coast between Inverallign and Diabeag. Over there was too much choice on too much rock. It felt better to be on the south side and look carefully for decent lines with nice moves on convenient outcrops.

The hills relaxed contentedly in the heat, they rested sharp and unhazed with upward sweeps and downward dips. Their silhouettes went from the swelling shoulder of Tom na Gruagaich to the hacked open gash of Alligin, and then switched down and up the Corbett that wanted to be a Munro, and then over the Mhic Nobuil glen to the rolling weaving extension dropping from the western summit of Liathach. We sat in the warm wind coming from the east as it seeped westward and spilled across the Highlands. We were relishing an early gift of summer with an anticyclone feeding its clean dry air across Scotland.

A fire had started on the lower slopes of Liathach. Its faint trail of blue smoke was creeping seaward from the base of the great gully that spills down from the main ridge of Liathach and gives a few acres of low ground behind the village of Fasag. The fire was on the windward side of the village and its smoke was curling about and trickling across the old fields behind the houses.

Lets ignore it, no problem there. It will never reach the house where we were staying at the far end of the village, and anyway its back garden is ringed by a stonewall abutting on a blocky scree slope that runs up between stepped buttresses on the mountainside. Any self-respecting fire should waft away in search of more glamorous bits to eat. Nonetheless between the fire and the house there was a highly burnable bramble tangle interwoven with abundant dry bracken and overshadowed by a mature Sitka spruce tree veined with combustible resins.

Forget the implications, because there are surely lots of local villagers ready to defend their curtileges, plus the second homers escaping for their extra holiday in celebration of the royal wedding day, the campers crammed onto the camp site, and the hostellers ready to respond to the challenge. There will be plenty of inferno fighters, and we won't forget the well equipped local volunteer fire crew whose calling is to defend the public good. This fire will be quickly snuffed out, it will be beaten to extinction and flailed to dusty ash. Anyway, it will give up its maurading habits when it runs out of ready fodder.

What about another short climb variation up this creamy fudgey rock, and perhaps there will be sufficient time even to go to the next outcrop and find if there is anything worth doing? The pitch didn't seem to take long but that is always the way when you are enjoying yourself. We got to the crest and were surprised by the look of the fire on Liathach. It seemed to have done a speedy race up the mountain and was burning within an smidgen of the ridge. It seemed improbable, but not impossible, that a couple of thousand feet of hillside could be consumed in an hour. We had better quit this sport, go home and do some firewatching, drink a relaxing cup of tea and enjoy a wee dram or two.

We turned off the main road by the National Trust information hut at the clump of old Scots pines and turned towards the village. We were looking at a blackened slope fringed with flickering flame where fresh vegetation was igniting. With the fire moving sideways across the hillside it was working in two opposite directions, going westward behind the village and also surprisingly backwards into the wind blowing down the glen. It wasn't under control, it wandered where it wanted, but it was still well away from the houses of the village.

We got home and refreshed ourselves, changed our shirts, and prepared for social stuffing and whirling. Outside the air reeked sweetly of the burnt ground and wafted billows of ochreous smoke blew low over our heads. We had a few doubts whether it was wise to leave the house unattended but were reassured when a heavily garbed and helmeted fireman came to the door to give advice. On going out, close all windows and shut the doors tight, he said. Right, okay, leave it to the experts; we

Glen Torridon, 30 April 2011. Photo: Roger Robb.

can leave to feast in Kinlochewe and forget that the slopes of Liathach will continue burning in our absence.

We came back suitably dined but glad to retire gracefully. The mountainside still was glowing deeply with fire, the drifting smoke reflecting every fresh flare-up in the trail of little outbursts edging across the hillside. The monster had found plenty to consume and most worryingly it had launched itself on to the ledges on the rock buttress above the house.

Close by it gobbled at a group of gorse bushes. Their massed prickles were toasting and crackling and throwing up a cloud of inflammable gases to spin around and ignite in midair. There were folk huddled in groups out on the street, watching and wondering what would happen next. Everything was stained in the red glow reflected down from the drifting smoke clouds. The firemen unrolled a hosepipe from their engine to pump up sea water to soak the slope behind the gardens. It looked like controlled chaos and we had complete trust in the outcome. This conflagration had to be subdued but I wouldn't be there to see it happen. I couldn't take any more for one day. I was too knackered to care. I crawled off to bed and slept the night away.

Next morning when I wafted into the kitchen Peter was stirring the porridge and looking rather wan. Through the night he had spent hours sousing the bitumen flat roof of the kitchen with buckets of water while higher up the fire crew had crept across the scree to maintain a sweeping spray of sea water on to the hot ledges.

The morning radio news had laid it on thick and had told the nation of the rampant infernos ravaging the Scottish Highlands. The biggest fire was claimed to be raging on the Torridon mountains where, believe it or not, ten square kilometres were burning, a village was under threat and the campers in a campsite had been evacuated at 2.30am. Most dramatically of all the police helicopers were water bombing the advancing fire. We accepted this was true because from the loch came the throbbing beat of a helicopter that waxed and waned as it flew around on its mission. We continued to enjoy our plates of porridge and and knew that another brilliant day was on the cards.

We stood at the front door to savour the view. Far up on the flank of the westernmost spur called Sgorr a'Chadail the faint wisps of tobacco-blue smoke still curled up against an unblemished sky. Gossamer cloud fragments wafted over the nearby buttress. We debated whether these vaporous fragments were high in the sky or were we looking at smoking remnants still burning behind the its crest. In contrast close by spring flowers were soaking up sunlight; snowdrops, aconites and early purple heaths, while on a ledge of the buttress the top branches of a single tall birch had survived the scorching and their fragile green leaves still waved gently in the breeze. Nonetheless it was a scene of desolation. Behind us everything burnable had been devoured and out of the dusty blackness covering the ground faint swirls of air lifted little clouds of ash.

Where should we climb today? Why not on the deep maroon sandstone by the seashore at Inveralligin? The sun would be glinting off the sea with the tide receding, the wind raising tiny wavelets and the coarse rock getting warmer by the minute, and best of all it was a mere stroll from the car. However first we ought to drive up the glen to see what damage the fire had caused and if any help was needed from two unskilled volunteers.

At the main road beside the abandoned campsite now fringed with the skeletons of scorched gorse the fire had done its worst to Wilseys Wood. Just beyond the campsite was a plantation of Scots pines established over thirty years ago in memory of two of my friends who perished down a wintery Glencoe gully. Now in an instant it had become a graveyard of stark blackened tree bones. Somehow it had been illfated from the day that the trees had first been planted in the poorly drained bogland. Its trees had always been stunted, ill-nourished and struggling to survive, and now they were gone.

We saw that high above us the fire was still alive and creeping slowly on along the rock terraces of Liathach, while up the road just before old wood by the river one of fire crews rested by their truck. Earlier the blown sparks had crossed the road and ignited the heather to put the dwellings in Annat close to the riverbank under threat. The crew had dealt partly with this but were still on standby and ready to respond to any further outbreaks. Take it easy and conserve energy, it was sensible to give the fire on the hill free rein, and let the helicopter do its stuff nearby. So backwards and forwards went the helicopter scooping its buckety bag into the sea and then peeling off to the smouldering burnline near the houses. Pull the ripcord, drop the load, splurge out a trailing curtain of salty water. We could contribute little so we backed away and set off to our rocks.

However unwittingly we were to get our moment of glory. We drove west out of the village on the winding road hugging the shore. High up on the hill the main fire was going round the shoulder of the mountain and was to die finally in a black boundary in the next valley, while lower down the fire was still breathing and sneaking imperceptibly into a mature birch wood and towards the fine old pine wood above Torridon House. My driver glancing upwards mouthed imprecations and prophesied dire disasters. We noticed at the roadside verge that some wandering flames were eating at the dead bracken. He was convinced that he had a semi-proprietary right to defend the wood. His time of vindication had come.

But did his van stop? Never a bit of it. It took off like a rally hotrod tearing up the hill, screeching round the sharp bends, through the wood and over the river, and across the open moorland. We drew up by a stacked bundle of long poles with flexible flappy heads, just the beating implements we needed. Pile them into the van and speed back to the fire.

We halted and in a flash the man of action was gone, plunging into the wood before I had got on my boots. I took a circuitous route and made sure I was well away from any taxing involvement. Where we had parked was close to a narrow boulder-filled gully that on demand carries the west coast cloudburst floods from far up the mountain but now it resembled a contorted dried-out wadi and was utterly devoid of water.

I could hear the unseen fire crackling gently on the far side of the gully. A few flickers appeared at the edge of the bank, gobbled some dry bracken, shed its ash and died above the gully bed. Such a feeble ineffective fire now would go no further today, so I ambled back to the roadside. The wind had gone and it was a morning made for indolence.

I lay down on a bank dotted with primroses above the shore, but soon Peter appeared dragging his weapon. He looked rather ashen, his clothes were smudged with dark sooty streaks, his T-shirt was wet with sweat, and he was well pleased. His honour and duty had been satisfied.

It was time to follow our plan of campaign, so off we went on our way to the wee cliffs of Inveralligin.

THE SALVATION OF ACHMORE[1]

By Peter Biggar

IT ALL BEGAN in that strange time between Christmas and New Year. Outside it was dark and a bitter wind was howling in across the loch, but here in the small village pub at the end of the working day all was warm and convivial. Old Archie was in fine form:

'The English,' he said, the eyes in his leathery face beginning to glitter, 'never discuss politics and religion. Here in Scotland we discuss *nothing but* politics and religion!'

'And the football,' said Tom the stalker.

'And sex and death,' said John from Glasgow.

'Och aye,' said Archie, the ghost of a smile playing about his cadaverous lips, 'one must have diversions. But you see John, as I was saying, the Capitalist System as we experience it here in Achmore...' but what he was saying was lost to me because at that moment a noisy bunch of young people erupted into the bar. We had seen a minibus by the mountaineering club hut at the other end of the village as Tom drove our battered transit back from the fish farm. Despite the fashion for global warming, this winter was turning out cold and the hills round Loch More were white and mysterious.

The students were rather loud and free with their opinions. Soon an argument was raging about the economic mainstay of the village. I felt no urge to take part. I had come to Achmore to get away from arguments, my intellectual and emotional life was frozen. I wanted only to exist. I sat back and listened.

The students canvassed all the usual tedious objections to fish-farming: the seabed below the cages was as dead as the Sahara; the wild salmon were having their genes polluted; the cages ruined the ambience – tourists would cease to come – and the empty feed bags blowing about the coast line were a shame and a disgrace. Having some personal experience of the trade, I couldn't help wondering how the students would fare standing on swaying cages in a south-wester trying to keep hold on a slippery bag while feeling sick – but they made some fair points.

One young fellow with curly reddish hair, gold specs, a purple fleece and a far south English accent – his name was Paul – was particularly adamant:

'The whole industry is plainly immoral!' he pronounced, 'and if your parliament really cared about the environment they'd shut it down tomorrow!' Considering that most of the locals made their livings at least partly from the fish-farm, this was a little inconsiderate. John in particular

---

1   This Achmore is purely fictional as are all the characters who inhabit it.

was getting riled. There was an angry silence. I could see that Archie had noticed John clenching his fist. His reedy voice broke the silence:

'I'll give you credit for knowing that we have a parliament,' he said. 'But, now, tell me sonny, what does your Dad do for a living?' Paul blushed furiously.

'That has nothing to do with the argument!' he blurted.

'Oh, fair enough,' said Archie mildly, 'but presumably you yourself want something to do when you grow up?' That was a bit unfair, but it got a laugh and changed the mood slightly. The young man stood his ground.

'Whatever I choose to do,' he said, 'it won't be something that causes harm to nature.' I had to smile. It sounded like something I might have said a thousand years ago.

'Ah, I see,' said Archie peaceably. 'You know, two things strike me about that. The first is that you'll be very privileged to have a choice. And the second is that you'll discover that most jobs get some dirt on your hands. We're an easy target,' he continued, turning to address the company more generally, taking the focus away from young Paul, 'the defects of fish-farming are gross and obvious. The average small town in the Midlands probably does more harm to the environment than the whole of the west coast fishery.' There was a murmur of agreement. His argument was a good one. 'Now,' he added with a twinkle, 'if it was the Capitalist System you wanted to dismantle…' The laugh that followed completed the work of defusing the tension and the discussion whirled on in great good humour.

'Phew! That was getting a bit heavy.' I hadn't noticed that a woman had sat down at my table near the fire. She had a lively, interested expression, longish dark hair and was dressed in climbing clothes. Although she was obviously with the student party, she was considerably older than them, a mature student or lecturer I guessed. 'Young Paul's a nice kid, but he's got a lot to learn about when to shout his mouth off. That could have got nasty. The old guy was really nice to him.'

'Archie can be a bit crabbed, but he's very kind underneath. The young chap made some good points though. I can't really judge the scientific effects of what we do, but the farms are visually intrusive and we do leave a bit of a mess I'm afraid.' I could see her looking at me more closely.

'You actually work on the fish-farm as well?'

'What else is there to do in Achmore?'

'Forgive me,' she said, 'but you don't sound like a fish-farmer.'

'And what does a fish-farmer sound like?'

Her green eyes made contact with mine.

'Much less educated, of course.'

'Not working class enough?'

'If we must use that kind of language, yes.'

'Anyway,' I said, 'all of this misses the point. You'd made some kind of judgment about me before I spoke, surely?'

She smiled and put her pint of Guinness down.

'I suppose I had, really,' she admitted disarmingly. 'Oh, I don't know, it's the way you sit there quietly taking it all in, the cut of the jaw, the intellectual features, whatever!' She laughed; it was a pleasant sound. 'You just don't quite fit the part.'

I enjoyed her company. We had a common interest in the hills. The other thing I do in Achmore is to help with mountain rescue. I was able to pass on a bit of local knowledge about the various climbing areas round about. She didn't ask why I had come to the far north-west, but I could sense a slight curiosity. Talking with her made me realise that I'd missed female company. At length her party got ready to go. They were to be in the area for a few days over New Year. I said I might see her around.

As I walked back down the dimly lit street I thought I could smell snow in the air and sure enough when I came out of the door the following morning, the ground was thick with it. I trudged back up the hill, pausing to read some of the notices on the wall of the village shop. The children were off to the pantomime in Inverness tomorrow; the New Year Dance was planned for 3 January in the hall; the adult Gaelic classes were starting again on the 8th in the school and the fund for the mini swimming pool had now reached over £12,000. With a twinge of conscience I remembered the sponsored walk I had rashly volunteered to take part in. Old Archie was very persuasive. While I was idly scanning the notices, Beryl brought the post bus to a slithering halt shouted a cheery greeting and dashed into the shop. As she came out again still stuffing things into her bag she paused long enough to tell me that the forecast for the next couple of days was poor: high winds and probably a thaw.

'I just hope they've gritted the road to Achbeg, otherwise I'm going to have fun.'

She set off, lumps of dirty snow peeling off the red bus as it weaved an erratic passage up the street. Achbeg was even more isolated than Achmore. The same company that owned our farm had one there too. There were rumours that the company was considering a 'rationalisation' plan and closing one or other of the farms, but in a small community there are always rumours.

While I was waiting to be picked up, my neighbour Donald-Alec came lurching along with his dog Lassie:

'Well, Patrick boy, and how iss your morale today?' He took his unlit pipe from his mouth and fiddled in his blue boiler suit for matches and his penknife.

'*Cem ara how* Donald?' I made my ritual attempt at a Gaelic greeting. 'And how are you today?'

'H'ach, not very great. There were one or two came in last night.' His eyes twinkled. 'That man from Bristol, the one that was the policeman; he can't hold his drink. And my niece was in from Achbeg – lovely girl she is. She's off to Glasgow to the university.' The old man's face clouded for a moment. 'She'll not be back. There's no work here for the young ones. She'll end in mucky England like as not. You're not English Patrick boy?' He knew perfectly well I wasn't.

'No Donald I'm a Scot.'

'Of course you are Patrick boy, you have the good Gaelic. Ach well, here is the van I'm thinking. Be sure to come in on Hogmanay. I'm telling you now, they're having it rough in the South and our turn's to come. Lassie! Come out of that bin! She's the devil of a beast, but I wouldn't be without her! Lassie!'

As we made our way out of the village we passed the hut and some of the students were just staggering out to look at the weather. Tom gave them a toot and they waved.

'They were a bit down on the fish-farming right enough,' he commented.

'They're just young,' said Archie philosophically. 'You don't really understand very much at that age: no experience.'

'All I hope is,' said John from the depths of the Daily Record, 'the eejits'll have the sense to keep off the hill. And that's a point,' he continued, 'what happens to the exercise tomorrow, eh? I don't suppose we can cancel it for bad weather can we?' There was a collective groan from the team members. Nobody fancied spending a precious Saturday carrying a stretcher through deep snow.

Work that day was awful. The fish cages lurched sickeningly in the grey swell, everyone, except Archie who had been a merchant seaman, felt ill. Several restorative half-bottles appeared at lunchtime and nothing much was done in the afternoon.

The students were in the pub again that evening. Big Dennis the barman - black as Hell and moody with it, he's from Lewis – had stoked up the fire and there was a cheerful blaze. The woman I had been chatting to was sitting by it with young Paul and one or two others. I caught her eye and she waved. When I got to the bar, Dennis gestured towards where she was sitting.

'There's one in the tap for you. The lassie with the long hair. She didn't know your name but,' he paused meaningfully, 'she described you.' I raised my glass to her from the bar and our eyes met again, but I didn't go across and sit down with her group. I was just glad to be still and quiet for a few minutes.

I was standing at the bar with one eye on the television – all the Scottish games were off because of the weather – when she arrived beside me.

'Thanks for the drink,' I said. 'And where did you get to today?'

'About half way up Ben More.' She smiled ruefully. 'It was just awful, high wind and spindrift. We turned back.'

'Very wise.'

'Paul and one or two others went round into Coire Dubh. Paul wanted to climb, but nobody would go with him.'

'Just as well.'

'Yes, he's a bit crazy I'm afraid. Not much experience.'

'Just as a matter of interest, what does his father do?'

'Oh, he's high up in a multinational; they have fingers in all sorts of pies, I believe. Paul and Daddy don't always see eye to eye on the environment and so on. I think that's why he gets so worked up. Youthful idealism, rebellion against father, you know the sort of thing.'

We chatted for quite a while about climbs we'd done and places we'd been. We were easy in each other's company. I got more drinks and she accepted a dram. By the time her group went off I knew her name was Julia and I'd invited her to bring some of them round to celebrate New Year. I could feel something starting to thaw inside myself.

We had more snow and the power went off. Apart from feeding the fish, all pretence at work stopped. In between the crackles on Radio Scotland we learned that the whole coast from Sutherland to Oban was in the dark and likely to remain so 'for some considerable while'; and even the English football was off.

After his ancient fowling piece had blasted away the Old Year, Donald-Alec came staggering in, '…and many of them, Patrick boy!' He had his funeral suit and his pork pie hat on. From one of his jacket pockets protruded a bottle of whisky, from the other a bottle of sherry 'for the women.' Archie and John arrived not long after, still chewing the fat over Socialism or some other forgotten creed. Beryl the Post and Arthur her husband were next – he's English, but naturalised.

Firelight flickered on the walls, candles glinted on glasses and picture frames. Outside yet more snow was falling and the wind was getting up again. The talk got round to the old days and the Clearances. Achmore and Achbeg are just two of the coastal settlements where people came to scratch a living by the sea.

'I'll tell you what,' said Archie, pausing as he put his bottle round. 'We'll have clearances all over again if we don't get the fish-farming sorted out.' The thought was uncomfortable. Adverse publicity and falling sales were already causing talk of closures and redundancies.

'Of course, there's the tourists,' I said.

'There's always the tourists,' said Tom.

'There'd be more if it wasn't for the midges,' put in Beryl.

'And the rain and the state of the pound,' said Arthur judiciously.

'Och, the tourists are all very well,' said John. 'But I don't want to live in a glass case for tourists to look at!'

'There's the sheep,' said Tom.

'I prefer women myself!' Old Donald piped up. In the midst of the hilarity that followed came an urgent knocking on the door.

Struggling, half drunk over rank tussocks of heather thickly coated with snow, falling in peat hags, slipping on iced boulders in the dark, the wind screaming in our faces was bad enough, but the position young Paul and his mate had got themselves into was the worst I've known. Roping down to them was like entering Hell with tongues of stinging spindrift for flames. There was an old ewe stuck on a ledge near the boys. Tom the stalker told me later it must have hit a big boulder in the corrie, for bits of it were scattered over forty yards.

The rescue went on all night. John had bad gloves and got frostbite in three fingers. He was off work for two months and started drinking heavily again, much to Archie's despair. No helicopter could fly in that storm. The fish-farm boat took the boys out to Kyle through mountainous seas and they pulled through, just.

Winter went at last and Chulia (as old Donald calls her) came for a visit. We were sitting in front of the cottage watching the worker bees busy on the lavender when an important looking car stopped and a thickly set man in a dark suit appeared.

'My name's Crawford,' he said. I must have looked blank, for he added, 'I'm Paul Crawford's father. I, er, I came to thank you for the part you played in the rescue.'

He accepted a dram and sat with us looking over the bay. He told us young Paul was well on the mend and wouldn't now lose any toes as had been feared. We were glad to hear it; he seemed to be a nice, spirited kid. He had written the team a pleasant letter from hospital.

'I'm sure you'll also be glad to hear that the future of the farm at Achmore is looking much more promising,' Mr Crawford said. Julia caught my eye. 'My fellow Directors take the view that we were, ah, not taking certain factors into account when closure seemed an option. You know,' he added, 'I was looking round at the village as I drove down, and I, err, I really shudder to think what might have happened if there hadn't been a thriving community at Achmore.'

The farm at Achbeg was closed two months later, making seven men and two women redundant.

As for me, I don't know if I'll be staying on at Achmore for ever, fish-farm or not. Julia has plans to drag me back to the city. But maybe we'll stay on and scratch a living somehow. We rather like it here.

THE RAILWAY CHILDREN

By Duncan Tunstall

SOME OF US WERE born to be compulsive tickers, and as such Ken Wilson books have had a significant influence on our lives. 'Hard Rock', for me, being the most important. Although, like many, I was driven by grade, 'Extreme Rock' has too many super hard routes which I will never do, so will never ever become a ticking target. What is strange is that despite this desire to climb the climbs in this book, I am surprisingly crap at it; struggling to do more than one a year and often many years go by with no additions. 'Why is that?' A question I can never really answer. In hindsight I don't have many excuses: although work has taken me overseas, for most of my career I was based in London which made the Devon and Cornwall sea-cliffs more available. What has shocked me is that, now having lived in Aboyne for more than five years, I have still been distracted.

Two of the routes I did manage were *Dragon* and *Gob* many years ago, inspired by the Mike O'Hara quote 'Carnmore is the most wonderful place in all Britain; remote, vast and beautiful in a fashion not found elsewhere in the Highlands.' Paddy Buckley describes *Dragon* as 'awesome, rather introspective; *Gob* is a mind-blower, packed with gusto and excitement: a star of the future.' Indeed I found them wonderful, and the chapter also reads that there are six climbs that are great – leaving *St George*, *Sword*, *Abomination* and *Carnmore Corner* still for me to do!

What is clear is that had I not climbed them when I did, they would still be on my list, and that is what shocks me. If, like me, you like solitude and long walks then it is a venue worth visiting as are many of the other Scottish Hard Rock venues. So why have I not visited more of these classic routes? The answer is I discovered some 'new' cliffs with good climbing that tempted me even more.

If one walks to the Fisherfield Hills from Dundonnell rather than Poolewe, one can't help but notice two substantial cliffs low down on these hills. Even more strange is that these cliffs get very little mention in the guidebooks. Both the cliffs were climbed on in the 1950s and several routes in the Very Difficult and Severe grade were climbed but they have probably not been repeated, certainly not in the last 20 years. In fact they appear to have been abandoned, and I have no idea why.

When I first moved to Scotland I was slightly flattered when Andy Nisbet said he was keen to go rock climbing on these hills and needed a partner. Of course, I was happy to go with him. We set off walking reasonably early in the evening and a Land Rover passed us. Me being me, I put out my thumb. We were shocked when it stopped and picked us up. I was even more shocked that the people in the Land Rover, fishermen and walkers, knew who Nisbet was. We rode in the Land Rover to about halfway to the cliffs before walking the rest of the way.

At the cliff called 'The Sidings', we roped up and, as expected, Andy led the first pitch, a fine crack which climbed to the obvious steepening. Here Andy belayed and brought me up. I expected to be handed the gear, after all I'd spent most of my life climbing alternate leads, but Andy had climbed the lines on either side. He thought the next section would probably be the crux. This was what Andy had walked in to climb. Oh god, what do I do? Do I stick to my principles as there are surely going to be thousands of routes with good pitches to do, or do I back down and let him, the leader, climb his chosen pitch? For reasons I will never know I backed down. Anyone who knows me knows that is something I will rarely do. From a climbing perspective, it made no difference. Sure, the next 15 feet of Andy's pitch were the crux, ten feet or so of a narrow crack that had a tricky exit which led to the continuation crack above. It was fine climbing but as it turned out the pitch above, was slightly easier but bolder. So, in summary, fun was had and *Flying Scotsman* (E1 5b) was a fine route. I am sure that *Little Red Train* (Hard Severe 4a) and *Thomas* (HVS 5a), earlier routes by Andy Nisbet and Sonya Drummond are equally fine.

What really opened my eyes was that the nearby 'Junction Buttress' seemed to be a much better cliff that also had not been visited since the 1960s. Hmm, I thought, why not? My eyebrows were raised. We walked out and the rain came down. In fact, the rain came down for several years and I understood why these routes had to be snatched when they're in condition. The combination of being north-facing and in the wettest part of the country means they are not often good for climbing.

However, over the coming years I spent a lot of time climbing with Andy elsewhere and we became close friends. I learnt that the route we'd done was the last of several he had pioneered on The Sidings. I swore to go back. However, I did not. Some time later, during a spate of good weather, Simon Yearsley asked me to go with him to Carnmore. I agreed, and a day and time were chosen. However, as the day approached the urge to return to the cliff I'd noticed while walking out on that previous visit was too strong. So I advised Simon that I was still keen to go but to a slightly different venue to the one which he'd suggested.

I phoned Andy to let him know we were going in case he wanted to come along. After all, I would not have known of this venue without him. He said yes and had a friend who was also keen to go, so I assumed we'd be a four. As it turned out, his friend was busy so we went as a three, and sharing gear is a very smart thing to do with such a long walk in.

When we got there, we noticed two significant aspects and chose the one which did not face true north. Andy took the first pitch and made slow but steady progress throwing the occasional clump of turf out of the

Andy Nisbet on the first ascent of Injunction (HVS), Junction Buttress, 3 May 2011.
Photo: Duncan Tunstall.

crack. Mutterings were made with regards to the benefits of abseiling and cleaning first, but he continued to make progress and the pitch was completed. Above, it looked like we could have continued straight up but a very distinct crack curved up and round to the right which I chose as the line. It was easy but fantastic. There were no easy belays and we climbed together as a three, in hindsight, for too long. So, we were pleased to get to a very big ledge. From here Simon had the lead for some more difficult climbing and chose to climb the slab to the left of an obvious crack which he managed with grace. I couldn't resist the obvious easier line and so led, from the slab, to the top.

At the top we were all quite happy but time was still available and to the right of us was a distinct continuation of the buttress now in the sun. We descended to its foot, managed to bypass the first pitch and Andy and Simon climbed a fine two-pitch route to the top. I followed with enjoyment. We then all headed back to the car.

After 20 minutes walking we stopped for water and I realised I didn't have my camera so I went back to look for it without success. It was the only blot on an otherwise fine day.

Last week (2012) Andy said he was keen to return and I was naturally excited. However, other stuff cropped up and I couldn't go, but I am pleased to say that Andy returned with another friend and ascended the central line. He said the direct was too bold to on-sight, but he'd found an enjoyable climb at a reasonable grade, similar in quality to the one we had climbed before – a fine VS. As we had done on our first trip, they had climbed another route on the slabs in the afternoon sun. It was at the bottom of the cliff that Andy found my camera, lost on that previous visit, rusted and damaged by the rains. He brought the camera back with him, and to my delight the photos we took were still recoverable.

So, in summary, the valley has gone from climbing idleness to being potentially an area of attraction to all those who like good rock in beautiful but isolated situations. Shenavall bothy makes the prospect of a long weekend there, with a combination of fine summits and many routes, an attractive proposition. Certainly as the sun shines through my window I am keen to return, one to repeat Andy's route, and two to have a closer look at some of the less obvious but still interesting lines on the cliff. Surely if Carnmore can have six lines around *Dragon* and *Gob*, so can Junction Buttress!

IS THE DISEASE COMING UNDER CONTROL?

By Nigel Suess

OUR LATE HON. President Bill Brooker was Clerk of the List for many years and wrote an amusing piece 'Rampant Munrosis, the Scottish Disease' over twenty years ago[1]. He commented that the growth in the number of (confessed) Munro Compleations had been exponential. This piece was reprinted with updating in Robin Campbell's Companion[2]. I briefly referred to the continued growth at around 11% compound annually in this Journal in 2001[3]. After another decade or so updated analysis may be of interest.

The word exponential has been co-opted into general usage after a long and illustrious period of possession by mathematicians and scientists. Indeed, one early user of its powers was Baron Napier of Merchiston, who produced a table of logarithms in 1614. As with many borrowed words the specific meaning has become corrupted. Recall that decay can be exponential. In mathematical terms exponential time-related growth/decay of a quantity implies that the rate of change is a constant proportion of the instantaneous value of the quantity. After this I shall refrain from equations and express my analysis with the data presented in graphical and tabular form.

Fortunately, there is a long record of the afflicted reporting their condition and allowing it to be publicised. The number of reported cases has now approached 5000. Indeed, that indicator point may have been attained by the time you read this. Nevertheless, I have enjoyed the company of several climbing partners who have kept their Compleation a secret from the pages of this Journal. I shall not 'out' them, but the price they pay is exclusion from the data set examined here.

For data on Compleations up to 1981, I have used the list given in Derek Bearhop's 1997 Edition of *Munros Tables*[4]. For the more recent period I have used the number reported in each year's *SMCJ* as a proxy for the number of Compleations for the previous year. That did involve allocating late reportings to the wrong year. However, their number is small and probably unbiased. As a result we have 110 years of records to analyse (1901–2010). I used a mathematical computer package, MAPLE.

1   WD Brooker, *SMCJ*, 34/182 (1991), 598–603.

2   Robin N Campbell, *The Munroist's Companion* (SMT, 1999), 309–13.

3   NM Suess, 'Plus Ça Change', *SMCJ,* 37/192 (2001), 510–12.

4   Derek A Bearhop, *Munro's Tables* (SMT, 1997), 75–91.

The questions to which I sought answers were:
i) what has been the mean annual growth rate of the number expressed as a proportion of the previous total?
ii) how has this mean annual growth rate varied in each decade?
iii) are we seeing a moderation in that growth rate in recent years?

The answer to the first question is 8.67%.
The answer to the second question is expressed in the Table below:

Decade	Increase over decade annualised in %
1901–1910	Infinite, but zero after AER
1911–1920	Zero
1921–1930	14.87%
1931–1940	7.18%
1941–1950	6.49%
1951–1960	10.84%
1961–1970	9.39%
1971–1980	8.92%
1981–1990	13.45%
1991–2000	11.42%
2001–2010	6.46%

The answer to the third question may be affirmative based on this Table. However, one recognises immediately that the trends are not smooth. For example, in the early years there was usually either one or no entry. More recently, one observes fluctuations about some perceived general trend. This irregularity was tackled by Brooker (here in Campbell's Companion) using the logarithm of a cumulative total and his resulting graph for 1945–97 is compelling. I have further updated this approach to 2010 (see graph A) and one may obtain a hint that the growth rate moderated after about the turn of the millennium. I also took a different approach, inspired by that branch of stockmarket analysis known as chartism. Do not ask me the reason but many chartists regard as significant the crossing of the chart of the price averaged over the previous 200 days with the price averaged over the previous 50 days. This may be mumbo jumbo but its adherents call it the 'Golden Cross', possibly in recognition of their profits from buying when the 50-day average rises above the 200-day average. I chose to adapt this notion to look at the chart of the mean number of new Compleations averaged over the previous 10 years with that averaged over the previous 3 years.

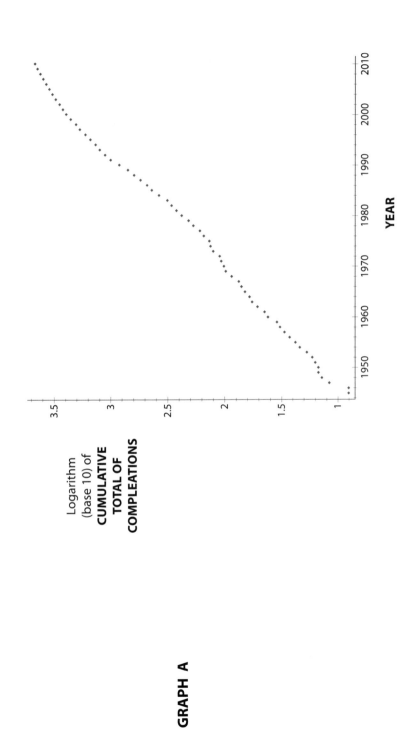

Logarithm
(base 10) of
**CUMULATIVE
TOTAL OF
COMPLEATIONS**

YEAR

GRAPH A

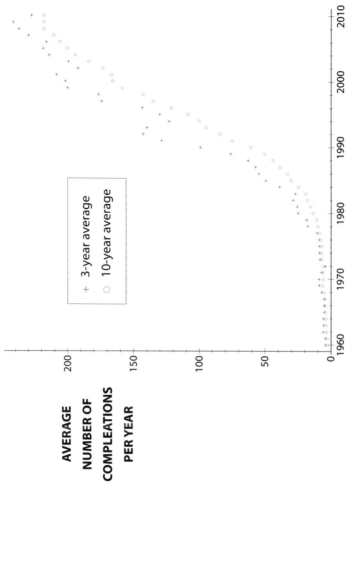

GRAPH B

The resulting graph B, covers the period 1960–2010.

My hypothesis is that any occurrence of the 3-year average falling below the 10-year average would indicate that the 'stock' has gone ex-growth. One does not see such a phenomenon in the period under review but the prospect of it occurring in the next few years appears more likely than it would have been a decade ago. One can observe that the 10-year average has stabilised at around 219 during the last three years studied.

Whether or not the Golden Cross applies in this scenario, my conclusion is that, after a period of rapid growth in the number of new Compleations during the 1980s and 1990s, we have returned to a more stable trend. That is not to say that walking the 3000ft hills of Scotland is in decline. A drive past certain Highland lay-bys is empirical evidence to the contrary. What appears to be the case is that the rate of recruitment to addiction has moved towards a stable level.

Perhaps the 'rampancy' of the Munrosis virus is now under better control?

PO AND JO IN ALBANIA

By Graham E. Little

Jim

Albania is the forgotten country of Europe due to long standing isolationist policies and subsequent political unrest and has only become reasonably accessible within the last decade or so. It has some very impressive mountains and a wealth of unclimbed rock. How about a visit in 2011 – I suggest a four man team.

Regards

Graham

PS Norman Wisdom, who died recently, is much loved in Albania as his films were the only Western entertainment available during the four decades of Enver Hoxha's repressive rule – we should take T-shirts!

THE IDEA BECAME a plan, the plan became a journey, and so it came to pass that an aristocrat, an actuary, an accountant (just retired) and I arrived at the splendid new Tirana airport in mid June 2011. To be honest, the plan was rudimentary, with a night in a hotel in the northern city of Shkodra our only firm arrangement.

Some climbing trips seem blessed and some cursed. This trip was blessed, with everything falling seamlessly into place as if we were but players in some cosmic choreography. Even taking into account that a shake of the head indicates yes (po) and a nod of the head means no (jo) we didn't have any trouble communicating as on every occasion things got a bit sticky, somebody would be there to help – often a teenager keen to apply their English language skills.

The mountains of northern Albania, known as the Accursed Mountains, span the border with Montenegro to the north and Kosovo to the east. Rising to a height of nearly 2700m they are spectacular by any standards and being Carboniferous limestone, display classic karst topography with challenging terrain and very little surface water. From Internet research, we knew that the area had recently been the recipient of a number of educational and environmental initiatives under the Balkan Peace Park Project and was starting to attract rock climbers from northern Europe.

A day after our arrival in Albania we found ourselves crammed into a battered minibus, with a bevy of young women, heading for Thethi, a village near the western edge of the mountain group. Our first night's accommodation had been smoothly arranged through the brother of a friend of the hotel owner – that's how thing happen in Albania.

We quickly gained height on the rough switchback track above Boga, to reach the Qafa e Terthores (a pass at 1630m), then plunged down into the depths of the Shala Valley. The head of the valley is dominated by a mountain that can only be described as iconic: in a land of spectacular peaks, Arapit, 2217m, for all its relatively modest height, is the El Cap of Albania. The first ascent of a direct line up its 1000m South Face was climbed by an international team as recently as 2010. Whilst our ambitions were more modest, this mountain had a mesmeric effect upon us, persistently drawing our eyes back from the wealth of other sights.

Our first night in the mountains was in a home-stay[1] with a local family. Lunch was served on arrival – the standard fare of rural Albania: lamb/goat, salad and chips with bread and cheese washed down with a glass of rough red wine. After lunch Eric (the actuary) and I took on the important task of sightseeing, including admiring bikini-clad models posing in the splash pool below the Grunas waterfall, whilst Ron (the retired accountant) and Jim (the aristocrat) whiled away the afternoon buying food and arranging horse hire.

Under a blistering sun we followed our well laden horse and owner across the near waterless boulder-strewn streambed and onto the path that zigzags up the steep pine-studded hillside to the east of Arapit. From the first col we took an ancient path that passes the strange lake of Liqenjte Pejes to a second col then eventually descends into the Ropojana valley in Montenegro. Our campsite was a little plain in a depression just off the path below the pine clad hill Point 1823m – an ideal spot, with spring water nearby. The whole area, called Stanet e Pejes, was obviously a summer sheep pasture at one time with walled enclosures and shepherds huts in various stages of decay.

Bursting with enthusiasm, Jim and I bashed up the hillside to the east of camp the following morning soon to be enveloped in a thick, damp mist that rendered navigation over the complex karst terrain near impossible. As the mist cleared, we found ourselves on the edge of a vast depression, with snow fields and looming limestone walls beyond. We contoured round the bowl and of course headed for the most striking line on the biggest face beyond. Our ambition was quickly tempered as we stepped from steep snow onto smooth limestone covered in pulverised rock debris. It was a mutual jo. Further into the back of the basin the pinnacles were lower and looked less scary and we traversed snowfields towards the col where ibex-like animals made a brief appearance. The second pinnacle from the col on the north side gave us a four-pitch climb with a bold 5a section and a final arête comprised of chaotically arranged limestone splinters. It was a modest top on a multi-topped ridge but it was a summit and almost certainly a first ascent.

---

1 Home-stay accommodation is well developed in the mountain valleys – expect to pay about 25 Euros for full board including drinks (the Albanian currency is the Lek but low denomination Euro notes are widely accepted).

Jim Lowther on top of 'the pinnacle' on the first ascent.
Photo: Graham Little.

The perfect campsite with Point 2205m behind. Photo: Graham Little.

Back in camp we heard of Ron and Eric's adventure in the mist resulting in them missing the main crag and climbing on a flanking face. Jim and I were already planning our next day out. Looking north-west from just above our camp the great towers of Lagojvet dominate the skyline with the right-hand main peak dropping a snaking ridge from summit to footing snow patch. Binoculars revealed grass and trees low down but higher up it looked cleaner and arête-like. The plan was set over a glass of whisky around a cracking pine-log fire.

The cool early morning air spurred us on over flower decked meadows and onto a grassy bench that cut an easy swathe through the rocky terrain. Soon we were to grips with steep grass and limestone slabs taking advantage of sturdy pine belays and heading up towards a huge roof that near barred the way to the middle part of our route. I belayed under a blazing sun as Jim climbed the barrier pitch, passing the great roof on the left. He dislodged a stone that whizzed past, thudded onto the ledge then arced out into space. I followed Jim's fine lead, acutely aware of the amount of loose rock all around. I moved a few metres above Jim on easier rock but not with much conviction. Every ledge was covered in loose blocks, it was past mid-day, there was still a lot of climbing above us and things just didn't feel right. My inner voice was advising retreat and I shared it with Jim. Was this a sound response to the risk of continuing the climb and the subsequent abseil descent or just a lack of bottle on my part? It is always easy to kid ourselves that a subjective

The Lagojvet Group with the sunlit arête attempted on the right. Photo: Graham Little.

perspective is an objective judgement. Jim did not question my voice and we commenced the descent with an airy launch over the middle of the great roof. The final abseil was down a vertical wall of polished limestone with a rash of large snails its only feature.

Back in camp my internal voice had a different story to tell and it was an uncomfortable one. The late afternoon sun picked out our ridge, the light and shade, the po and jo – mocking mere mortals, questioning our courage, playing with our emotions. With the fading light such introspection gave way to concern over the safety of Ron and Eric. We were relieved to spot them approaching camp before dark, Ron clearly hobbling. He had pulled off a large block that had sliced his thumb and caused an ankle-crunching fall onto a rock ledge. Whisky and first aid were administered and Ron, every the optimist, agreed that he'd better have a day's rest!

The lure of Arapit proved irresistible and Jim, Eric and I summited via a scrappy new route on the north side. The view into the green depths of the Shala valley and of the surrounding peaks was breathtaking. Descending the normal ascent route over the classic clints, grikes and sinkholes of schoolboy geography we came to a long runnelled wall that just had to be climbed. Our 80m HVS at the right hand end of the wall followed water-eroded flutes on perfect rock. The wall offered many similar lines but the sun was hot and Jim and I were tempted by a swim in the warm newt-filled water of Liqenjte Pejes.

Graham pushing the boat out on the first pitch of Norman Wisdom on FA (tiny figure just left of centre)
Photo: Ron Kenyon.

Ron needed another rest day so Jim, Eric and I decided that a big hill day was in order. Mt. Jezerces[2], at 2692m, is the highest peak in the Accursed Mountains and is truly Alpine in appearance. It proved a rewarding day with soft green meadows, vast snowfields, interesting route finding on shattered limestone and mountain panoramas drenching our senses. The summit book had no British entries since placed there a couple of years ago.

With just one more night to go at our high camp, Jim and I agreed that it was time for some meaty rock climbing. The nose of Point 2205m to the south of camp offered some striking lines, including a long chimney/crack running two-thirds of the way up the wall. Dashing up the hill after Jim was re-confirmation that effort and age have a direct correlation. As if to redress the balance I took the sharp end and launched up the steep and intimidating crack, quickly gaining height until an overhung narrowing brought me to an abrupt halt. The gear was good but a detached flake on the right wall was worrying and there seemed no alternative but to use it. Ron and Eric snapped shutters below whilst I wound myself up to launch up the flared, overhanging groove. A sidepull, a foot on the fractured flake, a cranking, sweating, scraping levitation and it was po, po, po to a niche above! Jim arrived looking very pale, telling of a stone I'd dislodged that had whirred past his head. His expression was a triple jo! I agreed to lead on but realised that continuing up the crack would be too risky and after a few metres took a diagonal line out left. After two pitches Jim, with regained composure, lead the fourth pitch with a steep and technical start. Two more long pitches took us to the foot of an open grassy groove and so the top. Our route, *Norman Wisdom*[3], was a real rat-feeder and we descended under a 30° sun-blast as cool as cats.

By a roaring fire, we watched the last rays of the sun turning the white limestone to flame, the jagged peaks silhouetting around us, with the deep satisfaction gained from turning an idea into an experience, of testing ourselves and not being found wanting – that rare satisfaction when endeavour, time and place form perfect union.

Our horse and horseman arrived spot-on the appointed time and, as we headed back to Tethi, we discussed how to spend our last few days in Albania. Ron was still limping so he and Eric decided to take our kit back to Shokdra. Jim and I were quick to plan a trek into and down the Valbona Valley with the intention of meeting Eric and Ron in the wild-east town of Bajram Curri.

After a lazy day in Tethi, drinking too many beers and playing lots of Bridge, the team split and Jim and I followed a snaking path up through superb natural beech woods to cross the Valbona Pass, 1812m and down

2 Mt. Jezerces, 2692m, is the second highest peak in Albania. The highest peak, Mt. Korab, 2764m, lies on the Albanian–Macedonian border.

3 *Norman Wisdom* was 210m, E2 5c, 5a, 4a, 5b, 4a, 4b.

into the flower meadows of the Valbona Valley. After skirting around a flock of sheep guarded by particularly vicious wolf-deterring dogs, we had our lunch-break with the local shepherd. With no common language we nevertheless enjoyed a full conversation.

Lower down the valley we searched for a home-stay and were lucky to find accommodation with the local teacher. His immediate offer of a cold beer set the scene for an enjoyable stay as we became part of the family for a couple of days. Our host's sons delighted in playing games on Jim's iPhone and his five-year-old daughter showed Jim how to play Chess!

With one spare day before our rendezvous in Bajram Curri, Jim and I decided on a big hill day. The walk into Mt. Roshit[4], 2522m, can only be described as magical – over flower-draped alps of outstanding beauty. As Jim said, there were many Julie Andrews moments. After some tricky route-finding we topped out as grey, cold skies briefly spat sleet upon us.

On the descent, with Jim well ahead of me, the temptation to bag another hill proved too great. I crossed the col and climbed to the knife-edged top of Point 2230m sitting in contemplation of the high and lows, the gains and losses of life; savouring the balm of high mountain solitude.

A hot bath (my first in Albania), sharing whisky with our hosts and eating a very late dinner with a room full of happy neighbours after the harvest had been gathered ended a near perfect day.

A large raki and strong coffee for breakfast and an emotional farewell to our host family saw us rattling down the Valbona valley. The rough track eventually gave way to tarmac and in a couple of hours we arrived in the strange town of Bajram Curri with its crumbling communist era housing, its long street market and shiny black Mercedes cruising the potholed roads. A lunchtime reunion with Ron and Eric, a wander round the town, followed by fried river trout for dinner, washed down with a surprisingly good Riesling, rounding off a day of contrasts.

Our penultimate day in Albania saw us on a battered old ferry chugging down Lake Komani, a flooded river gorge, which must be one of the most impressive boat trips in Europe.

A last night out in Shkodra and it was back to Tirana and the end of an amazing trip. Albania may be one of the poorest countries in Europe but it is rich in natural beauty, has mountains and unclimbed rock to satisfy every taste and when it comes to hospitality has few equals. Would I go again? Po!

---

4 Coincidentally, the Albanian word for carp, a national delicacy, is crap!

TRUST

By Donald M. Orr

I SUPPOSE THAT it is an age thing. Down sizing or, in the mountain sense, down scaling. Not necessarily the anxiety of managing to get up and down in the same day, but certainly a major concern is what physiotherapists jokingly refer to as 'recovery time'; which now, sadly, extends over a period of days rather than hours. One moves from Munros via Corbetts to Grahams and Donalds not through lack of fitness you understand, but purely from that desire for time spent away from the hordes seemingly directed out to advertise clothing from North Face, Berghaus et al. Not that I, I assure you, am not a hip hop and happening outdoor type – I too have a lime green T-shirt! However, I must admit that the knee joints are not what they were and do require the aforementioned amount of time to relax, or recover if you wish. Blasé as one may try to be, and not wishing to be aligned with the elderly and infirm, I feel that I am slipping into that group that the young French refer to as 'Citron pressé'. While you, as reader, are in no way requested to sympathise – you are all perfectly capable of crushing your own lemons, so to speak – you will, I am sure, agree that a certain amount of slippage can be found in any age group.

I am usually good with maps, or I was; never mind, lesson learned.

I had opted for myself and my veteran buddies a Graham in Argyll; an easy day, a little fresh air and exercise in autumnal grandeur; what could be better – true, but anyway, Western Ferries carried us over the Firth of Clyde to Cowal and we headed off in the general direction of Tighnabruaich. To save personal embarrassment I had resolved to omit the name of foresaid Graham, but anyway it was Cruach nan Capull; the heap of the mares, and a mare's nest it proved to be being the disordered circumstances of a discovery imagined to be important but proving worthless.

The sun shone, the air was golden, parking was available and there in front of us stood our objective rippling with cloud shadow and presented to us at the head of a small valley. All we had to do was walk up the forest road, turn off through the wood, clamber up the open hillside on to the ridge and follow it to the summit and Bob would undoubtedly have been our uncle.

I was not in any way taxed by problems of navigation; which on reflection may have been the problem. I cannot blame my friends, well, not for this specific situation, as I was happy to chat away as we warmed up on the road through the valley. I knew that the path through the woods was the first on the left and if we missed that the road ended at a stream which we could follow up on to the open slopes of the hill. Simple, as they say.

After a while I intuitively felt that we should be close to the path through the wood and looking about did see an opening which could have been the remains of an overgrown trail through the forest, but not the dirt road that the map assured me of. We went on and came to a stream crashing down the hill which did have a passing place but the road continued to climb whereas it should have stopped according to the map. We went on, climbing still, but the road becoming rapidly overgrown and narrow and finally, as I realized we were way off track, it collapsed into a muddy collection of imprints within a dense forest. I cursed which does no good and can leave a bad impression on the assembly. It must be noted that the foresaid assembly did not bat an eyelid at this which may suggest that perhaps my curses are now deemed invalid due to over use or that my navigation has been deteriorating for some time and they have become inured to suffering thus.

It was suggested that we strike up through the trees and make for the open hillside which they proceeded to do. This is not the way I like to conduct my compilation of Grahams. Getting seriously jagged…. anyway we got through it, and started tackling the vertical grass that awaited us towards the ridge. Struggling up this verdure was not easy and I was surprised to see a grey-haired gentleman sitting near the ridge watching us. How sad, I thought, coming up here for some solitude to have it broken by a group of aging hillwalkers grunting past your favourite spot. I raised my hand in a gesture of acknowledgement only to have it ignored. This very nearly drove me down the cursing avenue again but, having been ignored there also, I endeavoured to gain height and pass quietly by. Upon looking up again I saw that he was not content with mere gestures and was heading over to cut me off, presumably to lecture me about crashing through undergrowth, or the care and maintenance of trees act, or some other such reprimand. Only as he closed in did I recognise him as one of our own party who had got fed up waiting for me; which does rather suggest that I should at least take a pair of glasses with me occasionally, not that it affects my navigation you understand.

We gained a knoll on the ridge and the full glory of Cruach nan Capull spread out before us – unfortunately some miles away, with a very steep drop to the bealach and a fairly precipitous climb back up. The one bounty gained from being there was the fact that we could all see that the overgrown trail I had spotted originally was indeed the one we should have taken to get to the summit.

Apologies were offered. It did not matter they said, with a tinge of resignation in their voice, they had come out for some fresh air and exercise and the frisson of adventure off the beaten track had made it all memorable for them. I hesitated, then informed them that their bushwhacking was not over; the only way down would involve another crash through the undergrowth to gain the original stream and regain the forest road. Their eyes lit up. Here was a sense of achievement, the exercise of a skill recently developed and greatly enjoyed, the pursuit of the unknown and undiscovered. They tore off at a rate of knots, each choosing his own path and whooped and hollered their way down the hill like things demented. I followed trying to use my rucksack to push my way through but eventually turning my back and travelling backwards through the brushwood until we all met up on the road and started to get all the sticks out of our hair and clothing.

I apologised again. They were having none of it. This had been the best day out they'd had in the hills since I'd led them disastrously off Beinn a' Chreachain and down the Meall Buidhe–Beinn Achaladair gap which had involved what used to be referred to as 'combined tactics'.

On the way out I again scanned the section of map I had downloaded for the occasion. The features were all there, but the road had gone on much farther than indicated. Fergus peered over my shoulder, 'You do realise that the hardware may be new but the map was last revised in 1997,' he said, indicating a date in the corner that I had not noticed. I folded the map carefully, put it in my pocket and immediately started asking for their considered opinions on Saturday's sporting fixtures.

NO ONE SAID IT WOULD BE EASY
Part 1 – Coire nan Laogh

By Noel Williams

THE 'LAST' CORRIE on the south side of the Cuillin is rarely visited. It was first explored by Herford and Laycock exactly a century ago. In those days reaching Skye was an adventure in itself. They travelled up from Manchester and it was only after the 'labours of Hercules' that they reached their destination in Glen Brittle. Their journey was described by Herford in a letter to his father, which is quoted at length in Keith Treacher's fine biography of Siegfried Herford[1]. It is summarised here:

Friday 16/08/1912
2300 Took the train from Manchester to Wigan.

Saturday 17/08/1912
0030 Changed at Wigan for the train to Carlisle.
0300 Changed at Carlisle for the train to Crianlarich.
        Missed the train to Fort William by a minute – it pulled out before their eyes – so they lost the chance of crossing to Skye before Monday. They caught a train to Bridge of Orchy and sent on their baggage to Mallaig. They then set off on foot for the Kingshouse.
1700 Arrived at Kingshouse.

Sunday 18/08/1912
        Climbed *Crowberry Ridge*.
1500 Returned to Kingshouse.
        Walked back to Bridge of Orchy. Slept in an outhouse.

Monday 19/08/1912
        The train to Fort William didn't stop at Bridge of Orchy so they first caught the train back to Crianlarich. In Fort William they were told they had six minutes before the train left for Mallaig. They were only away four minutes getting refreshments, but the train had already left on their return. As all their things were on the train they couldn't climb Ben Nevis, so they caught the next train to Mallaig.
1400 Arrived at Mallaig.
        Sailed across to Armadale. Persuaded a local to take their baggage in his cart along a rough track to Point of Sleat. They camped one mile short of the Point. They expected to meet a fisherman who would take them to Glen Brittle, but he was away.

1   Keith Treacher, *Siegfried Herford* (The Ernest Press, 2000), 82–4.

Tuesday 20/08/1912

Laycock walked back to Armadale and wired a fisherman at Mallaig who agreed to pick them up and take them to Skye. Meanwhile Herford ferried 'a ton of baggage' the last mile to the Point of Sleat in the rain.

1400 Another fisherman turned up (the one wired couldn't come). The best he could manage was a lift to Rum. From there they'd have to get a steamer to Soay and another boat to Skye.

Once on Rum they discovered that the steamer might not call there. They wired another port to ensure that it did so. They were told it would arrive between 11 p.m. and 6 a.m.

1900 They pitched their tent and had a meal.

Then they were told to pack up quickly and they were rowed back to the fishing smack in the dark before eventually transferring to the steamer for Soay.

Wednesday 21/08/1912 (?)

On the last leg of their journey from Soay to Glen Brittle in a small sailing boat, they spotted two chimneys[2] cutting through the broad band of slabs in Coire nan Laogh.

— . —

Despite a week of rain Herford and Laycock ventured out every day and their ascents included the *Cioch*, the *South Crack* on the Inaccessible Pinnacle, *Slanting Gully,* and the Basteir face of the *Third Pinnacle* of Sgùrr nan Gillean. One day they were overtaken by a cloud burst on the Cioch and *Eastern Gully* became a river with pools in which they could almost have stood submerged. The worst part of the holiday was putting on wet breeches each morning.

One day after a wet morning they decided to look at the chimneys they had spotted in Coire nan Laogh from the boat. Despite originally identifying only **two chimneys** in his F&RCCJ article, Laycock went on to describe the ascent of **three gullies** which he called *A, B* and *C.*

A Gully was 'a mere walk.' *B Gully* had a severe pitch and was described as 'a remarkable place, of the most romantic, and a very worthy climb.' *C Gully* was 'a pleasant climb, perhaps a difficult.'

In the Club's guidebook to Skye, which was published in 1923, Steeple and Barlow describe three **prominent** [my emphasis] gullies which they called west, central and east. The identity of these three gullies has been confused in our guidebooks ever since.

As Laycock remarked, there are in fact only **two** prominent gullies in the corrie. It has been widely assumed that these were *West Gully* and *Central Gully,* (see for example JW Simpson's 1969 guide), because a third and less obvious chimney also lies a little further to the right.

2 J. Laycock, 'Impressions of Skye', *F&RCCJ*, 3/2 (1914), 61–4.

On a damp day in May a few years ago I set off by myself to ascend what I thought was *West Gully*. It looked quite intimidating from below, and certainly didn't look like a walk. But, hey, those old boys could climb. I soon encountered a steep little wall below an enormous chockstone. It felt very much like climbing to me, but I soon wriggled up through a tunnel and broke out into an easier section of gully. I assumed that I'd done the Moderate pitch at the bottom described in Simpson's 1969 guide. So all that remains now, I thought, is an uninteresting scramble over boulders. To my astonishment I then came to a dripping wet and overhanging chockstone that barred all progress. I had no gear with me and didn't really fancy reversing back down the tunnel. I stupidly thought it might be easier to escape from the gully by slanting down the east wall. It wasn't too bad to start with, although very exposed, but I then found myself at the base of a steep face with a great expanse of wet and slippery slabs below me. I ended up making a series of desperate moves and I got so gripped in the process that I was still trembling when I eventually managed to reach the corrie floor.

On the club meet to Skye this year, I was able to interest a large team in having a look at this gully. It had gone down to Easy in the various Mackenzie guides, but had then gone back up to Moderate again in the latest Cuillin guide by Mike Lates which appeared last September. So I was prepared to be humiliated if we managed to easily overcome my previous high point.

Paul Brian, Robin Campbell and Peter Macdonald set off a bit before us. Simon Fraser, Willie Jeffrey and I followed on behind. There is a good path now as far as Coire a' Ghrunnda, so it's not the flog it once was. We eventually spotted the scouting party ahead of us before losing sight of them again. We cut the corner by slanting diagonally up the hillside and soon realised that they'd stopped for lunch well below us beside the stream from the corrie. We also snatched a bite to eat and decided to press on to the mouth of the gully. Unfortunately the cloud was low and conditions were rather wintery with occasional flurries of snow and hail.

There are some minor steps in the introductory section of gully. I was surprised to find part of a digital camera among the scree. As we roped up beneath the first big chockstone we were pleased to see the others appear below us. Peter came storming up to join us. Willie offered to lower a rope for Robin, but the weather was worsening and he gave Willie a choice riposte. It wasn't a day for rock climbing and we wore gloves at times as well as cags and big boots.

All four of us had to remove our rucksacks before we could wriggle our way through the tunnel. It seemed tighter than I remembered. I then discovered a broken LED headtorch in the bed of the gully. People had been this way before.

We all gathered beneath the overhanging chockstone which had

Willie Jeffrey launches himself onto the left wall – to no avail. Photo: Noel Williams.

stopped me previously. It looked even more daunting than before. I thought perhaps Herford had used combined tactics to overcome this obstacle, so I kept encouraging Willie to stand on my shoulders. But Willie is made of sterner stuff. First he moved back down the gully slightly and tried to pull up onto a narrow ramp on the left wall. Despite several attempts he couldn't trust his fingers in the cold conditions. Then he tried to get round the left side of the chockstone, but no joy. Next he managed to fiddle a tape round a fist-sized rock on the right side of the

Willie Jeffrey leads a new variation on the right wall of Central Gully. Photo: Noel Williams.

chockstone, but it came out when he pulled on it and he landed in a heap back on the floor of the gully. I again suggested that he stand on my shoulders, but again he refused.

We had all seen a dyke running up the right wall of the gully, but had dismissed it as a possible option. The angular nature of the rock and its slimy appearance were off-putting. Willie decided it was worth a try. There didn't seem to be any gear and it wasn't clear if it was a blind alley. He edged up the feature with care, and we were relieved when he

Peter Macdonald at the top of the 'horizontal basalt columns' pitch. Photo: Noel Williams.

eventually managed to place a runner. It didn't look very good, but it was enough to encourage him on. After a few more moves and a much better runner he said he thought he would soon be able to get back into the gully above the chockstone. We were hugely relieved when he made it. We were grateful to have the rope above us when we followed. We all agreed it felt Severe in the conditions, though it might be easier in the dry.

The gully hadn't given up yet. We climbed up a pitch of horizontal basalt columns, which might have been pleasant in the dry. We were astonished to come across a length of fairly new climbing rope with a severed end hanging off a spike. Someone must have had an epic descending here? We continued up a long easier section of boulders before eventually escaping by a weakness on the left wall.

When the ground eased we traversed hard right and descended beyond the east end of the rock band back to the floor of the corrie.

For the last decade Stuart Pedlar has been transcribing every last word written about climbing in the Cuillin. I had already been in touch with him about Coire nan Laogh, and had suggested that either Herford and Laycock hadn't climbed *A Gully* or it had changed drastically since their visit. It didn't look like it could ever have been a mere walk.

A month after our visit Robin came up with the answer. It was so obvious I was embarrassed not to have thought of it myself, but I'm no

Simon Fraser solos up the delectable slabs immediately to the left of the mouth of East Gully.
Photo: Noel Williams.

lateral thinker. Robin suggested that we had in fact been in *Central Gully* (*B Gully* of Laycock). *West Gully* must lie further to the left. The other prominent gully to the right is *East Gully*, and the less obvious chimney further right again is unnamed. At first I wasn't sure, but on reading the full description of *B Gully* in Laycock's Fell & Rock article all became clear. Robin was undoubtedly correct.

> The first pitch was a large square chockstone bridging the gully—it was overcome on the left. The cleft steepened and the next pitch was hopelessly undercut. With a shoulder it might perhaps have been feasible, but the gully was very wet and shoulders were "off". We advanced up a slab on the left to a small corner with a spike, and thence a very delicate traverse led back to the head of the pitch. This pitch is severe. We now entered a deeply cut rift and walked up a natural staircase of small basaltic columns laid on their side for a hundred feet upwards and inwards. A big boulder closed the gully far outside of us, but a lower bridge half way out made the passage easier and safer. There only remained then a few feet of easy work.

Laycock doesn't mention a tunnel, but they must have climbed onto the ramp on the left wall that had repulsed Willie. Everything else fits. I've looked carefully at the left-hand half of the corrie, but can't identify an obvious gully worthy of a name. In any case since *West Gully (A Gully* of Laycock*)* is 'a mere walk' it has no place in a climbing guide.

Armed with this information I went back to Coire nan Laogh a month later with Simon Fraser. We thought we might look at the other prominent gully, *East Gully*, and the less obvious gully further right. It didn't take long for us to dismiss the 'Far Eastern Gully' as better tackled in winter – the first pitch was rather wet. We then transferred our attentions to *East Gully*. The lower part of the gully has an insurmountable chockstone, so we scrambled up the delectable slabs immediately to the left. We then regained the bed of the gully above the chockstone. Some giant boulders proved awkward but we eventually got past them close to the left wall.

The continuation up the gully looked wet and outrageous for Difficult. There's probably another tunnel pitch there, but we didn't investigate. Instead we traversed out on the left-hand side of the gully. We found some surprisingly pleasant climbing on the slabs above. The line we took is probably similar to a descent route used by McGuinness and Ainsworth in 1952. Stuart Pedlar found their description in the Glen Brittle House Log Book[3]. They graded their descent Difficult and called it *Mortuary Slabs*.

So, mystery solved. The two prominent gullies in Coire nan Laogh are *Central Gully* and *East Gully*. And, yes, those old boys could climb.

[There is a topo identifying all the climbs in Coire nan Laogh in the New Climbs section on page 161.]

---

3   Stuart Pedlar, *Across Unmeasured Space* (Unpublished manuscript, 2009), Vol. 2, p. 538.

A MUNRO JOURNEY

By Peter Gillman

WHEN THE SMC PRODUCED its infamous revision of the Munros table in 1997, I was one of those who took it as a personal affront. It had taken me almost 30 years to complete the original list, with the additional challenge of doing so from south London. My certificate from the SMC arrived just a few days before the publication of the new list, with its sanctimonious rider that it was 'a matter of conscience' for those who had completed under the old rules to decide whether to climb the new peaks. Well, I examined my conscience, and it was clear: I had completed the list in good faith as it stood. Besides, I had found the final summits an increasingly painful ordeal, as during the descents my knees felt as if they were grinding on broken glass. I had in fact climbed four of the 'new' eight anyway (and was dismayed to discover that one my original list had been demoted to the status of a top.) But at the age of 55 I thought that enough was enough, and resolved to continue my walking career in the softer (and sunnier) climes of southern England.

My resolve to abstain from Munros lasted fully eleven years. Then I was beguiled by a grandson into climbing a Munro again. That led me to reconsider my vow and tackle the four remaining new Munros. I am intensely grateful that I did so. Returning to the Munros not only evoked that profound sense of fulfilment familiar to SMCJ readers, but also took me on a personal journey of discovery, assisting me in coming to terms with feelings of loss and longing that had long been unassuaged.

I climbed my first Munros in illustrious company. In 1969, I made my first foray into the Scottish winter, working as a journalist on a magazine assignment with the photographer John Cleare, who conveyed entrée into the world of such celebrities as Hamish MacInnes and Tom Patey. I climbed Aladdin's Couloir with Tom watching my rope, then continued to the top of Cairngorm with him and John. A day or so later a party that now included Allen Fyffe and Jim McArtney went to Sgòrr Ruadh, where I put up my one and only new Scottish winter route, Easy Gully, which took us conveniently to the summit. That was also the week in which Tom made his celebrated girdle traverse of Creag Meagaidh – something way beyond my modest mountaineering capabilities, so I made my excuses and watched the proceedings from ground level. On several evenings we repaired to the hallowed Rowanlea in Carrbridge, where Jimmy Ross locked us in and we listened to Tom singing his irreverent mountain songs until close on dawn, when he would gulp amphetamines and speed back to Ullapool for his morning surgery.

From that scintillating start, climbing the Munros became more of a family affair. Nine years passed before I climbed my next set, doing so from the base of a primitive cottage on the Rhidorroch Estate near

Ullapool. Although I was by then a devotee of Scottish hill-walking, I still had only scant awareness of the Munros. My principal guidebook was Poucher's Scottish Peaks and we usually followed his recommendations, barely noticing the brief footnote he had provided about the Munros. Rather insouciantly, we set off one morning to climb a distant lump to the east, which proved to be Seana Bhraigh (not even mentioned by Poucher). There were five in our party, including my two sons, Danny, then 14, and Seth, 12. When Danny pushed ahead with the other two adults, Seth said he needed a rest, I offered to wait with him while the others went on to the top. Seth clearly regarded that as an affront and was soon on his feet again, determined to emulate his brother. My memory of the summit is of a view of a sea of peaks, nameless to me then but like old friends to me now. Later in the holiday we climbed Beinn Dearg via Gleann na Sguaib in swirling mist. Finally came that alluring pair, Conival and Ben More Assynt, where we picked our way along the bouldery ridge between them as clouds glowered overhead.

Over the next ten years, during further holidays with my wife Leni, Danny and Seth, I made a desultory pursuit of further Munros. They did include Liathach and Beinn Eighe, traversed on a blazing day when sun radiated from its quartzite blocks, and several of the Cuillin, including the In Pinn by the short side. Among the best was Blaven, snatched on an evening following rain when we reached the top and saw the Cuillin

Crossing the Cairngorm plateau on the approach to Sgòr an Lochain Uaine.

ridge emerging above a cloud inversion to the west. Although I had become aware of the activity known as Munro bagging I had resolved not to succumb to its thrall. Then came a fateful day in August 1987 when we climbed the entire South Cluanie Ridge. My total leapt up by another seven peaks to stand at 38, and the obsession took hold.

My quest took another ten years and brought a priceless gamut of experiences, peaks climbed in the gloaming of endless summer evenings, others snatched from the grasp of the Scottish winter. My most frequent companion was Danny, with whom I shared some of my most glittering memories. On Beinn Dorain we groped our way to the summit in a white-out, providentially locating a crucial cairn when we saw a single blade of rock protruding from the snow. On Schiehallion we battled on after a monumental gust of wind threw me the ground as if I had been struck by a giant hand. Attempting to reach Sgùrr a' Ghreadaidh in the Cuillin we escaped the hail blasting across the ridge like grapeshot by edging our way along the slabs that plunged down on the Coruisk side; our relief on reaching the summit was marred by the knowledge that we had to retrace our route in order to reach the sanctuary of the An Dorus notch. On such occasions we adopted the maxim of Bill Murray as he pondered whether to take refuge in the Corrour bothy during a winter tempest and concluded that it would be 'childish' not to press on.

One of our most transcendent days came when we headed up to the Grey Corries on a perfect February morning, when the air was utterly still, voices seemed to carry for miles, and our ice-axes rang out like tuning forks. When we saw the ridge extending westwards against an unblemished sky we resolved to savour every moment of what we knew would be a perfect day. By then Danny was a teacher in his 30s, I was in my mid-50s. On our first family walks in Scotland I had carried him on my back. On the Grey Corries he forged ahead, allowing me the luxury of tracking his steps in the snow. He patiently waited for me below the two Munro summits so that we could reach them together.

I selected Cairngorm as my final summit in keeping with the family undertaking that climbing Munros had become. I had of course been to the summit 28 years before, following my ascent of Aladdin's Couloir, but we had accepted a brief ride on a ski tow, thus disqualifying it as a 'clean' Munro. Cairngorm may appear a perverse choice, in view of its despoliation by skiing equipment. But by then I had three grandchildren, all aged four or less. Danny had two sons, Blake and Ben, and Seth a daughter, Orla. We arranged for them to take part in the celebrations by riding to the Ptarmigan Restaurant on the ski-lift and joining the summit party from there (a practice still permitted in 1997.) The culminating moment had a dreamlike quality, with the assembled company clapping and cheering, handshakes and hugs, and the fizzing of champagne. The partying continued back at ground level, with speeches, presentations and more fizz. I submitted my claim to the Scottish Mountaineering

Club and duly received a certificate recording that I was the 1726th person to complete.

So it was that I concluded that my Munro days were over, deterred above all by the pain in my knees. I eventually learned that the problem stemmed from an overactive parathyroid gland which had been pumping calcium around my body. The gland was excised (at the third attempt) but an orthopaedic surgeon showed me an X-ray which revealed needle-like shards of calcium in my knee cartilages, adding that they could not be removed.

There the matter rested, until the summer of 2008, when we took another holiday in Scotland, based at Aberfeldy. Leni and I were there with Seth, his wife, his daughter Orla, now a wilful teenager, and his son (and our fourth grandchild) Jake, who was six. One afternoon we went to the visitor centre at Ben Lawers. Jake, clearly intrigued by the mountain landscape, pointed at the nearest peak and said: 'I want to climb that.'

'That' proved to be Meall nan Tarmachan, the sensuous Munro above Killin which I had climbed on an immaculate winter day with Danny some 20 years before. Even though I was 66 and had suspect knees, six-year-old grandchildren are not to be denied. Besides, I told myself, Meall nan Tarmachan is one of the most forgiving Munros, with a starting point at 450m and a 'book' time of two hours. We embarked the next day, Jake bounding along ahead of his parents. He was not even out of breath as he stepped up to the cairn and proposed continuing to the next peak, a request which was firmly declined. I was apprehensive as we started the descent but was surprised and relieved to find that my knees were far less painful than ten years before, belying the surgeon's gloomy prognosis. By the time we had reached the car, inspired and reinvigorated by my grandson's performance, I was laying plans to climb the four missing Munros.

This time my partner would be my younger son Seth. During my original Munro campaign I had climbed more than 150 Munros with Danny compared to 25 with Seth. Danny was now living in faraway Cornwall but Seth, still in London, declared that he was ready for the challenge. Two of the peaks comprised the Glen Coe pair, Stob Coire Raineach on Buachaille Etive Beag and Stob na Broige on Buachaille Etive Mòr. We arrived on a chill April weekend the following year, finding them streaked with snow and seared by a bitter wind. It was something of a culture shock, climbing in semi-winter conditions again, but that added to the relish and we accomplished them without undue difficulty.

The final two would pose a stiffer challenge: An Stuc in the Ben Lawers range, 34th in the Munros list, and, most daunting, Sgòr an Lochain Uaine in the Cairngorms, shown as fifth in height, with the long approach across the Cairngorm plateau, notorious for its lack of refuge and demands for accurate navigation. How I rued the day in October

1990 when Danny and I had been some 40 minutes away on the summit of Cairn Toul, but were deterred by a gale from continuing along the ridge. Seth and I returned in August and tackled An Stuc first, forging a route below the Lawers ridge to Lochan nan Cat and striking up from there, with a final scramble over the steep buttress guarding the summit to the north-east. The top was wreathed in mist during our approach but it cleared just as we arrived, bringing breath-taking views of the Cairngorms, Mamores and Ben Nevis. The round trip took us seven hours and we felt ready for the culminating challenge. But the weather was against us: rain and wind for the rest of the week allowed no window large enough for the rigours of Sgòr an Lochain Uaine. Unable to find another date before the days grew too short, we postponed the denouement until 2009.

Although I was apprehensive about retaining – or regaining – my fitness for the following year, the pause gave me time to reflect on the extent to which walking in Scotland had become a family enterprise. Leni and I had taken Danny and Seth along their first Scottish glen in the early 1970s, hoping they would share our love of the wild places. Now that I was in my late 60s, it was gratifying to know that Seth took pleasure from walking with his father. But that realisation also brought me a reminder of what I had missed.

My father died of cancer when I was 11, leaving me wanting to know so much about him. He had served in the Army throughout the First World War but I knew only fragments of where he had fought. His regiment, the Civil Service Rifles, had been posted to the Somme in 1916 but escaped the slaughter when it was diverted to the Balkans and then Palestine, where my father marched into Jerusalem with Allenby after defeating the Turks in 1917. He returned to the western front in 1918 and was granted leave on the eve of an attack across a canal that he would have been lucky to survive. That much I knew from the tales my mother told; it was only when I started reading the poetry of Wilfred Owen, documenting the carnage and the horror, that I began to glimpse what he must have gone through. In the Second World War he served as a fire-watcher, looking out for bombs from the roof of his office in the City. There were so many questions that I longed to have asked him had I known him into adulthood, as Seth knew me now. My sense of loss for my father had never dissipated and even 50 years after his death I would have dreams of meeting him again, waking afterwards suffused with joy.

Seth, I was pleased to find during our walks and drives, wanted to hear about my father. After a chequered time at a school and an uneven start to his career, Seth had obtained a degree to qualify as a counsellor, with a speciality in child bereavement. He gently suggested that I still had grief to process, particularly as I had not attended my father's funeral, for

Seth beside a burn above Loch nan Cnapan.

my mother had felt it would be too distressing for an 11-year-old boy, and what Seth said rang true.

Our conversations turned to my mother, who had brought me up alone until she died, also of cancer, when I was 20. I knew her to be resolute and loving but somehow had never assembled the pieces of her life. She had lost both her parents at a younger age than me: her father when she was ten, her mother at 13. After living with her grandmother for three years, she travelled to a convent school in Cahors in France – this was during the First World War – in order to qualify as a teacher in the French education system. In the summer of 1917, when she was 17, she took a train from Cahors to the Basque town of Durango to achieve the equivalent qualification in Spain. In the 1920s she and her younger sister took holidays together in Spain and Portugal. After she married in 1929, she and my father embarked on ambitious motoring trips throughout Europe, from Scandinavia to southern Spain. In 1938 they planned to drive to Prague (I still have the guidebook they purchased) but the turn of events diverted them to Skye instead.

My parents spent most of the war in south London where, in 1945, I survived a V2 incident. Soon afterwards my mother contracted breast cancer from which she recovered. When my father died in 1953, my mother, by then in her 50s, repeated some of her pre-war journeys with me, determined as she was to pass on the experiences and the values she had shared and enjoyed with my father. And so we drove through France and Spain, with her at the wheel of a Standard Pennant, later replaced by a Renault Dauphine, reaching as far south as Granada and Seville. She took me to the Louvre and the Prado, taught me about music and poetry, introduced me to French and Spanish cuisine, and crossed the passes in the Alps and the Pyrenees that she and my father had traversed 20 years before. When my mother's cancer returned her first thought, as with my father's death, was to protect me, insisting that her doctor broke the news to her and preventing me from knowing for as long as possible. As I related all this to Seth, constructing a narrative of my mother's fortitude and selflessness that had previously eluded me, I was overwhelmed with a grief that had somehow remained captive too.

Seth and I returned to the Cairngorms in May 2010, with just two days at our disposal to attempt Sgòr an Lochain Uaine. Wind and rain swept across the A9 as we drove into Aviemore but the following morning was miraculously clear. We were in Glen Feshie by 8 a.m., allowing ourselves 12 hours of daylight. I felt intimidated by the long walk in from Auchlean, even though I had trained at our local leisure centre and spent a weekend in the Lakes a month before. Seth was in far from top shape: he was recovering from a heavy cold and after an hour had to deal with a blister. He did not say it, but I realised later there was not the remotest chance he would consider turning back. It was not just that he had insisted on continuing on Seana Bhraigh; in life too he had fought against setbacks.

After his brother Danny won a place at Cambridge from a Croydon comprehensive, Seth, who had suffered from weak and inconsistent teaching, had dropped out of the academic race. In his 40s, after working as a teaching assistant, he had achieved his counselling degree in the teeth of a series of administrative cock-ups that would have tested anyone's resolve. This was not a man who was going to turn back on his father's final Munro.

After two hours we breasted the last rise from the Coire Fhearnagan glen to see the Cairngorm plateau, dappled with snow, stretching before us, our peak worryingly distant at its eastern edge. Although there were no navigational problems, the prospect ahead brought the sense of exploration and discovery that I counted among the rewards of venturing into the wild places, deepened now through being shared with Seth. As we headed down towards the dip in the plateau, my apprehension over how far we had yet to walk, not only to the summit but also on the return, ceded to the sensuous pleasure of the landscape: the patches of crisp snow, the ruffled lochs, the music of meltwater. In that awesome setting, something else was happening. The feelings of loss I had expressed to Seth were being replaced by a fuller sense of fatherhood: an awareness of the story of my parents' lives and how that extended through the generations. Seth had helped me reach this point and I felt fulfilled that he knew who they were and acknowledged that they were part of him too.

Seth and the author on his final summit.

The author descending from his final summit. Photo: Seth Gillman.

As we crossed the burn that flows from Loch nan Cnapan the sky was radiant, the air breathlessly still. We headed upwards again, picking our way through the rough ground, then gasped in wonder as we reached the rim of the plateau and saw the monumental cliffs of Braeriach rising from the Lairig Ghru. As always, the final snow slope was steeper than it looked but a familiar surge of adrenalin kicked in. Seth had gone ahead, picking his way through the summit boulder field, then waited ten metres short of the cairn. We embraced at that point and reached the top together, tears brimming in my eyes.

In contrast to the partying 13 years before, we had the summit almost to ourselves. We shared a miniature of Glenmorangie with a solitary walker who took our photograph and spent a full hour savouring the moment and the view. A snow bunting hopped among the rocks, enchanting us with its rippling song. At last it was time to return. We found a better route back across the plateau and stopped to rest beside Loch nan Cnapan. We took our time reaching the crest of the rise above Glen Feshie where, as evening set in, blue lines of hills stretched away towards the west. We were back at Auchlean at 7.15 p.m. It was raining again as we headed south down the A9 the following day, leaving us to wonder at our good fortune. In more than 40 years of climbing Munros, this day was among the very best.

NOTES ON W.H. MURRAY'S CLIMBING AND WRITING
Based on his application for membership of the Scottish Mountaineering Club

By Michael Cocker

W.H. MURRAY requires no introduction to readers of this journal, some of whom were his friends, so I must state at the outset that I never met Bill Murray and that I am aware of my presumption in addressing this subject amidst those more able and better qualified. When I first started climbing, Murray's two books, *Mountaineering in Scotland* and *Undiscovered Scotland*, had just been republished in a single volume by Diadem. Like others before me, I found them both inspirational and enlightening. More than thirty years have passed since then and despite having acquired a small library of mountaineering material they remain my favourite climbing books and the ones to which I return most often. They have also sparked a wider interest in the era in which they are set and the man behind the words.

A decade or so of casual enquiry eventually led to interviews with some of Murray's climbing contemporaries and a more focused endeavour to document what I could of Murray's pre-war climbing, as a context to the adventures described in his books. One interesting discovery was Murray's application for membership of the Scottish Mountaineering Club (SMC), which appears to be a complete record of all his mountain days prior to joining the club in December 1945[1]. This made a convenient framework on which to build a chronology and the climbing diaries of Dr. J.H.B. (Jim) Bell, Ben Humble, Douglas Scott, Alex Small and Ted Zenthon[2], along with the archival records of the Junior Mountaineering Club of Scotland (JMCS) and the SMC, provided much of the rest. What follows is a series of observations based on this chronology and a discussion of some the anomalies that have become apparent in Murray's writing.

It is common knowledge that Murray spent three harsh years in prison camps during the Second World War and that it was here that he wrote

---

1 Only two ascents are known to be missing from Murray's application: The Douglas Boulder (Ben Nevis) with Lister (no initials) on 17 May 1940, which is recorded in the CIC hut log and The Chasm with Douglas Laidlaw and W. Redman (an Englishman) on 16 June 1940, which is mentioned in a letter to his sister quoted in *The Evidence of Things Not Seen* (p. 327).

2 J.H.B. Bell and Ben Humble's diaries are in the National Library of Scotland. Douglas Scott's diaries were lent to the writer by Audrey Scott. Alex Small's have recently been donated to the SMC archive. Ted Zenthon's were published privately as *The Life and Work of Edward R Zenthon* in 2011.

the majority of the twenty-three chapters comprising *Mountaineering in Scotland*[3]. After he was released, in April 1945, he was given two months leave from the army and went to stay with his mother and sister who had been evacuated to a farmhouse in Wales. The address of the farmhouse is recorded on the first page of Murray's SMC application and so it is likely that he started compiling it there and that he probably took several weeks over the task for he didn't sign it until 3 September, when he was back in Scotland attached to a unit of Royal Engineers. He was proposed by Jim Bell and seconded by Bill Mackenzie.

Prospective SMC candidates are asked to provide details of their mountaineering experience and, at the time Murray applied, the official form consisted of two sides of foolscap with an option to add further pages. Murray filled nine additional pages. The original document is now yellowed with age but Murray's hand writing is clearly legible with asterisks in red ink used to identify the climbs he led. The list starts with an ascent of the Cobbler in April 1935 and concludes with the climbs he did with the Commando Mountain Training Unit based at Llanberis, in Snowdonia, in July and August 1945. Between these he recorded over three-hundred ascents that involved climbing, scrambling or hillwalking, in all weathers and in every season, sometimes alone, and it is interesting to see the ones described in *Mountaineering in Scotland* and some of those in its sequel *Undiscovered Scotland* set amidst other quite ordinary days when the weather was poor or opportunities limited.

For the record to be as detailed as it is Murray must have referred to the diaries he is known to have kept[4] and may have used the application as a way of revisiting his pre-war experiences whilst checking details for the manuscript *Mountaineering in Scotland*. Perhaps, also, he wanted to demonstrate that he was an all-round mountaineer, a quality appreciated by the SMC, and not just a specialist climber[5]. The minimum requirement

---

3 Murray published four articles in the *SMC Journal* that were subsequently rewritten for *Mountaineering in Scotland*: 'Defeat: (A December Night on the Crowberry Ridge)' [21/124 (1937), 237–44]; 'The Great Gully of Sgor Nam Fiannaidh, Glencoe' [21/126 (1938), 414–17]; 'Night Up There – Hogmanay on Ben Nevis' [22/130 (1940), 244–7]; 'The Last Day on Buachaille' [23/133 (1942), 1–7].

4 Murray makes several references to his diaries in *Mountaineering in Scotland* and *Undiscovered Scotland* and occasionally quotes from them.

5 After 1935 the JMCS saw a rapid expansion in its membership and became so vibrant that some of the more experienced members, who by then were expected to join the SMC, chose to remain with the younger club. When Murray informed the SMC committee of this he recalls being fixed with the steely-eyed glare of a 'brass-hat' who barked, 'We don't want climbing gorillas in *this* club!' [*SMCJ,* 30/166 (1975), 322], an exchange that probably occurred at the SMC rooms, in Edinburgh, on 11 October 1938, when Donald Campbell (President of the Glasgow JMCS) and Murray attended a meeting with Alex Harrison, John Osborne and Logan Aikman to discuss the matter.

for SMC membership at the time that Murray applied was 40 ascents involving either a summit of 3,000 feet or some technical climbing – his application far exceeded this.

In the 1930s most people, including Murray[6], worked a five-and-a-half- or six-day week and were not free to head to the hills until Saturday afternoon or early Sunday morning. Consequently the bulk of Murray's climbing occurred on a Sunday, sometimes with a late return to Glasgow in the early hours of Monday morning. His application reflects this pattern of regular weekend climbing with the addition of statutory holidays and three weeks annual leave. His activities were mainly concentrated in the Southern and Central Highlands with occasional forays to the Cairngorms and longer holidays on Skye. His application records 25 days on the Cobbler, 63 on Buachaille Etive Mòr, 29 on Ben Nevis, nine traverses of the Aonach Eagach Ridge (four in winter) and the ascent of 84 Munros. He only made one visit to the Northern Highlands (Torridon) before the war, one to the English Lake District and one to the Swiss Alps. Between 1937 and 1940, the period when he climbed most intensely, he averaged 65 days climbing and hillwalking each year.

Murray was amongst the first generation able to climb regularly at weekends; a change that had been facilitated by the availability of cheap cars and petrol, improvements in the state of the roads and the formation of locally-based climbing clubs. Prior to this mountaineering was almost exclusively a holiday activity and clubs like the SMC were nationally-based with few official meets. Murray joined the Glasgow section of the JMCS in autumn 1935 and, although this was a national club established as a feeder into the SMC, the regional branches held regular indoor and outdoor meets, shared transport and, in addition to hotels, used economical alternatives, like camping and bed and breakfasts[7]. The Glasgow section was the largest of these branches, with around 70 members in 1935 rising to 115 by 1940. Murray was elected a committee member in December 1936 and was the club secretary from December 1937 until May 1940 when he was called up by the army so handed this over to George Marskell[8].

Archie MacAlpine, Bill Mackenzie and Kenneth Dunn were all in the

---

6 Murray worked as a trainee with the Union Bank of Scotland.

7 The Inverarnan Hotel at Glen Falloch was the unofficial headquarters for the Glasgow JMCS in the pre- and post-war years. It used to be run by Nancy and Hannah Girvan and remained a popular venue with climbers and skiers until the late 1960s when it changed hands and was renamed the Drover's Inn.

8 W.G. Marskell often climbed with Murray in the pre-war years and participated in the first ascent of the Clachaig Gully (1938) and the second ascent of Raven's Gully (1939). He worked at Babcock & Wilcox Ltd, an engineering company that manufactured tanks and munitions during the war, which made this a reserved occupation.

(l to r) Anderson and Murray on the summit of Sgùrr Alasdair, 17 June 1936. Photo: Douglas Scott.

Glasgow JMCS and with Murray formed one of the strongest climbing teams operating in Scotland between 1936 and 1940. Mackenzie in particular was a bold leader with an aptitude for matching route choice with conditions and Murray attributed much of their success in winter to this and to planning their campaigns in advance. Douglas Scott, 'Hamish' Hamilton, Alex Small, Ben Humble and Tom MacKinnon were also prominent members who climbed with their own groups. These groupings, however, were not exclusive and there were frequent interchanges as Murray's application demonstrates. In addition to those mentioned above, Murray names another forty individuals that he climbed or walked with in the years prior to the Second World War. The majority of these were JMCS members, but, from 1938 onwards, he also climbed regularly with Jim Bell who was in the SMC. As the JMCS secretary Murray was usually the first person approached by prospective members. Applicants had to be seventeen or over but no previous experience was required and the record shows that Murray climbed or hillwalked with a number of the new members introducing them to the mountains and the club.

During the inter-war years the Cuillin on Skye were a popular alternative to the Alps. Murray spent three summer holidays there. The first, in June 1936, coincided with an unusually fine spell of weather. He went with Ross Higgins and on the boat from Mallaig met Douglas Scott and Rob Anderson. They recognised each other from JMCS meets, but at this stage were not familiar. Two days later, on 17 June, Murray, Scott and Anderson climbed Abraham's Route on Sgùrr Alasdair together.

(l to r) Murray and Anderson on the summit of Sgùrr Thearlaich, 17 June 1936. Photo: Douglas Scott.

Scott took a photograph of the other two at the summit cairn that was later published in *Mountaineering in Scotland*[9]. Ben Humble and Douglas Scott's diaries both contain detailed descriptions of this holiday. Murray returned to Skye the following summer and again in August 1939 when he made the third traverse of the Greater Cuillin Ridge with Gordon Donaldson. In July 1938 he went to Arolla, in Switzerland, with Alan Garrick and his wife, but the weather was poor and they achieved little aside from a traverse of the Petite Dent de Veisivi. Murray's only pre-war visit to the Lake District was in October 1938 when he spent five days climbing at Wasdale Head with Mrs Garrick.

Murray was unequivocal in his preference for winter to summer mountaineering and completed over 50 snow and ice climbs in the years before the Second World War, with a similar number of days spent hillwalking on snow covered ground. His first winter climb was Central Gully (grade I/II) on Bidean nam Bian with Ross Higgins and Archie MacAlpine on Sunday 1 March 1936, and the hardest, and the one he later described as 'the best winter climb I ever did'[10], the first ascent of Shelf Route (grade IV, 6), on Buachaille Etive Mòr, with Bill Mackenzie,

9 This photograph was also published in *A Century of Scottish Mountaineering* (1988) and *The Evidence of Things Not Seen* (2002). Scott told the writer that he thought the picture revealed something of the two personalities – Anderson reclining and laid back, Murray upright and wanting to be on with the next route. They completed the day with a round of Coire Lagan and the Inaccessible Pinnacle.

10 Letter to Ken Wilson in 1979.

in March 1937. It is a debatable point as to whether Murray and his generation advanced winter climbing or consolidated the achievements of their Victorian and Edwardian forebears. What is certain is that there was a return of hard winters in the 1930s and 40s and that, due to lax recording, Murray and his contemporaries were not always fully aware of the accomplishments of their predecessors[11]. They had a slight advantage over the earlier climbers in that some of the developments in equipment – windproof jackets, down sleeping bags, lightweight tents, pitons and snap-link karabiners (a spin-off from the Antarctic and Everest expeditions) were available to them. However, they also introduced innovations of their own such as short axes, longer rope lengths and head torches.

Murray's significant winter routes from this period included the second ascent of Observatory Ridge (grade IV, 4), on Ben Nevis, in February 1938; the third recorded ascent of SC Gully (grade III), on Stob Coire nan Lochan, in March 1939; the first ascent of Deep Cut Chimney (grade III/IV), on Stob Coire nam Beith, in April 1939 and three early ascents of Crowberry Gully (grade III/IV), on Buachaille Etive Mòr – the last of these, on 1 February 1941 with Gordon Donaldson, being Murray's final climb before being posted abroad with the army.

Despite his preference for winter climbing Murray was a keen rock climber and involved in several significant ascents in the summer months; most notably, the first ascent of the Clachaig Gully (Severe), in Glen Coe, in May 1938, a route that had previously defeated several strong parties; the third ascent of Rubicon Wall (Severe), on Ben Nevis, in August 1937; the second ascent of Raven's Gully (Hard Very Severe), on Buachaille Etive Mòr, in June 1939, at the time the hardest route in the Central Highlands, and the first ascent of Parallel Buttress (Severe), on Lochnagar, in May 1939. All of these are described in *Mountaineering in Scotland.*

Jim Bell's diaries are particularly well written and, in addition to the climbing, contain details of the transport arrangements, accommodation, visits to pubs and chip shops and late returns home in the early hours of a Monday morning often omitted in Murray's accounts. Whilst not directly relevant to the climbing they are interesting in that they capture something of the atmosphere of the time and give an earthier hue to Murray's roseate tendency.

Two differences from modern practice are evident in Murray's record. Firstly how often they were prepared to climb in wet weather or marginal conditions. With only one day a week available for climbing and limited annual leave they couldn't afford to be too particular about the conditions and a factor in their favour was that nailed boots, routinely worn on

---

11 For example Harold Raeburn's ascent of Crowberry Gully in April 1909. For further discussion on this see Robin Campbell's article 'The First Scottish Ice Climbers', *SMCJ*, 30/163 (1972), 48–57.

W.H. Murray on the approach to SC Gully, Stob Coire nan Lochan, 26 March 1939.
Photo: Douglas Scott.

climbs up to Very Difficult or even Severe, were almost as effective on wet and icy rock as on dry. Gym shoes or 'Rubbers' were only used on more difficult routes. And secondly, in summer, the frequent use of climbs such as Tower Ridge on Ben Nevis, or North Buttress on Buachaille Etive Mòr, as a means of descent. In the era of no running belays and the maxim that 'the leader never falls', the ability to down climb and retreat from a route was as important a skill as safety in ascent. This type of climbing would also have been considered good training for the Alps. For this generation it was the exploratory aspect of mountaineering that held the greatest appeal; technical difficulty, although interesting, was generally a secondary consideration.

One of the things that became apparent when reviewing Murray's application is that there are discrepancies between the information he recorded in this and in his published work. The application is almost certainly the true record. Some of these were probably simple oversights or changes made for literary effect, but for others, although apparently deliberate, there is no discernible reason and they remain something of a mystery. Some of the more obvious examples are considered below.

The first entry on Murray's SMC application reads: 'April 1935, the Cobbler and Narnain, climbed alone.' The exact date was probably Friday 19 April. Murray refers to this event on several occasions; two are quoted[12]:

> The yearning to explore hills was born in myself in 1934, when I, a confirmed pavement dweller, overheard a mountaineer describe a weekend visit to An Teallach... At the first opportunity, then, I went to one of the few mountains I knew by name – the Cobbler at Arrochar. It was a fine April day with plenty of snow on the tops... From that day I became a mountaineer. *Undiscovered Scotland* (p. 1)

> When nineteen and lodging at Maclay Hall (a Glasgow student's residence) I overheard the Warden talk at table of his traverse of An Teallach... and my attention was gripped... I made no move. I knew no one who climbed mountains. A year later, in April 1934, I at last bestirred myself and went to the nearest I knew by name, the Cobbler, at Arrochar. *The Evidence of Things Not Seen* (p. 21)

Already there is a discrepancy in these accounts. In the first Murray writes 'the yearning to explore hills' was born in 1934 and that at the first opportunity he went to the Cobbler. In the second he says that after hearing about the traverse of An Teallach he 'made no move' and that it was 'a year later, in April 1934' when he went to the Cobbler. In his published work Murray consistently suggests that his initial ascent of the Cobbler was made in 1934, only in his SMC application and in the obituary he wrote for Archie MacAlpine in the *SMC Journal* [35/186 (1995), 749] does he state this occurred in April 1935. The obituary reads:

> I persuaded him [MacAlpine] to think of Glen Coe, to which I had not yet found my way... On a sunny September morning of 1935, we

12 Murray also writes that he first ascended the Cobbler in April 1934 in 'Present Moments' in the *Alpine Journal* [86/330 (1981), 47] and 'High Tops', a chapter in *Wildlife in Scotland* (Macmillan, 1979).

rounded the last bend of the Rannoch road and for the first time saw the huge rock-cone [Buachaille Etive Mòr] lift high out of the moor... We found our way up by the easy route from Glen Etive. Archie, not yet fit, dubbed the trudge laborious, but his attitude changed on reaching the summit screes, where we could walk in delight to the cairn. He needed just one look over that wild, far scene – and was hooked, just as I had been five months earlier on the Cobbler.

A substantial portion of this obituary was transcribed into *The Evidence of Things Not Seen* (p. 23/24). The only significant alteration was to the sentence referring to Murray's ascent of the Cobbler, which, in the obituary reads 'five months earlier' and in *The Evidence of Things Not Seen*, was changed to 'the previous year', shifting the date from 1935 back to 1934. The alteration must have been done deliberately, probably by Murray, but could have been made by his editor[13].

A further hint that 1935 is the correct year is in *Undiscovered Scotland* (p. 110), where Murray says 19 April was the anniversary of his first ascent of a mountain. He doesn't tell us which anniversary, but as 19 April 1935 was Good Friday, a day when he would have been free to leave Glasgow, and a Thursday the previous year, when he would probably have been at work, 1935 is the more likely year.

There is no obvious reason for this discrepancy and Murray was clearly aware of it for when compiling a formal record – the SMC application and MacAlpine's obituary – he was unequivocal about the date. The weight of evidence suggests that Murray first became inspired by the idea of mountain climbing when he overheard the warden's conversation sometime in 1934, and that he made his first visit to the mountains in April 1935 and that, when writing about this at different periods in his life, he rather loosely interchanged the year that he started hillwalking with the one when he first became interested in the idea of mountain climbing.

Another anomaly in Murray's writing concerns the crossing of Cain Toul and Braeriach in a storm one May, accompanied by a chance companion Mortimer, as described in chapter 21, 'Cairngorm Blizzard', in *Mountaineering in Scotland*. This adventure is mentioned in *The Evidence of Things Not Seen* (p. 31) when Murray writes that in May 1936 MacAlpine attended a JMCS meet in Glen Coe whilst he was in the Cairngorms. The *SMC Journal* [21/122 (1936), 160] records the Glen Coe meet was 16–18 May and described it as a washout due to bad weather. When referring to his first visit to the Cairngorms in June 1935 (*The Evidence of Things Not Seen*, p. 22) Murray tells us that the following May he was caught by a blizzard on Cairn Toul, and, in MacAlpine's obituary, he says that on the weekend of the JMCS meet in Glen Coe he was 'absent fighting a blizzard in the Cairngorms.' All three

---

13 *The Evidence of Things Not Seen* was edited by Anne Murray. The publisher, Ken Wilson, advises me that he was not responsible for the alteration.

references suggest that Murray was in the Cairngorms in May 1936; two of them point specifically to the weekend 16–17 and mention a blizzard. What is curious is that there is no record of this in Murray's SMC application and the identity of his companion, Mortimer, is also unknown. However, as Murray was not at the JMCS meet in Glen Coe, it remains possible that he was in the Cairngorms, and the appalling weather in Glen Coe would be consistent with there being a blizzard.

The absence of any reference to this excursion has to make one wonder if the account in *Mountaineering in Scotland* is essentially fiction or a composite event based on a number of experiences. The only other explanation is that Murray accidentally missed this out when completing the application, but with the detailed chronicling of many other quite ordinary days this seems unlikely.

It is worth noting that Murray's account in *Mountaineering in Scotland* bears some similarity to an incident on Ben Macdui that occurred in May 1934, when three hillwalkers were caught in a white-out near the summit and lost their way with tragic consequences. This received considerable attention in the press at the time and Murray would almost certainly have been aware of it. Could Murray's account have had an educational motive warning of the possibility of being caught unprepared in unseasonable and unexpected winter conditions?

In chapter 20, 'Castle Buttress', in *Undiscovered Scotland*, Murray describes an attempt on The Castle (Grade III), on Ben Nevis, made one January (he doesn't say which year) with Douglas Laidlaw. They climbed three-quarters of the way up the route to find unstable snow overlying smooth slabs and considered it prudent to retreat. The Castle had been the scene of several narrow escapes and one fatal accident due to similar conditions and was known to be a serious although not technically difficult undertaking. There is no record of a January ascent of this route by either Murray or Laidlaw in the CIC hut log or in Murray's SMC application. The only pre-war ascent known to have been made by either of them is the one recorded in the CIC hut log in May 1940 when it was in summer conditions (Very Difficult). The entry in the hut books reads:

> May 15th. <u>The Castle</u>. Wet. Down No 3. Good glissading. Good visibility on top – Ireland, Barra Head etc and Cuillin.

At the beginning of the 'Castle Buttress' chapter Murray writes:

> During our day on North-east Buttress I told Laidlaw of the Castle problem... I had climbed with him only two or three times so far, but found him a born mountaineer, remarkably speedy and safe for a man of just less than eighteen years. *Undiscovered Scotland* (p. 187)

Murray's first recorded climb with Laidlaw occurred in October 1939, which would make January 1940 the most likely period for the ascent of The Castle described in *Undiscovered Scotland* (according to his SMC application their ascent in May 1940 was their twenty-second climb together). However, when Murray writes about the North-East Buttress (referred to in the quote above), he says this climb was made 'one March' and that he and Laidlaw had climbed together 'only two or three times so far' (*Undiscovered Scotland,* p. 164 & 187), which, if the order of events he describes are true, would have to have been March 1939 or, less probably, March 1940. Like the 'Cairngorm Blizzard' chapter, the 'Castle Buttress' account is difficult to locate and appears to be partly fictional. Another similarity between these chapters is that they both have an educational quality; the former warning of the risk of getting caught out in unexpectedly severe winter weather; the latter of the avalanche risk on a climb known for this danger, and that retreat is sometimes the prudent option.

As mentioned above, Murray writes that his ascent of the North-East Buttress with Douglas Laidlaw was made 'one March', but doesn't say which year. Murray made three ascents of the North-East Buttress before the Second World War, the first at the beginning of May 1939 with Jim Bell, the second in April 1940 with Gordon Donaldson and the third in May 1940 with Douglas Laidlaw. There is no record of a March ascent with Laidlaw or anyone else and it appears likely that the account of the North-East Buttress, like those of 'Castle Buttress' and the 'Cairngorm Blizzard', is also a composite or semi-fictional event. Whilst many writers alter details to make a better story, with such a wealth of experiences to draw upon, it is curious that Murray chose to stray into the realms of fiction. Laidlaw was killed in the Second World War when his plane was shot down over Germany and it is possible that the two chapters – 'Castle Buttress' and 'Ben Nevis by the North-east Buttress' – were written in the form of idealised days to honour his memory.

Murray had no doubt that the pre-war climbing years were his best and that nothing that came after, in the Alps or in the Himalaya, ever brought the same intensity of experience as those of his youth when he was least distracted, his enthusiasm highest and the bonds of friendship strongest[14].

Author's Note:

The writer is responsible for the observations in this article, but gratefully acknowledges the assistance he has received from Bob Aitken, Robin Campbell, John Fowler, Olive Geddes (National Library of Scotland), Robin Lloyd Jones, Ken Wilson and Audrey Scott. An abridged chronology and commentary on Murray's climbs 1935–45 is to be published as an appendix in Robin Lloyd Jones' forthcoming biography of W.H. Murray, *The Sunlit Summit*. The full version of the chronology will be made available to any interested SMC members at a later date.

---

14 Interview with Tom Weir in the 1970s, published in *Weir's Way* (Edinburgh: Gordon Wright, 1981), 173.

EXPECTING TO FLY

By Andy Tibbs

WITH FOREARMS pumping I hang below the bulge on a welcome but flat hold comforted by a good nut I am reluctant to leave behind. The position is strangely familiar as it is my high point on a previous attempt nearly 25 years ago in 1987. Above to the left I can see the peg I had placed which marked a high point on an even earlier attempt. It is well off route in no mans land.

Stac Pollaidh is Scotland's midget gem mountain and I had been attracted for many years to the impressive wall directly below the summit which is now home to its hardest routes. A strong Alness climber, Alan Winton, and myself had already dubbed it 'The Great Wall'. Made from finest featured Torridonian sandstone and receiving plenty of sunshine the height of the wall increases towards the left hand side as it drops off down the gully towards the road by Loch Lurgainn. An upper wall of 15m is protected by a band of overhangs which girdles the entire face. Rab Carrington and John Maclean had climbed Felo de Se in 1969 but this is to the left and the central challenge of the wall remained unbreached.

In June 1985 I abseiled down the line, placed a peg by the band of overhangs, then failed to even reach it on the lead. Alan fared better than me and arrived at the sanctuary of the peg only to be repelled by the bulging overhangs above. Two years later on a very windy May day I was back with a different climbing partner for a fresh attempt. New route paranoia had set in with a vengeance and worries about being beaten to the route were foremost in my mind. As we approached from directly below, I saw to my horror that there was a party ahead of us. Surely they couldn't have the same objective? It had just become clear that the first ascent of such a prize was to be snatched from under our noses when nature intervened in our favour.

The party ahead had stopped at the bottom and were about to gear up when a particularly strong gust of wind caught one of their rucksacks and sent it tumbling off down the hillside towards the road. Conditions were far from ideal but I latched on to the wall immediately despite the buffeting wind which was more than just off-putting. While Simon Richardson headed off down the hill to retrieve his rucksack Tom Prentice looked on as I battled up to the point where I now find myself. To tease me further he took some photographs and I subsequently appeared in two guidebooks including a crag diagram despite again failing on the route. Tom returned a few weeks later, belayed by his wife, to unlock the crux and complete the route by moving right where we had tried left.

From the welcome flat hold I boulder up strenuously fiddling a small,

Alan Winton enjoys some flying time on a retreat from Expecting to Fly in 1985.

Photo: Andy Tibbs.

poor wire into a thin, slanting crack before retreating. Up again I go to place another unhappy wire. Each foray is strength sapping and on my third attempt a bigger and more secure placement is found. With strength starting to wane it's now time to go or run out of steam. Up, foot across right, and commit. No going back now. Focussing on a hold above I climb on instinct placing two cams which I am almost too pumped to clip. I know I should extend them but no energy for that. 'Thank you Gary'[1] I mutter to Jason waiting patiently below as a No. 3 friend is hastily shoved into a flared slot.

I push on to the promise of better holds and I'm committed again. My arms are pumping and I look down at the No. 3 below my feet and consider jumping off. One of the last three pieces would surely hold and

---

1 A reference to Gary Latter's guidebook which mentions a No. 3 friend placement. (Describing gear placements in descriptions is not a practice I generally agree with!)

Andy Tibbs on Expecting to Fly (E4 6a).
Photo: Jason Walker.

the fall could be big but safely into space. I don't like the jump and grit my teeth. Fear leads me to the conclusion that if I'm going to come off I should at least fall trying. With failing arms I heave onwards till finally the weight is on my feet but I quiver nervously with the upper part of my body on the less steep headwall. It's one of those scary, awkward places, with a good foothold but little for the hands, and I have to remain calm to avoid gibbering myself off towards the void below.

No new gear materialises and I attempt to relax to regain strength and salvage some willpower which is now running low. I've been on the pitch too long and feel guilty about Jason's mundane belay task below. Finally I make the move and there's good gear and I'm in the upper crack proper. I know the route is in the bag but I tell myself it's not, as I've come to grief before by making that mistake. I forge on up the crack till my nose is embedded in the moss over the top of the crag – almost smelling success. It's a sloping, insecure and dirty top-out, and the runners I should have extended are coming back to haunt me. A high runner is not very good but holds the weight of the ropes enabling a flop onto the summit ledge. This climb has done for me and I need to rest and clear my head before finding a belay. Expecting to fly? I certainly was!

EXPLORING EILEAN DUBH AND EILEAN NAM MUC

by Chris Dickinson

SEEING THE INSPIRING photos of Erraid in Gary latter's guide prompted me to call a few friends and suggest an excursion out there in August, complete with sea kayaks. We all arrived on Mull around the same time and in mixed weather arrived at Fidden to load up. This was to be no lightweight trip. John Peden, Don McLeod, Chris Ravey, David Shortt and I crammed stuff into those sea kayaks as if our lives depended on it. I managed to get a double gas burner and a cylinder inside mine. Once they were full, stuff started getting strapped on the decks, chairs, fishing rods, Don's crutch, and the proverbial kitchen sink.

The paddle through Tinker's Hole between Eilean Dubh and Erraid is a delight. Granite skerries littered across the sparkling sea. At the south end of Erraid is a wonderful bay Traigh Gheal with two white sand beaches, sheltered from the open ocean and ringed by granite cliffs and crags. We spent a truly wonderful week here, climbing some of the Erraid routes, sea kayaking, swimming and fishing. We enjoyed the company of otters, mink, seals, basking sharks, sea birds and the hardy Erraid sheep.

Quite by chance, paddling back to camp one day, David and I decided to paddle the west side of Eilean Dubh and were intrigued to see a proud buttress facing west. The next day we nipped ashore and investigated the steep, lichen–covered cliff. I led the classic crack line that faces west, *Eileen Doo*, VS, and then we turned our attention to a fine overhanging crack on the south face.

This had a scary sword of granite wedged into the top of the crack that looked and felt like it could come away at any moment. I managed to haul myself up it on a rope, but left a first lead to a bolder man. We headed back to camp, contented, but curious to paddle the west and south sides of Eilean nam Muc, just to the southwest. This island has a fine but forbidding east wall facing Erraid. It rises straight from the sea and finishes on steep grass and the routes looked hard. On the west we noted a sheltered landing, two very steep isolated buttresses, before rounding the south end. Here we found a long wall of featured granite, set above a glacis at the east end and largely protected from the sea by a fin of rock at the west end. Right away we decided to come back next day and climb on the Dream Wall.

The following day was a bluebird day. Sun splitting the sky. David and I worked our way over the summit of the island with magical views to Iona, Mull, Jura and Islay, and established an easy way down onto the glacis at the southeast corner of Eilean nam Muc. There we spent a wonderful day ticking off routes from Diff to HVS on perfect granite,

until our toes could take no more. Stand out routes were *Flakey Friends*, Severe 4a, and *Slab and Tickle*, HVS 5a. We headed back triumphant and baked by the sun

Back on Erraid dinner was full of tales of fine new routes in a perfect setting, but next morning Dave's toes were too sore for another session so Anthony and Chris came instead. We had another spectacular day climbing routes in the deep Islay Cleft at the east end of the Dream Wall and also the western sector. Stand-out routes this day included, in the cleft, my *Islay Wall*, VS 4c, and *Starboard Tack*, *Port Tack*, VS 4c. This last starts with a fine diagonal hand traverse followed by a step up onto a hanging slab and finishing high above the start. Two fine cracks mid wall gave *Xenophobe*, Severe 4a, and *Xenolith*, HS 4b, by Anthony and Chris respectively.

It was a couple of weeks later that I returned to Eilean nam Muc, this time with James Kinnaird, and in plastic river kayaks instead of sea kayaks. We camped at Fidden farm and made a day trip out in breezy conditions which made the paddle pretty exciting for James. We enjoyed another sun drenched day filling in gaps on the Dream Wall and adding a first route on the East or Erraid Walls, *Cat's Causeway* VD. Best routes of the day were my lead, *I Come From a Land Down Under*, VS 4c, at the bottom of the Islay Cleft below the jutting prow, and a lead by James of *Robster Lobster*, HVS 5a, a steep roof and wall on the western sector of the Dream Wall.

Those days on Eilean nam Muc are vivid. The sparkling ocean, the impeccable granite, the wonderful lines, the good company. All at a special place we had not even suspected was there.

I guess the moral is to always take a peek around the corner, as you will never know what you may find.

— . —

Nearly forty new routes have been done on these two small islands. They are 8–25m long and grades range from Moderate to HVS, though the majority are Severe. Details of these and many other new climbs can be found in 'NewClimbs2011' which is available for download from the SMC website:
<http://www.smc.org.uk/Downloads/NewClimbs2011.pdf>

Top left: Don McLeod soaking up Erraid sunshine on the beach at Traigh Gheal.
Top right: Chris Ravey using jams and nubbins on Xenolith (Hard Severe 4b).
Bottom left: Davis Shortt on Flakey Friends (Severe 4a).
Bottom right: James Kinnaird on the slab and diedre of The Pooch (Severe 4a).
All photos: Chris Dickinson.

NO ONE SAID IT WOULD BE EASY
Part 2 – An Doras Gully

By Noel Williams

THERE IS A DIP on the Cuillin main ridge which on current OS maps is called An Dorus (847m), although I'm told the modern Gaelic spelling is An Doras. It means 'the Door', and it's a popular starting point from which hillwalkers bag the two Munros on either side – Sgùrr a' Mhadaidh to the north and Sgùrr a' Ghreadaidh to the south.

At one time this feature was confused with another dip a little higher up the ridge towards Sgùrr a' Ghreadaidh called Eag Dubh (881m). In the first climbing guidebook to Skye, which took up a whole issue of the SMC Journal in September 1907[1], William Douglas described these dips as follows:

> Eag Dubh = black notch, 2,760 ap. This on the map is called An Dorus. The pass is fairly easy on the Coire a' Ghreadaidh side but troublesome on the other, owing to slippery slabs. In Coire an Uaigneis take left side of the burn...
> An Dorus = the door, or Macleod's Gap, 2,890. (N.B.—A pass said to be used by the Macleods.) There is an easy descent into Coire a' Ghreadaidh by a scree gully.

So when Steeple and Barlow explored the gullies in Coire an Uaigneis on the Coruisk side of the ridge a few years later they continued the confusion by calling the lower dip Eag Dubh[2].

How this confusion came about is unclear, but, in an SMC Journal shortly after this, Colin B. Phillip seemed to lay the blame on John Mackenzie[3].

> There is considerable doubt as to the true position of An Dorus, at the head of Coir a' Ghreadaidh. John Mackenzie holds that it is not the obvious gap at the foot of Sgurr a' Mhadaidh as given in O.S., but the deep cut a little further up the ridge of Sgurr a' Ghreadaidh. It may be mentioned here that Mr Campbell at Glen Brittle always calls the neck of the pass at Bealach Coire na Banachdich, An Dorus, not that this means that the other is not also An Dorus...

---

1   William Douglas, 'SMC Guide Book: The Island of Skye', *SMCJ*, 9/54 (1907), 293–367.

2   E.W. Steeple, 'The Gullies of Coire an Uaigneis', *SMCJ*, 13/73 (1914), 13–16.

3   Colin B. Phillip, 'Nomenclature of the Cuillin', *SMCJ*, 14/79 (1916), 11–17.

It seems strange that Mackenzie took this view. The name Eag Dubh, *dark slit*, much better describes the impressively deep slot which lies on the Glen Brittle side of the higher dip.

When Steeple, Barlow and Doughty investigated the gully on the Coruisk side of Eag Dubh [their An Dorus Gully] in 1913 they found a 'decidedly difficult climb' of eight or nine pitches, so they rubbished the idea that this was a practical pass. Instead they suggested that the only feasible pass hereabouts was at An Dorus [their Eag Dubh], although they conceded that it 'may be considered difficult'.

By the time Steeple and Barlow brought out their masterpiece of a guidebook in 1923 the names of the dips had settled down to their current usage[4].

AN DORUS, 2700 = the door. (This is marked An Dorus on the O.S. map.) The descent into Coire na Dorus is easy. On the Coruisk side there is a narrow gully with several small pitches.

From this pass the ridge rising to Sgurr a' Ghreadaidh is interrupted by a narrow gap now known as EAG DUBH, 2890 = black notch. An easy scree gully leads into Coire na Dorus, but the only approach on the Coruisk side is by a difficult gully, and it is therefore no longer possible to regard this as the Macleod's Gap, a pass said to be used by the Macleods and called An Dorus.

This seemed to imply that Macleod's Gap was the lower dip now called An Dorus, but could it really be regarded as a pass? In Simpson's 1969 guide, the feature on the Coruisk side called An Dorus Gully was described as 'mainly scree, but with a few easy rock steps' and graded Easy. In his 1996 guide the Earl of Cromartie went strongly for the pass idea. 'Much used as a pass in the bad old days of rape and pillage.' He kept the Easy grade and described it as a 'prominent gully that is largely scree.'

When I was working on a revision of Skye Scrambles a few years ago my friend Simon Fraser, who lives near Portree, offered to help. I'd not visited Coire an Uaigneis at that time, so I mentioned that it would be interesting to know if An Dorus Gully offered a straightforward exit route from the corrie. I should perhaps have warned him that Steeple had described it as 'not altogether easy', but surely it wasn't all that hard?

Simon got the boat in from Elgol to Coruisk and walked all the way up to Coire an Uaigneis. He was by himself and was travelling light so didn't have any climbing gear. He failed at the very first chockstone. He'd planned on getting over to the Youth Hostel in Glen Brittle where he'd left his car, so he was reluctant to give up. He retreated a short distance back down the gully and tried to climb the right wall instead. All went well to start with and he managed to get up a stretch of slabby rock, but he then came to a grinding halt below a wall. He didn't have many options at this point and only managed to extricate himself by very

4   E.W. Steeple, G. Barlow et al, *The Island of Skye* (SMC 1923).

carefully reversing what he'd done. He eventually escaped by traversing round to Bealach na Glaic Moire.

Now Simon doesn't pretend to be a great climber, but he can solo Moderates and he'd never failed on an Easy before. It seemed unlikely that his route finding was at fault. Maybe he'd just had an off day.

It's not often that Skye gets sweltering weather, but for a few days in late May this year it was exceptionally hot. Where better to go than the superb suntrap that is Coire an Uaigneis?

Simon Fraser suns himself on the Costa del Cuillin (it was hotter than Barcelona), 25 May 2012. Looking across Coire an Uaigneis to Sgùrr a' Ghreadaidh. Photo: Noel Williams.

We set off up Coire na Creiche at a steady plod and then headed right for Coire a' Mhadaidh. We took separate lines up the delightful slabby buttresses at the back of the corrie leading to Bealach na Glaic Moire. I'd forgotten how enjoyable these routes are in the dry.

We dropped down on the Coruisk side and then traversed hard right into Coire an Uaigneis. The whole place was like a cauldron. We made the mistake of going too high at first and made life difficult for ourselves, but we eventually reached the broad scree slope below An Doras. Brown's Buttress looked impressive to the right and we also spotted a possible virgin buttress to the left. The whole corrie is completely unspoilt with virtually no sign of human passage. Everywhere was bone dry so we'd have no excuses.

We headed up the scree and as the gully narrowed we started to come across various bits of abandoned gear. 'Not far to the ridge now,' I thought. Simon carried on up to the first chockstone. When I joined him I realised immediately that this wasn't Easy. We both made a couple of half-hearted attempts at getting up the left-hand side, but there was so much scree over the top it didn't feel at all inviting. We could reach a loop of thin cord hanging from the lip, but we couldn't see what it was attached to and weren't prepared to pull up on it.

Simon thought that since we had a rope with us we might be better off trying to force his route up the right wall, so we retreated down the gully. The slabby rocks were completely dry and we soloed up as Simon had

Simon Fraser is reacquainted with the first chockstone in An Doras Gully. Photo: Noel Williams.

Looking back down Right Wall (Very Difficult), An Doras Gully. Photo: Noel Williams.

done before. I was impressed that he'd been able to reverse an awkward step on his previous visit. 'Needs must', he explained. 'Needs must.'

At Simon's high point I managed to traverse hard left to reach a position overlooking the initial chockstone in the gully. Simon didn't fancy following without a rope so I struggled to uncoil it one-handed. I found a rather iffy belay round a boss of rock and Simon quickly joined me.

We might have been able to get back into the bed of the gully at this point, but it didn't look easy and we spied three more chockstones with various bits of tape and climbing rope hanging from them. I pressed on up the wall and after a short harder section, I was delighted to reach a horizontal ledge which led back easily into the final section of gully above all the difficulties.

Back home we checked the new Cuillin rock guide and noticed that An Doras Gully is now given '(Moderate)' though I suspect the brackets mask some uncertainty about the grade. We also couldn't find it in the First Ascent list. At first I thought this was a mistake because Steeple said in his Journal article that he had 'explored' it with Barlow in 1910. We also found no mention of a route on our virgin buttress.

When I checked in Stuart Pedlar's Cuillin treatise[5] I was amazed to discover that Steeple and Barlow hadn't actually climbed An Doras Gully after all, as this extract from Steeple's personal diary reveals.

---

5   Stuart Pedlar, *Across Unmeasured Space* (Unpublished manuscript 2009).

Simon Fraser descends the Easy Rake to Coire an Uaigneis. Photo: Noel Williams.

We had understood that the Coruisk side of the Eag Dubh [i.e. An Doras] pass was 'troublesome owing to slippery slabs,' a description which we found a little mysterious. Slabs there were, it is true, skirting the base of the Mhadaidh cliffs, but immediately below us was a narrow gully, which we **descended** [my emphasis] by a series of amusing little chock-stone pitches.

Steeple and Barlow may have found it amusing to descend the gully, but they don't seem to have repeated the experience. On subsequent

Looking up Scrambled Eag Buttress with Eag Dubh Gully on the left and An Doras Gully on the right.

visits to Coire an Uaigneis they descended either 3/4 Gully, or the Easy Rake.

The only other mention of An Doras Gully in Stuart Pedlar's great work is a descent by JW Simpson when he was researching for the 1969 guide.

Simpson made ascents of Brown's Climb, 2/3 Gully, and top of 1/2 Gully as well as descents of 3/4 Gully and An Dorus Gully.

Judging by the amount of 'tat' around the various chockstones it looks as if a number of parties must have roped down An Doras Gully in recent times. But as far as I can tell there is no record of an actual ascent. It is highly unlikely that An Doras was ever used as a pass by the Macleods. Why would you when Bealach na Glaic Moire (760m) is a lower and easier crossing point?

A couple of days later Simon and I returned to a baking hot Coire an Uaigneis. This time we approached by Coire a' Ghreadaidh and scrambled up the North-West Ridge of Sgùrr a' Mhadaidh. We then descended to the gap between the third and fourth tops, and continued down the long Easy Rake to the floor of the corrie. In dry conditions this makes a scenic and relatively straightforward scramble.

We then traversed across the corrie to look at the buttress to the left of An Doras Gully. We moved well over to the left-hand side close to Eag Dubh Gully. At first we thought that we might just be able to scramble up

Simon Fraser on Scrambled Eag Buttress (Difficult), Coire an Uaigneis. Photo: Noel Williams.

the slabby rocks. However, when we reached some awkward overlaps, we decided to rope up. It's not every day that you have a whole corrie to yourself in perfect weather. We called our route Scrambled Eag Buttress. We eventually crossed over the main ridge at Eag Dubh and scrambled straight down the deep cleft the other side into Coire an Dorais. All in all, it was a fun outing, and nothing like as hard as An Doras Gully.

I'm not sure what grade 'not altogether easy' really is, but this much I know – it's not Easy.

THE TIDE WAITS FOR NO MAN

By Mike Jacob

We were at the point of contact of a world vanishing and a world arriving
John Buchan

HE WAS A TYPICAL retired army-officer – slightly stooped but nevertheless of upright bearing and with a subdued air of authority, impressive military moustache, twinkling eyes moist with dew – in fact, distinctly Tilmanesque. He seemed to have a problem. Could I help? So I found myself on his yacht tethered to the floating pontoon at muddy Kippford. The silty Solway seawater flooded by, gently rocking the boat. By dint of younger eyes, a more flexible spine and a length of twisted cable, I managed to recover a crucial steel pin from its greasy recess in the bilges. He was delighted. Would I join him for a gin-and-tonic or, with greater enthusiasm and brandishing a bottle of malt whisky, perhaps a dram? However, it was mid-morning and I needed to hurry if I was to catch the tide so I declined the invitation, a decision I now reflect upon.

Moonbeam, my little green lugger, skipped over and around the estuarine wavelets, a few salty drops splashing my face. A silver salmon leaped clear of the water, heading in the opposite direction up the Urr. Further out, beyond the smugglers' isle of Hestan, the motion of the boat changed, reflecting a different wave pattern and I could sense the powerful oceanic swell of the sea whose surface sparkled with blue diamonds in the bright sunlight. In conditions like this you could sail on and on … and dance through the horizon over the Irish Sea … where in 1915 the liner *Lusitania* bound for Liverpool was torpedoed, with terrible loss of life, by a German submarine.

The gravitational pull of the moon is, perhaps, the least sensed of Nature's mighty forces but the canny sailor ignores it at his peril. It was time to turn for home. The tan sails filled on a broad reach as the wooden dinghy matched the ebb, my face now turned northwards towards the pine-clad shore and beyond.

*

My thoughts flew onwards toward the heather-covered hills where in John Buchan's 'The Thirty-Nine Steps' the hero, in 1914, is pursued by a gang of German agents aided in their hunt by the use of an aeroplane. Buchan, later Lord Tweedsmuir and famous for his literary output, was a multi-talented and widely accomplished man. It is not generally appreciated, however, that he was also a member of both the Alpine Club and the SMC, which he joined in 1903. Born in 1875, he was 23 years old when he first went rock-climbing in Glen Coe, with later trips to Ben Nevis, Skye and Wester Ross, and had several Alpine holidays in

The Urr estuary at low tide. The hills in the distance are Bengairn and Screel. Photo: Mike Jacob.

Chamonix, Zermatt and the Dolomites. His obituarist wrote in the 1940 *SMC Journal* [22/129, 202]:

> His assets were strong fingers and arms, rather short legs of enormous lifting power, an enviable poise, which reminded me of Raeburn's marvellous balance, and a body that had limpet qualities.

Buchan spent his boyhood fishing the hill-burns of Tweedsdale and exploring the Cheviot and Galloway hills. He almost certainly based his novel on reports in Dumfries and Galloway's local newspapers about sightings of hostile aircraft, suspicious lights on Cairnsmore of Fleet, submarines in the Solway Firth and strangers asking their way to lonely spots. There was an imperturbable conviction that, hidden in the hills, the enemy had a secret base which could be used to monitor vital naval movements in the Irish Sea, the Clyde and even the Forth Estuary. All this may seem very melodramatic now, some hundred years on, but intrigue and rumour about German military intentions was rife and a fearful part of everyday life. You could scarcely open a national newspaper without reading an article or letter about the subversive business of a very devious enemy. In addition, U-boat activity in the North Channel was intense and there was speculation that they could have been obtaining supplies at sea and then helping to provision the nearby land-base. C.W. Dick, a close friend of Buchan, wrote about a rumour in Newton Stewart one forenoon that a discovery of fifteen-hundred tins of fuel had been made in the hills; by the afternoon the quantity had reached fifteen-hundred tons. The area off Corsewall Point, north-west of Stranraer, became an ideal place for German submarines to lie in wait for the many ships plying to-and-fro on the approach to the Clyde from the Irish Sea – with devastating results.

If you ever go rock-climbing on the greywacke cliffs of Portobello or Larbrax spare a thought for the poignant tragedies which have occurred in the sea that pounds these coastal bastions. One of them, the sinking of HMS *Bayano* on 11 March 1915, was to be the forerunner of a darker tale. The converted merchant vessel was torpedoed by submarine *U-27* some 10 miles from Corsewall Point, with the loss of 196 men. Some six months later, south of Ireland, *U-27* was about to sink another captured ship, the SS *Nicosian*, when she was approached by the decoy Q-ship *Baralong* flying the Stars and Stripes. Moving in, *Baralong* dropped her disguise, raised the White Ensign and opened fire. Small-arms fire killed a few of the German survivors as they swam from the sinking submarine. The rest, including the U-boat commander, were later executed by a party of marines from the *Baralong*.

All the fore-going may help to explain why the level-headed Harold Raeburn made the apparently eccentric suggestion that members of the SMC were in an ideal position to act as potential lookouts for enemy activity in the hills – quite possibly having gleaned his information from Buchan. In October, 1914 the committee discussed his letter, which proposed that they:

> circularise the Keepers and Shepherds in remote districts asking them to report on any suspicious circumstances and form a small committee to sift, analyse and if necessary investigate such reports; all with a view to locating enemy wireless sending stations or aeroplane depots.

Although involvement in subterfuge and spy-catching appear to have been considered unlikely pursuits for Scottish mountaineers, at least officially, it is now clear that some members did decide to act as volunteers in an adventurous escapade straight out of *Boys' Own Paper* or an episode of *Dad's Army*.

In January 1915, residents of remote Glen Trool in the Galloway hills reported hearing an aeroplane engine and witnessing the obligatory flashing lights. Colonel V.E. Lawrie – a descendant of Burns' celebrated Annie Laurie – dispatched men from the King's Own Scottish Borderers on a concentrated search of the Rhinns of Kells and Merrick ranges and the numerous hill lochs where a plane on floats could supply a hidden base. Suspicions seemed to have been confirmed when a tent was found in the snow on the west-facing slope of the 2,350ft Millfire, apparently strategically placed to cover the area between Loch Enoch in the north to Loch Dee in the south. As a result, a troop under the command of a Lieutenant William Dinwiddie was dispatched to Glen Trool 'to watch for hydroplanes which are thought to be landing on the lochs in Galloway and to look for signalling'. They set up headquarters at Glen Trool Lodge

The Solway Firth and Hestan Isle. The Isle of Man can just be discerned in the distance. Photo: Mike Jacob.

– owned by the 12th Earl of Galloway, then a PoW having been captured at Ypres – on the northern side of the loch and hatched their plans. As an aircraft leaving the area would probably fly down Glen Trool, ropes were stretched across the western end of the glen in an attempt to trap any unsuspecting German pilot. He later recounted the story to H.V. Morton who wrote:

> an ancient postman … remarked 'ah weel, there'll be no more lichts seen in the glen the noo, I'm thinkin', for I hear they've got a teetotal officer up at the lodge'.

It's easy now to laugh at the wires that once were stretched across the Caldons meadow to slice the wings off the German aeroplane and at the inspecting general officer who, on entering a shepherd's hut, pounced on the primitive apparatus for making candle dips as a sinister signalling machine.

Under the leadership of John Rennie (SMC President 1906–7) a group of SMC spy-watchers did indeed assemble at Glen Trool in an attempt to help separate fact from fiction. Interestingly, Raeburn's friend and long-time climbing companion, W. Ling, was a member of this irregular troop. He wrote in his diary that on 19 March 1915:

> G. Sang, C.W. Walker and I with Sergeant Patterson and 2 men of the Kings Own Scottish Borderers left Glentrool Lodge at 2.30 on service. We rowed across the loch then struck up the hillside towards Mulldonoch and the Nick of the Lochans. We got into mist and reached the top at

4.45 where the soldiers had made a rough shelter at the end of the wall. Our escort descended and we unpacked our stuff and made things as comfortable as possible. It was very cold. We made tea and boiled eggs. Later about 7 it cleared somewhat and later was clear to the E and S with occasional mist. The burning heather interfered with our duty of watching for lights. At sea we saw 2 vessels signalling and round the coast the lighthouse showed, but we found nothing tangible. Later it again got thick and we retired to our shelter, a strong cold N wind blowing. About 3am a blizzard began and covered us with 4 to 6 inches of snow. About 6 when it got light we descended with difficulty to Glen Trool in the face of driving snow. The weather continued bad and we received instructions from the C.O. not to go to the top. The snow had drifted badly. On the 21st we again ascended in fine clear weather to the summit [Lamachan Hill, 2340ft] and had a fine view of the bays, the Isle of Man and the coast of Ireland. We carted down our stuff, heavy loads to Loch Trool and all night went on patrol but heavy rain and mist rendered signalling out of the question and observations impossible.

Another participant was SMC member Major A. White who:

… formed one of Mr Rennie's party in the spy-hunting expedition in March 1915. There, under the exceptionally trying weather conditions, his powers of endurance, skill in signalling and strength of purpose were of great aid to his companions on their chilly vigil.

Major White was killed shortly afterwards from wounds received at Gallipoli [*SMCJ*, 14/79 (1916), 26].

So, the weather had the last say, as usual, and the spy-watchers withdrew in much the same manner as the English knights after Robert the Bruce's guerilla force had routed them here in 1307. Ironically, my source[1] states that the mystery of the tent was only eventually revealed when a member of the Scottish Alpine Club informed the army that they had abandoned the tent after members had sheltered in it during a severe snow-storm. **No!** Did not W.W. Naismith originally propose the formation of a 'Scottish Alpine Club' in 1889, a club which came into existence a couple of months later as the Scottish Mountaineering Club? Had the whole embarrassing situation, then, been precipitated by the actions *in extremis* of unspecified club-members who had also inadvertently compromised the SMC's reputation?

Fortunately, however, it may be possible to point the finger in a slightly different direction for the Scottish Alpine Club did actually exist – but not as we might understand it. In the May 1892 *SMCJ* [2/2, 90] Dr Charles Stuart wrote:

The late Professor Balfour of Edinburgh University instituted the Club, in John Cameron's Hotel, Bridge of Lochay, Killin, on the 10th of August 1870. It consisted of ten original members, and at least five of these are dead. The object of the excursions, which are annual, was to explore the higher parts of our mountains in search of the rarer alpines.

Phew, we can blame these botanists then. I have a sneaking suspicion, though, that John Rennie of Helensburgh might have known more about the background to this episode than is apparent now. At the time he would have been in his mid-fifties and was described [*SMCJ*, 21/124 (1937), 277] as a naturalist rather than a mountaineer, a characteristic, perhaps, of an *alpines-ist*?

*

Mud banks were beginning to appear but I was able to raise the heavy metal centre-plate a few inches and, avoiding the stake nets, hold to the edge of the estuary. Out in the tideway the retreating surge, reinforced by the river's outflow, gained lunatic force, accelerating between the constricting sandbanks. You don't have much time to cheat the impatient, unforgiving Solway tides and, if the wind drops, you can forget rowing. Without an engine your only option is to drop anchor, wait several hours for the planet to pirouette on its axis and pray that the wind stays fair. I barely reached the end of the slimy slipway and then went through the usual packing-up routine, finally using a hose to wash mud from the dinghy, the trolley and myself.

I looked round but the yacht was back on its mooring and Lieut-Col G.M. Dinwiddie of the 7th Galloway Battalion, KOSB, had gone. What was his relationship to the young officer of Glen Trool? I had lost my opportunity to have a blether with him and, sadly, he died a year or two later. However, in all honesty, I don't think that I would have traded my exhilarating sailing trip for the answer and I feel that the old soldier would have raised his tumbler to that ...

... joy is wisdom, Time an endless song

(Yeats)

***

Sources

1. Peter Connon, *An Aeronautical History of the Cumbria, Dumfries & Galloway Region. Part 2: 1915 to 1930* (Penrith, Cumbria: St. Patrick's Press, 1984).
2. C.W. Dick, *Highways & Byways in Galloway & Carrick* (London: MacMillan, 1916).
3. H.V. Morton, *In Scotland Again* (London: Methuen, 1934).
4. The diaries of W. Ling (permission to quote courtesy of the Alpine Club, London).
5. The SMC Archives (National Library of Scotland, Edinburgh).

NEW CLIMBS SECTION

OUTER ISLES

LEWIS SEA-CLIFFS, Bernera, Creag Liam:
Exact Epicentre   20m   F7a+ S2A **. Julian Lines. 20 Jun 2012.
A direct line on *Epicentre* (2007). Where *Epicentre* goes left at the impasse, go up and undercut the overlap making hard moves to gain the flat hold in the blank wall. Make a further hard move using a slot on the right to gain a flake hold above. Follow flakes more easily up and right to a ledge and the easy groove to the top.

Hypercentre   20m   F7b S3 **. Julian Lines. 20 Jun 2012.
Climbs the wall right of *Epicentre*. Traverse in from the right to gain the centre of the wall. Climb easily to a big pink pocket where a thin seam leads to the overlap where it turns into a tiny corner. Climb just left of the seam to layback off the corner to reach small holds on the wall above. Flake holds soon appear and are followed to the final easy groove as per *Exact Epicentre*.

Mega Tsunami – Prow Finish   F7b S2 ****. Julian Lines. 20 Jun 2012.
Brilliant, world class DWSing. As for *Mega Tsunami* to the jug/ sidepull where the original goes up the pocketed crack on the right. Reach left around the prow and climb the underside of the prow via a wild series of compression moves to the break. Move to the right side and then back left to finish on the very prow.

Aftershock   20m   F7a+ S2 **. Julian Lines. 20 Jun 2012.
Climbs the wall left of *Mega Tsunami*. Climb the wall just left of the arete to a notch at the overlap. Layback the crack-line to a vague quartz seam. Find a hidden finger slot on the right and cross through for a good flat hold. Slap up the hanging rib to gain a pink boss hold and continue up the line on hidden slots and which bends slightly into a blocky finishing groove.

Tremors   20m   F6c S2 *. Julian Lines. 20 Jun 2012.
Climbs the buttress between *Mini Tsunami* and *Shock Waves*. Climb a vertical wall, moving left at the top to beneath a slight tapering ramp. Climb this to a ledge. Using small sidepulls, move out left over the void to use the hanging prow to gain the ledge above. Scramble out easily on the left.

Painted Geo:
Tigger   25m   E6 6b ***. Ally Coull, Gordon Lennox (both led). Jul 2011.
Start as for *Gneiss is Nice*. Climb the steep short wall onto the slab and move up to the overlap. Pull over this and head directly up to below the bulge. Climb straight up through the steep bulge on positive holds then trend right to the obvious large flake. Launch directly up the striped wall to eventually gain good holds and the top.

Trojan Wall, Far Right Buttress:
Tidal   West facing

The cliff immediately right (south) of Trojan Wall is loose and unstable. Thirty metres south of the wall is another buttress with two prominent right-facing corners in the lower section. The left shallow corner angles up leftwards; the right is vertical to a shallow roof and bounded by a rib on the left. The two routes provide good climbing but also some loose rock. Access from old in-situ stakes.

Wit Amidst Folly   35m   HVS 5a. Ross Jones, Clare Jones. 16 Apr 2012.
Start below and just right of the left corner. Climb the wall right of the corner trending slightly rightwards to pull out on to a halfway ledge just left of a broken hanging rib. Step left and directly up with care to finish right of the detached corner/crack.

Another Case for Dr Lightfoot   35m   E1 5a. Ross Jones, Clare Jones. 16 Apr 2012.
Start below the second corner. Climb the corner and then the right side of the rib to a halfway ledge. Climb a shallow chimney and pull out left on to a shallow roof. Climb up for 3m and then traverse rightwards to finish up a right facing corner.

Beannan Mòr, Tolsta Chaolais:
(NB 381 198)   Alt 25m   North-West facing
The broken crag on the west side of Beannan Mòr overlooks Loch a' Bhaile and the village of Tolsta Chaolais. It provides a single sheltered line on its north end that remains relatively dry when everywhere else is wet. Approach 10mins.

Beannan Crack   10m   E1 5b **. Ross Jones, Clare Jones. 18 Apr 2012.
Climb the hanging crack pulling out left through the roof.

HARRIS, Sròn Ulladale:
Note: A possible FFA of *Premonition* at E6 6a,6b,6b,6a *** by Ally Coull & Gordon Lennox in Jul 2011. On the second 6b pitch, a slightly different line was taken. Follow the initial groove as described but instead of climbing out onto the right arete into another groove, follow it up and left before pulling over the roof in an amazing position to rejoin the described pitch at the thin crack which is followed to the hand traverse right to the belay. It was thought a more obvious way to go and puzzling that the FA didn't.

MINGULAY, Geirum Walls:
Hot Enough for Ya?   30m   E2 5c **. Gary Latter, Matt Harding. 16 Aug 2011.
Scramble down left from the main platform to a lower ledge system directly beneath the 45 degree roofs. Hand-traverse left to gain a large ledge (may be better to gain this directly by abseil). Climb direct by grooves and through a roof on good holds to gain the left end of the long tapering ledge below the main roofs. Continue to a large flake at the left side (up and right of similar smaller feature on *Horizontal Hamish*). Pull through the roof leftwards in a fine position, then climb direct up a wall, pulling out right at a horizontal crack to finish up a crack on the right.

Sunshine's Better   15m   E4 6a **. Gary Latter, Matt Harding. 16 Aug 2011.
From the left side of the ledge system, climb the easy wall to the roof (as for *Hot*

Tamsin Gay enjoys the immaculate rock on Okeanos (E2 5c), Guarsay Mòr, Mingulay.
Photo: Tim Blakemore <www.northernmountainsports.co.uk>.

Enough for Ya?), then directly through this on good holds (good cams) to finish up the crack above.

Little Miss Sunshine   15m   E3 6a **. Matt Harding, Gary Latter. 16 Aug 2011.
Climb straight up from near the left end of the ledge to gain a juggy break beneath the main roof. Using a good hold, launch up to a flat jug on the lip (Camalot 2 above) and pull over into the hanging crack which leads to the top.

Pragmatist's Folly   15m   E5 6a **. Gary Latter, Matt Harding. 15 Aug 2011.
The impressive-looking offwidth crack, climbed on surprisingly good holds, mainly on its right side. Large cams useful, including Camalot 4.

It Ain't Half Hot Mum   10m   VS 4b *. Lee Fleming, Alan Anderson. 15 Aug 2011.
The crack and easier continuation above the second bad step, gained from the right.

Gunner Graham   10m   VS 4b *. Gary Latter. 15 Aug 2011.
A line of good holds up the wall 2m right of the above route, keeping right at the top.

Guarsay Mòr, The Aga:

The Aga Sanction   125m   E4 ***. Henry Tyce, John Crook, Gary Latter. 17 Aug 2011.
Superb climbing up the centre of the wall. Start just right of the long narrow pool, about 10m right of *Taking the Hump*.
1. 35m 6a Climb the vertical pegmatite band, with difficult reachy moves to gain good holds beneath a prominent right-slanting flake/groove system. Continue up this, then go direct to a sloping ledge below a small roof.
2. 25m 5b Traverse right 4m, then go straight up the corner/groove above to a comfy ledge.
3. 30m 5c From the right end of the ledge, climb the steep wall on rounded holds, then straight up to beneath the roof.
4. 35m 5c Traverse left, then climb straight up to gain and climb the hanging roof-capped corner. Climb this, then step right onto a small slab, pull out rightwards on superb holds in a stunning position and finish directly on good holds.

Hot White Spider   120m   E4 ***. Henry Tyce, Gary Latter, John Crook. 18 Aug 2011.
Another superb varied route up the wall. Start beneath the short hanging right arete, just left of a large low roof and the leftmost of two deep caves.
1. 40m 6a Climb the twin hanging cracks in the arete with difficulty to good jams leading more easily to the large open groove. Continue fairly directly steeply on big holds to guano-covered ledges. Traverse right and up to a perfect clean triangular ledge.
2. 40m 5b Move out right, then directly up wall on incut holds, trending rightwards on easier ground, heading for a prominent leaning pegmatite band breaking through the right side of the second last roof system. Belay on large guano ledges, just left of a large (possibly suspect) spike.

3. 40m 5c Climb initially gritty rock up to the roof; move left then up through the overlap on good holds. Continue up the fine sustained overhanging groove with good gear to a small roof. Cross this slightly leftwards on surprisingly good holds, then directly, then move out right to follow a crack up the wall in a superb position to the top.

Note: *Taking the Hump* starts about 30m right of *Rayburnt*, up a prominent right-facing grey groove, the most obvious feature on the wall. There is a long narrow pool tucked in against the base, perhaps 10m long. *Taking the Hump* starts at the left end of this. *The Aga Sanction* is at the right end, with *Hot White Spider* about 20m right again.

RUM, Creag Loch an Dornabac:
These routes, in a picturesque spot at NM 358 981 (near Loch an Dornabac), have easy access and are on good rock with good protection. Approx. 500m from the road (High's Brae) and clearly visible, is a steep brown peridotite crag facing SW. The left side of the crag descends into a small unnamed loch, 80m right of which is a sloping, almost triangular slab, about 14m wide at the base. To the immediate left of the slab, at 15m height, is a 5m long horizontal overhang. Descend by an easy grassy slope to the right.

Tabby's Smile 19m Severe 4a. Sean Byron, Rob Murray. Jun 2011.
Straight up the face to the immediate left of the overhang. The crux is well protected at 15m where the climb is at its steepest.

Immy's Song 20m Severe 4b. Sean Byron, Rob Murray. Jun 2011.
Straight up the face following a crack through the centre of the overhang (well protected crux).

Orly's Composition 20m H.Severe 4c. Sean Byron, Rob Murray. Jun 2011.
Follow the crack leading to the right end of the overhang, then pull over (crux) and climb directly to the top.

Emily's Kiss 21m Diff. Sean Byron, Rob Murray. Jun 2011.
Easy climbing straight up the middle of the triangular slab.

TIREE, Pigeon Cave:
(NL 966 387) Tidal South-East facing
The Pigeon Cave area offers very smooth, water worn undercut starts with good quality rock on steep walls to finish. Quick drying.
Approach: Park at West Hynish just before the last house. Go past Dun Shiabar, through a small rocky valley, then ascend rightwards and access the top of the routes.
    The routes are on the right-hand side looking out of the Pigeon Cave. They start at the mouth of the cave above a smooth overhanging base formed by waves. Abseil from a good boulder to reach the starts.

The No Hope 20m V.Diff. Adrian Henderson, Andy Spink. 17 Sep 2011.
From a hanging stance, follow the obvious right-trending crack and corner. Pleasant climbing.

Catch the Pigeon   20m   Severe. Adrian Henderson, Andy Spink. 17 Sep 2011.
Start 3m left of *The No Hope* from a hanging stance. Climb the steep initial wall
on good holds to a small bulge; continue above on a slabby wall with good
protection.

ERRAID, Main Crag, Lower Tier:
Above   6m   HVS 5a *. Gary & Karen Latter. 4 Jun 2011.
The hanging crack springing from the apex of the hole.

Beyond   8m   HS 4b **. Gary Latter. 4 Jun 2011.
A left-slanting fault-line up wall left of *Weeping Corner* on surprisingly
accommodating holds. May be easy for the grade?

Main Crag, Upper Tier:
Dubh Artach   7m   E5 6b **. Gary Latter. 5 Jun 2011.
The brutal twin cracks 2m right of *Stonecrop Groove*.

SKYE

GLEN SLIGACHAN, Sligachan Buttress:
The following routes are on the slabs (named Salvation Slab) immediately to the
right of the main buttress. All the 25m routes can be continued for a further 25m
of pleasant scrambling to finish at the same point as *The Good Book*.

Resurrection   25m   H.Severe 4b. Paul Cunningham, Brendan Croft. 4 Jun 2011.
A bold route that heads direct into the open groove on the left side of the buttress.
From the top of the buttress head left to find easier ground.

Jacob's Ladder   25m   H.Severe 4b **. Paul Cunningham, Brendan Croft. 4 Jun
2011.
A nice line with all the difficulties in the first 10m. Follow the crack all the way
to its top.

Cross   25m   E1 5b ***. Brendan Croft, Paul Cunningham. 4 Jun 2011.
In the centre of the buttress two cracks cross in an obvious feature. Start from the
right and climb the crack right to left. Finish easily on the slabs above.

The Good Book   50m   V.Diff. Brendan Croft, Paul Cunningham. 4 Jun 2011.
At the far right of the buttress is a fine corner and wide crack. Climb this to a slab
above, and follow this to a block exactly 50m.

SGÙRR NAN GILLEAN, Lament Wall:
Nae Bother Pal   25m   VS 5a **. Paul Cunningham, Brendan Croft. 4 Jun 2011.
A route just left of the big overhang reached on first arrival at the buttress. Follow
a direct and straightforward line up to the left-facing corner to the left of the
overhang. A tough move with good protection gains the corner followed by some
fine delicate climbing above. Finish direct.

SGÙRR NAN GILLEAN, Bhasteir Face (5th Pinnacle):

Bull's Eye 90m HVS. Mike Lates, Lucy Spark. 27 Jul 2011.

Gains then climbs the crack-line on the wall left of *Forked Chimney*.

1. 20m 5a Start by climbing the open-book groove rising left from the toe of *Forked Chimney* until forced right by a bulge to a small horizontal break (wires). Climb up and left to gain the obvious ledge and the start of the crack. Climb the corner at the left end of the ledge to a cramped hanging stance.

2. 30m 4c Step back right to regain the crack-line which gives excellent climbing to a good ledge (15m). Continue direct before reaching an overhung bulge and vegetated loose bay. Turn this either left (loose) or right (bold) to reach a slabby hanging belay below an overhung corner.

3. 20m 5a Climb the corner steeply to a recess. Avoid the next (very loose) overhang by traversing out to the right edge of a steepening wall. Climb the crack (crux) to a large ledge and awkward belay (possible descent).

4. 20m 4b A worryingly loose pitch. Turn the loose roof above the belay on the right-hand side before climbing delicately to an open bowl.

Continue with care to gain either the West or North Ridges of Gillean.

Note: A suggestion for future ascents would be to split the climb into two 35m pitches and avoid the final pitch by traversing left down a narrow rake to gain *Fourth-Fifth Gully* and the foot of the climb.

Notes: *Second/Third Gully* will always be at least Grade II and could be as much as IV when lean.

Mike Lates and Susan Jensen thought *Flutings Climb* to be 125m V,4 (6 Feb 2012). Good ice was necessary in the initial shallow chimney.

SGÙRR NAN GILLEAN, Lota Face:

White Lies 270m IV,5 **. Mike Lates, Mark Francis, Ben Weir. 15 Dec 2011.

Takes a continuous line of ice 50m right of the central icefalls of *White Dreams*.

1. 20m Climb straight up to a perched flake.

2. 40m Step left, then go fairly direct to the foot of a prominent slab that slants left. Gain this and belay below an open book corner.

3. 30m Climb the steep corner (crux), then bear left more easily to the foot of the broad fat ice smear.

4. 50m Climb the ice (20m), then easy snow to a spike.

5 and 6. 90m Climb easy angled ice to a spike at the top of an open bay.

7. 40m Head up and right below the final steepening. Mixed ground for 10m leads to the SE Ridge 30m from the summit.

SGÙRR A' MHADAIDH, Upper Rake:

Wildcat Flap 60m V,6. Paul Cunningham, Brendan Croft. 3 Feb 2012.

Start as for the summer chimney, *Fox Trap*.

1. 20m Follow the snowy gully up to the base of the chimney.

2. 40m Climb the chimney for a few metres until a right-trending line becomes possible. Continue to climb up and right until a snowy ledge is reached at 30m (possible belay). Step left into an awkward corner using good hooks, and make some delicate moves (crux) to reach easier ground.

SGÙRR NAN GOBHAR, Creag an Gobhar (NG 432 226):

A clean slab lies high on the flanks of Sgùrr nan Gobhar above Coir' an Eich at about 550m altitude. A very loose gully runs up left from the toe of the buttress. Descent is by an easy traverse right and a short abseil down the right-bounding gully.

Techno-Snob 40m E2 5c **. Malcom Airey, Mike Lates. 3 Jul 2012.
Starts by the most obvious fault splitting the crag 10m left of centre. A boulder problem (5b) through the undercut face gives access to the main fault. Follow this for 10m. Hand-traverse a prominent ledge for 3m to good flakes. The weakness continues and finishes with 10m of committed thin climbing using positive holds on the right wall. Finish more easily to belay on the grassy terrace.

SGÙRR DEARG, Coire Lagan, South Crag:
Southern Comfort 240m IV,5 *. Mike Lates, Matthew Holmes. 18 Dec 2011.
Gains, then climbs ice in the gully bounding the right side of South Buttress. Start 50m west of the more obvious *In Pinn Fall*.
1. 50m Mixed turf, ice and rock leads to a horizontal rock rib. Surmount this easily.
2. 40m Descend slightly left, then climb the obvious main corner line. Belay in rocks below the steep ice step.
3. 50m Climb the ice step direct (crux), an iced corner above, then bear right to the foot of a large icefall.
4. 50m Climb good ice for 30m. Easy snow and ice continues above.
5. 50m Easy ground leads to a shoulder on the long narrow ridge that leads off the top of South Crag. Follow the exposed rib for a further 100m (III) until easier ground leads to the crest of Sgùrr Dearg 100m west of the In Pinn.

SGÙRR THEARLAICH, Stone Shoot Face:
E is for Eejit (Gully E variation) 50m III. Susan Jensen, Mike Lates. 5 Feb 2012.
Follow *Gully E* directly as opposed to the indirect version climbed in 2011.

Curse of the Hobgoblin 70m V,7. Mike Lates, Andy Huntington. 4 Mar 2012.
Follows the obvious line immediately right of *Gully E*.
1. 30m Climb into the recess, then exit by the right wall to gain the steep crack. A belay was taken on the left wall at 30m.
2. 40m Continue up the steep crack with thin moves initially (20m). Traverse easier ground left to reach *Gully E*.
Note: Climbing the main feature in one continuous 50m pitch to a good thread belay would be better.

High Visibility 80m VI,6. Susan Jensen, Mike Lates. 3 Feb 2012.
Fifty metres right of *Gully E* the buttress steepens noticeably. Ten metres up is an impending square shaped bulge 10m in width. The route climbs the line that forms the left side of this feature.
1. 35m A snow ramp leads to the first steepening. Turn this to reach the left side of the square shaped overhang. Tackle the steep corner above on positive hooks. Delicate climbing follows the continuation of the fault to beneath a small roof.
2. 40m Turn the roof easily. Head to the left side of a prominent fin of rock above. Steep moves using the fin lead to a good spike immediately above (20m).

Step left to gain the groove that leads to a small cave 10m above. Easy terrain for 15m leads to a block belay on the Ridge.

Notes: The squeezes on *Gully C* are extremely tight.
Paul Cunningham and Charlie Hill completed a direct finish to *BC Buttress* on 6 Feb 2012 (V,6). Where the description says to traverse right, instead follow a delicate corner above to finish on easier ground.

COIRE A' GHRUNNDA, Sròn na Cìche, North Crag:
The crag is characterised by a prominent central corner with a roof at about two-thirds height. The routes finish on the left-rising terrace/rake below the Stack and which provides a convenient descent to the right (east).

Pole Dancer   75m   HVS 5a **. Steve Kennedy, Andy MacDonald. 2 Jun 2012. The central corner. Scramble to the foot of two short right-facing corners. Climb the right-hand corner to a grassy ledge at the foot of the main corner (25m). Climb the corner, stepping right at 5m, until just below the roof. Traverse left onto a slabby wall via a thin horizontal break, then make exposed moves up the rib to reach the upper wall. The wall is climbed fairly directly by a crack system on impeccable rock to reach easier ground and the terrace (50m).

Lapdancer   75m   Severe 4a *. Steve Kennedy, Chris Docherty. 27 May 2012. This route follows the crack system up the wall right of *Pole Dancer*. Climb the right-hand of the two lower corners as per *Pole Dancer* to belay on the grassy ledge at the foot of the main corner (25m). Move right and follow the crack system up rightwards to reach a short right-facing corner. Climb the corner, then move up and left into a large niche. From the niche, traverse out left to easier ground leading to the terrace (50m).

Come Dancing   75m   VS 4c *. Steve Kennedy, Cynthia Grindley. 9 Jun 2012. The wall right of the main corner, starting midway between *Pole Dancer* and *Stack Buttress Direct*. Climb easily into a recessed area, surmount a bulge on the right and follow a deep crack rightwards to a belay below a small roof (25m). Move right a short distance until below a prominent flake-crack in a scooped area. Follow the flake-crack, then move up leftwards until below a large roof. Climb steep cracks right of the roof, then move left across a wall to reach a grassy ramp leading leftwards to a belay just right of a large niche (junction with *Lapdancer*) – 35m. Finish up steep cracks just right of the niche (15m).

90 Years On   75m   HVS 5a **. Steve Kennedy, Cynthia Grindley. 4 Jun 2012. The attractive cracked rib between the main corner of *Pole Dancer* and the upper chimney of *Red Wall Variant*. Scramble up to the two short right-facing corners as per *Pole Dancer*. Climb the left-hand corner. Continue up leftwards, passing a large flake, to belay at an unusual 'leg' of gabbro at the foot of the rib just left of the main corner (30m). Climb deep cracks leading up the rib until *Pole Dancer* is joined just below the upper wall. Finish up the fine upper wall as for *Pole Dancer* (45m).

Hidden Causeway   70m   VS 4b *. Steve Kennedy, Cynthia Grindley. 4 Jun 2012.

The red basalt wall on the lower left section of the crag (*Red Wall Variant*) is bounded on the left by a groove which develops into a chimney. Climb the groove and chimney. From the top of the chimney, move up left to belay below a prominent right-trending basalt intrusion (25m). Follow the stepped intrusion to a large flake-crack. Step left at the flake, then climb directly to the top, finishing up a short steep wall (45m).

Paul Brian examines the perched boulder in Coire nan Laogh on the SMC Skye Meet, May 2012. Photo: Robin Campbell,

Zeus 38m E3 5c ***. Steve Kennedy, Cynthia Grindley. 9 Jun 2012.
The striking slab, containing thin snaking cracks in the upper part, located on the right side of *North Crag Gully* near the top of Slab Buttress. Situated almost opposite the foot of the slabby terrace/rake leading to the Stack. An excellent, sustained main pitch with spaced but adequate protection. Low in the grade. Start at the lowest point of the buttress below the slab at a basalt intrusion.
1. 26m 5c Climb the intrusion over a small bulge to a ledge at 6m. Step left onto the slab and climb up to the base of a crack-line. Thin cracks lead to a small spike below the upper wall. Finish up the deep left-hand crack to reach a good ledge. The much easier upper pitch can be avoided by scrambling off right from the belay along a fault.
2. 15m The wall above the ledge (left of a prominent corner) provides a straightforward finish.

Note: *Red Wall Variant* may not be accurately shown on the photo diagram on p195 of *Skye, The Cuillin*. The line shown on the diagram goes up a steep smooth wall which looks sustained and bold (5b?). It appears that the true line may be a few metres to the right up the right edge of the red wall. At that point a short red wall leads to a basalt flake close to the right edge then a rib of gabbro, and corresponds roughly with the description. It looks much easier than the smooth red wall to the left.

COIRE NAN LAOGH:
The two prominent gullies in the corrie have been wrongly identified in SMC guidebooks for many years. The left-hand one is *Central Gully* and the right-hand one is *East Gully*. See the topo opposite. *West Gully* – a much less obvious feature further to the left – is only a walk and is not worthy of inclusion in a climbing guide. To the right of *East Gully* there is a less prominent chimney (here labelled *Far Eastern Gully*) which does not appear to have been climbed.

Kappa 155m Diff *. Simon Fraser, Noel Williams. 25 Jun 2012.
Start at the mouth of *East Gully*. Scramble up the delightful slab on the left side of the gully and, just before a steepening, descend rightwards into the bed of the gully.
1. 25m Climb up a groove formed by a giant block and the left wall of the gully. Traverse left out of the gully and continue traversing left to a good stance in a corner.
2. 30m Climb a short but tricky wall to gain a broad recess. Ascend the left side of a giant flake and step right to gain a large mossy alcove.
3. 50m Step left and make a couple of moves up a dyke before slanting leftwards up delightful slabs. Eventually slant back rightwards between twin cracks to gain a stance with poor belays immediately below a prominent cone sheet.
4. 50m Pleasant but easier slabs lead to the top.

COIREACHAN RUADHA, SGÙRR NA BANACHDAICH,
Summit Buttresses North:
Midget Ridge 120m IV,4. David Ritchie, Neil McGougan. 10 Jan 2011.
The top of the initial slab was gained from the left, then the crest of the ridge was followed turning a steep wall on the right at half-height. Recommended.

COIRE NAN LAOGH

Central Gully

East Gully

Far Eastern Gully

1. Mu — Severe * — Mason & Shallice (1958)
2. Central Gully — Severe * — Herford & Laycock (1912)
3. Lambda — Difficult — Mason & Shallice (1958)
4. Kappa — Difficult * — Fraser & Williams (2012)
5. East Gully — Difficult — Herford & Laycock (1912)
6. Far Eastern Gully — ? — ?

COIR'-UISG, COIRE AN UAIGNEIS:
This little-visited corrie can be reached either by descending from Bealach na
Glaic Moire and traversing in, or by scrambling down the 'Easy Rake' from the
dip between the 3rd and 4th tops of Sgùrr a' Mhadaidh.

Scrambled Eag Buttress   150m   Difficult. Noel Williams, Simon Fraser. 27 May
2012.
This is the obvious buttress between *Eag Dubh Gully* and *An Doras Gully*. Start
close to Eag Dubh Gully and scramble up easy rocks at first. Continue up a right-
slanting groove to an overlap formed by a basalt cone sheet, then step left to a
stance. Continue traversing some distance left before breaking through to easier
rocks. Climb up just left of a large cracked block. Traverse left again and break
through another steepening to a stance below a large rock scar. Cross broken
ground slightly rightwards and climb slabs to the top of the buttress. Scramble up
easier ground and scree to the main ridge at the top of *Eag Dubh Gully*.

Right Wall, An Doras Gully   70m   V.Diff. Noel Williams, Simon Fraser. 25 May
2012.
Start a short distance down from a rock rib in the bed of the gully. Climb easily
up the right wall parallel to the gully. Ascend a more difficult section of slab by a
small right-facing corner, then continue up easier slabs to a wall. Traverse
delicately leftwards and pull up into a position overlooking the gully – poor
belay on a boss of rock. Continue up steeper rock to reach a good horizontal
ledge which leads back easily into the bed of the gully above all the chockstones.
Easy scree leads to the top.

CARN LIATH:
Notes by Ian Taylor: *Bengal Lancer* was thought to be solid E3 5c and very
serious at the start of the second pitch. It would be safer to do as one pitch to
reduce the fall factor. *Prospect of Rona Direct* was E2 5b,5c.

RUBHA HUNISH:
Notes by Ian Taylor: *Whispering Crack* grade and stars confirmed. *Northern
Exposure* was E2 5c *. Very dirty, grassy and disappointing given **** in the
new guide.

NEIST, Conductor Cove:
The Breach   10m   H.Severe 4b. Ben Barnard. May 2012.
A corner-crack line left of *Ruby Groove* and right of the descent chimney. A
blocky start takes you easily up to gain a committing sequence of moves up the
crack.

Sonamara Area:
Reconnection   25m   VS 4b *. Ben Barnard. May 2012.
Start 1m left of *Baywatch* at a rib directly beneath the left corner of a triangular
overhang. Climb the rib, then continue past the overhang to gain an obvious
flake-line directly above. Follow this to the top.
Note: The party though that *Prog* was Severe and *Portrait Gully* worth a star.

Tim Blakemore on Whispering Crack (E3 5c), Rubha Hunish, Skye. Photo: Tamsin Gay.

Foghorn Cove:
The following are deep water soloes given French grades.

Saline Solution   12m   F7a * S0. Julian Lines. 26 May 2012.
Start as for *Hypertension* and move right on undercuts before pulling through the bulge on sidepulls to reach a jug rail. Rockover onto the rail and step up left and crimp to a horizontal break. Move up and right more easily.

Chemistry   12m   F7a ** S0. Julian Lines. 26 May 2012.
A far better and more direct line than *Toxic Chemistry* that climbs on the left side of the arete all the way to the top.

Bay Four:
Notes by Ian Taylor: *Inanimate Objects Fight Back* is very good, worth ***.
Unfortunate Prey to Genetic Infantry Men looks to be the same route as *Starfish Enterprise*.

Cumhann Geo, Seaward Wall:
The following DWS routes start from the ledge at the bottom of *End of an Era*.

Sundial   14m   F7a+ ** S1. Julian Lines. 25 May 2012.
Traverse left from the ledge to the pillar/arete where the wall changes direction. Climb the pillar to a knee-bar rest on the arete under an overlap. Make hard moves up the arete to an easy finish up the sea grass wall.

Sea Biscuit   14m   F6a ** S0. Julian Lines. 25 May 2012.
The small left facing corner to the right of *Sundial*. Finish up and left on the sea grass wall.

Timeline   14m   F4 * S1. Julian Lines. 25 May 2012.
The right-hand crack-line to the right of *End of an Era*. Finish up the same upper groove.

Cumhann Geo, Main Face:
In the centre of the geo (between *Quantum Tunnelling* and *Bagpipe Deadline*) is a fine looking right-angled corner *(The Parcel)* that plunges straight into the sea. The first four routes (DWS) are accessed from here.

The Hot Tub   15m   F6a+ * S0. Julian Lines. 21 May 2012.
The left-hand arete of the corner is gained by a traverse and a set of flat, ramp-like holds. The top half is much easier.

Pawprints   15m   F6b * S1. Julian Lines. 21 May 2012.
The hand crack between the arete and the corner fizzles out at half-height. Continue up the wall using the only hold and some frantic moves up and left to reach the arete.

The Parcel   15m   F4+ * S2. Julian Lines. 21 May 2012.
The right-angled corner, passing a parcel-like chockstone at 3m.

Ang Mo   15m   F6b * S3. Julian Lines. 21 May 2012.
The right arete of the parcel. Make very technical moves (crux S0) to gain the obvious jug. The arete is easier and the final groove above a small ledge is S3.

Theory of Attachment   14m   F6a+ S1. Julian Lines. 23 Jun 2012.
Start as for *Silent Witness*. Go up the crack for a few metres to pull up and right onto the wall. Make thin moves to get onto the arete. Follow it to the top.

Coriolis Effect   12m   F7b+ S0 *. Julian Lines. 23 Jun 2012.
Five metres right of *Theory of Attachment* is a hanging arete with two yellow lichen strips. Start on the left and make a thin traverse right to better holds. Move up to an overlap and span left to the arete. Climb the arete via an excrutiatingly technical sequence.

Geopod   12m   F5 S0 *. Julian Lines. 23 Jun 2012.
The podded groove to the right of *Coriolis Effect*. If the initial traverse is done then it is F6c

SUIDHE BIORACH:
Overhang Cure   20m   E2 5a. Mike Lates, Ian Hey. 25 May 2012.
A prominent large triangular cave lies at the right-hand end of the section that contains *Mother's Pride*, *Hovis* & *Cameron's Climb*. Scramble up into the cave to start. Climb up and right to the roof of the cave before pulling out on large steep holds to gain a ledge 3m above. Finish up the top 5m with care. A stake belay is required, but is not in situ.

SUISHNISH AREA, Carn Dearg Buttress:
Walking on Eggshells   30m   Severe. Bob Hamilton, Steve Kennedy. 19 May 2012.
The ridge left of the open gully opposite *So Where Are The Dolphins?* Start above and right of the foot of the ridge. Scramble to a steep wall which is climbed by a steep crack. Slabs lead to the upper arete and the top. Fairly loose in places.

RAASAY, An Caol:
The Great Silkie of Sule Skerry   10m   VS 4c. Tom Last, Chester Robinson. 8 Aug 2011.
Follow *Cave Crack* for a short distance, then step right across *Cave Crack* and delicately onto the face to join a steep crack which is followed on good holds to the top.

The 39 Steps   10m   H.Severe 4b. Chester Robinson, Tom Last. 8 Aug 2011.
At the right end of the crag are three obvious cracks. Enter the rightmost of these steeply and follow it to the top.

Path Boulders:
The Loneliness of The Long-Distance Runnel   6m   E3 5b *. Andrew Barker (on-sight solo). 23 Jun 2012.
Climbs the runnel on the east side of the large boulder on the shoreline (Runnel Project, p268 Syke Sea-Cliffs and Outcrops guide). Pull on at a flake and follow sharp snappy pockets to the runnel which is laybacked with trepidation to an exit

right onto the forest-covered top. The descent is to the left and is reached by thrashing up and over the top of the boulder. No pads used and graded as such.

NORTHERN HIGHLANDS NORTH

BEINN DEARG, Silver Slabs:

Meridian   145m   HVS ***. John Mackenzie, Eve Austin. 2 Aug 2011; John Mackenzie, Colin Tarbat. 27 May 2012 (top 3 pitches).

A direct line up the middle of the slabs, bold in places but with good climbing, taking the top overlaps at their most interesting. Small to large Friends needed. Start below the bottom overlap, midway between the jutting block of *Boom Time* on the left and a wet corner to the right.

1. 25m 5a Climb up to a thin left-slanting crack and surmount the well protected overlap to an initially steep slab. Climb this direct to an overlap just right of a clean-cut corner.
2. 55m 4b Climb the overlap to a steep slab. Go up this in the centre via hidden holds and continue with minimal protection up the easier clean slabs and small overlaps to the terrace that cuts across the slabs below the overlapping headwall slabs. Belay on the right at a big cracked block.
3. 20m 4a Climb up a left-slanting corner with possibly suspect blocks, keeping to their left and move left to a ledge.
4. 25m 4c/5a Climb over an undercut overlap, step left then straight over the next overlap to a break in the top overhang just left of a large block. Climb over via the slanting crack and continue up and left to reach grass and a cracked block. An excellent pitch, well protected and surprising.
5. 20m Move up left more easily to finish.

CAIRN CONMHEALL, South-East Face:

This steep groove-lined face is reached by continuing up past the more open West Face to near the top of the gully where a very narrow heather ledge above broken rocks bottoms the face.

Centrepiece   30m   HVS 5b ***. John Mackenzie, Eve Austin. 14 Jun 2012.

To the left of three deep set corners lies a continuous S-shaped groove above a lower corner-ramp. Large Friend belay below the ramp. Climb the ramp leftwards past a thread and up a steep flake-crack and difficult landing on a ledge, possible belay. Continue to and up the narrow crack above to the top in a fine position. Very good varied climbing and well protected by a good range of cams.

BEINN MORE COIGACH, Cadh' a' Mhoraire:

Hyperborea   300m   IV,5. John Higham, Iain Young. 3 Feb 2012.

Takes a direct line up the buttress that leads to the highest point at the back of the hanging corrie, Cadh' a' Mhoraire, south of the east end of Lochan Tuath. From the base, follow a turfy ramp rightwards, then cut back left to the bottom of a prominent groove. Follow the groove (crux), move slightly right and follow a chimney come gully that leads back left to gain the buttress crest. Follow this to the summit ridge.

Stac Pollaidh: Carlos Las Heras climbs Vlad the Impaler (HVS,5a) on the SMC aspirant meet 2012.
Photo: Andy Nisbet.

STAC POLLAIDH, Pinnacle Basin:

Cinch Crack 30m   VS 5a *. John Mackenzie, Eve Austin. 9 Jun 2012.
Immediately above the path leading into Pinnacle Basin from the west is a short steep wall with a prominent layback crack at its left-hand end. Perhaps done before.
1. 15m 5a Climb the layback crack and the capping bulge, then up the groove to a ledge. A good pitch, well protected.
2. 15m 4a Climb the crack then up the clean slab directly above.

Andy Tibbs on Dangerous Dancer (E3 6a), Ardmair. Photo: Martin Hind.

REIFF, Stone Pig Cliff:

Jolly Roger 7m HVS 4c. John Dyble, Graham Stein. 5 May 2012.
Climbs the middle of the slab between *Chalk Block* and *Walk the Plank*. Using poor holds to start (possibly 5a), gain the horizontal break and place the only gear on the route. Continue with long reaches up the centre of the unprotected slab.

Pinnacle Area, First Geo:

The Cleft 20m H.Severe 4c. Michael Barnard. 11 Nov 2011.
The antithesis of sunny Reiff climbing! Walk into the cave left of *Octopus' Garden* to belay below a corner on the left wall with a small pool at its foot. After a gymnastic start (crux), move rightwards along a ledge to gain the obvious fault-line leading to the top.

Bouldering Cliff:

Dab Chick 25m E3 6a/b. Tess Fryer, Ian Taylor. 3 Jun 2012.
Right of *One Scoop or Two?* is a hanging corner that leads to the right arete of the slab. Climb the steep little corner, then the right edge of the slab.

Platform Walls:

Pali Gap 20m Diff. Michael Barnard. 12 Nov 2011.
The slabby corner left of the descent (below *Mad Dogs and Englishmen*) has an obvious hole. Climb through it.

Note: The route *Thumper* (p176, NH North) was first climbed by Paul Allen & Wilson Moir in May 1995 and named *Spring Sonatina*.

Spaced Out Rockers Cliff:

Shortcut to Oblivion 35m E4 6a ***. Tess Fryer, Ian Taylor. 19 Aug 2011.
Start 5m right of *Culach* and just left of the sea cave. Climb up and make committing moves to gain a shallow guano splattered groove and follow this to a junction with *Spaced out Rockers*. Continue up *Spaced out Rockers* to its belay ledge, then carry on more or less directly to a large roof, which is passed on its left via keyed-in blocks to gain a ledge. Steep bulges above lead to another roof. Move left and make a final long reach for the top.

Aqua Rambling 20m E5 6a ***. Ian Taylor, Tess Fryer. 19 Aug 2011.
Start as for *Spaced out Rockers*. Swing left onto the front face and follow the edge and crack above to gain a good break. Move left, make some thin moves and continue to another break. Go up to a roof and pull over using flat holds, step right and climb up to finish on a ledge just below the cliff-top. Low in the grade with good protection where it matters.

Slime Time 30m E3 6a **. Tess Fryer, Ian Taylor. 23 Jun 2012.
The always wet corner-line at the left end of the cliff. Needs a drought or a positive attitude to damp.

Leaning Block:

Pirates Direct 15m HVS 5b *. Tess Fryer, Ian Taylor. 23 Jun 2012.
Start 4m right of *Harold* and climb the wall direct, cutting through the ramp of *Pirates of Coigach*.

Edges and Spaces   18m   E3 6a ***. Gary Latter. 11 Jun 2011.
Very well protected climbing up the wall midway between *Caoraich Mhor* and
Sixteen Men… Climb direct on good edges to the first break, then continue with
difficult reachy moves between good breaks at mid-height. Finish more easily.

Rubha Ploytach:

Past *The Joker* is a tidal square-cut bay with a black and tan north facing wall.
The following two routes are accessible in calm seas for two hours each side of
low tide.

King Prawn   10m   H.Severe 4a. Steve Lenartowicz, Clare Humphry. 25 May
2012.
The shallow corner on the left, often wet but on good holds.

Black Queen 10m   VS 4c ** Steve Lenartowicz, Clare Humphry. 25 May 2012.
The steep line of flakes gives a fine sustained route, without using the rib on the
right.

ACHMELVICH, Creag Rodha Mòr aka Super Crag (NC 056 236):

The crag is situated on the south shore of Loch Roe, near Achmelvich. The crag
consists of a very steep west facing 40m wall and a couple of south facing
stepped walls (aka The Burnished Walls). Despite some big guano ledges no sea
birds appear to nest on the Main Wall (probably too scared), but on The Burnished
Walls there are a few shags right of *Rolling Foam* and the odd fulmar on a grassy
ledge. A pdf file is available with topos, a map and the descriptions.
Approach: 40mins, but may take a bit longer the first time!
   Although it doesn't look far on the map the approach feels fairly complex and
the ground is quite rough. Take the single track Achmelvich road from the B869
Lochinver to Stoer road and after about 1km turn left down a narrow road
(signposted footpath to Baddidaroch). Park at the top of the hill where the tarmac
ends. This is the same parking as for Loch Dubh Crag.
   Continue along the new track, go through a gate and after 250m look out for a
small stream coming in from the right. A very vague path follows the stream past
some ruined crofts and then onto the open ground above. Cross a fence and
continue following the stream to a narrow lochan. From here head west over
ridges and drainage channels until the ground starts dropping down to the sea. If
you're lucky then off to the left you'll spot a large, heather covered mound at the
end of a ridge running out to sea. This is the top of the crag. Dropping down to
the left (facing out) allows a good view of The Burnished Walls with the Main
Crag beyond. There's also a handy small stream near the viewing point.

The Burnished Walls:

The south facing Burnished Walls are about 40m at the right end and 20m on the
left. Above the shorter section is a luxurious grassy ledge known as Ant Ledge.
This is easily accessed from the landward end via a sloping ramp and short down
climb. A 35m abseil from a big block on Ant Ledge gains non-tidal ledges below
the walls. The walls are a real suntrap.

Upper Wall:

Falconer Cracks 15m VS 4b *. Tess Fryer, Ian Taylor. 1 May 2011.
Climb the obvious crack above the big block on Ant Ledge.

Bogie Wonderland 6m E2 6a *. Ian Taylor, Tess Fryer. 1 Jun 2011.
Above the step in the descent ramp to Ant Ledge is a perched block. Climb the most continuous crack right of the block.

Lower Wall:

The most prominent features of the Lower Wall are the short arete on the left *(Rusty Buckets)*, the central crack below the step and the steep hanging corner to its right.

Crystal Shell 20m E3 5c **. Ian Taylor, Tess Fryer. 24 Apr 2011.
Just left of the arete is a flake-crack and *Crystal Shell* climbs the vertical crack to its left. Start by stepping left to the whacky crystalline hollow, then follow the surprisingly steep crack to a ledge. Finish up a red corner and short walls above.

Champagne Rhubarb 20m E2 6a **. Ian Taylor, Tess Fryer. 22 Apr 2011.
Climb the flake-crack just left of the arete until below the roof. Swing rightwards onto the arete and go up a crack at the right end of the roof to a ledge. Belay here or on Ant Ledge just above. Finishing leftwards as for *Crystal Shell* is E1 5b.

Rusty Buckets 20m E3 5c ***. Tess Fryer, Ian Taylor. 22 Apr 2011.
The thin crack-line, just right of the arete, gives a pumpy little gem. Finish up a brown slab above the break.

The Shiner 20m E4 6a **. Tess Fryer, Ian Taylor. 30 Apr 2011.
Start up the left side of the hanging block. Go up, take a diagonal crack leftwards for a couple of metres, then make hard moves up the wall above. Another pumper.

Read my Lips 20m E3 6a **. Tess Fryer, Ian Taylor. 24 Apr 2011.
Start up the right side of the hanging block to follow a right-trending crack to below a nose. Make a mean move to go round the left side of the nose and finish more easily.

Small Time Girl 20m E2 5b/c *. Tess Fryer, Ian Taylor. 29 Apr 2011.
This takes the vague crack-line right of *Read my Lips* until below the very steep headwall. Follow a break rightwards until able to gain the ledge above and finish up the short wall.

Vive la Republique 20m E1 5a *. Ian Taylor, Tess Fryer. 29 Apr 2011.
Start at an easy ramp and go up a crack to a break. Move right along the break to a flake and go up this to Ant Ledge.

Burnt Umber 20m E1 5a *. Ian Taylor, Tess Fryer. 7 May 2011.
From the easy ramp go up rightwards to the top of a nose, just left of the central crack. Continue using the crack and the wall to its left.

Blair Fyffe belays Richie Betts on Rusty Buckets (E3 5c), Creag Rodha Mòr. Photo: Ian Taylor.

Watch out for a bit of loose rock at the top of the following three routes.

Mega Flake   40m   E2 5b *. Tess Fryer, Ian Taylor. 22 Apr 2011.
Start at the central crack and climb this for 10m, then follow a diagonal line
rightwards heading for a big bleached flake in the middle of the right side of the
wall. Monkey up the flake and at its top go right and follow a line to the top.

Shades of Glory   30m   E2/3 5c *. Tess Fryer, Ian Taylor. 24 Apr 2011.
Start as for *Mega Flake* but move right and go up a shallow groove and golden
crack above to reach easier ground (junction with *Mega Flake*). Go slightly left
and climb a steep flake 2m left of the big bleached flake. Belay on the ramp
above.

Rolling Foam   45m   E3 5c ***. Ian Taylor, Tess Fryer. 24 Apr 2011.
A well positioned route up the hanging corner round to the left. Traverse right
into the corner and follow it steeply until able to pull onto a welcome ledge on
the left. Go straight up the wall above then trend right to gain some grey flakes
and follow these over a final bulge to the ramp.

Main Wall:
The impressive west facing Main Wall rears up from a sloping non-tidal ledge
system, which can be gained by a short 10m abseil from Ant Ledge. Although it's
hard to get a good view, the right side can be seen from Ant Ledge. The major
features are a brown corner at the right end, two large guano covered ledges right
of centre (one at 20m and one at 30m) and a big groove line left of centre, with a
smooth wall to its left.
   The rock varies from solid juggy grey gneiss to a disconcertingly smooth
brown variety. As with any big sea-cliff there are occasional loose sections and in
general it feels a bit snappier than Sheigra. It comes into the sun about 3 p.m.
Apart from at high tide it is possible to scramble down to sea-level and escape off
leftwards. There is a 6m E2 5c up an open corner in the centre of the small steep
wall below *Guanissimo*. From right to left.

Ruddy Glow Corner   30m   E4 6b **. Ian Taylor, Tess Fryer. 22 Apr 2011.
This is the big obvious brown corner at the right end of Main Wall. Start below
and right of the corner and go up easily until a diagonal line, over large grey
blocks, gains the corner proper. Make some committing moves up the corner,
then get burly.

The All Abilities Path   40m   E4/5 **. Tess Fryer, Ian Taylor. 19 Jun 2011.
Climbs the steep wall right of *Guanissimo*, followed by an 'escape' up the top
section of *Personal Mingulay*. Start just right of the yellow ramp.
1. 20m 6a Go boldly up the wall to good holds and gear. Make hard moves to
gain a flake-line and follow this into the left-hand groove above. Exit from the
groove to a sloping ledge below a dauntingly steep brown wall.
2. 20m 6a Hand-traverse left below the steep wall until below an open brown
groove just right of the higher guano ledge. Go up the groove, pulling left onto a
sloping ledge at a black band. Continue via a hanging flake, pulling onto a slab to
finish.

Richie Betts leads pitch 2 of (My Own) Personal Mingulay (E4/5 6a), Creag Rodha Mòr, Achmelvich. The abseil rope shows the angle. Photo: Ian Taylor.

Guanissimo 60m E3 ***. Tess Fryer, Ian Taylor. 1 May 2011.
A fine natural line that wanders around to give the easiest route on Main Wall. A hanging ramp leads up and left to the lower guano ledge and a right-facing flake system leads to the right end of the hanging ramp. Start from an easy yellow ramp.
1. 20m 5c Gain and climb the flake passing the right-hand of two black 'eyes'. At its top follow the ramp easily leftwards to the lower guano ledge.
2. 20m 5b Go up the steep flake-crack to reach a juggy handrail and follow this leftwards to the higher guano ledge. A cracking pitch, Friends 1 & 2 are handy for the belay.
3. 20m 5b Traverse left 4m, then make an awkward move onto a sloping ledge. Continue easily to a herbaceous finish.

(My Own) Personal Mingulay 45m E4/5 ***. Ian Taylor, Tess Fryer. 7 May 2011.
An excellent direct route with two great pitches. Start just left of *Guanissimo*.
1. 20m 5c Go up a line of steep flakes, passing the left-hand of the black 'eyes', to gain the middle of the sloping ramp. A rattling block in the flake-line seems to be well keyed-in. Move left and belay as for *Guanissimo*.
2. 25m 6a Go up the flake-crack above to gain the juggy handrail as for *Guanissimo*. Move left, then go up an open brown groove, pulling left onto a sloping ledge at a black band. Continue via a hanging flake, pulling onto a slab to finish.

The Pabbay Express 20m E3 5c ***. Tess Fryer, Ian Taylor. 20 May 2012.
An alternative first pitch to *Personal Mingulay*. Slightly harder and slightly better. Start just left of *Personal Mingulay* and go straight up past two horizontal breaks to gain a shallow groove line that leads to a belay at the left end of the lower guano ledge. Continue up *Guanissimo* (E3) or *Personal Mingulay* (E4/5).

Unnamed 40m E7 6b ***. Iain Small, Niall McNair (both led). 23 Jun 2012.
Excellent pumpy climbing followed by an exhilarating crux. Possibly low in the grade. Start 2m left of *Undertoad* and climb via big flakes, breaks and blocks for 10m. Go up the wall right of a corner on pockets and flakes to a good break and good cams. Hand-traverse this for 3m, then go up on obvious left-facing flakes to a second break system. Go along the break (small cam), then up on flakes again to jugs. Move up to flat holds, then boldly trend left past a rock scar to a hidden sidepull (crux)and make a long reach for a hand rail on the edge of the guano ledge. Tackle the overhanging wall at the right end of the ledge to gain a good foot ledge, then trend up and right to the top.

The Under Toad 40m E5 6b *** Ian Taylor, Tess Fryer. 17 Jun 2011.
Start left of *Personal Mingulay* at a step in the sloping ledge. Climb up via flakes to gain a ledge below a thin, slightly right-trending crack. Follow the crack all the way to the left side of the lower guano ledge. Move left along a flake to a small rock scar and make hard moves up a thin crack to the upper guano ledge. Move right off the ledge to the open brown groove of *Personal Mingulay* and finish up this.

Ian Taylor leads The Ambassadors (E6 6b), Creag Rodha Mòr. Photo: Richie Betts.

The Ambassadors   40m   E6 6b ***. Ian Taylor, Tess Fryer. 20 May 2011.
The central line on Main Wall starting up an obvious groove with two downward pointing grey flakes at 15m. Intricate and committing on the crux section. Gain the groove by following a thin flake rightwards to a ledge, then moving left to another ledge. Go up the groove past the downward pointing flakes and make a long move from undercuts to gain a horizontal break in the brown rock. Hard moves up and left lead to a precarious ramp, at the top of which small wires can be fiddled in. Move right, then make more hard moves up to a line of improving holds and follow these rightwards until able to pull awkwardly onto the high guano ledge. Move left 4m, pull onto a sloping ledge and finish easily. Belay well back.

Rodha Mor   40m   E5 6a ***. Tess Fryer, Ian Taylor. 7 May 2011.
A big route with exciting climbing up the big left-hand groove line. Start below and to the right of the groove at a 3m flake. From the flake steep moves up and left lead to a small guano ledge at the base of the groove. Follow the groove for 20m, then continue up a thin crack heading for a downward pointing flake. From the flake move up and left to another flake, then go straight up to a horizontal seam. Go left then finish up a slightly creaky flake.

Ramp it Up   45m   E3 5c **. Ian Taylor, Tess Fryer. 1 May 2011.
This route goes up the groove of *Rodha Mor*, before escaping off to the left. Climb the groove for 20m to a large lump of black amphibolite, then hand-traverse left to gain a yellow ramp and follow this leftwards to gain ledges. Continue left, then pull onto a lichenous slab to finish. Scramble off leftwards.

The Cullinan 35m E6 6b ***. Ian Taylor, Tess Fryer. 1 Jun 2011.
Another great route up the centre of the smooth wall left of *Rodha Mor*. Start at a bowl shaped depression. Climb more or less straight up on positive holds, till a move left at 10m gains a large flake. From a big jug at the top of the flake, make a move up, then round to the left to gain a positive hold (good gear down and to the left), then make further hard moves to an easing on a yellow slab. Go up a final crimpy wall to a ledge (possible belay) then finish up and left as for *Ramp it Up*.

Brow Beaten 55m E4 *. Ian Taylor, Tess Fryer. 30 Apr 2011.
Takes a line just right of the left edge of the wall. Below and left of the main cliff is an undercut cave, gained by scrambling down leftwards from the sloping ledge (not at high tide). Start on the right side of the cave at a protruding nose.
1. 20m 5b Move up from the nose to an undercut ledge and shuffle left along this. Surmount the bulge above to gain an open groove, then move left into a hanging corner. Go up this to a small ledge below the main cliff.
2. 35m 6a Climb up to gain a ledge, hand-traverse 2m rightwards, then make a committing move up to a diagonal break. Continue up to a flake of lighter coloured rock, then hand-traverse right and pull over onto an overhung ledge. Go steeply up and left for a few moves, then follow a line diagonally rightwards on lichenous slabby rock to easier ground.

CULKEIN STOER:
A number of unrecorded routes have been done on these easily accessible cliffs. The two tier black wall gives a good E3 6a **, starting up a thin crack to a ledge, then following the obvious continuation. There is a two bolt belay just left of the top, but there are also plenty of natural placements. Just to the west are two strange bolt routes on a black north facing wall. Abseil in to hanging belays. They are about 15m long. The left-hand line is F6c and the right-hand line is F6b. Both routes were apparently drilled by Creagh Dhu climbers a few years back. Further west is 30m cliff above a non-tidal platform. Facing north it seeps quite badly. The following route may be new. Approach by abseil.

Omission Impossible 15m E2 5c ***. Ian Taylor, Tess Fryer. 22 Aug 2011.
At the shorter left-hand end is a good looking hanging flake-crack. Gain this by following some grooves, then moving right. A wee gem.

TARBET SEA-CLIFFS, Balmy Slabs, Eastern Sector:
The Serpent 12m E3 5c *. Michael Barnard, John Nelson. 6 May 2012.
The thin crack in the slab right of *Scuttlefish*. Start on a small triangular block at the base of that route and step right to climb the crack.

White Slab:
Slabitus 25m Severe. Michael Barnard. 25 Mar 2012.
Climbs the slabby west side of the obvious narrow pillar left of *White Slab* (approached by abseiling the line of the route).

FAR NORTH-WEST CRAGS, Creag an Dubh Loch:
Note: *Updraught* (Northern Highland North page 240). The pitches are more

like 30m and 20m. The descent gully is pretty wet, loose and unpleasant even in a week of dry weather.

Ridgeway View Crag:

Michael 15m Severe. Colin Lesenger. 5 Aug 2011.
Start just right of the grassy line between *Classic Crack* and *Row the Boat*. Climb clean cracks, step right to an inverted V-niche and pull over direct.

Groovy 10m Severe. Colin Lesenger. 5 Aug 2011.
The left-facing corner as for *Rodney's Gneiss Route* but climbed direct.

Red Slab:

Lady Jane Direct 10m HVS 5b *. James Duthie, Michael Barnard. 16 Jun 2012.
Climb straight up into the crack of *Lady Jane*.

Heart of Stone Direct 15m E1 5b *. Michael Barnard, James Duthie. 16 Jun 2012.
Climb the obvious flake and crack right of *As Good as it Gets* to join *Heart of Stone* at the end of its traverse.

Big Yellow Caterpillar 10m HVS 5a *. Michael Barnard, James Duthie. 16 Jun 2012.
Right of *Heart of Stone Direct* is a steep wall. Climb the vertical crack at the far right end of the wall, moving right then left at the top.

Moves Like Jagger 10m VS 4c. James Duthie, Michael Barnard. 16 Jun 2012.
Climbs the shallow right-facing ramp/corner at the right end of the crag.

Notes: *Heart of Stone* is 20m (not 25m) and has become too lichenous for **.
Little Red Rooster was thought to be VS 5a (not HVS 5b) and is 15m (not 20m).
As Good as it Gets is the best route on the crag but still worth **.

ARDBEG, West Geo:

The Greater Black Crack Gull 15m VS 4c **. Steve Perry, Katie Long. 29 May 2012.
The corner to the left of *Cabin Fever*. The clean-cut corner is not as hard as first appears and gives good protection. Layback away to a crux move at half-height leading to easier ground.

CAITHNESS SEA-CLIFFS, Sarclet, Big Buttress North Face:

The black wall on this face is north facing and can take time to dry. It is best accessed by abseil but there is a scramble out on the north side of the bay, but beware of the fulmars.

The God of Suspended Sediments 35m HVS 5a ***. Rob Christie, Harald Ramsoy, Charlie Macleod. 14 Jul 2011.
Start below a massive hanging block immediately left of *Silver Darlings*. Move up and right past a jammed boulder, then to the right of the block. Step out left onto the block and into the groove behind. Climb easily up the groove to finish.

Rune Magick 35m HVS 5a ***. Charlie Macleod, Rob Christie. 29 Jul 2011.
Right of *Silver Darlings*, climb a pillar to a ledge with a square block below a crack leading into a groove to the top.

Americana 25m VS 4c. Rob Christie, Charlie Macleod. 29 Jul 2011.
From the birdlime covered ledge at 10m, step onto the right wall. Climb cracks to the top. Avoid during the nesting season.

Sarclet, Wee Buttress (ND 343 421):
The Wee Buttress is directly north of the Big Buttress. Access is by abseil. Four lines were climbed in 2010 on the left section of the buttress (SMCJ 2011). The following were climbed on the central and right sections.

Central Section:
Italian Rover 25m Severe 4a. Giacomo Marchi, Kirstin Carmouche. 2 Jul 2011.
Climb a shallow square corner on the left arete to half-height. Traverse left into the gully and finish up a straightforward crack.

Scottish Ferrari 25m VS 4b. Charlie Macleod, Rob Christie. 6 Jul 2011.
Climb to a small roof 2m right of *Italian Rover*, step right, go up to a ledge and finish through the broad notch.

Shaken All Over 25m HVS 4c *. Charlie Macleod, Rob Christie. 13 Aug 2011.
Two meters right of *Scottish Ferrari* is a blank wall with thin cracks. Move up and right into a groove, then on to the arete and back left at the top.

Unnecessary Egyptian 25m E1 5b **. Charlie Macleod, Kirstin Carmouche, Giacomo Marchi, Rob Christie. 2 Jul 2011.
Start at extreme right of the central section. Step up and right to cross the gully onto the right section. Follow a ledge to the crack below the right end of the roof. Move out onto the wall and go directly up to finish.

Right Section:
Eat your Greens 25m VS 4b **. Rob Christie, Charlie Macleod. 29 Jul 2011.
At low tide, follow the crack 2m from the right edge for 5m, then go right onto the arete. Turn back onto the front face near the top.

Sarclet, Gloup Ledge:
(ND 341 417) Non-tidal
South of the Tilted Ledge there is a 20m clean wall, above a good ledge, accessed by abseil. The central feature is a slim rib to the right of a water filled surging gloup. Left of the wall above the gloup is a right-facing corner below a small roof.

Molly Cough Cocktail 20m E1 5b *. Raymond Wallace, Charlie Macleod, Rob Christie. 29 Apr 2011.
Climb the corner and turn the roof to the right. Climb to the top on easier ground.

Bublicious   20m   HVS 5a *. Raymond Wallace, Rob Christie. 27 Jul 2007.
Climb the wall above the gloup on the left. Traverse across the ramp at half-height. Climb to a big roof which is turned to the right.

Domino Rib   20m   HVS 5a **. Charlie Macleod, Giacomo Marchi, Allan Sinclair, Rob Christie. 4 May 2011.
The route up the left of the rib. Make steep moves onto the arete, then over easier ground to a roof. Move left to finish.

Big Fat Calzone   20m   Severe 4b. Charlie Macleod, Kirstin Carmouche, Giacomo Marchi. 3 Jul 2011.
Right of the route is an easy gully with much birdlife at the top. This is the first clean line to the right taking a straightforward route to the ledge above, just below the cliff-top.

Scary Jacuzzi   20m   VS 4c **. Rob Christie, Charlie Macleod, Kirstin Carnmouche, Giacomo Marchi. 3 Jul 2011.
The blunt arete to the right of *Big Fat Calzone*. Climb a broad juggy pillar on to the arete, pass small roof on the right before finishing on the slab above to the left.

Experimental Pizza   20m   HVS 5a **. Rob Christie, Charlie Macleod. 3 Jun 2011.
Start at the right-facing corner. Climb onto the wall above to the roof. Move right and climb the cleft through the roof.

Extra Chilli Pepper   20m   E1 5a *. Charlie Macleod, Rob Christie. 3 Jun 2011.
Start to the right of *Experimental Pizza*. Climb to a roof, traverse round a bulge and go up to the right (poorly protected). Climb to the roof, move right and pull through the cleft on big jugs.

ORKNEY, Yesnaby:
A large number of routes have been climbed by Neil Morrison, Tim Rankin, Julian Lines, Danny Laing and others. They will be reported next year.

SHETLAND, Bressay, Bard Head:
(HU 516 357)   Mainly non-tidal   South-South-East facing
The sandstone headland below the Bard Gun has a large hanging slab capped by a broken overhang at the top with a right-facing curving corner on the left. Climbs start from ledges below overhanging walls beneath the slab. Ledges should be clear except in a large swell.
Approach: Abseil from the large Bard Gun to tidal ledges at the south-east end of the wall below the large slab. 100m rope required.

Poetic License   90m   E1 5b *. Ross Jones, Andrew Hunter. 27 Mar 2012.
Start below a hanging groove/corner system at the left end of ledges. A fine and atmospheric route with an excellent first pitch, marred by some lose rock and poor protection on the second pitch.
1. 30m 5b Climb the hanging corner and belay directly above it.

2. 30m 4a Go left and up onto the slab above. Climb this directly to the arete to the left of the main slab.
3. 30m 5a Climb the wall just left of the arete with a tricky pull up and small overhang to surmount at 20m.

Bard From Bressay 95m E2 5c **. Ross Jones, Paul Whitworth. 23 Mar 2012.
1. 35m 5c Pull up into the hanging corner as for *Poetic License*. Pull out right and traverse 3m to a small left corner. Climb this and the corner above for 8m. Pull out right 4m below the capping roof on to the arete and make an airy traverse rightwards to a hanging corner. Pull up into this.
2. 30m 5a Climb the corner to ledges beneath the slab. Make an easy rising leftwards traverse up the poorly protected slab to the corner above the first bulge.
3. 30m 5a Climb the corner for 10m, then pull out leftwards and up into a hanging groove. Climb this, pulling out leftwards to finish.

Eshaness, Stuvva Head:
The Unforgiving Sea 15m H.Severe 4a. Ross Jones, Al Whitworth. 24 Mar 2012.
The wall and shallow groove left of *A Single Cask*.

NORTHERN HIGHLANDS CENTRAL

STONE VALLEY CRAGS, The Valley Walls:
FarNorth Slab 15m VS 5a. Jeannie Northoven, Stuart Macfarlane. 2 Jul 2011.
Just to the left of *Round the Block* there is a slab with a corner on its left. Climb the slab, which widens with height. Climb using the slab only and do not use the holds of the corner on the left or the higher holds of *Round the Block* on the right. The corner is used for gear lower down.

Game of 2 Halves 15m H.Severe 4c. Jeannie Northover, Stuart Macfarlane. 2 Jul 2011.
To the left of the route above and to the left of the corner, climb a steep rib to a platform. The start of the route involves a tricky bouldering move. Avoid finishing left from the platform and climb the face to the right and up using bridging moves.

Rum Doodle Crag:
Note: The variation finish to *Rum Doodle Arete* (SMCJ 2011) was in fact done on the first ascent, so is not new.

Stone Valley Crag:
Cheeseslice 10m V.Diff. Stuart Macfarlane, Jeannie Northover. 3 Jul 2011.
To the left of *Cheesegrater Slab* is a prominent crack. Climb the crack.

Albatross 25m VS 4c. Jeannie Northover, Stuart Macfarlane. 3 Jul 2011.
A wandering and anti-social route. Climb the crack on the right edge of the slab of *Touch and Go* and veer left up steps at the top of the crack to finish at a niche

with the main slab. Traverse across the main slab of *Open Secret* to the finishing corner of *Inside Information*. Climb this awkward corner (crux).
Note: This may have been the line of the original exploration on the crag, but it was graded V.Diff, although nothing of that grade seems possible.

AZTEC TOWER:

Texcoco 15m   H.Severe 4b. Stuart Macfarlane, Jeannie Northover. 2 Oct 2011.
Climb up *Warrior God* to the middle ledge, then follow an obvious left-diagonal crack which joins the upper part of *Conquistador*.

Sacrificial Stone 10m   Severe 4a. Jeannie Northover, Stuart Macfarlane. 2 Oct 2011.
Between *Sun God* and *Infanta* is a vague crack-line leading to the top. The crack is attained by a tricky move to gain a ledge with a large clump of heather. Easier climbing up crack-line leads to the top.

Note: *The Inca Trail* has been renamed *Coatlicue* and graded H.Severe 4b.

RUBHA MOR, Camas Point:

The following routes are on a fine west facing slab at Camam Point to the landward of the area described in the guidebook.

Niece Wall 10m   Severe 4b. Stuart Murdoch, Jane Murdoch, Geena Murdoch. 30 Apr 2012.
The obvious central crack-line, continuing directly above to gain a steep undercut wall (crux).

Escalator 10m   Diff. Stuart Murdoch, Jane Murdoch, Geena Murdoch. 30 Apr 2012.
The obvious line of weakness about 5m right. An ideal beginners' route.

Notes: *Mr Freeze* was thought Severe 4c.
Traction Control – correct grade at H.Severe 4b and maybe worth a star.
To Infinity and Beyond was thought Severe for the step round the nose at half-height.

GRUINARD CRAGS, Inverianvie Crag, Bayview Wall:

Alluring Complexity   15m   HVS 5a. Jeannie Northover, Stuart Macfarlane. 28 Apr 2012.
Climb the arete immediately to the right of *Double Matured* and before *Cask Conditioned*. A tricky start that involves climbing/squeezing under tree branches. Good climbing continues on the arete above where protection is adequate with small wires and cams.

Dome Crag:

Welcome to the Terror Dome 50m   E8 6c ***. Ally Coull. 2 Oct 2011.
Takes a line between *Dead Calm* and *Majordomo*. Start mid-way between the above routes directly below a small diagonal roof right of the three obvious white streaks. Climb up to the roof and turn it on the right, then climb up and right over another overlap to a rest below the obvious small roof (bold). Pull over

this roof and climb diagonally up left passing good gear to a diagonal crack and small overlap. Make hard moves directly up to reach a good flat hold; gear can be arranged to the right (crucial). Use an undercut and poor holds to gain the next break (hard) and continue boldly into a niche. Climb left out of the niche to an easing in angle. Climb the obvious groove more easily to the top. Head pointed, all gear placed on lead.

Jetty Buttress, Back West Wall:
Big Flapper 20m E5 6a ***. Ian Taylor, Tess Fryer. 24 Oct 2011.
An excellent clean route up the left edge of the wall that contains *Gogmagog*. Sustained with good protection where it matters.

AN TEALLACH AREA, Junction Buttress:
Via Duct 130m VS. Andy Nisbet, Jonathan Preston. 23 May 2012.
This climbs the highest line of continuous rock, which is a ridge left of *Injunction* (SMCJ 2011). It could again be described as lying at the change of aspect of the cliff. Left of *Injunction* is a steep wall at the cliff base. This leads up to clean walls forming the ridge and bounded on the left by a groove system with a wet overhanging base (this lack of access means it can't be one of the original routes). Start left of this overhanging base.
1. 50m 4b Start up the left side, but soon move into the centre of a clean slabby wall to reach a ledge below trees.
2. 50m 4b Traverse right across the wet fault to gain the ridge above its steepest section. Climb the first step of the ridge on its left side, then continue up the longer second step.
3. 30m 5a Climb a steeper final step to easier slabs.

Spaghetti Junction 130m HVS. Andy Nisbet, Jonathan Preston. 23 May 2012.
Climbed on its 40th anniversary. Start just right of *Rightward Slant*, at the left end of the slabby ground which forms much of the west side of the crag. Right of this are polished waves of steep smooth ground.
1. 30m 4c Follow a right-slanting crack to a bay.
2. 45m 5a Move on to the right arete of the bay and gain its top. Follow a ramp rightwards to its end, then climb up through a tricky bulge to easier slabby ground which leads to a ledge.
3. 25m 4c Climb a pocketed slabby wall, then walk behind a block to *Rightward Slant*.
4. 35m 5a Cross this and climb a right-slanting crack in a fine clean slab.

AN TEALLACH, Ghlas Tholl:
Haymaker 90m VI,7. James Edwards, Roger Webb. 28 Jan 2012.
There is a prominent buttress between the forks of *Hayfork Gully*. Start at the equally prominent groove just left of the toe of the buttress.
1. 30m Enter the groove via a well protected boulder problem start, then climb it with less protection to an excellent pinnacle on the left.
2. 30m Gain the ramp above with difficulty and climb diagonally up and right crossing an interesting slab to belay on the crest of the buttress.
3. 30m Climb grooves in the crest to finish.

Toll an Lochain, Gobhlach Buttress:

Haggis Raclette   310m   IV,3. Sandy Allan, John Lyall, Andy Nisbet. 6 Feb 2012.
An ice and turf line on the left side of the buttress. Start up the first step of *Gobhlach Ramp* (SMCJ 2011), then move right to a parallel icy fault-line. Go up this to a deep narrow chimney, then move out left to a ledge (40m). Go back right to the top of the chimney, then follow the fault up left (40m). Continue left to a large icy ramp leading up right and make a start up it (50m). Climb ice on the ramp to where it begins to peter out, then traverse right and go up on turf to easier turf (40m). Go left up a shallow turfy chimney (50m). Climb straight up via a short icy step (40m). Take a slabby ramp leading right to the crest above the long final groove of *Gobhlach Buttress*. Go up the crest to easy ground near the top of the buttress (50m).

Narrow Buttress   200m   II. Andy Nisbet, Jonathan Preston. 19 Feb 2012.
The buttress between *Central Gully* and *Chockstone Gully*. Start up *Central Gully* and move right after about 100m to reach the start. An initial tier was climbed via a right-slanting ramp, followed by easy ground. The steepest tier was climbed by a shallow chimney on the crest, then finish more easily on the crest, including two small pinnacles.

THE FANNAICHS, Sgùrr Breac, North-East Nose:

Hugh's Groove   100m   III. Ewan Lyons, Barry Middleton. 15 Dec 2011.
This climb follows a line on the other side of the rib to the right of *Heather Horror*. Start just right of *Heather Horror* at a short icefall. Climb this with a step to the right (crux) and continue to the back of a bay (50m). Follow an icy groove up left or an easier finish trending right under a wall (50m).

THE FANNAICHS, Creag Dubh a' Gorm Lochain (NH 237 693):

Roseroot   300m   V,5. James Edwards, Martin Hind. 5 Feb 2012.
A big rambling route with the occasional ice pitch. Start up an ice pitch in a chimney just up from the base of a big easy gully which has been named *Gormless Gully* (30m). Follow up easier mixed ground (80m) before another band of rock with an ice pitch (50m) leads up to the final obvious ice pitch on the headwall of this section (45m). Above easier ground leads to the top (100m).

GLEN AFFRIC, Tom a Choinich:

John Mackenzie notes that the East Ridge of Tom a' Choinich is a very attractive way up the hill, holds snow well and is approached from Gleann nam Fiadh and the track up into the corrie via the Allt Toll Easa. The east ridge is set further into the corrie than the curved SE ridge and tops out at around 950m with a base around 750m. It is well defined with Grade I climbing near the top following the crest directly. Map ref NH 174 267.

GLEN AFFRIC, Sgùrr na Lapaich:

Central Gully   150   II. Matt & Vicky Smith. 29 Apr 2012.
The obvious easy gully splitting the face gets steeper with height and was climbed direct. A left-hand exit (*Swansong* II, SMCJ 2010) may be useful if the cornice is too large.

SGÙRR NAN CLACHAN GEALA:

The Last Lap   120m   IV,4. Simon Richardson, Magnus Stromhall. 27 Jan 2012.
Facing north, the short steep buttress on the north end of the south-east ridge is a
useful back up if the climbs on Lapland Buttress are not fully frozen.
1. 40m Start 30m right of *Practice Lap* and climb a ramp up and left to gain a
ledge with several prominent yellow blocks. Move up and right to another ledge,
then trend left and belay just right of the crest.
2. 10m Climb a steep corner to reach easier ground.
3. 70m Continue up easy mixed ground on the broad front face of the buttress to
the top.

Creag Loch Tuill Bhearnach:

The following route is on the lower crag immediately above the loch. This is the
right-hand of two obvious lines on the buttress and starting from its toe.

Peat Bog Faeries   90m   V,5. Martin Hind, James Edwards. 10 Nov 2010.
Climbs the gully/chimney line on the buttress. Easy climbing leads to a thrutchy
corner, or easier up and left and back round above.

STRATHCONON, Creag Ruadh, North-East Face (SMCJ 2011):

Feint Rib   115m   II. John Mackenzie, Eve Austin. 2 Feb 2012.
A faint rib runs from the highest point well right of *Creag Ruadh Corner* with a
lower tier split by a groove but with avoidable broken ground above ending at a
small isolated outcrop. This seems the longest of several ribs.
1. 25m A short ice step then leads left into the groove and a stance in a grotto.
2. 50m Move right then up left over a thin slab and follow the faint turfy line
after a level section to turf belays.
3. 40m Follow the more obvious rib, some ice, to the isolated outcrop, turned by
either side.

BEN WYVIS, Creag Coire na Feola:

Forties, Cromarty   225m   IV,4. John Lyall. 8 Feb 2010.
The parallel and narrower ice line to the left of *Gael Force Grooves*. Start on the
left side of the snow bay and climb an icy right-facing corner. Continue straight
up on snow and iced slabs to the easier upper slopes.

Quiet and Peacefall   210m   VI, 5/6. John Lowther, John Lyall. 2 Feb 2012.
The elegant but rarely formed icefall down the steepest part of the lower wall,
between *Proletariat* and *Laird of the Rings*.
1. 15m Climb short icy steps leftwards to a thread.
2. 55m Move steeply right and follow the thin right-slanting line of ice to a steep
exit. Continue up a thinly iced groove and shallow gully to a small spike and
blade crack to the left.
3. 30m Go straight up to the steep diagonal wall.
4. 50m A blue pillar of ice leads onto a hanging ramp of ice (left of the groove
on *Laird*) which is followed to the last rock.
5. 60m Easy snow and a final short tier.

STRATHVAICH, Black Bridge Crags:
Route 4.5 10m VS 4b. Iain Thow. 5 May 2007.
A thin crack between *Routes Four* and *Five*.

Note: Continuing diagonally on *Route Three* makes a pleasant Severe 4b. Iain Thow. 5 May 2007.

NORTHERN HIGHLANDS SOUTH

DRUIM SHIONNACH, West Face:
Castle in the Sky 60m Harder than X **. Dave MacLeod. 1 Feb 2012.
Near the right side of the crag is a large recess with a smooth 5m horizontal roof at its top. The route climbs directly across the widest point, just left of a diagonal crack which also crosses the roof. Start below a system of steep flakes leading to the centre of the roof. Climb these to a good rest underneath the roof. Launch directly across this with footless moves and multiple figure fours, passing a poor blade near the lip. Further thin and hard climbing leads over the lip and to easy ground after a few metres. The last half of the roof and headwall is poorly protected and serious. A belay is possible on the turf ramp above if you have a strong second. Otherwise pull the rope through and continue boldly up the ramp until it is possible to climb direct past a flake to the top.

CREAG COIRE AN T-SLUGAIN:
Gorillas in the Missed 300m III. Jon Ison, Mark Ward. 21 Feb 2011.
Start at the right end of the lower crag (a long way right of *Double Gully*) and climb an easy gully to an ice cave/narrowing. Two short pitches gained the top of the lower gully. The first was difficult under powder and verglas. From the top of the upper gully, a traverse leftwards and up for approx. 100m leads to the base of some overlapping left-leaning small rock slabs. The start of the second section is a little ill defined. From a rock belay a pitch leads directly upwards over a couple of bulges to a boulder. Above is an obvious narrowing and the crux ice bulge leading to a slab and a boulder approx 15m below the cornice. Topo provided.

THE SADDLE, Sgorr na Forcan:
South Face Direct 120m I/II. Duncan Robb, Michael Ramage. 7 Feb 2012.
NG 942 129. An obvious gully line to the right of the southern spur leading to the summit ridge of Sgùrr na Forcan. A straightforward route with an airy top out on the ridge to the east of the summit.

SGÙRR NAN CONBHAIREAN:
Note: Starting well below and left of the gullies, the East Ridge proper, more of a broken buttress, is open to considerable variation. Grade II, George Allan, John Thomas, 28 Jan 2012.

COIRE LAIR, Whispering Wall:
Will of the Wisp 30m E2 5c. Pete Macpherson, Martin Moran. 15 Sep 2001.
Start on the terrace at the left end of the crag below an obvious clean triangular niche. Climb with difficulty into the niche using the handrail on the left. Move

right again and place the first runners before continuing up and right (bold) to three incut foot holds. Continue straight up, placing poor gear until easier climbing gains the top. Beautiful clean rock!

Kirsty Two Squeaks 30m HVS 5a. Pete Macpherson, Martin Moran. 15 Sep 2001.
Start 2m to the left of *Society of Whispers*. Pull left onto the ledge and continue up a groove until a hard move gains a break below a bulge. Pull over the bulge on big holds and continue more easily, trending slightly left to the top.

Harry's Lair 30m E2 5c. Pete Macpherson, Martin Moran. 15 Sep 2001.
About 3m right of *Society of Whispers* is a steep cracked groove, with another 2m right again. Start below this second groove. Bouldery moves lead to a steep crack on good holds. Go up the crack and mantel left onto a ledge (bold). Step left and continue up to gain a crack between the grooves. Continue fairly direct on easier ground to the top.

Note: *Society of Whispers* was thought E1 5b as against E2 5b/5c; Ross Jones (FAist) is happy with this.

SGORR RUADH, Raeburn's Buttress:
Note: Ken Applegate climbed a line up the face right of *Easy Gully* (Grade II, 19 Feb 2012) but since it crosses the descent from the top of the lower section of Raeburn's Buttress, a full description is not given.

KISHORN Note: The prominent waterfall on the north side of the road from Lochcarron to Kishorn (SMCJ 2011 p462) had previously been climbed by Morris MacLeod and partner in 1978.

MEALL GORM:
The Blue Lamppost 120m VIII,8. Pete Macpherson, Martin Moran. 7 Dec 2011.
Start from the bottom of *Lobster Gully*, zigzagging up slightly right through broken turfy ground to the bottom of a slightly left-leaning turfy groove.
1. 30m Climb the groove to reach a snow terrace and belay directly behind at the next rock band.
2. 30m Move right and head up turfy grooves leftwards to reach a steep corner which is at the left end of a long roof 15m further up. Climb the groove with sustained technical interest to reach the roof and belay at its left end.
3. 18m Directly above is a fine clean fist jam crack which splits the roof and goes up the wall above; this is the summer line. Avoid this and instead move right 4m and climb up to the roof, then pull through to gain a crack (bold). Climb diagonally up and left for about 8m to gain a ledge and big flat block.
4. 40m Directly above is a right-facing groove which continues up to a hanging chimney with an offwidth to the right. Gain the groove with difficulty and commitment (crux) and continue up steeply with sustained climbing to reach the bottom of the chimney (beware of a protruding loose block). Pull left into the chimney and climb in a fantastic postion to reach easier ground which is follwed to the top. A brilliant pitch!

SHIELDAIG CRAGS, Creag Ob Mheallaidh (SMCJ 2011):
Choppy Waters   15m   Difficult **. Michael Barnard. 20 May 2012.
The fine blunt arete down and right from the main crag (passed on the approach).

BEINN DAMH:
The Bulldog Spirit   70m   V,5. Simon Richardson, Roger Webb. 18 Dec 2011.
The prominent line of weakness, just left of centre, cutting the vertical quartzite cliff directly below the summit of Beinn Damh.
1. 35m Climb up into the gully-fault, and follow it trending right under a roof to reach a good ledge.
2. 35m Move right and climb a rib (which borders the left side of a deep gully) and finish up a steep corner-crack.

BEN DAMPH, Little Corrie:
Slender Buttress   120m   II. Peter Biggar, Roger Robb. 15 Dec. 2011.
This is the narrow buttress between *The Thin White Line* and *The Slanter*. Two pitches of mixed ground lead to a steepening with a prominent chimney. Climb the first part of this to a ledge; go left to a system of cracks and grooves in the edge. Quite sustained for the grade.

SEANA MHEALLAN WEST, Pink Walls:
Something Fine   15m   E1 5b **. Gary & Karen Latter. 18 Apr 2011.
Fine well-protected climbing up the right-slanting groove just right of *Fish and Chips*. Climb the groove mainly by its right arete, then step left and pull over a roof easily.

Bedrock Buttress:
Sky Blue and Black   10m   E3 6a **. Gary Latter. 18 Apr 2011.
Well-protected climbing up the fine arete up the left side of the corner of *Dolphin Friendly*. Start as for that route, pulling left and climb up the arete with difficult moves to good breaks at the top roof. Pull over this on good holds to finish.

BEINN EIGHE, Far East Wall:
Rudolf   100m   VIII, 8/9 ***. Murdo Jamieson, Martin Moran. 23 Jan 2012.
A superb winter route, very sustained and at the upper end of the grade. Pitch one climbed the iced crack left of the cave to a belay in a niche at the first roof (25m serious). The second pitch has a hard start (maybe 9), then climbs past wedged pillars to a layback crack which would be very hard if iced, before traversing 3m left to a hanging belay (20m). The top section was broken into two pitches. The first goes up to a roof, makes a delicate traverse into the upper corner, then climbs strenuously up cracks in the leaning right wall before regaining the corner and climbing to a constricted belay under a capping roof (30m). The top pitch moves left past the roof with difficulty then follows the monolithic final corner to the top (25m).

King of the Swingers   VIII,10. (one fall, one rest) Martin Moran, Pete Macpherson. 11 Jan 2011.
1. 25m As for the summer line following turfy grooves up to the base of the corner.
2. 25m Climb up the corner until about 2m below a small overlap which is about

Andy Nisbet on the first ascent of Wild West (V,6) Beinn Eighe, 16 March 2011. Photo: Garry Smith.

4m below the big roof. Travese horizontally left on extremely thin moves for both tools and feet to reach the fist width crack on the left (very difficult!) Climb up the crack with sustained difficulty until desperate moves over a bulge gains a sloping ledge.

3. 20m Climb the excellent corner on great hooks and gear before pulling out left below the roof onto a ledge.

4. 20m Step left and climb up the slabby wall before pulling round the right side of a roof. Continue up via a turfy corner to below a final steep corner.

5. 10m Climb the steep corner to easier ground.

Eastern Ramparts:
Note: *The Unknown Soldier* was climbed free at E2 5c by Andy Nisbet & Jonathan Preston on 20 Jun 2012; worth a star or two. Very well protected on the crux, so perhaps E1.

Far West Buttress:
Occidental VI,7. Andy Nisbet, Duncan Tunstall. 4 Apr 2012.
The big corner of the summer route and an unclimbed short chimney above gave good enough climbing to be content to finish up other routes.

1. 20m Climb the big corner as for summer (axe with a big adze recommended), and belay on top of the three wedged blocks.

2. 20m Step right and climb a short chimney past its capping block. Climb the wall above (as for *Athame*), then move right and gain the terrace as for *Chalice*.

3. 30m There are many possible finishes but this ascent moved 10m right along the terrace, then finished as for *Chock-a-Block*, starting with the through route.

Pineapple Cliff:
Jammy Dodger 120m III,5. Andy Nisbet. 5 Mar 2012.
Left of *Sidestep* is this gully, much deeper than it appears from below. The grade could well be much lower with a good build-up. The gully is straightforward to a final cave. Step right on to a ledge and make a hard but well protected move up to turf. Continue into the upper gully and finish easily.

CAIRNGORMS

COIRE AN T-SNEACHDA, Fluted Buttress:
Brute Force and Ignorance 105m VI,7 *. Michael Barnard, Pat Ingram. 29 Jan 2011.
The main feature of this route is the obvious cracked corner line on the steep left wall of *Broken Gully*. Rather unbalanced, with the first pitch the crux by far, but interesting and with a fun finish.

1. 30m Climb up to the cracked corner line and follow this directly to a ledge below the top section. Traverse right 3m and move back up via flake-cracks to belay on *Broken Gully*.

2. 60m Move up left and climb a groove through the rocks above, continuing up the snow slope to the base of the upper tower.

3. 15m Climb the obvious corner-crack on the right-hand side of the tower.

COIRE AN LOCHAIN, No. 1 Buttress:

The Hyperventilator IX,10. Greg Boswell, Will Sim. 22 Jan 2012.
The route takes the steep faint overhanging crack-line on the left wall of the Vent (to the right of the '*Big Daddy* corner'). The route is still waiting a clean ascent as on the last ground up attempt, GB came off one move from easy ground. But pulled back on and finished the route. The second pitch takes the obvious large corner above and right of the terrace.

No. 2 Buttress:

Minute Man Direct Start 30m VII,7. Andy Ingles, Guy Robertson. 16 May 2012.
Start about 5m right of *Chute Route*, below a groove with a rockfall scar on its left wall. Climb the groove until just below where it peters out, then pull right onto the rib and climb steep cracks up to join *Milky Way* just below the upper tower of *Minute Man*. No change in overall grade.

No. 3 Buttress:

Siberian Tiger 70m IX,10. Greg Boswell, Pete Macpherson, Guy Robertson. 12 Dec 2011.
Exceptionally strenuous and technical climbing with large fall potential on pitch 2 which is the crux. Start as for *The Vicar*.
1. 25m Climb the groove for about 7m and break out onto the right wall as soon as possible. Climb the wall via useful cracks to gain a belay ledge (common with *The Vicar*). A lovely well protected pitch which would make a more logical start to *The Vicar*.
2. 45m Gain the arete via a crack to a small ledge and pull tenuously around onto the slab. Climb the slab via tenuous thin flared cracks heading leftwards until under the left side of the roof on the arete. Rest as best you can before climbing the overhanging flake above which proves very strenuous. Once over the roof, trend boldly rightwards to the right edge of the slab and pull round the corner. Climb more easily to the top.

Pfugga-Lule 60m VIII,9 ***. Charly Fritzer, Matthias Wurzer. 22 Jan 2012.
Start at the bottom of a small left-facing corner 3m right of *Happy Tyroleans* start.
1. 30m Climb the corner to gain a ledge and small terrace on the right. Step back left and climb a steep crack to swing left at its top to gain a large undercut flake. Climb the flake up and right to gain a right-facing corner and follow this to belay on the large terrace as for *Overseer Direct*.
2. 25m Move up the stepped ground to climb the obvious overhanging chimney exiting left at its top to reach easier ground.

Never Mind, Mindless Finish IX,10. Nick Bullock, Bayard Russell. 23 Jan 2012.
A full winter ascent of the *Mindless Finish*. The route described in the Cairngorms guide finishes further right. The name *Pic n' Mix* for this seems to have stuck and has settled at VIII,9.

CREAGAN COIRE A' CHA-NO:

International Rib   65m   II. Ibrahim Aboudiwan, John Lyall, Mike Rigby, Huw Williams. 26 Jan 2012.
Start at the toe of the rib to the left of *Plasma Gully* (the following route). Follow a slanting fault just right of the crest, then by a groove between two pillars to finish right of the final tower.

Plasma Gully   50m   I.
The gully to the right of *International Rib*, exiting on the right of the big cornice.

Next is the broader Blood Buttress.

True Blood   50m   III. John Lyall, Eric Pirie. 13 Jan 2012.
Start about 15m left of the left edge of the buttress, and go up a gully and over a big wedged block. Continue to a recess, pull out left and follow corners until a wide crack on the right leads to the finishing slope.

Blood Thirsty   50m   III,4. Scott Frazer, John Lyall, Mick Twomey. 28 Jan 2012.
Start just right of the left edge of the buttress and climb an easy fault, then a short steep corner with a wedged block.

The Blood is Strong   50m   III,4. John Lyall, Eric Pirie. 13 Jan 2012.
Start at the lowest rocks on the right side of the buttress, just left of a short vertical wall. Take the left-slanting slabby corner to start, and the continuation corners to the top.

There are a couple of very short but steep walls on the left of *Wide Gully* (the following route).

Wide Gully   40m   I.
The gully left of *Short Ridge*, passing the cornice on the right.

Short Ridge   50m   IV,4. John Lyall, Andy Nisbet, Jonathan Preston. 12 Dec 2011.
The next ridge south of *Cutty Sark*. Take a short chimney on the left side to a ledge, then follow the ridge to the top.

Mainmast   35m   IV,5. John Lyall, Andy Nisbet, Jonathan Preston. 12 Dec 2011.
The steep chimney-crack left of *Cutty Sark*. Climb this and pull out left at the top of the crack, then follow the gully behind the pinnacle, finishing right of the cornice.

Auld Reekie   30m   IV,4. John Lyall, Eric Pirie. 13 Jan 2012.
On the steep right flank of the *Cutty Sark* buttress. Climb an icy groove, then move left and pull up into a short deep chimney, exiting left of the capping roof.
Direct Start   V,6. Neil Adams, Gwilym Lynn. 22 Jan 2012.
Take a more direct entry up a wide crack to gain the short deep chimney.

Note: *Chimney Rib* is now thought to be III,4 rather than its original IV,4. An alternative start (IV,6) to *Chimney Rib* was made by Martin Holland & Steve

Langton on 24 Jan 2012. Climb the short (7m) wall down and left of the chimney to gain the platform left of the chimney and step right to gain the chimney itself.

Frozen Planet 40m IV,6. John Lyall, Andy Nisbet, Jonathan Preston. 12 Dec 2011.
An escapable line on the left flank of the Anvil Buttress. Start beneath *Flaked Out* and climb two short corners leading left, then up a wide open chimney to a ledge (30m). Climb the bulging flakey edge above, and move left behind a block to the top (10m).

Wile-E-Coyote 60m IV,4. Steve Crawford, Alex Parmentier. 19 Jan 2012.
A deep groove round the arete right of *Anvil Corner*.

Kerplunk 60m III. Stuart Lade, Liam Fleming, Jill Plummer. 13 Jan 2012.
The broad ledgey buttress between *Anvil Corner* and *Duke's Rib*. A rambling line finishing by a 20m corner.

Arch Rival 60m V,5. Sylvain Baboud, Simon Richardson. 26 Jan 2012.
A counter diagonal to *Arch Wall*, taking the prominent groove-line just left of the rockfall scar in the upper part of the face. Start 10m left of *Arch Wall*.
1. 30m Climb a right-trending series of turfy shelves leading to a short steep corner. Climb this to reach the alcove stance of *Arch Wall*.
2. 30m Move up and right to gain the foot of the prominent left-facing corner (*Arch Wall* goes left then up from here through the roof of the arch), and climb it in good but well spaced turf to a snow bay. Move left and climb a short corner to the top.

Ptarmigan Rib 60m IV,5. Simon Richardson, Roger Everett. 12 Feb 2012.
The right-bounding rib of the gully-line of *Fingers and Thumbs*. A prominent line, but most of the climbing coincides with existing routes.
1. 30m Climb directly up the rib until the way is barred by a blank bulge. Move right to join the upper continuation of *Mac's Crack* to belay in the notch of *Fingers and Thumbs*.
2. 30m Continue up the steep section of *Fingers and Thumbs*, but instead of exiting left up the gully continue right to a ledge. Move up and left up a final wall to finish.

Note: An alternative finish to *Tower Chimney* was climbed by Ross Mathers & Edvin Mellergard on 27 Jan 2012. An obvious line that continues straight up instead of veering right up the squeeze chimney of the original line.

Flying Rib 100m IV,5. Simon Richardson, Sylvain Baboud. 26 Jan 2012.
The cracked slabby rib that runs down and left from the upper part of *Boundary Ridge*.
1. 30m Start at the lower right end of the rib and climb a crack to the crest. Move left along the crest, step left onto a cracked slab and climb to a stance below the upper slab.
2. 20m Move up to an overlap and pull over onto the slab above. Climb turfy cracks to its top.
3. 50m Continue up snow slopes to the top.

Boundary Ridge 180m III,4. Sylvain Baboud, Simon Richardson. 26 Jan 2012.
The right bounding ridge of the corrie. Start 10m up and left from its foot below
a broken crack-line leading up the left wall. Climb this with interest for 60m,
then continue more easily for two pitches to the top.

COIRE AN SPREIDHE:
Goulotte Cachee 300m IV,4. Roger Everett, Simon Richardson. 12 Feb 2012.
A good mountaineering line up the right side of the face. Not sustained, but the
crux pitch is steeper than it looks. Start approximately 50m right of *Central
Couloir* and climb low-angle ice in a shallow runnel for 60m into a large snow
bay. Exit the snow bay from its top left corner via a steep ice step (crux) to reach
a gully (hidden from below) and climb this for 30m to reach easier ground.
Continue straight up for 150m through a section of mixed ground in the upper
part of the face, to the top.

STACAN DUBHA:
Atlantis 160m III. Andy Nisbet, Jonathan Preston. 30 Dec 2011.
A line of grooves between *The Shuttle* and the following route. Start just left of
the lowest rocks below the grooves. Climb the right-hand of two turfy grooves
rightwards to a ledge. Ignore the groove above and move right to another groove
(not another one further right). Climb this groove before moving left to a bay. Go
to its top left corner and climb a line of weakness trending slightly right to reach
easy ground.

Upper Crust 150m VI,6. Ross Cowie, Andy Nisbet, Helen Rennard. 20 Dec
2011.
The buttress immediately right of the chokestone gully. Start up a snowy ramp
leading left towards the crest overlooking the gully and reach an overlap.
1. 45m Step right and climb an inset slab to the crest. Make steep moves up to
gain a turfy groove and climb it to its top. Step left on to slabby ground and climb
a left-facing corner to its top where moves right reach a flake.
2. 35m Climb turfy ground up a slight crest before moving left to a steep barrier
wall. Traverse left to a big corner system.
3. 40m Climb the corner to a snow bay, above which is a steep groove. Climb the
groove to a ledge on the right.
4. 30m Climb a short wall above to easy ground.

Mr. Blobby 160m V,5. Andy Nisbet, Jonathan Preston. 15 Dec 2011.
The buttress between the chokestone gully and *Transavon Gully*. Start just inside
Transavon Gully and climb a groove to a bulge. Move right to the crest and step
left over a huge flake (30m). Climb a groove directly above the lower one, step
over its right arete and traverse the steep face on the right over flakes until
possible to go up to a point above the belay (30m). Climb the easier crest of the
buttress to where the buttress peters out at the junction of *Transavon Gully* and
the chokestone gully (50m). Finish easily up the chokestone gully (50m).

Red Dwarf 160m VII,7. Simon Richardson, Markus Griesshammer. 24 Jan
2012.
The prominent corner-line defining the right side of the buttress between *Zigzag*
and *Tangent*.

1. 60m Start at the foot of the buttress and climb a prominent V-corner that curls up and right to reach easier ground below the upper buttress. The corner is deceptively steep and smooth, and the steep bulge at 20m was climbed by moving across the left wall of the corner, and returning right along a dwindling ramp.
2. 20m Move easily up to the foot of the right-facing corner.
3. 40m Step left and sit astride a flake below shallow cracks in the rounded gully guarding entry to the corner. Climb the cracks with difficulty and then continue up the right-facing corner system above to a good belay on the left.
4. 40m Continue up the corner that opens out into a gully and the top of the buttress.

Goldilocks   160m   VI,6. Roger Everett, Simon Richardson. 11 Dec 2011.
Good mixed climbing up the pronounced pillar left of the previous route. Start below and left of the pillar.
1. 70m Climb easy snow up and right to below the foot of the upper pillar. Belay below the right-hand of two fault systems.
2. 15m Climb the right-hand fault to a ledge.
3. 15m Transfer to the left-hand fault and climb it via an overhanging chimney to a ledge.
4. 40m Continue in the same line up the left-hand fault to a large terrace.
5. 20m Finish easily up and right to the top.

Zig-Zag   150m   IV,4. Andy Nisbet, Jonathan Preston. 30 Dec 2011.
The relation to the summer route is unsure. Climbed in fairly lean but icy conditions; the lower half could bank out under heavy snow. Start at the left edge of the crag, just above and left of a prominent overlap. Move right on to the face and climb a thin but prominent line of turf snaking up the slabs above. Move left to the top left corner of a snow bay. Gain and climb a corner right of the buttress crest before moving left on to the crest. Go up the crest, then rightwards to another corner. At the top of this move right above steep ground and gain slabs above. Climb these trending right to the top.

CÀRN ETCHACHAN, Upper Tier:
Jumping Jupiter   VIII,8. Greg Boswell, Ian Parnell, James Dunn. 21 Dec 2011.
Thin and slightly bold climbing with a hard crux through the first overlap. Belay under the roof above the slab. Turn the roof via the arete on the left and make a right-trending traverse to regain the summer line.

GARBH UISGE CRAG:
Garbh Gully, Right Exit   35m   II. John Lyall. 15 Jan 2012.
Take the fault going out right from below the crux of the normal route. An escape if the final pitch is not formed, and makes the route grade II overall.

Garbh Gully, Left Exit   90m   IV,6. Scott Frazer, John Lyall, Mick Twomey. 27 Jan 2012.
The thinly iced chimney forming the left fork of the gully. Passing the final chokestone was the crux, but it may become easier with a bigger build-up of snow. There were signs of retreat from below the crux.

STAG ROCKS:

These routes are on the small buttress on the top right-hand side of the Y-shaped gully, just below the fork. It has a steep rib on the left and an alcove on the right with a slab and big roofs.

Summer Rib   30m   Severe 4a. John Lyall, Andy Nisbet, Jonathan Preston. 28 Mar 2012.
Start on top of a small shattered buttress below the steep rib. Follow cracks on the right side of the rib, and move left at a steepening to finish up a groove on its left side.

Midnight Tiles   45m   VS 4c. John Lyall, Andy Nisbet, Jonathan Preston. 28 Mar 2012.
Start at the top of the alcove and climb the initial short wall by a sharp edged flake and step right to a ledge. Head up left through a small curving overlap, then follow a corner to break through the left end of the long roof and continue straight up to finish by a right-facing corner.

Black and Blue   45m   E1 5b. John Lyall, Andy Nisbet, Jonathan Preston. 28 Mar 2012.
Start 3m to the right and go straight up the clean slab to break through the long roof at a flake-crack (crux). Continue boldly up the left-facing corner and fault above.

Note: Gordon Smith notes that when he did *The Tenements* in winter 1978/79, he started up a prominent corner system just right of *Stagnant Gully* and joined the summer route above its clean first two pitches. John Lyall has winter climbed the summer start at a higher grade but the normal winter route starts to its right.

STAC AN FHARAIDH:

To the left of the Western Sector are three distinct buttresses cut by well-defined gullies. The following two routes lie on the prominent central buttress that is defined by a prominent undercut niche at its base.

Ice Axe Elbow   85m   V,7. Simon Richardson, James Edwards. 30 Dec 2011.
Good mixed climbing up the left side of the lower section of the central buttress.
1. 25m Start in the undercut niche and move up and left through steep blocky terrain to near the left the arete. Continue up just right of the arete, passing a difficult rounded section to a short prominent hanging crack. Climb this into a triangular niche.
2. 40m Climb the right-angled corner at the back of the niche to reach a ledge. Continue up the line of turf leading up and right to a terrace below the right side of the final tier.
3. 20m Finish up the left-hand of two right-facing corners inset into the top right side of the buttress.

Wrist Flexor   85m   VI,7. Iain Small, Simon Richardson. 8 Jan 2011.
The steep central section of the central buttress. Start in an undercut niche.
1. 30m Climb straight up via a crack through a roof. Ignore the crack above and then trend right to join a crack system 5m to the right. Climb this steeply, through

a bulge to reach a good ledge. A sustained and strenuous pitch.
2. 30m Move 5m right and climb the slabby corner system moving right to the
right crest. Continue up this on rounded holds to the terrace below the right side
of the final tier.
3. 20m Climb the right-hand of two right-facing corners inset into the top right
side of the buttress.

Wobble Block Chimney 80m V,5. Simon Richardson, Roger Webb. 2 Jan 2012.
The left side of the rightmost buttress is cut by a long straight gully with an
impending chimney at its top.
1. 45m Deceptively steep moves up a vegetated offwidth crack lead into the
gully. Climb this over a steep step to reach the easier angled gully above, and
follow this to a pronounced steepening.
2. 15m Continue up the steep section to a good ledge below the impending
chimney.
3. 20m Climb the chimney (easier than it looks) to a good platform. The
eponymous wobbling block was trundled, and is no more.

The Glassy Cherry V,5. Jason Currie, Guy Robertson. 17 Jan 2010.
A pure ice line approximating to the route *Cherry*. Unbalanced, with a hard
section on thin ice through the central steep wall, but very good. Finish direct up
a steep ice pillar.

SRÒN NA LAIRIGE:
Park Life 220m IV,4. Hamish Irvine, John Lyall. 16 Dec 2011.
A line between *Lairig Ridge* and *Kasbah*, starting just right of the foot of the
buttress in a snow bay.
1. 20m Slant left up the obvious fault to the base of a big right-slanting slab on
the right flank of the ridge.
2. 45m Climb turf up the slab.
3. 40m Go up leftwards to a slight gully overlooking *Kasbah*, and up to a bay
and large spike.
4. 15m Ignore the easy gully on the left, and climb steeply on the right of the
flake to gain a hanging gully and belay below the crest.
5. 30m Go right on turf, taking a slanting line rightwards and gain the crest at a
pinnacle.
6. 70m Follow the ridge to the top.

Goths' Corner 120m IV,4. Sandy Allan, Andy Nisbet. 8 Jan 2012.
An iced corner formed between the buttress with *Polar Bear* and a slabby
buttress to the right. Grade III in better conditions. Start below a steep iced entry
to snow leading to the corner. The ice was too thin, so the route was started up
the next groove to the right, then moving left into the snow which was followed
to below the corner. Climb the corner on turf and ice to easy ground.

Blood Brothers 120m III. Sandy Allan, Dave McGimpsey, Andy Nisbet. 30 Jan
2012.
The slabby buttress to the right of the previous route holds a right-facing corner
in the centre and a roofed groove to its right. This route climbs the right-facing
corner after an easy start up a snow groove.

Kowloon 120m IV,4. Sandy Allan, Dave McGimpsey, Andy Nisbet. 30 Jan 2012.
Start as for *Blood Brothers* but soon stay right of it and climb up into the groove. The more ice, the easier the groove (thin but adequate this time). At the roof, step left on to the left arete and soon reach flakes. Step off these and go up to a sharp rib. It is easy to escape right here but the route climbs the rib.

The following routes are on the next buttress right and which is the rightmost major buttress. It has right-slanting lines across the slabby left flank and a prominent block on its crest.

Swerving Gully 170m II. Scott Frazer, John Lyall, Mick Twomey. 31 Jan 2012.
The gully that curves up the left side of the buttress.

Beaufort Groove 110m IV,5. Scott Frazer, John Lyall, Mick Twomey. 31 Jan 2012.
The left-hand of two parallel grooves on the left side of the buttress. Start 60m up *Swerving Gully* and climb the groove – a good pitch (45m). Then easy mixed ground to the top.

The Three Buffeteers 140m IV,4. Scott Frazer, John Lyall, Mick Twomey. 30 Jan 2012.
The right-hand groove system, starting 15m up *Swerving Gully*, level with a diagonal overlap going out right.
1. 35m Go right under the overlap until overlooking the curving slab of *Passmaster*, then go straight up the fault to blocks.
2. 30m Cross the next diagonal break and climb the roof directly into the groove. Follow this past another roof to a bay.
3. 40m The continuation groove to the crest left of a pinnacle.
4. 35m Easy to the top.

Passmaster 160m III,4. Scott Frazer, John Lyall, Mick Twomey. 30 Jan 2012.
Start at the foot of *Swerving Gully*.
1. 40m Climb the big right-curving slab to its end below an overlap.
2. 30m Climb the groove on the left and take the first fault on the right, leading to the buttress crest.
3. 45m Follow the shallow chimney above, then easier ground to the right of the prominent block.
4. 45m An easy crest leads to the top.

Storm Force 160m II. George Clowes, John Lyall, Andy Rook, Roger Winterburn. 20 Feb 2012.
Climbs the right flank of the *Passmaster* ridge. Start 15m up the gully on the right of the ridge.
1. 40m Follow turf into an icy groove on the left, and up to a block on a big ramp.
2. 45m Continue up the ramp to its end, then step down right into a shallow gully and follow this to a belay.
3. 45m Follow the gully to the second pinnacle.
4. 30m Continue to the top.

SGOR GAOITH, A' Phocaid:

Headfirst 150m III. Sandy Allan, John Lyall. 14 Jan 2012.
Climbs the rib on the right of *Pick Pocket*. Start in the fault of *Pursed Lips* and climb ice up left to gain the vegetated rib. Follow this and easier mixed ground to the top.

Carn Ban Gully 180m I.
The gully to the left of the waterfall.

COIRE GARBHLACH, Lower Corrie:

Solitude Standing 100m IV,4. Sandy Allan, John Lyall. 18 Dec 2010.
The big easy angled gully right of *Hermit's Ridge* is followed towards the cave, then the left branch is taken to a point where an easy ramp runs left to the top of the ridge. Avoid this ramp, and follow a left-slanting icy ramp across the steep right wall past a big fang of ice to a mixed exit. Easy slopes lead to the top.

COIRE GARBHLACH, Upper Corrie:

Fraudster 100m II. Andy Nisbet. 18 Dec 2011.
Curving Gully is on a buttress further right from the pinnacled one. This route climbs the rib to its right. Start just inside *Curving Gully* and take a line of weakness leading out right to the crest. Follow a ramp leading back left and regain the crest again. Follow this easily to the top.

Corkscrew 120m IV,3. Andy Nisbet, Jonathan Preston. 6 Jan 2012.
The right side of the pinnacled buttress has easy slopes leading to a central crest. Left of the crest is a steep wall leading down to a gully. This route climbs the gully, which is lower angled to start and leads leftwards to a steep narrow section. In good conditions it could be climbed direct, but this ascent went out right after 10m, then back left across the gully and up to a recess, before climbing back right across an arete to the easy upper section of the gully.
Corkscrew Direct IV,3. Dave McGimpsey, Andy Nisbet. 20 Jan 2012.
When fully frozen, the gully is climbed direct.

Cribbage 120m III. Dave McGimpsey, Andy Nisbet. 20 Jan 2012.
The rib left of *Corkscrew*. Start at a wide groove midway between the two gullies. Climb the groove moving left across a bowl, then back right up turf until close to *Corkscrew*. Follow the easy rib to a steep wall. Traverse left along a turf ledge overlooking the following route, step across a groove and climb steep turfy ground first up and then left to a snowy finish.

Moss Ghyll 120m III. Andy Nisbet. 18 Dec 2011.
A gully at the left end of the pinnacled buttress. Easy to start, it steepens and finishes on a slope leading up to the cornice.

Sharp Edge 120m III,4. Andy Nisbet. 5 Dec 2011.
Climbs the leftmost ridge on the pinnacled buttress, immediately left of *Moss Ghyll*. Start easily to reach a steep sharp crest. Gain this from the right and climb it to an apparent pinnacle which is climbed to a level crest. A snow slope leads to the cornice at the same place as *Moss Ghyll*.

CAIRN TOUL, Coire an t-Saighdeir:

Much of this corrie banks out in the depth of winter, but the south end has number of short buttresses.

Resolution Buttress 100m III. Simon Richardson. 25 Feb 2012.
The convex buttress defining the left edge of the corrie at NN 967 963. Start at the foot of the buttress below a prominent left-facing corner-ramp (the most natural line of weakness) and climb this, and two successive corner-ramps, to easier ground. Finish up this to a scrambling exit.

Dogged Groove 60m II. Simon Richardson. 25 Feb 2012.
The icy corner cutting the centre of the rock bluff lower down the corrie at NN 964 964.

Decisive Rib 70m III. Simon Richardson. 25 Feb 2012.
The low-angled buttress starting at NN 965 963. Climb a turfy runnel to gain a ramp running up the centre of the buttress that leads to three well defined grooves. Climb the deep right-hand groove and exit right at its top.

Resolute Gully 60m II. Simon Richardson. 25 Feb 2012.
The shallow gully right of *Decisive Rib* with a steep step at half-height.

Coire Lochain Uaine:

Double Helix 80m III. Simon Richardson. 5 May 2012.
To the right of *Solitude Rib*, the broken headwall of Coire Lochain Uaine is cut by two well-defined gully lines. This route takes the deeper left-hand line. Approach by climbing snow slopes and short mixed walls to reach the foot of the gully which is guarded by a short steep ice step. Above easier ground leads to a chokestone that is avoided on the left.

Double Trouble 70m II. Simon Richardson. 5 May 2012.
Follow the right-hand gully directly, with a short icy groove at two-thirds height.

CAIRN TOUL, Coire of the Chokestone Gully:

The Angel's Share 200m III. Simon Richardson. 5 May 2012.
The triangular rib defining the left side of *South-East Couloir*. Start 15m left of *South-East Couloir* at a short gully, climb this through a short steepening, then trend left up snow and short mixed walls to the left side of the steep section of the rib. Here, a hidden shallow gully leads up to the crest which is climbed on large blocks. Finish up the final easy crest above (which is joined from the right by *South-East Couloir*) to bypass the cornice.

EINICH CAIRN, Coire nan Clach:

Sourdough Grooves 60m IV,4. Roger Everett, Simon Richardson. 7 Nov 2010.
The buttress to the right of *Yukon Gold* is cut by a shallow groove system. Climb this in two pitches to an easing finish.

Cheechako Corner 40m II. Simon Richardson, Roger Everett. 7 Nov 2010.
Right of *Sourdough Grooves* is a shallow left-facing corner that defines the right edge of the buttress.

The Forgotten Pinnacle   70m   VI,7. Simon Richardson, Roger Everett. 7 Nov 2010.

The prominent buttress defining the right side of *Schoolmaster's Gully* consists of a pinnacle (not seen from directly below) and connecting ridge. This route climbs the steep groove on the right side of the pinnacle before finishing up the ridge.

1. 40m Climb deceptively awkward slabs (banks out later in the season) to the foot of the steep groove. Enter this from the right and climb it with difficulty to the top of the pinnacle.

2. 20m Descend to the col behind and finish up the easy connecting ridge to the plateau.

BRAERIACH, Garbh Choire Mor:

Left Wing Extremist   180m   III. Andy Nisbet, Duncan Tunstall. 14 Jan 2012.
Start at the very left corner of West Buttress. Climb the easy gully which forms the left edge of the buttress for a few metres until a line leads on to the buttress. Climb snowy grooves always keeping left of the crest to reach the final steep tier. Move left to climb an icy groove (crux by far) which led to the upper slopes and no cornice on the day.

West Buttress Right Edge   200m   II. Andy Nisbet. 9 Jan 2012.
Start at the bottom right corner of the buttress and climb an icy flake-chimney. This could be hard if not fully iced. It is now possible to move left into the central groove line of the buttress but this is the original winter route. Instead climb the rounded rib above and move right below the steeper upper section of the rib. Return left up an icy groove and climb direct to the cornice. There was a break in the cornice on this occasion but it is probably unusual to have this when there is a good build-up of snow on the buttress.

Cthulhu   150m   II. Andy Nisbet, Jonathan Preston. 17 Feb 2012.
The buttress to the right of the twin shallow gullies, at the right end of the Upper Corrie. Graded for good snow conditions. Start just inside the right of the twin gullies. Take a ramp-line up right to the crest and follow this to the cornice. The crest rather peters out into snow slopes above half-height.

Coire Ruadh:

Persistence Wall   80m   II. Simon Richardson, Roger Everett. 27 Nov 2011.
The buttress defining the corrie headwall provides a useful early season route. Start below the centre of the crag and climb mixed ground to the prominent left-slanting ramp. Follow this to where it fades then climb a short slab to the left edge (60m). Continue up and right to the top.

Coire an Lochain:

Dereliction of Duty   200m   II. Simon Richardson. 11 Mar 2012.
The rocky edge left of *Derelict Gully* (the proposed name for the prominent gully defining the left side of *Derelict Ridge*).

Eagle Grooves   80m   IV,5. Roger Everett, Simon Richardson. 4 Mar 2012.
A prominent groove-line cuts into the left side of *Derelict Ridge*.

1. 30m From half-height in *Derelict Gully*, climb the groove over a steep section to a ledge on the right.

2. 30m   Continue up the groove to below the final tower on *Derelict Ridge*. Climb this directly via steep cracks to its top.
3. 20m   Finish along the crest to the cornice.

Cameo Rib   140m   III,5. Simon Richardson, Roger Everett. 4 Mar 2012.
Right of *Derelict Ridge* is another rib that trends up and left to meet *Derelict Ridge* below the final tower. Start at the lowest point of the buttress.
1. 60m   Climb easy mixed ground to where the rib steepens.
2. 30m   Move up through a short wall to a left-trending ramp. Climb this to its top and climb a triangular wall (crux) exiting left at the top. Continue up blocks to the start of another left-trending ramp.
3. 30m   Follow the ramp to below a steep wall on the right side of the final tower. Pull steeply up directly to its top.
4. 20m   Finish along the crest to the cornice.

Dishonorable Discharge   70m   II. Simon Richardson. 11 Mar 2012.
The well-defined gully left of *Derelict Buttress*.

Derelict Buttress   70m   III,4. Simon Richardson, Roger Everett. 4 Mar 2012.
The short squat buttress up and right of *Derelict Ridge*.
1. 30m   Start below the centre of the buttress and climb the left-facing line of corners and grooves to a ledge that crosses the buttress at half-height.
2. 40m   Trend left then climb the central corner line, again trending left, through the centre of the buttress. Finish along a short crest to the cornice.

Nuclear Football   120m   II. Simon Richardson. 11 Mar 2012.
The rightmost feature in the corrie. Follow grooves up the centre of the triangular-shaped buttress approximately 100m right of *Derelict Ridge*.

Coire Domhdail:
Tempest Rib   70m   II. Simon Richardson. 5 May 2012.
The furthest right buttress on the north wall of the corrie. Climb turfy grooves on the right side of the buttress to a break. Continue up the groove above to the top.

Thunder Groove   70m   II. Simon Richardson. 5 May 2012.
The prominent buttress left of *Tempest Rib* is cut by a prominent groove. Climb this to where it narrows, step right to the continuation groove, and follow this to the top.

BEN MACDUI, Coire Lochain Uaine:
There are two prominent ribs on the right side of the broken North-East Face of Sròn Riach. The gully between the two ribs is Grade I.

Unnamed   100m   II. Simon Richardson. 12 May 2012.
The left-hand rib starts easily, and narrows to a steeper section before curling up and left along a narrow crest to the plateau.

Unnamed   80m   II. Simon Richardson. 12 May 2012.
The right-hand rib is better defined and has more sustained climbing directly up the crest.

Coire Mòr:

The cup-shaped corrie directly east of the summit of Ben Macdui contains several low-angle ribs. A cluster of three ribs on the north wall, approximately 100m south of the memorial cairn provides the best-defined routes.

Cenotaph 100m II. Simon Richardson. 12 May 2012.
The most prominent and rightmost rib which defines the right side of a well-defined wide gully (useful descent). Climb a shallow groove on the right side of the initial barrier wall and continue around a series of towers to a broad final crest leading to the plateau.

Commemoration Rib 100m II. Simon Richardson. 20 May 2012.
The rib left of well-defined wide gully. Interesting climbing, but unfortunately escapable to the left.

Keyhole Rib 100m II. Simon Richardson. 20 May 2012.
The leftmost rib. Pass the steep initial wall by climbing a groove on the left and move up and right to the crest by a prominent perched block. Continue up short walls to the to the broad snow crest leading to the plateau (possible cornice).

There are three prominent ribs on the west-facing back wall of the corrie.

Memorial Rib 100m II. Simon Richardson. 20 May 2012.
Straightforward climbing up the prominent rib leading to the plateau about 50m right of the memorial cairn.

Avalanche Rib 80m II. Simon Richardson. 20 May 2012.
The left-hand of twin ribs at the centre of the west wall is split by a gully depression. Follow this easily to steep section that leads to a broad snow crest and the top.

Right Central 100m II. Simon Richardson. 20 May 2012.
The right-hand of twin ribs at the centre of the west wall is similarly split by a gully depression. Follow this to a steep section that leads to a steepening crest and the plateau.

BEINN A' BHUIRD, Coire an Dubh Lochain:

Sniffer Buttress 80m VIII,8. Guy Robertson, Simon Richardson, Piotr Wisthal. 15 Apr 2012.
A winter version of the summer route. Start 10m right of the crest (the summer start).
1. 25m Climb a steep cracked wall over a steep bulge to a turfy shelf below twin rounded cracks. Start up the left-hand crack, mantelshelf on to a ledge (hard) then continue up the right-hand crack (harder) to good turf and a welcome ledge.
2. 10m Move up to the base of the offwidth crack directly above, then make a long stretch to the chimney on the left and exit to a good stance.
3. 45m Move up and right up a turfy slab to the exit gully which leads between two rounded pillars to the plateau.

Andrew Melvin leads pitch 3 of Vertigo Wall (VII,7), Creag an Dubh Loch.
Robbie Miller on the stance. Photo: Henning Wackerhage.

Garbh Choire:

The Primate VIII,8. Pete Davies, Donnie O'Sullivan. 5 Feb 2012.
By the summer line. Summer pitch 1 was largely banked out, so the first pitch went straight to the belay of pitch 2 up the 4c crack (30m). The second pitch was the summer pitch 3, traversing left, through the roof and straight up the headwall. Positive climbing, good hooks, excellent protection and some nice turfy bits higher up. Belay on the biggest and highest ledge (45m). Finish up the left-trending ramp to top out on the left arete (20m). Low in the grade.

The Simulator 90m VII,8. Guy Robertson, Simon Richardson. 22 Apr 2012.
The right edge of *Slochd Wall* is cut by steep inset right-facing corner that is not visible from below. Start by climbing *North-West Gully* for 30m and belay just below the jammed blocks directly underneath a vertical crack that leads up and right into the corner. One fall was taken on the first pitch and a rest point on the second.
1. 30m Climb the crack for 10m and pull out at its top (crux). Make a difficult step right and climb a right-facing corner-ramp to below a steep undercut niche.
2. 10m Climb the right side of the niche, then pull out left up a steep groove to reach a good ledge.
3. 20m Step left onto snowy shelves above *Slochd Wall* and follow these to below the final headwall.
4. 30m Follow the right to left ramp-line that cuts across the headwall to finish up the final few moves of *The Primate*.

LOCHNAGAR, Southern Sector:

Rendes Vous Manque 100m II. Bill Church, Duncan Tunstall. Feb 2011.
An ice sheet for 60m on the left of The Sentinel. As the angle eases, an easier gully can be followed to the top.

The Cathedral:

The Cracker 100m VII,8 **. Guy Robertson, Jason Curry. Jan 2012.
A quality route providing good value which takes the short corner and bulging crack-line on the lower left wall of *Cathedral Chimney*.
1. 15m Climb a short introductory pitch past a short chimney step to a commodious platform and huge block below the groove.
2. 25m Climb the groove to a ledge, then continue up the sustained crack (ignoring a right fork) to a final strenuous pull directly over the capping overhang.
3. 20m Climb easier ground slightly right to belay below a short steep crack with an obvious chimney slot above, just right of a steep tapering groove.
4. 40m Climb the crack into the chimney and continue direct, before stepping left into a narrow gully to finish.

Mullahmaloumouktou 90m VIII,8 ***. Guy Robertson, Pete Macpherson. Jan 2012.
Superb climbing, following the summer line, except on the final pitch take the constricted right-trending groove just right of the final chimney of *Transept Route*. The second pitch is the crux (bold).

Pete Macpherson moving up towards the overlap and crux ramp of The Mummy (VIII,8), a winter version of Mullahmaloumouktou on Lochnagar.. Photo: Guy Robertson.

Black Spout Wall:

Black Spout Wall   90m   IX,9 ****. Guy Robertson, Nick Bullock. Feb 2012.
An outstanding, sustained and varied route with generally excellent protection.
The winter ascent started up the wall right of the summer line. Gain and link the
groove right of the first pitch of *Steep Frowning Glories* into that route's second
pitch to gain the first belay of summer *Black Spout Wall*. The section up into and
across the traverse was the technical crux. The summer route was then followed
(very sustained but technically reasonable) to the headwall, where the
Inhospitable Crack led with difficulty (in darkness) into the crux of *Link Direct*
and so to the top.

West Buttress:

Blue Velvet   IV,5 **. Dave Almond, Greg Parsons, Duncan Tunstall. Dec 2010.
A very distinct ice line early in the season halfway between *Black Velvet* and
Black Spout Buttress, and which makes an excellent first pitch if the two towers
are climbed direct above. Almost certainly been climbed before. Climb the ice
for two pitches with a short tricky section starting the second pitch.

Osiris   270m   VII,8. Iain Small, Simon Richardson. 19 Feb 2012.
A sustained expedition up the full height of West Buttress starting first right of
Isis, and finishing to its left. The first pitch is bold and serious and would be
more secure with ice in the grooves.
1. 60m Start at the bottom right side of the lower buttress (at the foot of the gully
of *Western Slant*) and climb a turfy ramp for up onto the buttress for 10m. Make
an awkward step into a right-facing groove and climb this to below a steep,
smooth right-facing corner. Climb the corner (crux) and exit into a smooth
groove. Climb this for 5m to its top to reach a ledge. Traverse the ledge to the
right, dropping down a couple of short walls to gain the prominent corner-line
running up the right edge of the buttress. Climb this over a series of short steps
and belay on the left.
2. 40m Continue more easily in the same lime too where the right side of the
lower buttress merges with the snowfield on the right.
3. 60m Move up easily right into the wide gully above and belay at the foot of
the 'square-cut gully' of *Isis*.
4. 50m Climb the square-cut gully and its continuation line up and left (*Isis*
moves right after the first step) to its top. Junction with *Western Slant*.
5. 60m Continue up the left-facing corner in the buttress above and finish
directly up easier ground to the top.

Horus   270m   VII,7. Simon Richardson, Magnus Stromhall. 28 Jan 2012.
A sustained expedition up the full height of West Buttress starting first left of
Isis, and finishing to the right. Start 20m right of *Black Spout Buttress*.
1. 50m Climb the right-facing chimney-corner system running up the apex of the
lower tier.
2. 60m Continue up the same line to near the top of the buttress.
3. 60m Move easily right and up a wide gully to belay at the foot of the square-
cut gully of *Isis*.
4. 40m Climb the prominent corner cutting the right wall of the square-cut gully
to a good ledge. An excellent pitch.
5. 40m Follow *Isis* for 10m to below the cul de sac. Instead of moving left on to

the front face of the buttress (as for *Isis*), pull through the overhanging cul de sac and move up to easier ground.
6. 20m Finish directly by taking the right-trending ramp through the final wall to the plateau.

Coire Loch nan Eun:
Come Back Buttress   100m   II. Simon Richardson. 24 Oct 2010.
There are twin buttresses at the head of Coire Loch nan Eun. Unfortunately much of this cliff banks out during a heavy winter, so this route and the following one, are best climbed early in the season. Start at the base of the most prominent buttress at NO 237 852 and climb a right-facing corner trending right to a midway terrace. Continue directly up the cracked crest above, in a fine position to reach the top. Moderate in summer.

Return Rib   100m   II. Simon Richardson. 24 Oct 2010.
Start 50m left of *Come Back Buttress* below a steep wall and climb this via a line slanting right on turf before continuing up the broad buttress crest to the top.

Gondola Edge   40m   II. Simon Richardson. 24 Oct 2010.
The well defined turfy groove close to the left edge of *Balloon Buttress*.

CANNESS GLEN:
La Palme d'Or   200m   IV,4. John Higham, John Hutchinson, Iain Young. 18 Dec 2011.
Takes the narrow rib on the immediate left (looking up) of the gully taken by the *Red Carpet*. It is not obvious as a line until virtually beneath it. Start at the lowermost rocks and climb the crest directly in four pitches comprising steeper sections linked by fine snow aretes, to the plateau. The obvious triangular tower high on the route is taken direct. At times too heathery to provide continuously fine climbing; the situations and sunny, south-easterly aspect makes for a very alpine experience.

GLEN CLOVA, Coire Farchal:
Elder Crack Buttress   160m   III. Roger Everett, Simon Richardson. 5 Feb 2012.
The wide broken buttress to the left of *Farchal Gully*. Start 10m left of *Farchal Gully*.
1. 40m Climb a short ice smear through the lower band of slabs. Continue up then trend right to near *Farchal Gully*.
2. 40m Trend up and left to enter a hidden right-slanting gully cutting through the steep tier above. Belay halfway up on the right by a niche.
3. 30m Exit the gully via a steep icicle and move up and right to a terrace.
4. 40m A steep snow slope leads to the top.

Winter Corrie:
Waterfall Buttress Direct   60m   VI,7. Roger Everett, Simon Richardson. 5 Feb 2012.
The centre of Waterfall Buttress is cut by a prominent corner and crack-line.
1. 30m Climb directly up the steep left-facing corner to ledges, then move right to the prominent halfway ledge.
2. 30m Struggle up the short offwidth crack behind a short pinnacle and stand on

its top. Make a difficult step into an overhung niche and pull out steeply to easier ground. Move up, then right, to the top.

Coire Fee:

Alphabet Soup 200m I/II. George Allan. 18 Dec 2011.
Just beyond the first steep wall on the right flank of *A Gully* is a wide groove. Climb this and its continuation fault past some trees to a point overlooking *A-B Integrate*. Traverse left and climb the snowfields. A pleasant romp.

Craig Maud Area:

Note: The squat buttress separating the two broad gullies towards the right end of the Craig Maud escarpment is Grade III (George Allan, David Windle, 3 Feb 2012).

MAYAR, North Craig:

(NO 239 733) Alt 700m South facing
Approach: Ascent the Kilbo path, walk for about 500 m towards the summit of Mayar and then contour to find the crag. It is not named but marked as one black line on the OS 1:50000 map about 500m SW from the summit of Mayar. Topo provided.

White Plains Drifter 45m IV,5 *. Arno Alpi, Henning Wackerhage. 17 Dec 2011.
Climb the obvious iciest corner. If the ice is thin or hollow the last 10m can be precarious.

Whitewash 50m IV,5. Arno Alpi, Henning Wackerhage. 17 Dec 2011.
To the right of *White Plains Drifter* climb the obvious gully line with an ice step one-third up. The route will probably be a grade easier if there is good neve.

White Sun of the Desert 45m III,4. Arno Alpi, Henning Wackerhage. 17 Dec 2011.
On the first ascent the ice in the gully was fragile so the buttress to the left was climbed to gain the upper part of the gully via a few airy steps.

GLEN ESK, Carlochy Buttress:

Access is best from the Shank of Inchgrundle. Follow the track up the Shank to where it becomes horizontal. The top of the cliff is about 20m down to the left. The base of the cliff can be reached by losing height down to the left. The Carlochy is to the right and 100m or so lower. There are three main buttresses.

Stalkers' Buttress 100m II. Bill Church, Duncan Tunstall. 13 Dec 2011
Start up the gully between the left and central buttresses. Below a steepening in the gully, take either of two possible ramp-lines out on to the easy upper crest of the central buttress.

Fallow Buttress 160m III. Andy Nisbet, Duncan Tunstall. 17 Dec 2011.
Climbs the central buttress from its base. Start below a steep groove which leads leftwards. Gain the groove from the right, then follow it left and right to the easy upper crest, gained higher up by the previous route.

Rutting Buttress   70m   IV,4. Andy Nisbet, Duncan Tunstall. 17 Dec 2011.
The fine looking right buttress, which unfortunately eases off to a steep slope after 70m. Start below its steep left wall. Climb an icy ramp to the crest. A steepening leads to a tree and the easing of the angle. Either follow a snow slope to the summit or descend to the right.

Craig Maskeldie, North Face:

Snowlake Reunion   200m   IV,5 **. Duncan Tunstall, Stephen Venables. 7 Feb 2012.
Dochty Gully is actually the rightmost of a trilogy of gullies. The centre one is very direct with a severe steepening at 100m where an icefall forms. This can be climbed direct for 30m with good rock protection. The angle reverts back above to the same as the gully below.

Earn Craig:

Gobma   130m   VS 4c. Duncan Tunstall, Greg Parsons. 11 Mar 2012.
The wall just to the left of *Eagle's Fall* has an obvious line. Start at the lowest point of the cliff.
1. 20m Climb the groove up diagonally rightwards to a ledge. This can also be reached by descending easy ground that starts up and to the right.
2. 35m The short step is passed on its left and then climbed up and diagonally left to a large ledge.
3. 40m 4c Above the ledge is clean rock. Climb this diagonally rightwards for 30m to the bottom of a short steep wide crack. This is climbed (escape is now possible up and to the left).
4. 35m 4b Above is a clean line which is followed to easier angled grass and a good belay can be found 10m higher.
Either scramble easily off left or continue along the obvious ramp-line past a short rock step to reach the top of the cliff (60m).

What Dentists Earn   90m   E1 5b. Mark Atkins, Duncan Tunstall. 31 Aug 2010.
A pleasantly sustained line that leads directly up the cliff apart from the traverse connecting pitch 2 to pitch 3. Start on the right end of the raised low angled grass in the centre of the crag about 10m up.
1. 25m 5b Climb a steep crack. Where it ends, traverse left below the steepening to a belay.
2. 30m 5b Continue straight to a grass ledge. Traverse easily right for 20m.
3. 25m 5b Climb the corner on the right of the ledge, then the hanging ramp that leads diagonally left.
4. 40m 5b Climb to a roof, then traverse down to its left end. From here the wall can be followed up and right. A tricky move gains the left edge which leads to a tree. Bash through the undergrowth for another 10m.
5. 40m 5b Climb straight up for 30m to a tree. Use this to climb steep grass before drifting right to a good crack.
6. 20m 5a Surmount the initial overlap, then traverse left to overcome the overhang beside the corner. Traverse immediately back right to above the belay, then follow easy ground to the top.

High Grade Low Grade 160m VII,8. Dave Almond, Duncan Tunstall. 9 Dec 2011.
A direct line starting up *Right-Hand Route*, then climbing direct to join *What Dentists Earn* with a short direct finish.
1. 30m Climb pitch 1 of *Right-Hand Route* but belay at the bottom of the cracks.
2. 20m Traverse left across to the bottom of the ramp-line with the overhanging wall above.
3. 35m Climb up the ramp and steep steps and into a corner at half-height, moving on to the left wall to exit (crux).
4. 55m Climb the rock pillar, then trend left and up past the tree to belay by an icefall.
5. 20m Either climb the ice direct or take the right wall moving left around a roof.

Bruntwood Craig:

The Artist 90m HVS. Duncan Tunstall, Stephen Venables. 30 Mar 2012.
Start at the foot of the steep section of *Gro'lryc Gully*, at the trees halfway up the cliff.
1. 40m 5a Climb easily to where the rock steepens and becomes very clean. Climb this moving right to avoid the short steep sections.
2. 50m 5a Continue up the left edge of the good rock. A short step is passed further left. Follow the grass to the next steepening which quickly leads to the top and a good belay.

NORTH-EAST OUTCROPS

STUDY HEAD:

Matterhorn Stack 40m VS. Simon Richardson, Ben Richardson. 5 Aug 2011.
This impressive stack lies in the bay 300m east of Silver Wall and is mentioned on p208 of the North-East Outcrops guide. Approach by swimming 50m to a platform on the east side of the stack.
1. 20m 4a Climb a deep chimney-groove to a poor stance on the slab above.
2. 20m 4c Move left around a protruding block, and climb diagonally up and left across a wall (surmounting a gap) to a ledge. Finish up the short wall above to gain the summit ridge.

LONGHAVEN CRAIG (NK 122 402), Buff Pinnacle:

Frank Buff 60m VS 5a **. Christian Ellis, Duncan Tunstall. 26 Apr 2011
1. 40m 5a Start easily up the right side of the lower wall. Climb the steeper wall above to a roof-like edge. From here climb diagonally right up to a tricky move to reach the Buff Ledge.
2. 20m Descend from the tower by the short west ridge to the col and then up steeper rock to the summit.

Buffday Boy   60m   HVS 5a ***. Christian Ellis, Duncan Tunstall. 26 Apr 2011.
A fine pitch.
1. 40m 5a Climb the left side of the steep wall up a fine crack over a steep exit
to gain the wall above. Climb this straight up, then diagonally right to gain a
crack which leads leftwards on fine rock to the Buff Traverse.
2. 20m Descend from the tower by the short west ridge to the col and then up
steeper rock to the summit.

Rebuffed   40m   E2 5c ***. Christian Ellis, Duncan Tunstall. 26 Apr 2011.
1. 20m 5c Climb the crack in the centre of the lower wall to the roof. Traverse
left to the below the left edge of the roof. A tricky move gains a ledge below the
roof, good gear. The roof is passed up and left leading to a diagonal break (1
rest). Hanging belay.
2. 20m 5b Cross a smaller roof, then climb the sustained wall direct to *The Old
Buff* belay.

LONGHAVEN, South Face of Scimitar Ridge:
Pussy Galore   20m   E7 6c ***. Ally Coull, Russ Birkett. Aug 2006.
The right arete of the steep end wall containing *Comfortably Numb* and *The
Trial*. Abseil down the line of *Sea-Scoop* to belay on a ledge. From the ledge step
left and climb up just to the left of the arete to a short, shallow green corner-
crack. Step up and onto the right side of the arete. Arrange protection, then climb
the left side of the arete to a small flat hold (crux). Climb the edge of the arere to
the top. The perfect potential DWS.

LONGHAVEN QUARRIES, Seaward Face of Scimitar Ridge:
Two for a Squid   20m   E4 6a **. Russell Birkett, Tim Whitaker. 25 Mar 2012.
This links features on the slab to give a good sustained climb. From the ledge
below Peapod climb boldly up trending left following edges to join *Squid Vicious*
at the top of its crack below the ledge. Hand-traverse this left to make technical
moves along a thin break to gain the finishing crack of *Octopussy*. Superb rock.

CUMMINGSTON:
Buda's Arete   15m   HVS 5b. Steve Bate, John Hall. 23 May 2012.
Start as for *Centre* until under the arete, gear on the left. Pull onto the hanging
arete and follow direct to the top resisting the temptation to bridge into *Left*.

Crown of Thorns   20m   VS 5a. Martin Collins, Graeme Jones. 1 Sep 2011.
Start 1m from left end of Prophet Walls below a crown of thorns. Climb a scoop
and bulge (crux) to a flake. Go up left on easy ground, then traverse right under
overhangs. Break through at a spike.

COVESEA, Covesea Crag (SMCJ 2010):
Ledge Route   8m   HVS 5a. Jonathan Preston, Pete Amphlett. 24 Jun 2010.
Between *Prestonpans* and *Preston Regardless* is a sloping ledge with a steep
wall above. Gain the ledge from the right and climb straight up the wall, moving
to the left of a nose at the top.

Tidal Surge   8m   VS 4c. Jonathan Preston, Pete Amphlett. 24 Jun 2010.
On the right of the cliff, where it turns the corner there is a blunt arete with a roof

above. This climb starts just left of the arete and climbs straight up to pass the roof on the left.

Face Off 8m VS 4c. Jonathan Preston, Pete Amphlett. 24 Jun 2010.
There is a deep chimney on the seaward face of the crag. Climb the chimney, which is harder than it looks!

Sandbag 8m VS 4c. Jonathan Preston, Pete Amphlett. 24 Jun 2010.
Right again is a hanging corner. Gain the corner and climb to the top. The clue is in the name!

FINDOCHTY:
Pointy Stack 20m HVS 4c. Tom Prentice, Simon Richardson. 16 Oct 2011.
The spectacular leaning stack (as viewed from the west) is the showpiece of the bay west of Tronach Head. The route can be accessed two hours either side of low tide. Traverse right to left along the diagonal break (large Friends useful) to reach a good ledge. Move right across the headwall and scramble up and left to the top. Abseil descent.

Boulder Stack 20m Severe. Simon Richardson, Tom Prentice. 16 Oct 2011.
The sister stack to *Pointy Stack* has a curious conglomerate boulder perched near the summit. Approach by swimming to the north arete and climb an easy groove to the final headwall. Climb this by a steep crack on the left on huge holds to reach the top. Abseil descent.

Double-Headed Rock 30m Moderate. Simon Richardson, Tom Prentice. 16 Oct 2011.
The island-stack 50m to the west of *Pointy Stack* provides a fun scramble up the south-east ridge with a continuation to the sharper subsidiary summit.

PORTNOCKIE
Bow Fiddle Rock, Catgut Pillar and Traverse 85m VS. Simon Richardson, Tom Prentice. 15 Oct 2011.
An excellent adventure and a potential North-East sea-stack classic. The route climbs the prominent pillar on the steeper left skyline of Bow Fiddle Rock, traverses the summit and then descends The Fiddler's Bow. In true mountaineering fashion, all access equipment (wetsuits etc) will need to be carried over the summit. Start by swimming 200m to the foot of the pillar.
1. 30m 4c Pull through a bulge to reach a prominent groove-line on the left side of the pillar. Climb this on good holds to a prominent hanging block on the right. Move right over the block and finish up the steep wall above.
2. 55m Continue easily along the ridge to the steep step leading to the summit. Climb this on good holds in a spectacular position to the top. Abseil down the hanging slab of The Fiddler's Bow and return back to the beach with another 200m swim.
Note: The obvious line up the hanging slab forming the fiddler's bow on Bow Fiddle Rock was climbed by Simon Richardson, Ben Richardson and Chris Woodward, 11 Sep 2011 (40m Moderate). This is a spectacular feature has almost certainly been climbed before, but no evidence of a prior ascent was found, although the route may have been ascended by coasteering parties now

operating in the area. (An ascent of Bow Fiddle Rock was a rite of passage for young men of Portknockie, but it is not clear which line was taken. The easiest route, which minimises swimming, would have been to approach at low tide and avoid the bow slab by climbing slabs on the east side to gain the summit ridge. This would also have maximised the egg collecting potential). Approach by swimming 200m to ledges on the far side of the bow. Climb the bow slab, approaching from the right. Low in the grade, but some loose rock. Abseil descent.

White Craig Rock   25m   Moderate. Simon Richardson, Ben Richardson, Chris Woodward. 11 Sep 2011.
The triangular guano-covered rock (also known locally as Shitten Craig) lies about 100m west of Bow Fiddle Rock. Climb the east side of the rock up easy cracked slabs. Approach by a 200m swim.

ROSEHEARTY, Murcurry Walls, South Wall:
Romancing the Stone   18m   E8 6c **. Guy Robertson. Aug 2011.
The obvious direct line into the upper flake and crux of *Big Stone Country* provides superb if painful fingery climbing. Start directly below the flake, just left of a hairline crack. Climb up slightly left to a tiny flake sidepull, then step back right and forge straight up to the flake which leads with a little respite into the crux section of *Big Stone Country*. Finish up this.

ROSEHEARTY:
Stack One   30m   Severe. Simon Richardson, Tom Prentice. 14 Oct 2011.
The southerly stack is the most impressive-looking of the Quarryhead sea-stacks. Gain the west face of the stack either by boulder hopping at low tide, or by swimming. Climb the deep chimney splitting the face to a ledge on the left, then move up and right in an impressive position to gain the top by the right arête (20m). From here an easy but airy traverse along the crest of the stack leads to the top. Abseil descent.

Stack Two   25m   VS 4b. Tom Prentice, Simon Richardson. 14 Oct 2011.
This route climbs the broad pillar on the west face of the northerly stack. It lies to the right of the narrow arch that almost splits the stack into two. Approach by boulder hopping at low tide (awkward) or by swimming. Climb the pillar on good rock with a steep exit. Abseil descent.

Stack Two Point Five   12m   Moderate. Simon Richardson, Ben Richardson. 20 Aug 2011.
Stack Two has a subsidiary triangular-shaped stack on its north side separated by a narrow cleft. Approach by swimming. Climb easily up a slanting crack on the west face.

Stack Three   25m   Severe. Simon Richardson, Ben Richardson. 20 Aug 2011.
Approach by swimming 100m from the eastern approach ridge to Murcurry Walls. Climb the west ridge of the stack, easy at first, to a prominent gap. Move right and climb a crack just right of the arete on the landward side to the top. Abseil descent.

DEESIDE, VAT BURN:
A complete set of descriptions is available on the SMC web-site. Many more routes have been climbed in the last year.

HIGHLAND OUTCROPS

BEINN BHEAG, Lochailort:
The Rebellion 12m E6 6b. Kev Shields. 23 May 2012.
Start as for *Frustration* but go direct up the blank slab. There is gear in a crack on the right at around half-height. No further use of the crack or anything to its right. Committing and bold.

POLLDUBH, What Wee Wall:
What Wee Ramp 12m HVS 5a. Julian Lines. Apr 2012.
The dwindling ramp-line on the left side of the wall.

Honeycomb 12m E4 6a. Julian Lines. Apr 2012.
Climbs the left side of the highly textured wall. Start at a head-height finger hold and go directly up the wall to reach the ramp at half-height. Finish up the ramp.

Honey Thief 12m E5 6a. Julian Lines. Apr 2012.
An eliminate line with great climbing. Start just right of centre of the wall (just left of the tiny groove ramp of *Carpe Diem*). Climb directly up the wall into the vaguest of grooves at 6m, then climb up and left on more positive holds to finish at the top of the ramp. Hardest at the start and very sustained if the holds aren't chalked.

ASHIE FORT:
Roost Wall 10m HVS 5a. Davy Moy, Peter Langlands. 24 Mar 2012.
Start at the foot of *Raeburn's Original Route* and surmount the overhang to access the steep right wall. Go straight up via a bird roost spot to the top.

CREAG DUBH, Little Rock:
Bulgarian Biceps 15m HVS 5a. Andy Nisbet, Jonathan Preston. 2 Jul 2011.
Based on the left arete of the wall left of the second pitch of *Hungarian Hamstring*. Pleasant climbing but escapable. Start below the arete and climb a wide crack to the right end of a ledge (unfortunately you can walk off here). Move right and climb trending slightly right to an easy slabby finish.

CRAIG A' BARNS, Polney Crag:
Blast Off 30m HVS 5b. Michael Barnard, Ron Dempster. 27 Mar 2011.
Climbs a line of weakness through the short steep headwall overlooking *Holly Tree Groove* (right of *Scram '79*). Start below a crack leading up to the short corner/niche of that route. Climb the crack and move through the bulge above to reach the headwall. Launch up this (crux), before moving right to finish up the chimney of *Holly Tree Groove*.

GLEN LEDNOCK, Balnacoul Castle:

Alasdair Fulton notes that *Central Groove* is much harder than E2 5c and poorly protected with rusty pegs.

CREAG NAN SPEIREAG:

Big Slab   55m   VS 4b. Keith Alexander, Graeme Diack, Karin Helwig. 8 Apr 2011.

A route on a a big slabby rock between Creagruie and Bleater's Wall and visible from the road.

1. 10m   Climb the corner-crack on the left flank of the giant slabby boulder, moving up right to a big sloping ledge with an in-situ peg at the right-hand end.

2. 45m 4b   Round the corner, on the slabby face, traverse right along a narrow ledge with a large horizontal crack for hands, then step up to gain a thin vertical crack which leads up the right side of the slab. When the crack ends, continue more easily up the right edge of the slab to a tree belay.

Note: The rock has been climbed before, as there was abseil tat at the top, but the line unknown.

Monachyle Glen Crag:

(NN 481 282)   South-East facing

This small crag is located some 200m further up the glen from Bleaters Wall (Highland Outcrops, pp350–2) and overlooks Monachylebeag Farm. The crag is best described as slabby, with an angle of around 75 degrees. A compact mica schist crag with few weaknesses and protection sparse. Well drained. Poor belays at top, but can be found some 10m back from the edge. The two hardest routes were top-roped. Parking is difficult but can be found. Do not block passing places.

Monachyle Edge   15m   V.Diff. Alan Wilson. 27 May 2012.

Gain the left arete from a grassy ledge a few feet right from the end of the crag. Follow on good jugs to the top.

Marching On   15m   VS 4c. Alan Wilson. 27 May 2012.

Start below a series of small flaky holds, some obvious flakes lie near the top.

Spring Break   15m   5b. Alan Wilson. 27 May 2012.

Start directly beneath a small overlap at mid-height. Gain a stance below this on poor holds, pass the overlap on its left end with some thin moves to gain the better flaky holds to finish.

An Dealg   15m   5a. Alan Wilson. 27 May 2012.

Follow a very thin quartz line which runs vertically up the wall. Where it runs out, make a slight rightwards move past two quartz bands to gain the obvious narrow slightly right-trending crack and follow this to the top.

March Mongrel   15m   VS 4c. Alan Wilson. 27 May 2012.

Follow the line of obvious right-facing flakes to the top.

Nick Bullock making the possible second ascent of Le Panthere Rose (VI,6) on Raeburn's Wall, Ben Nevis in January 2012. Photo: Keith Ball.

Tess Fryer leads the corner pitch on The Bat (E2, 5b), Ben Nevis. Photo: Ian Taylor.

BEN NEVIS, AONACHS, CREAG MEAGAIDH

Tower Ridge East Flank:

Ride of the Wild Bullhorn 55m VIII,10. Nick Bullock, Douglas Tavener. 16 Dec 2011.

The climb is the obvious overhanging groove/corner crack on the left side of the steep buttress to the right of *Great Chimney.*

1. 30m Follow ice smears to reach a large ledge beneath the main face of the buttress.

2. On the left side of the ledge beneath the overhanging groove/corner is a broken right to left crack system. Follow this with one quite hard pull until on a ledge just to the left of the groove. The belay is an in-situ red hex and a large block on the far left of the ledge.

3. Climb direct into the steep groove, then using a variety of techniques, continue to climb the overhanging corner past a small pod with a quasi-rest, past another overhang (crux) and into a tight V-groove to exit steeply onto *Tower Ridge.*

Douglas Boulder:

Flash of the Blade 95m VS *. Michael Barnard, Aoibhinn Bradley. 26 May 2012.

Good climbing up the fine hanging corner immediately right of *Cutlass.*

1. 30m Climb easy slabs to below the wall leading into the corner.

2. 30m 5a Climb the wall (bold for a few metres until the crack is gained) and the corner above to a tricky finish (crux).

3. 35m 4b Move up the crack then directly up the arete above to a ledge. Climb the steep wall above on good holds to gain easier ground leading to *South-West Ridge.*

Garadh na Ciste Note:

Two teams climbed separate lines close to *Cryotherapy* on 20 Jan 2012. Jeremy Windsor, Piers Harley & Rob Marson climbed the obvious line of icy ramps up the centre of the face (*Thea*, III). Dafydd Morris & Matt Buchanan climbed the line of mixed grooves to the left to give *Crying Out Loud* (IV,5).

South Trident Buttress:

Cyclops 100m V,5. Simon Richardson, Helen Rennard. 3 Dec 2011.

The groove-line right of *Polyphemus Pillar.* Start 30m right of *Polyphemus Pillar* below a left-trending ramp.

1. 30m Follow the ramp to its end and continue up a vertical groove-line in the steep wall above to belay on a small snow patch.

2. 40m Continue up an icy groove into the prominent gully above. Climb this over two bulges to exit onto a large snowfield. Surmount a short slabby wall to belay in a smaller snow patch above.

3. 30m Climb a short hidden chimney on the right and continue up the upper crest of *Pinnacle Arete* to the plateau.

Moonlight Gully Buttress:

The Big Cheese 110m VIII,8 **. Greg Boswell, Harry Holmes, Jim Higgins. 4 Dec 2011.

Start at the bottom of the main central slab capped by a roof.

1. 50m   Climb the slab to gain the small pod below the ice capped roof (ice needed over the roof). Swing wildly around the roof to gain and climb the bold icy groove above. Continue following the groove to reach easier ground and follow this for 20m to reach a belay.
2. 60m Climb easier ground to gain a steep ice groove with a distinctive cracked left wall. Climb the grove and ice bulge above to reach easier ground wich leads to the top of the buttress.

Limelight   95m   Severe. Graeme Tough, Brian Shackleton, Graeme Morrison. 21 Aug 2010.
Start immediately left of the start of *Right-Hand Chimney*.
1. 45m Climb a steep rib. Continue with interest to a further steepening left of the chimney (crux)and reach a ledge.
2. 25m Continue immediately above to a steep nose with *Right-Hand Chimney* just to the right. Climb the nose and exit left onto slabs which are followed to a small ledge.
3. 25m Follow more broken rocks to the top of the buttress.

Take Off   70m   IV,5. Richard Ashton, Peter McCallum. 29 Dec 2011.
Start behind a rocky outcrop on the left-hand side of *Number Five Gully*, almost opposite the start of *Ledge Route*.
1. 30m Climb a short right-slanting slab to gain the actual right wall of Moonlight Gully Buttress. Climb straight up through iced cracks and grooves to reach a chimney. Climb this to a spike belay on the left-hand wall.
2. 40m Climb the thinly iced, broken slabby wall directly above without much protection to gain the snow shelf above Moonlight Gully Buttress.
Note: Ken Crocket thinks this route starts right of *Phosphorescent Grooves* and climbs fairly directly upwards crossing that route. At the belay *Phosphorescent Grooves* goes rightwards, making an awkward step down and across a gap, whereas this route goes up.

MAMORES, Stob Ban, South Buttress, East Wing:
Shining Edge   80m   III,4. Helen Rennard, Simon Richardson. 4 Dec 2011.
The prominent crest right of *Eag Blanc*.
1. 40m Trend right from the foot of *Eag Blanc* to gain the crest and follow ramps and grooves to belay just below a prominent notch on the right skyline.
2. 40m Move up and left to a turfy corner on the left side of a prominent tower. Climb the corner (technical but well protected) and continue up the crest above to where the angle eases.

AM BODACH:
An area of ice in the centre of the steepest section of crag left of *Central Buttress* (SMCJ 2011) – topo provided.

The Hemulen   80m   V,5. Andy Turner, Ruth Taylor (alt). 24 Jan 2010.
1. 35m From the toe of the buttress, follow up the left side of the ice streak heading for an icicle. Pull onto the icicle and follow to the top and an ease in angle into a bay.
2. 45m From the left side of the bay, follow steeper ice which soon eases. Continue up until reaching the top of the ice and more mixed terrain which

continues as a pleasant ramble. One could continue to the top of Am Bodach but the party abseiled off.

Little My 80m IV,4. Andy Turner, Ruth Taylor. 24 Jan 2010.
1. 35m From the toe of the buttress, go straight up and climb the ice to the right of the icicle until reaching the bay.
2. As for *The Hemulen*.

Snufkin 80m IV, 5. Andy Turner, Ruth Taylor. 24 Jan 2010.
1. 35m Starting approx 5m right of *Little My*, follow the obvious rightwards trending ice until it steepens on the left. Climb the short steep section and continue up to arrive at the right side of the bay.
2. 45m As for *The Hemulen*.

AONACH MOR, Coire an Locain:
The Prow 55m VIII,8 **. Adam Hughes, Guy Steven, Luke Brooks. 26 Jan 2012.
The prow left of *Stirling Bridge* gives very committing climbing.
1. 30m Start underneath the prow and climb the slab to reach a ramp below the obvious groove. Climb the turfy groove with good gear to make a tricky step right on to a good foothold. Here the groove narrows and becomes blank. Make some thin moves to gain the steep wall out right, and make even thinner moves on poor flat hooks to reach the thin hanging crack/corner. More thin moves up the crack gains some good, but hollow hooks halfway up the corner (poor bulldog protects). From here a committing move left leads to a rest on a good turf ledge. Move up and then move right across the face to regain the crack, then the arete. Easy climbing leads to a good belay.
2. 25m Climb easy snow to the top.

AONACH BEAG, An Aghaidh Garbh:
Goblet of Fire, Right-Hand Finish 50m VI,6. Nick Turner, David Ritchie. 2 Jan 2011.
Takes the obvious icefall situated to the right of the original route. Follow the first pitch of *Goblet of Fire* to belay. Climb the obvious thinly iced slab leading out right to gain a niche below the icefall. Awkward moves gained very steep ice which was followed to reach a poor belay on the right.

An Aghaidh Garbh, Summit Buttress:
Passage a Droite III,4 70m *. Bob Hamilton, Steve Kennedy. 15 Apr 2012.
The short right-hand gully in the narrow buttress just below the summit *(Le Passage)* follows the left-hand gully – see SMCJ 2009, p459. Climbed late in the season after the usual massive cornice had collapsed. Steep snow slopes lead to a belay below the narrow gully. A nice ice pitch leads up gully to open slopes and a belay below the final snow arete. The short arete leads to the cornice finish.

Note: *Le Passage* (SMCJ 2009) should be renamed *Passage a Gauche*.

STRATHOSSIAN, Creagan nan Nead, Lower Slab (SMCJ 2010):
Niamh 50m E4 5c ***. Brian Davison, Andy Nisbet. 5 Jun 2012.
Start at a white streak midway between the corner marking the left side of the

slab and the prominent left-hand of two black streaks. The start is close to *Fionn*. Climb 3m to a ledge, then from its left end make a move up and leftwards to the top of a flake-crack and protection. Move back right and up using a protruding knobble on the left (which is directly above the flake and can be reached more easily from the flake). The knobble can be tied off as a runner. Climb up the slab on the right past three pockets to a thin horizontal crack-line and make hard moves left along this to a Friend placement in a letterbox. Move up and right to three holes in the slab and up to a pegmatite band. Move up to a further band and a horizontal slot for a Friend 1 on the right. Move up to another horizontal pegmatite band and a spherical intrusion above it. An awkward move past this leads to more slab and gear in an overlap. Pass the overlap and climb the slab above to easier ground and a abseil tree.

Basilisk   50m   E3 6a **. Brian Davison, Andy Nisbet. 5 Jun 2012.
Climbs the left-hand black streak; a selection of Friends zero to 2.5 are useful for protection in pockets. Slow to dry and a bit mossy. Start in the centre of the streak. Climb up to a ledge and protection in a pocket. Make a thin move to another pocket and protection then a pocket just right of the black steak. Step right at this point with feet just above the second pocket and make a thin traverse left for a move to gain the easier angled slab to the left of the black streak. Move up to a pegmatite band in a depression in the slab and arrange protection in pockets, a Friend 2.5 on the right (as for *Oisin*) and a Friend 1 on the left (as for *Niamh*). It is possible to climb straight up from the third pocket to the pocket for the Friend 2.5. Continue up the depression past further pegmatite bands to where the angle in the slab eases in the slab. Move left to a right-facing corner. Climb the corner and the slab above to the abseil tree.

BEN ALDER, South Buttress of Garbh Choire:
Raeburn's Gully Left Branch   70m   II. Ross Heyburn, Karen Heyburn. 28 Jan 2012.
Shortly after passing the upper snow terrace, a narrow gully on the left leads with one short pitch onto open snow slopes below the top of the crag.

The Diamond:
Right of *Raeburn's Gully* is this large triangular buttress. The following route climbs its left rib, adjacent to *Raeburn's Gully*.

Raeburn's Edge   200m   III. Dave McGimpsey, Andy Nisbet, Duncan Tunstall. 16 Jan 2012.
Start at a groove on the front face below and left of the crest. Climb this towards the crest and follow further turfy grooves just left of the crest until the crest is gained high up. A final steep groove on the right is optional.

Thrills and Spills   200m   V,4. Dave McGimpsey, Andy Nisbet. 28 Jan 2012.
A line up the left side of the front face of the buttress. Start at the lowest point of the buttress, below a big snow patch some 10 to 20m up and above which is a left-leaning corner. Climb icy slabs to the left edge of the snow patch (thin ice may be necessary here). Move left and climb a shallow corner to better turf. Go diagonally left to reach a turf ramp leading diagonally right (this is the higher and better defined of two ramps). Climb the ramp to a steepening (60m).

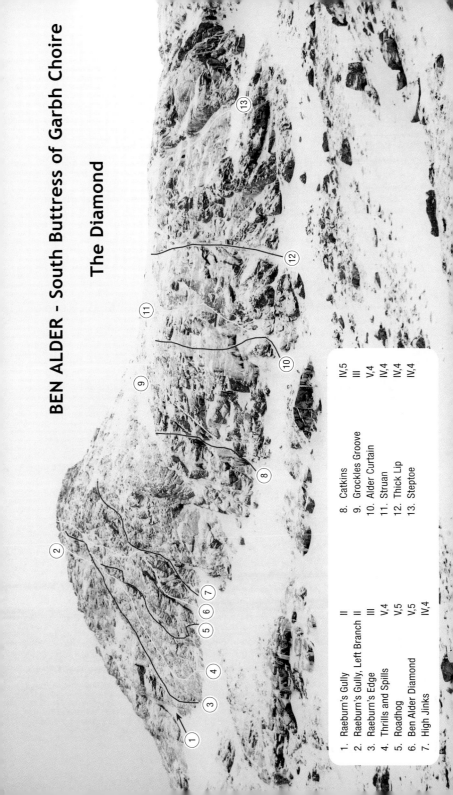

BEN ALDER – South Buttress of Garbh Choire

The Diamond

1. Raeburn's Gully — II
2. Raeburn's Gully, Left Branch — II
3. Raeburn's Edge — III
4. Thrills and Spills — V,4
5. Roadhog — V,5
6. Ben Alder Diamond — V,5
7. High Jinks — IV,4

8. Catkins — IV,5
9. Grockles Groove — III
10. Alder Curtain — V,4
11. Struan — IV,4
12. Thick Lip — IV,4
13. Steptoe — IV,4

Continue up the diagonal line past a steeper thin section to reach a big snow bay high on the face (55m). Climb a gully which leads out of the top of the snow bay towards the crest, but then move right and go up turfy ground to more snow (50m). Climb the groove in the tier above (the optional groove of *Raeburn's Edge*) to reach easy ground (35m).

Roadhog 200m V,5. Sandy Allan, Andy Nisbet. 31 Jan 2012.
A line based on chimneys right of centre on the face. Start below the chimney-fault line right of *Thrills and Spills*. Move left on turf to a line of turf leading back right to the base of a big shallow chimney (which is very steep). Make a descending traverse left before tricky moves up gain another right-slanting line of turf which leads close to the top of the shallow chimney (50m). Continue up to a snow bay, then climb a deep chimney above its right side (hidden on the approach) – 50m. Move up to a bigger snow bay. The logical line would be up the gully above it, but this is taken by *Thrills and Spills*, so a groove on the right was climbed until *Thrills and Spills* was joined (50m). Finish as for this route (50m).

Ben Alder Diamond 260m V,5. Simon Richardson, Roger Webb. 15 Jan 2012.
A varied mixed line running the full height of The Diamond.
1. 30m Start 15m left of *High Jinks* below a short deep gully that leads up into an impenetrable-looking niche. Climb up the gully into a niche that curls up and right behind a hidden pinnacle. Step off the summit of the pinnacle up a short steep wall to gain the start of a right-tending ramp.
2. 60m Move right along the ramp to where the gully of *High Jinks* comes in from the right. Instead of taking the continuation gully groove straight ahead, climb the diagonal fault leading left into the centre of the buttress. Belay in a bay above a series of steep steps.
3. 50m Quit the diagonal line and climb straight up via grooves and snowfields to a terrace.
4. 50m Continue in the same line up easing ground to a large snowfield at the top of the lower buttress.
5. 50m Ascend the snowfield and belay below the obvious square-cut gully cutting through the headwall.
6. 20m Climb the gully with interest, to the top.

High Jinks 130m IV,4. Dave McGimpsey, Andy Nisbet. 16 Jan 2012.
A gully which forms the right edge of the buttress. Easy snow and a little ice leads rightwards to a large recess. Climb an icy groove at the back of the recess before a move left and back right above leads to a V-groove on the right. Climb this to a thread on the right (45m). Continue up the groove to easy ground at the right edge of the crag (50m) and traverse right to descend.

The following ice routes are on a the smaller section of cliff right of the previous routes and thought to include the route *Thick Lip*. The smaller section is separated from the main cliff by a diagonal fault and just right of this is a deep right-slanting groove.

Catkins 70m IV,5. Andy Nisbet. 9 Feb 2012.
An icefall which flows into the base of the groove. Start up the groove before

moving left up an icy slab. Follow the ice right over an overlap, then left up a short vertical section to an easing. Climb another steep section to an easier ice finish.

Grockles Groove 80m III. Andy Nisbet. 9 Feb 2012.
Follow the deep right-slanting groove throughout; could be harder without a good build-up.

Alder Curtain 80m V,4. Dave McGimpsey, Andy Nisbet. 28 Jan 2012.
A wide ice smear near the centre of the smaller section of cliff. Its base ended in icicles so a start on the right was made (10m). The main smear was gained by a left slanting groove and climbed on good ice but too thin for ice screws (60m). Finish by an easy groove (10m).

Struan 80m IV,4. Andy Nisbet. 9 Feb 2012.
Start as for *Alder Curtain* to gain and follow an iced right-slanting groove. The best ice left the groove and climbed the slab on the left. This led to an easier corner to finish.

Right of here is a gully formed by a stream in summer and thought by Andy Nisbet to be *Thick Lip*; the grade was agreed at IV,4.

Steptoe 50m IV,4. Sandy Allan, Andy Nisbet. 31 Jan 2012.
An ice sheet in a left-facing corner at the right end of the smaller section of cliff. Could be easier with snow on the easier sections.

CREAG MEAGAIDH, Bellvue Buttress:
Note: Ken Applegate & Viv Wallace repeated *Crow Road* on ice on 3 Feb 2012 but with a different start. Start 100m right of *The Scene* (and about 10m right of *Crow Road*). Climb directly up steep ice to belay right of a steep icefall, beneath a roof (30m). Make steep moves out left (crux), as for *Crow Road*.

Haste Not 120m VI,5. Bjorn-Ovin Bjornstad, Ben Tibbetts. 13 Feb 2012.
A line about 40m to the right of *Post Haste*. Pitch 1 was 40m of steep ice. Pitch 2 was sustained ice, turned the steepest section on the right (30m). Pitch 3 eased a little, with an exit right under an overhanging rock prow to avoid a vertical snow exit.

Inner Corrie:
Gully of the Sods 150m VI,6 **. Donnie O'Sullivan, Pete Davies. 29 Jan 2012.
A steep gully cutting through the imposing right wall of *Crescent Gully*. The route is graded for icy conditions.
1. 40m Climb the gully on ice to belay at a snow terrace.
2. 40m Above the belay is a large overhanging recess barring entry to the upper gully. Continue up to the left of the recess until above the level of the roofs. Make an exposed rightward traverse across a wall to regain ice leading into the upper gully. Follow the upper gully to block belays on the left.
3. 70m Easier ground leads to the plateau.

Fly Me to the Moon   130m   VII,8. Simon Richardson, Iain Small. 22 Jan 2012.
A spectacular climb taking the fault-line cutting through the overhanging wall
right of *Crescent Gully*. Start by climbing the first easy 30m of *Crescent Gully* to
below the foot of the wall.
1. 50m Straight ahead is the steep gully line of *Gully of the Sods* and to the right
is a turfy corner-line leading up and right. Climb the corner to the midway
girdling ledge of *Quasimodo* and belay on blocks just to the right of the diagonal
fault.
2. 40m Climb the fault, which is a ramp-line to start, and step left at its top.
Continue up the vertical crack above and pull through the tiered roofs (crux) to a
boulder belay at the top of the wall.
3. 40m Continue up the crest of the buttress, following an easy wide gully to the
final snow slope and the top.

GLEN COE

STOB COIRE SGREAMHACH EAST:

The neglected eastern corrie of Stob Coire Sgreamhach offers a range of mixed
routes with a surprisingly remote feel, easily accessed from the lower slopes of
the Sron na Lairig ridge. The unnamed Grade I gully mentioned in the existing
guide, located just right of the ridge, provides an interesting and worthwhile
route to the summit. The name *Eilde Gully* is suggested. Left of the gully are a
series of buttresses forming the right (north) side of the Sron na Lairig ridge,
referred to below as the Ridge Buttresses. Immediately right of *Eilde Gully* is
Summit Buttress (SMCJ 2011, p500) which is bounded on the right by another
easy gully which provides a convenient descent route. Right of the easy gully is
the sprawling westmost buttress referred to as Monolith Buttress.

Ridge Buttresses:

Return   60m   V,6. Simon Yearsley, Chris Pasteur. 3 Feb 2012.
Just inside the left (true right) side of *Eilde Gully* is a small subsidiary gully/
chimney. Start 3m right of this. Climb the steep awkward wall, then move up and
into the right of two left-leaning grooves. Climb the groove to easier ground to
finish in an excellent position, right on the narrowest part of the Sron na Lairig
ridge.

Diminishing Return   55m   III *. Steve Kennedy, Bob Hamilton. 19 Feb 2012.
An easier indirect version of *Return*. Start about 10m above the foot of *Eilde
Gully* and follow the most prominent ramp leading out left onto the buttress to
join *Return* above the crux section of that route. Continue by following *Return*
up interesting mixed ground to the summit ridge.

Summit Buttress:

Gun Slinger   70m   IV,4 **. Steve Kennedy, Andy MacDonald. 18 Dec 2011.
The obvious gully/groove line immediately right of *The Slot*. Start up a
deceptively steep groove (almost a right-facing corner) leading into the right side
of a snow bay below the gully proper. Trend left into the confines of the gully
and continue to a point where the gully becomes blocked by a rock wall.

Circumvent the wall by moving out right, then up and left via a groove to rejoin the open gully above. Continue up mixed ground trending rightwards to a a small snowy col (55m). Finish up easier ground (15m).

Lamed Scout   60m   II/III. Andy Macdonald, Steve Kennedy. 10 Dec 2011.
The broad buttress forming the right side of Summit Buttress. Start just left of the Grade I gully and climb the straightforward lower section to reach ledges leading up leftwards below the steep upper wall. Follow the ledge system into a short chimney which leads to the top.

Monolith Buttress:
The westmost buttress contains a prominent monolithic block in the lower section, just left of the steeper right-hand section. The following routes are described by reference to the monolith.

Caballero   60m   II/III *. Steve Kennedy. 28 Jan 2012.
Start at a snow bay approximately 25m left of the monolithic block. Start up a short right-slanting groove at the top of the bay, about 10m right of the small steep buttress forming the left boundary of the buttress. Continue up an open groove to finish just right of a rocky pinnacle.

Wagon Train   60m   III,4 *. Steve Kennedy, Katie Long, Andy MacDonald. 5 Feb 2012.
Follows a line up the buttress, starting about 5m left of *Caballero*, just before the buttress steepens considerably. Climb an awkward slabby wall, continue up mixed ground for a short distance, then move left into a deep groove. Follow the groove and finish by steep moves on the left side of the final rocky pinnacle.

Left Draw   70m   III,4 *. Steve Kennedy, Andy MacDonald, Katie Long. 5 Feb 2012.
Scramble up to a belay at the foot of the monolith. Move onto the slabby wall just left of the monolith and climb steep mixed ground to belay at the top of a large snowfield (45m). Finish easily up rightward slanting snow slopes (25m).

Right Draw   70m   IV,5 *. Bob Hamilton, Steve Kennedy. 19 Feb 2012.
The steep groove running up the right side of the monolith leading to a snow terrace below the upper buttress (35m). From the terrace, continue directly up the buttress to finish close to *Left Draw* (35m).

Lone Rifle   80m   II/III *. Andy MacDonald. 14 Dec 2011.
This route generally follows a system of ledges leading diagonally right across the buttress starting about 5m right of *Right Draw*. Climb up and rightwards to reach a snow terrace. Continue rightwards following the prominent ledge system to reach a bay below the steep upper buttress. Finish up a deep groove on the left.

High Noon   70m   IV,4 **. Steve Kennedy, Andy MacDonald. 22 Jan 2012.
The most obvious feature on the steeper right section is an open gully which fans out at the bottom. Climb the right side of the initial fan until the gully narrows. A steeper section leads to a wide snow terrace (junction with *Lone Rifle*) - 35m. Climb the upper buttress by a line leading up leftwards to reach easier ground and finish directly (35m).

Tim Blakemore on Crocodile (E3,6a), Aonach Dubh, Glen Coe. Photo: Tamsin Gay.

Sharp Shooter   70m   V,6 **. Steve Kennedy, Andy Macdonald. 29 Jan 2012.
A fine route, nicely exposed in the upper reaches. To the right of *High Noon* is an
open groove with a slabby left wall. The lower groove forms the crux where it
forms a steep thinly iced slab and was climbed by strenuous moves up the
vertical right wall. The groove opens out above and leads to a wide terrace at
mid-height (35m). From near the left end of the terrace follow a right-trending
ramp (awkward initial moves) above a steep wall to a thin slab. Traverse left
along a narrow ledge in an exposed position. Continue rightwards to finish up the
right edge of the buttress (35m).

Twin Ridges Area:
Well right of Monolith Buttress, in the upper reaches of the north-west corner of
the corrie, lie two prominent parallel ridges leading to the summit ridge. The
ridges are situated above a lower broken buttress and offer pleasant routes in a
fine setting with a remote feel.

Comanche Ridge   60m   III *. Bob Hamilton, Steve Kennedy. 19 Feb 2012.
The left-hand ridge. Clmb the lower broad buttress by an obvious right-slanting
groove leading onto the ridge. Follow the ridge to the top, skirting a small rocky
buttress on the left.

Cherokee Ridge   60m   III, 4 *. Bob Hamilton, Steve Kennedy. 19 Feb 2012.
The right-hand ridge. The lower buttress is climbed by a steep open groove near
the centre just right of a block belay. Interesting mixed ground leads to the broad
upper ridge.

BEINN FHADA, West Face, Summit Buttress:
The Rampart   200m   II. James Roddie. 3 Feb 2012.
Climb the turfy crest to the right of *The Ramp*.

The Rhyme   80m   II/III. James Roddie. 3 Feb 2012.
On the right-hand side of the Summit Buttress are two narrow buttresses divided
by a narrow snow gully. *The Rhyme* takes the right-hand buttress. Climb a steep
wall to turfy ledges above. Then climb a higher steep wall by either a narrow
chimney on the right or rocky shelves on the left. Easier ground leads to the ridge
crest above.

Last Orders   80m   II/III. James Roddie. 3 Feb 2012.
The left of the two narrow buttresses on the right side of Summit Buttress. Climb
an initial short rock wall via a corner on the right. Easier angled turfy ground
leads to another rock wall. Climb this via a left-slanting crack, and move more
easily to the ridge crest above.

STOB COIRE NAN LOCHAIN:
Langsam Direct   100m   IV,4 **. Michael Barnard, Ron Dempster. 10 Dec 2011.
Climbs the central fault-line in the short steep wall avoided by *Langsam*.
1. 50m Follow *Langsam* up to below and slightly right of the fault-line. Continue
up, then move left to a large spike. Step left and climb the steep groove (serious
but on plentiful turf) to the halfway ledge. Continue with further interest up the
icy corner above to a large block.

2. 50m Continue direct up easier ground to the top.

The Inbetweeners 60m VI,8, **. Mark Garthwaite, Andy Sharpe. 27 Nov 2010.
Climbs a groove, then a very steep crack right of *The Struggler*. Start on the front
of the buttress right of *The Struggler*.
1. 15m Climb an open groove to belay below the steep wall.
2. 10m Climb the very thin overhanging crack on thin hooks and torques to a
ledge at its top next to the pinnacle.
3. 35m Finish as for *The Struggler*, up the slabby V-groove and chimney on the
buttress behind the pinnacle.

Twisted Chimney 30m V,6 **. Michael Barnard, John MacLeod. 17 Dec 2011.
The obvious steep chimney-groove cutting into the right wall of *Twisting Gully*
(up and left of *Moonshadow*).

AONACH DUBH, West Face:
No.3 Gully Rib 50m II/III. James Roddie. 5 Dec 2011.
Approach the Middle Ledge via the lower easy slopes of B Buttress. Once at the
Middle Ledge break right onto a small rib running up the left side of *No.3 Gully*.
After the first initial steepening, take easier ground to a final wall. Climb this
either by a short narrow chimney or take the wall direct on either side. Top out
onto the upper rake.

SGOR NA H-UDLAIDH, West Buttress:
Nicholson's Sneer 200m II. Colin Lesenger. 5 Mar 1996.
Start in a bay in the centre of the large sprawling buttress and just left of a
prominent left-trending ramp. Climb a short awkward gully to a snowfield.
Halfway up, take a shallow gully line on the right and follow this trending left at
the top to gain the broad buttress crest. Take the easiest line up mixed ground to
the top.

BEINN FHIONNLAIDH, Coire a' Chait, Alasdair's Buttress:
Ian Stennet notes that he would reduce the stars on the routes described in SMCJ
2010. *Maximus* **; *Commodus* *; *Proximo* III; *Caesar* II/III (downgraded).

ARDNAMURCHAN, Beinn na Seilg, Hebrides Wall:
Oldenbold 30m H.Severe 4a. Ian & Mhairi McCabe. 6 May 2012.
Start 5m right of *Unknown Warrior*, as the crag forms a grassy corner. Climb the
steep groove in the wall to gain a little left-facing flake crag. Use this to surmount
the steep initial wall, then trend up diagonally right over slabs to access two short
easy corners which lead to the crest of the SW ridge. Good climbing, sparsely
protected.

Coire Creagach (NM 501 681):
The crag is adjacent to Lochain Mhic Dhonuill Dhuibh, to the east of Meall
Meadhoin.

Where Eagles Glare 12m Diff **. Neil Henson, Mark Collins. 19 May 2012.
The leftwards curving crack-line at the centre of the crag via some loose blocks.

Where do the Memories Go?   10m   H.Severe 4a. Neil Henson, Mark Collins. 19 May 2012.
The blunt arete and shallow crack at the right end of the crag. Unprotected climbing on suspect holds.

Wish you were Here   12m   Severe 4a. Neil Henson, Mark Collins. 19 May 2012.
Climb direct up the slab just left of a loose horn of rock. Care required with hold selection. Scruffy rock that offers nice moves – better than it looks.

SOUTHERN HIGHLANDS

BEINN AN DOTHAIDH, North-East Corrie:
On the left of *Easy Gully* lie two crags, split by an easy gully trending left. This climbs the obvious corner in the centre of the right and upper crag, mostly on thin ice and frozen turf.

Consolation Corner   65m   IV,5. Erick Baillot, Stuart McFarlane. 15 Jan 2012.
1. 40m Climb the corner, with a steepening at half-height (crux), to a snow bay beneath overlaps.
2. 25m The natural fault continues up through these overlaps. Instead, step left onto a ramp which leads to a slot through the headwall.

BEINN A' CHAISTEAL:
Corax   170m   III. Fiona & Robert Kincaid. 3 Feb 2012.
Start up a left-sloping watercourse from the base of the ramp that spilts the face directly above the cattle grid. Belay on the right just before the first steepening. Follow the stepped watercourse over several steeper sections to gain the terrace. Descent is right along the terrace to the ramp.
Note: To its right is a parallel unclimbed line, which seems to have a very thin start.

THE COBBLER, North Peak, North Face:
Zig-Zag Gully   150m   II. Andy Bain, Jake Thackrey. 11 Dec 2011.
Climbs direct to North Peak. NN 263 061.
1. 25m Climb a snow gully to a headwall with a large crack.
2. 25m Climb an ice pitch then a gully.
3. and 4. 100m Climb the broken shoulder to the top with variation possible.

Groovie Crack   85m   IV,3. Andy Bain, Jake Thackrey, Dougie Beck. 31 Jan 2012.
Start at the rightmost section of crag at an open gully.
1. 25m Climb up a prominent gully between a large ridge on the left and a small ridge on the right to a large ledge with a huge flake boulder resting into a groove.
2. 35m Either climb the flake left or right to the groove and go up turf ledges to its top. Trend rightwards onto a block buttress and go under a chockstone into a large gash. Climb up on good hooks onto a large terrace.
3. 25m Climb leftwards around the terrace headwall to easy ground.

THE COBBLER, Fin Crag (NN 262 062):
This crag is on the north facing shoulder of the North Peak looking over to Beinn Narnain.

32 Inches and Under   55m   II. Andy Bain, Jake Thackrey. 17 Jan 2012.
Start at the rock face under the fin.
1. 30m Climb ledges on to a snowfield to belay on the middle gash.
2. 25m Climb up ledges and go through a small gap to enter a hidden cave and up into a small rocky amphitheatre.

Finders Keepers   75m   II. Andy Bain, Jake Thackrey, Dougie Beck. 31 Jan 2012.
Start 10m right of *32 Inches and Under* at an iced wall with a ramp.
1. 40m Climb up a small iced wall onto a right-slanting ledge under an overlap Follow this to a corner and go delicately around a corner crossing the chimney pitch of *Ordinary Route* to reach a large open corner.
2. 35m Follow rightwards along a ledge to a good headwall at the top.

Wee Ordinary Route   50m   III *. Andy Bain, Jake Thackrey. 11 Dec 2011.
A line of weakness starting about 30m left of the lowest point of the buttress. Climb an 8m cascade, then head for and climb an obvious chimney before crossing a snowfield. Finish up a small V-chimney on the left.

Lost and Found   IV,3 *. Andy Bain, Jake Thackrey. 17 Jan 2012.
Start at the lowest point of the buttress 40m right of *Ordinary Route*.
1. 35m Climb a shallow groove on a slab to a slanting ledge with a niche. Head up to a overhang with a good ledge at a corner.
2. 30m Climb a slab under the roof, then down climb 1m and go up a ramp to a good stance. Climb the left wall on good turf, then move left to the top.

BEINN NARNAIN, Yawning Crag (NN 266 065):
Don't Stop till you see Smoke   60m   IV,4 **. Andy Bain, Jake Thackrey, Douglas Beck. 18 Dec 2011.
Start left of a steep triangular buttress.
1. 25m Climb up and under a chockstone to a deep chimney. Climb this to a large ledge on the left.
2. 15m Move back into the chimney and go up to a niche. Climb a right-slanting crack to an overhanging bulge and go up to a large terrace.
3. 20m Climb blocky grooves to a ledge. Move left to a flake and up rightwards over slabs to a corner with a wide crack. Climb up and over a bulge to a terrace.
Note: As an alternative to pitch 2, move left for 5m and climb an easy blocky groove rightwards to the terrace.

G13   65m   III. Jake Thackrey, Andy Bain, Douglas Beck. 18 Dec 2011.
Climbs the right side of the triangular buttress.
1. 25m Climb a ramp to the bottom of a chimney .
2. 35m Climb the deep chimney, then move left on to the buttress. Climb this, then traverse left to easy ground and a large terrace.
Various finishes are possible.

THE BRACK:

Great Central Groove, Variation Finish   40m   VII,9. Pete Macpherson, Pete Benson. 22 Dec 2010.

1. and 2. Climb the first two pitches of *Great Central Groove*, belaying below the barrier headwall. On the left is a steep wall with an obvious crack system to the left of the chimney.

3. 20m Climb up the steep crack and pull onto a small ledge. Climb up the blank looking slab above and continue up turfy ground to belay beside a huge block on the right.

4. 20m Directly behind the block is a recess with a right-trending ramp. Gain the icy ramp and climb as it tapers with increasing difficulty until it becomes a groove and a steep exit is made onto icy turf.

BEN DONICH:

A large jumble of boulders is located at NN 225 054 and is passed on the ascent up the NE ridge (before one gets to the main crags).

The Squirmer   20m   H.Severe. Michael Barnard, Eve Bradley. 8 Aug 2011.

Takes the obvious vertical crack-line splitting the west face of the largest block and lying just right of a large roof. The lower half is overhung and is overcome by means of an entertaining through route. Start at the back of the cave.

1. 10m Move up into the gap in the roof. Follow a ledge outwards past a tight sqeeze to belay on the edge.

2. 10m 4b Climb the steep crack above to the top.

STOB DIAMH, Sron an Isean, North-North-East Buttress:

Approach: Go directly SSW from the end of the track that goes NW along Allt Mhoille from the farms on the NE corner of Loch Awe. This is the approach track for Beinn a' Chochuill and Beinn Eunaich to the north, as well as Stob Diamh if approaching from the north.

V-Gully   150m   I/II (left) II/III (right). Ole Kemi. 22 Jan 2012.

The main buttress is split by a gully which splits at one-third height into two narrow gullies. The right has a harder crux section with a passage on rock. Climbed in poor conditions, but after a good freeze, the climbing should be toward the easier grade. Both lines become easier toward the top.

ARRAN

No routes to report.

LOWLAND OUTCROPS

AYRSHIRE, Clifton:

The Arete Direct   15m   E3 5c. Brian Davison, Paul Wood. 24 May 2012.

Climb the original route direct without entering the corner and continue to the spike knobble above. Instead of moving right into the crack continue straight up the arete.

Note: The guide gives the start of this E4 6a but it seems to have been a guess and not actually climbed.

Squidge   10m   HVS 5a. Stephen Reid, James Kinnaird. 19 May 2012.
An enjoyable eliminate up the rib right of *Overground*. Good strenuous climbing but the grade assumes that the crack of *Overground* is only used for protection. Start just left of the niche of *Outcast* at a diagonal crack. Make a hard move to gain the rib and follow it, avoiding holds in *Overground* with difficulty.

DUNGEON OF BUCHAN, Cooran Buttress:
Cooran Gully   125m   III/IV *. Stephen Reid, John Biggar. 2 Feb 2012.
The open gully to the right of Cooran Buttress gives a good climb but is seldom in condition. It requires both a long freeze and a big dump of snow. From down and right of *The Colonel's Corner*, traverse right about 25m passing under two deep corners to an amphitheatre. Starting here, climb up easily towards the left side of this then wend your way rightwards and then back leftwards through a steeper band to gain a more defined gully and a belay (30m). Continue up the gully, bypassing a narrowing chimney just to its right and take a stance a little higher (30m). Continue up the gully until it turns into an overhanging offwidth and take an obvious traverse out to the right arete via a big block (25m). Step across rightwards into a groove and climb this and a short rock rib then more easily to the top (40m). The second of the two corners has also been climbed as an alternative first pitch at much the same grade though more sustained.
Note: The same team also did the alternative start on the same day.

Brown Study   125m   II/III. Ian Brown, Jonathan Grubb. 2 Feb 2012.
Gain the huge easy angled right-slanting ramp just right of *Cooran Gully* via rocky scrambling. At the top of the ramp climb the short gully on the right.

Note: *Saddle Tramp*. An alternative way on pitch 2 is to avoid the niche by traversing above it to the same point. R.Whitworth, D.Boothman, 20 Aug 2011.

WOLF SLOCK:
(NX 457 894)   Alt 350m   North-East facing
This large rambling cliff lies on the north-east end of Hoodens Hill, a northerly outlier of Mullwharchar.

Connoisseurs' Choice   135m   E2 **. Andrew Fraser, Iain Magill, Stephen Reid. 27 May 2012.
A tremendous adventure up the most continuous and clean pillar of rock on the left side of the crag, situated to the right of twin heathery gullies and left of waterworn slabs. A good drought and a double rack of cams up to Camalot 3 size are recommended. Start at a slim rib below the right side of the pillar.
1. 15m 4b Twin cracks in the rib lead to a grass ledge.
2. 15m 4b A crack in the wall culminates in an awkward exit onto a grass ledge.
3. 25m 5b The steep cracked wall is climbed centrally. Start 1m right of a smooth corner and follow flakes and cracks to a small niche. Move up then rightwards into cracks that lead to the top and belay immediately. A very sustained pitch but with excellent protection; 2 rest points taken.
4. 45m 4c Move left up grass and overcome a short wall via a little groove to

gain a grass ledge. Follow a left-trending line of flakes to an awkward mantelshelf onto a narrow grass ledge. Follow a crack and rib above then turn the headwall by a short chimney on its left.

5. 35m 4c Follow a left-curving crack in the centre of the face for a move, then step onto the slab on the right and overcome a slight overlap. Traverse left and climb a short cleft, taking care with a poised pinnacle. Traverse right under a block and climb the open corner in the wall above.

DUNGEON OF BUCHAN, Corwar:

The Return of the King   23m   HVS 5a **. Stephen Reid, Chris King, James Kinnaird. 15 Sep 2011.

Direct variations on *Corwar Wall* and just as good. Start 1.5m right of *Corwar Wall* and climb the wall directly to a small overhang, then climb up to the left-slanting break of *Ruta Aurelio*. Make one move leftwards along this and then launch directly up the wall above via a jug to gain the hand traverse of *Corwar Wall*. Stand on the traverse holds, step left into a shallow scoop and finish direct.

STIRLING AREA, North Third:

Sybiline Slab   18m   E2 5c **. Keith Alexander, Graeme Diack. 8 Aug 2011.

Lies on the same buttress as *Faulty Towers*. Excellent well-protected climbing up thin cracks on the slab in the middle of the buttress. At the last small roof, follow a crack leading right and up to finish.

EDINBURGH AREA, Blackford Quarry:

Note: Nigel Suess notes that the route *Good Craic* (SMCJ 2011) has been climbed many times before and is V.Diff.

MISCELLANEOUS NOTES

THE W.H. MURRAY LITERARY PRIZE

As a tribute to the late Bill Murray, whose mountain and environment writings have been an inspiration to many a budding mountaineer, the SMC have set up a modest writing prize, to be run through the pages of the Journal. The basic rules are set out below, and will be reprinted each year. The prize is run with a deadline of 1 May each year.

The Rules:

1. There shall be a competition for the best entry on Scottish Mountaineering published in the *Scottish Mountaineering Club Journal*. The competition shall be called the 'W.H. Murray Literary Prize', hereafter called the 'Prize'.
2. The judging panel shall consist of, in the first instance, the following: The current Editor of the *SMC Journal*; The current President of the SMC; and two or three lay members, who may be drawn from the membership of the SMC. The lay members of the panel will sit for three years after which they will be replaced.
3. If, in the view of the panel, there is in any year no entry suitable for the Prize, then there shall be no award that year.
4. Entries shall be writing on the general theme of 'Scottish Mountaineering', and may be prose articles of up to approximately 5000 words in length, or shorter verse. Entries may be fictional.
5. Panel members may not enter for the competition during the period of their membership.
6. Entries must be of original, previously unpublished material. Entries should be submitted to the Editor of the *SMC Journal* by 1 May for consideration that year. Electronic contributions are preferred and should be submitted via e-mail, although double-spaced typewritten hard copies will also be accepted by post. (See Office Bearers page at end of this Journal for address etc.) Any contributor to the SMC Journal is entitled to exclude their material from consideration for the Prize and should so notify the Editor of this wish in advance.
7. The prize will be a cheque for the amount £250.
8. Contributors may make different submissions in different years.
9. The decision of the panel is final.
10. Any winning entry will be announced in the *SMC Journal,* and will be published in the *SMC Journal* and on the SMC Website. Thereafter, authors retain copyright.

THE W.H. MURRAY LITERARY PRIZE 2012

There was a slight hiccup with The Prize this year. The judges picked one outstanding submission only to discover, late in the day, that the contributor did not wish his article to be considered for the prize. There was no obvious second choice so it was decided not to make an award this year. However, many of the articles were much enjoyed by the judges and again all the contributors are thanked for their efforts.

There were a lot of articles about climbing abroad this year. *Mount Cameroon* is 'an informative, enertaining introduction to a largely unknown area not normally associated with high mountains. Full of charming and at times alarming details of travel in this part of the world.' Little is generally known also of the rock climbing possibilities in Albania. *Po and Jo in Albania* certainly gives of a good taste of the climbing in that country. Two contrasting articles describe ice climbing in Norway and Austria. The scale of the frozen waterfalls described in *Fjordland* is quite breathtaking, but the article about *Das Gully* is also very interesting and told in an entertaining way. *Countering Wisdom* is another amusing article, this time about climbing in the Canadian Rockies. And, if you need any help, it gives some clear advice about how to organise an epic!

Neil's Fall is a fine account of a scary accident on the Orion Face of Ben Nevis. The tale is charged with adrenalin even though it is told twenty years after it happened. The author is clearly impressed by the night-time efforts of the rescue team. He was not to know that big lowers had become routine on Ben Nevis by that time. His own efforts, in finishing the route alone and navigating safely off the summit without map or compass, were perhaps more impressive.

A scholarly piece about W.H. Murray and his writing raises some questions about the veracity rather than the essential spirit of his accounts.

Early evening light on Marsco.   Artist: Helen Forde.

SCOTTISH WINTER NOTES 2011–12

After the warmest November on record, winter started with a bang in early December as a series of blizzards swept across the Highlands. After the long and frustrating wait for winter conditions to arrive, activity levels were high for several weeks, but unfortunately it began to warm up in late February. After an unusually mild March, temperatures were consistently cold through late April and most of May. To the delight of ski mountaineers, there was more snow on the Cairngorm plateau in May than during the rest of the season, and there were dozens of mountaineering routes ripe for the taking in the high corries on Ben Macdui and Braeriach.

A notable feature of December and January were strong north-westerlies that often kept the Northern Corries windblown and bare and did not allow significant snow and ice build up on the Ben. In many ways it was the 'thinking climber's season, where careful consideration of wind direction, temperature and precipitation levels meant that good winter climbing could be found every weekend (except during March), but only if you disregarded the more popular venues. December and January for example, were perfect times to climb on some of the high south-facing crags in the Cairngorms, which typically, are rarely in condition.

As always it is difficult to single out the most significant events, but Greg Boswell's 20-day blitz in December stands out as something special, with pride of place going to the first ascent of *Siberian Tiger* (IX,10) in Coire an Lochain and the outstanding second ascent of *Stone Temple Pilots* (X,9) on the Shelter Stone with Will Sim. It is unusual for the highlights of a Scottish winter season to be repeats, but there were several second ascents of legendary routes such as *Don't Die of Ignorance* (XI,11) on Ben Nevis. Arguably the finest new route took place on Lochnagar in February, when Guy Robertson and Nick Bullock climbed *Black Spout Wall* (IX,9) – an outstanding line climbed in superlative style.

Another feature of the season was the number of visits from accomplished overseas climbers. The BMC International Meet in late January attracted several talented climbers such as Takaaki Nagato from Japan and Bayard Russell from the US, which resulted in many high standard repeats and a handful of first ascents. Earlier, in the middle of January, Charly Fritzer and Matthias Wurzer added the steep *Pfugga-Lule* (VIII,9) on the Happy Tyroleans wall in Coire an Lochain in the Northern Corries. The Austrians first climbed the route on almost dry snowless rock, but when they heard feedback that these conditions were not acceptable, they returned and reclimbed the route in bona fide winter conditions after it had snowed a few days later. Swiss climber Dani Arnold of recent Eiger record fame, eclipsed everyone however, with the fourth ascent of *The Hurting* (XI,11) in Coire an Lochain during his first ever winter climbing trip to Scotland.

But if anything demonstrated the relentless rise in standards, it was Guy Robertson's back-to-back ascents of *Guerdon Grooves* (IX,8), *The Duel* (IX,9) and *Satyr* (IX,9) in Glen Coe. Three Grade IXs on consecutive days was an unprecedented feat, requiring outstanding technical ability, supreme fitness and the crucial Scottish winter ability of being in the exactly the right place at the right time.

The Boswell Blitz

The month of December was dominated by one man – Greg Boswell. The

20-year-old started his campaign on Ben Nevis on 2 December when he made the second ascent of *The Minge* (VII,8) on South Trident Buttress. Conditions were appalling that day with blowing spindrift and half-frozen turf, but even so, Boswell and Fiona Murray climbed the route in rapid time. The weather was even worse next morning, so wary of avalanche danger, Boswell climbed the prominent direct line up the centre of the low-lying Moonlight Gully Buttress. *The Big Cheese* (VIII,8) was climbed with Jim Higgins and Harry Holmes and sported a very bold first pitch up a narrow hanging streak of newly formed ice.

Two days later, Boswell teamed up with regular partner Will Sim and visited Creag an Socach in the Southern Highlands for the second ascent of *Defenders of the Faith* (IX,9). This route was first climbed by Dave MacLeod and Fiona Murray in 2006 and was Scotland's first on sight Grade IX. Boswell dispatched the crux pitch in double quick time, and Sim later commented that 'I expect this one will become a proper classic, similar in popularity to the neighbouring Messiah.'

They then moved up to the CIC Hut on Ben Nevis with James Dunn. After climbing *The Great Chimney*, they were confined to the hut next day as the Great December Storm ripped off the roof covering of the sleeping quarters. The wind calmed down overnight, and undeterred, the trio made the second ascent of *The Knuckleduster* (VIII,9) on Number Three Gully Buttress. This was first climbed in winter by Steve Ashworth and Blair Fyffe in February 2007 with a finish up *Sioux Wall*, but Boswell, Sim and Dunn stayed independent and climbed the steep final summer pitch.

Three days later, Boswell was in Coire an Lochain in the Northern Corries with Guy Robertson and Pete Macpherson attempting a winter ascent of *Siberia*, a spectacular summer E3 that takes the arête between *The Demon* and *The Vicar*. Unfortunately, Macpherson took a long fall from the crux, narrowly missing his belayers heads, so after another attempt he pulled the ropes through and Boswell took the lead. Boswell powered through the crux sequence onto a bold and very tenuous section before reaching easier ground. Guy Robertson compared *Siberian Tiger* (IX,10) to *Crazy Sorrow* on Lochnagar, and it ranks as one of Scotland's most technical winter routes.

Full of confidence Boswell teamed up with Will Sim three days later for *Stone Temple Pilots*. They started the route at 6.30 a.m., and fourteen hours later they were on the summit of the Shelter Stone with one of Scotland's most prized second ascents in the bag. *Stone Temple Pilots* is an eight-pitch super directissima, which links the summer lines of *Steeple*, *Haystack* and *Spire* directly up the front face of the crag. It was first climbed last winter by Guy Robertson and Pete Macpherson, and at a grade of X,9, it is generally considered to be the most technically sustained Scottish winter route climbed to date. Finally, to cap an exceptional period of climbing, Boswell made the first winter ascent of *Jumping Jupiter* (VIII,8), a summer E2 on Carn Etchachan, in the company of Ian Parnell.

Boswell's 20-day climbing spree is not just outstanding for the difficulty and volume of routes. It is tempting to think that high standard winter climbing is all about gymnastic ability, but Scottish winter makes far more demands than just pulling hard on tools. Boswell has been climbing since he was 13, but even so the maturity and depth of experience required to gauge conditions, assess the potential of new lines and combine this with navigation and general mountain skills are remarkable for someone so young. 'I'm speechless,' Guy Robertson exclaimed after Stone Temple Pilots. 'I'm so, so impressed. It took me twenty years to get to that route – it's taken Greg two seasons! Brilliant – just absolutely brilliant.'

BMC International Winter Meet

The BMC Winter Meet was held in Glenmore Lodge during the last week of January. Forty overseas guests from 26 different countries teamed up with a similar number of British hosts and climbed for six days all over Scotland.Routes were climbed at all standards, from straightforward hill walks up to Grade IXs, with the majority of the visitors enjoying a rich sample of Scottish winter climbing. There were smiles all round at dinner every night and in total eight new routes were climbed. The most technically difficult was Nick Bullock and Russell Bayards' ascent of *The Mindless Finish* (IX,10) to *Pic 'n Mix* in Coire an Lochain, with Nick later describing this run out pitch as an 'emotional experience.'

On Ben Nevis, Simon Frost and Takaaki Nagato from Japan made the first ascent of *Sake* (VIII,9) which lies to the right of *Babylon* on Number Three Gully Buttress. Nagato and his colleague Ryo Mastumoto were the technical stars of the meet, and impressed everyone with their quiet and efficient climbing style that resulted in a string of impressive ascents such as *The Vicar* and *Daddy Longlegs* in Coire an Lochain, *Where Eagles Dare* on Lochnagar and *Unicorn* in Glen Coe. Other new routes included *Red Dwarf* (VII,7) on Stacan Dubha by Markus Griesshammer from Germany, and *Horus*, a new six-pitch VII,7 on the West Buttress of Lochnagar by Swedish climber Magnus Stromhall.

Guerdon Grooves – Second Ascent

On 28 January, Guy Robertson, Nick Bullock and Bayard Russell made headlines with the second ascent of *Guerdon Grooves* (IX,8) on Buachaille Etive Mor's imposing Slime Wall. *Guerdon Grooves*, was first climbed in winter by Arthur Paul and Dave Cuthbertson in January 1984, and originally graded VI, it was the earliest route to be given Grade VIII when the grading system was extended in the early 1990s. Following a number of attempts over the years, its reputation had built considerably and it is graded IX,8 in the current guidebook. The second ascent went relatively smoothly in nine hours, but as Nick explained afterwards, with the burden of 28 years of history, 'the crux of the route was actually starting it.'

Robertson, Bullock and Russell were assisted by relatively good conditions and some helpful ice, whilst some previous repeat attempts had made attempts in less than helpful powder conditions. But choosing the appropriate conditions is an essential component of Scottish winter climbing, and Guy Robertson excels at this aspect of the sport. As if to emphasise the point, Robertson made it three Grade IXs on consecutive days. He climbed *The Duel* (IX,9) on Stob Coire an Lochan with Pete Macpherson the following day, and the pair were joined by Nick Bullock again the next morning for the second ascent of the neighbouring *Satyr* (IX,9). This route saw its first winter ascent last season after a number of attempts by Donald King and Andy Nelson. The Robertson-Macpherson-Bullock trio on-sighted the route with Bullock leading the crux. 'It's a brilliant route and the consensus was IX,10,' Nick told me. 'I can't believe Nelson and King went back to climb it again with that first pitch. Those boys are stronger and braver than they think!'

Don't Die of Ignorance – Second Ascent

On 29 January, Greg Boswell and James Dunn pulled off the coveted second free ascent of *Don't Die of Ignorance* on Ben Nevis. This sensational route, which traverses around the steep front nose of The Comb to gain the attractive central groove system, was climbed as a partial aid route in February 1987 and graded VI,6 and A2. In March 2008 Dave MacLeod succeeded in freeing the climb with Joe French on his sixth attempt. The route was graded XI,11 making it not only the highest graded route on Ben Nevis, but along with *The Hurting* (another Dave MacLeod route), the most technically difficult winter route in Scotland. Over the last couple of seasons several strong teams had attempted the repeat, but it was an on form Greg Boswell who took the honours after attempting the route two days before. 'I got it first time on my second visit with a fairly smooth ascent,' Greg told me. 'The crux traverse was powerful and thin, but the icy wall above the crack was utterly terrifying!'

Black Spout Wall

Big news in February was the first winter ascent of *Black Spout Wall* on Lochnagar by Guy Robertson and Nick Bullock. The 170m-high Black Spout Wall towers above the prominent gully of The Black Spout and is the steepest feature on the mountain. It was first climbed in summer by Dougie Dinwoodie and Bob Smith in 1976 at E3 5c and is one of the most sought after rock climbs in the Cairngorms. Such a prominent route was a clear winter target and it had been probed by a number of teams, but all had failed on the steep, wide, rounded crack of the first pitch.

Nick Bullock made an ascent of the nearby *Link Direct* (which takes a less direct line up the wall) with Tim Neill and Keith Ball on 2 February and was intrigued by the route's winter potential. He prompted Guy Robertson into action, who being well aware of the nature of the summer first pitch, he hit upon the inspired idea of starting up the first two 5c pitches of *Steep Frowning Glories*, a neighbouring E6, to access the line. Four days later the pair returned to Lochnagar and put their plan into action with Robertson leading the crucial entry pitches and Bullock leading the difficult second pitch of the summer Black Spout Wall and the 'Inhospitable Crack', a desperate finish up the impending headwall. The result was an outstanding IX,9 and one of the most brilliant on-sight first winter ascents ever made in Scotland.

Castle in the Sky

Dave MacLeod's six-metre wide roof, *Castle in the Sky* on Druim Shionnach in Glen Shiel, was another significant climbing achievement, and typical of so many Dave MacLeod routes, it pushed the boundaries. The pre-protected nature of the route means that it is more in the realms of a continental M-climb rather than a traditional Scottish winter route, but this does not mean that it was a safe undertaking. An upside down Pecker and a blade peg as the key protection must have offered little reassurance, and the route is so unlike any other that it is virtually unclassifiable. A key point perhaps, is that MacLeod has demonstrated that roofs of this size are physically possible on Scottish winter rock.

All Go in the Cuillin

Some of the most remarkable discoveries of the winter took place on Skye in the hands of Cuillin mountain guide and guidebook author Mike Lates. Together with Ben Wear and Mike Francis in late December, he made the first ascent of

Bjorn-Ovin Bjornstad on the first ascent of Haste Not (VI,6) on Creag Meagaidh's Post Face.
Photo: Ben Tibbetts.

White Lies (IV,5), a seven-pitch ice line on the South Face of Gillean, and three days later, he was back with Matthew Holmes to climb *Southern Comfort* (IV,5), a 240m-long ice route in Coire Lagan. 'This week was one of the best I've known up here,' Mike told me. 'It was just amazing to get two long ice lines in the Cuillin, and ironic having spent all the effort trying to persuade folk to think of it as a mixed venue. I have a variety of south facing lines in the "fantasy bank" but never expected any of them to ever come off!' Lates also organised a very successful winter climbing meet on Skye, which resulted in several new routes including *Wildcat Flap* (V,6), a new route on the Upper Rake of Sgùrr a' Mhadaidh by Paul Cunningham and Brendan Croft, and *High Visibility* (VI,6) on the buttress right of Gully E on Sgùrr Theàrlaich by Lates and Susan Jensen. Finally in early March, when everyone thought the season had come to a premature end, Lates used his intimate knowledge of the Cuillin when he teamed up with Andy Huntington and Robin Clothier to add *Curse of the Hobgoblin* (V,7).

Central Highlands

Apart from the activity on the Winter Meet reported above, it was not a particularly eventful season on Ben Nevis. Early in December, Helen Rennard and I added *Cyclops* (V,5) on the upper tier of South Trident Buttress, and later in the month Nick Bullock and Dougal Tavener added a fiercely difficult route to the East Flank of Tower Ridge. *The Ride of the Wild Bullhorn* (VIII,10) takes the groove to the right of *The Pretender* and was described by Bullock as 'George Smith territory in winter – knee bars, hand jams and pretty savage pulling.' Nearby on Aonach Mòr, Adam Hughes made a bold lead of *The Prow* (VIII,8), the prominent feature left of *Stirling Bridge*. This committing climb involved precarious hooking on poor flat hooks and protected by a bulldog halfway up a steep hanging corner.

Across on Creag Meagaidh, the mixed potential of the steep bounding wall to the right of Crescent Gully was explored. First on the scene was Iain Small and myself who added *Fly Me to the Moon* (VII,8), an unlikely-looking fault-line through a series of roofs, closely followed by Pete Davies and Donie O'Sullivan who climbed *Gully of the Sods* (VI,6) the overhanging ice gully to the left. 'It was like a mini Great Overhanging Gully on Beinn Bhan,' Pete enthused afterwards. In February, Ken Applegate and Vic Wallace visited Bellevue Buttress and made the second ascent of *Crow Road* adding the two pitch long *Feathered Friend Start* (V,5), and across on the Post Face, Ben Tibbetts and Norwegian visitor Bjorn-Ovin Bjornstad added *Haste Not* (VI,6), a line of steep ice joining the finish of *The Lost Post*.

Northern Highlands

Activity in the Northern Highlands was limited too, although Martin Moran and Pete Macpherson made a winter ascent of *The Blue Lamppost* (VIII,8), a summer HVS on Meall Gorm, and Roger Webb and I climbed *The Bulldog Spirit* (V,5) up the centre of the previously unclimbed summit cliff of Beinn Damh. Elsewhere in the Highlands, activity was rather limited in early in January due to storm force winds, but some superb new routes were climbed later in the month. These include the first winter ascent of *Rudolf* (VIII,9) on Beinn Eighe by Martin Moran and Murdoch Jamieson. (Moran considers this his hardest new route on the mountain.) Warm weather sweeping across the country limited activity for much of February, but there was some worthwhile exploratory activity before the

Martin Hind leading pitch 4 of Roseroot (V,5), a new 300m-long route in the Fannaichs.
Photo: James Edwards.

temperatures soared. In the Northern Highlands, Martin Hind and James Edwards climbed the intriguing-sounding *Roseroot* (V,5), a 300m route on a previously unclimbed cliff deep in the Fannaichs.

Cairngorms

The weather most favoured the Northern Cairngorms, and the Loch Avon Basin proved especially popular with the Shelter Stone seeing ascents of *Western Union*, *Sticil Face* and *Citadel*, and an ascent of *The Needle* (VIII,8) by Martin Moran and Murdoch Jamieson. New route activity focused on the nearby Stacan Dubha where Andy Nisbet, Helen Rennard and Jonathan Preston and Ross Cowie added *Upper Crust* (VI,6), *Atlantis* (III) and *Mr Blobby* (V,5) in the centre of the crag as well as making the first winter ascent of *Zigzag* (IV,4). Roger Everett and I also nipped in for some of the action with the first ascent of *Goldilocks* (VI,6) up the crest of the pillar left of *Tangent*.

In Coire an Lochain, Greg Boswell and Will Sim repeated *The Gathering* (VIII,9), Guy Robertson and Pete Macpherson's test-piece from last season on the Pinnacle, and on the day before the Winter Meet they added *Hyperventilator* (IX,10), the faint overhanging crack line on the left wall of the Vent. The route still awaits a clean ascent as Boswell fell one move away from easy ground.

On the southern side of the Cairngorms, the first winter ascent of *The Primate* (VIII,8) on the West Wall of Mitre Ridge on Beinn a' Bhuird in early February by Pete Davies and Donie O'Sullivan was an impressive achievement. This rarely climbed E1, which tackles the wall right of Slochd Wall, breaching a large overhang at mid-height, was another obvious Cairngorms winter target, but most had been put off by the 16km approach. Davies and O'Sullivan's matter-of-fact on sight ascent demonstrates that remoteness is now no barrier, for even the most imposing of objectives.

Across on Lochnagar, Guy Robertson made first ascents of *The Mummy* (VIII,8) and *The Cracker* (VII,8) on The Cathedral with Pete Macpherson and Jason Currie, and later in February a cold snap allowed Iain Small and I to climb a counter-diagonal to *Isis* on West Buttress. The 300m-long *Osiris* (VII,8) featured a steep and bold first pitch leading to sustained Grade VI climbing above. Nearby on Earn Crag at the head of Glen Esk, Dave Almond and Duncan Tunstall made the first ascent of the five-pitch *High Grade Low Grade* (VIII). Finally, the cold weather at the end of April allowed Guy Robertson, Piotr Wistal and I to make the first winter ascent of *Sniffer Buttress* (VIII,8) in Coire an Dubh Lochain.

Ben Alder Magic

Ben Alder saw a number of good additions, but the prize for the most determined piece of exploratory climbing goes to Andy Nisbet who concluded his exploration of the remote South Buttress of Garbh Choire with an audacious solo visit just as the mid February thaw set in. Nisbet had previously added seven routes to the cliff earlier in the season with Duncan Tunstall, Dave McGimpsey and Sandy Allan, but three ice lines remained. The 24km approach demands a big commitment, and Nisbet arrived at the foot of the still-frozen crag in a determined mood 'with no rope, no ice screws and no excuse'. The result was the ice smear of *Struan* (IV,4), the imposing icy groove of *Catkins* (IV,5), and the more amenable ice line of *Grockles Groove* (III). He couldn't resist making the second ascent of *Thick Lip* (IV,4) before starting on the long journey home. 'I should

Dave McGimpsey on the first ascent of Thrills and Spills (V,4) on the South Buttress of Garbh Choire on Ben Alder. Photo: Andy Nisbet.

have been on a high for the cycle out,' Andy explained, 'but the frozen track had turned to glue and it was a very tired and muddy person who reached the car with leaden legs.'

Simon Richardson

100 YEARS AGO: THE CLUB IN 1912

The 23rd Annual Meeting and Dinner took place on Friday 1 December 1911 in the St Enoch Hotel, Glasgow, with Godfrey Solly presiding. Treasurer Nelson announced a balance of £119 6s. 3d., which together with the Life Membership Fund of £299 2s. 8d., and Gaiter Club 'legacy' of £100, brought the Club's total funds to £518 8s. 11d. Recurrent expenditure had been much higher than usual, on account of £77 12s. 1d. for the exceptional item of the 10-Volume Index. Secretary Clark announced 9 new members, the membership thereby increasing to 196. A vote of thanks was given to William Garden and James Parker, who had compiled the 10-Volume Index, a mighty work of a quality not since approached in this or any other mountaineering club (3s. 6d.; 4d. postage). Parker also compiled a 24-year table of membership (*SMCJ,* 12/67 (1912), 50), showing a big shift in the balance of membership from Glasgow to Edinburgh, and a steady rise in the proportion of English members from 14% to 31%.

The New Year Meet was held at the Tarbet Hotel with 32 members and 13 guests attending, another record turn-out. The weather was poor – warm, wet, and snowless, as usual, and the only climb of consequence was a repeat ascent of the *McLaren-Shadbolt Gully* on Creag Tharsuinn by Goggs, Goodeve, Ling and McLaren – McLaren leading – on the 29th, probably the most difficult route in the district at that time. On the 30th, various routes on the Spearhead and Cobbler North Peak were climbed. On Saturday evening there were curling matches on the billiard table, and on Sunday two members bathed in Loch Lomond!

Lochearnhead 1912
(L to R) Mabel Inglis Clark, Mrs & Mr Robert Watson, Harry MacRobert, Charles Inglis Clark.
Photo: SMC Image Archive.

On 10 February, the *Aberdeen Evening Gazette* carried a report of a discovery on Ben More, Perthshire, made by new member Alastair McLaren then resident at Inverardran just west of the hill. When climbing Ben More, McLaren

> came to small chasm, which was almost imperceptible. Pushing his way in, he saw a funnel-like opening, and by strenuous endeavours he got to the top, where he found a large cave, which he thinks has never been explored before. He then saw a ray of light, and succeeding in reaching the opening, he emerged on the side of the hill, and one-eighth of a mile from where he had entered.

No record of this remarkable discovery seems to have appeared in our publications, although there is a note in *CCJ* (8, 180), from which the text given above is taken.

On 27 February there was a Special Dinner of the Club in Ferguson & Forrester's Restaurant, 129 Princes Street. This was held to honour the first Editor, and composer of the Club's Song – Joseph Stott, who was making his first (and very brief) return from New Zealand. The Dinner was chaired by Solly, and four ex-Presidents attended along with 23 other members.

On 9 March C.I. Clark, S.F.M. Cumming, J.R. Young and W.G. MacAlister climbed Stobinian in mild conditions. Passing to Ben More, Young and MacAlister descended the North Corrie where they were caught up in a major new snow over old snow avalanche. MacAlister, after a fall of 850 feet, found himself bound to the waist in snow, frozen by the pressure. He began to extricate himself using his pocket-knife, shouting the while. Fortunately, Young was unscathed and after some time found MacAlister and freed him with his ice-axe.

The Easter Meet was held at Ballachulish, Clachaig and Kingshouse Hotels,

Avalanche debris, North-West flank of Ben More, March 1912.
Photo: by JR Young (SMC Image Archive).

Glen Coe. A fourth venue, the Tartan Hotel, Kinlochleven, attracted no members. 28 members and 9 guests were spread across the three centres. The Meet enjoyed four days of heavy rain, occasionally spiced by gales, that prevented all but the more primitive sorts of climbing. Because of a miners' strike, trains were few and stopped short, so that those attending were obliged to walk or cycle long distances to reach their destinations. For example, J.C. Thomson and his guest W.B.I. Pollock walked from Rannoch to Kinlochleven via Sgùrr Eilde, and thence came to Ballachulish by steamer. The vilest route march was undertaken (predictably enough) by Galbraith, Goggs, and Russell, who walked from Taynuilt via Benn Sgulaird to Clachaig through incessant rain. Their journey took 15 hours, and ended with a perilous river crossing in Gleann Leac na Muidhe at 8.15: 'We were getting desperate now, and as Galbraith was the oldest, we tied a rope around his waist and threw him in', wrote Goggs (see 'A Fifteen-Hour Walk in Benderloch', *SMCJ*, 12/71 (1913), 258–66).

In late May, Wm. Ling (*Diary*, Book 10, pp. 9–15) continued his explorations of the Far Northern Highlands, in the company of Gibbs, Mounsey and Sang. From Aultguish, they explored Beinn Dearg (see Sang's 'The Forbidden Mountains', *SMCJ*, 12/70 (1913), 215–20), then from Ullapool Sgùrr an Fhidleir, and from Inchnadamph they visited Quinag and Suilven. An attempt was made on the Fiddler, but the party were eventually forced off to the left. On Suilven, Sang climbed a difficult chimney on the lower band of rocks (*SMCJ*, 13/76 (1915), 201).

On 22 June, Ling, Raymond Bicknell and Claude Elliott (Head Master of Eton College from 1933) made the third ascent of Pillar's *North-East Climb* (*Diary*, Book 10, p. 20–1), returning from the summit by descending the *New West Climb*. Bicknell climbed frequently with Ling. He went on to become a leading alpinist, but eventually died in an accident on the Aiguilles d'Arves in 1927. The *North-East Climb* had first been climbed just two months before by the Abrahams on 21 April. On 25 April, Ling and McLaren had looked for the new route (knowing of it) but 'failed to hit it off' (*Diary*, Book 10, p.7). The second ascent (adding an improved 3-pitch finish avoided by the Abrahams) was made on 30 May by C.F. Stocks, Miss Capper, C.S. Worthington & J. Gaspard. This chronology is interesting: it shows that Ling was absolutely *au fait* with Lake District climbing. In fact, along with his usual companions (Glover, Raeburn, J.H. Bell, Goodeve and Bicknell – rough chronological order) Ling & Co. were just off the pace in the central Lake District area of Scafell, Gable and Pillar – a remarkable achievement, since all of their expeditions began with long marches from Seathwaite Farm in Borrowdale, or from Buttermere, and were carried out without benefit of the latest news from the Wasdale Climbing Book. The best effort of this group was probably Ling and Raeburn's early ascent of Pillar's Very Severe *North-West Climb* on 11 July 1908 (first ascent 1906), which added a new and harder variation finish (*Diary*, Book 7, p. 37–9). I regret to say that I was unaware of this bold ascent when I wrote my review of 'the Club in 1908'.

In July, John Hirst and Robert Workman climbed the *Crack Climb* on Stob Coire nam Beith (*SMCJ*, 12/69 (1912), 186), the first summer route on that peak. Also in July, Howard Drummond and James McCoss made the first ascent of the Shelter Stone Crag's *Forefinger Pinnacle* (*CCJ*, 7, 229)

The Alpine season was troubled by very poor weather, and most parties achieved little or nothing. In the Mont Blanc group, Ling, Sang, Charles Walker and Bicknell managed the North Ridge of the Pointe des Periades before the

Easter Sunday, 7 April 1912: *This group were on the Easter Meet at Ballachulish/Glen Coe. They took a motor boat to Inversanda for the day, and six of the party climbed Garbh Bheinn in awful weather.*

(L to R) Stuart Cumming, E.O. Wheeler (guest & President of the Canadian Alpine Club), obscured inside the doorway is C.I. Clark with his father W.I. Clark in front of him, in the striped suit is Henry Hoek, Lamond Howie, John Watson (guest), the Keeper 'K', J.C. Thomson and John Hirst (guest).

Missing is J.R. Young, who presumably took the photo. Photo: SMC Image archive.

weather broke. The party then walked round to Courmayeur, but had no better luck there. Bicknell then left to cross the Col du Géant to Montenvers. From the Val du Rhemes, they traversed the Bec de Zambeina, Cima d'Entrelor and Cima dell'Aouillié to Valsavarenche, and then crossed to Cogne where they met Harry Walker. From Cogne, the Herbetet was climbed. Later, Ling and the Walkers climbed Punta Patri and the West Ridge of the Punta Garin. Elsewhere, Goodeve and Backhouse made guided ascents of some Oberland peaks, the Inglis Clark family climbed Piz Cengalo, and permutations of Team MacRobert (MacRobert, Greig, Jeffrey, Menzies, Workman, Young) struggled up Mont Blanc de Seilon, the Dent Perroc, L'Eveque, and a few peaks in the Western Oberland on the handful of decent days in August.

In Norway, W.W. King spent July at Turtegro in the Hurrungane, and enjoyed glorious weather there. He climbed Store Skagastøltind with the proprietor Ole Berge, up by Vigedal's route and down by Heftye's. He then joined forces with two Norwegians, Grøndahl and Dybwad, to make a complete traverse of the three Skagastøltinde, and what may have been a first ascent of the North Ridge of Styggedalstind (Norwegian climbing history defeats me). Then with Dybwad and a Miss Hoff he climbed Riingstind by a new route, and continued over Midtmaradalstind. Finally, he climbed Dyrhaugstind with Mrs King.

Towards the end of the year, Raeburn appears in the record tied to a rope for the first time since January 1911. On 15 September, he and Ling climbed Pillar's *North-East Climb* (Ling's 3rd ascent of it in 1912! – see *Diary*, Book 10, p. 45). Raeburn visited Arran on the following weekend. Along with sister Ruth,

MacRobert and Young, he explored the rib between B1 and B2 Gullies on Cir Mhòr (*SMCJ*, 12/70 (1913), 236). Peering into the upper chasm of C Gully, he remarked that 'The slabs which form the sides .... are built on a really grand scale. Even the adepts of the most modern oromaniacal school, the "Naked-footed slab-crawlers" or "Adhesives" we might term them, would find it difficult to make anything of such a place.' Finally, he took part in a mass ascent of *Elephant Gully* of the Brack along with his sister and the entire Clark family on 3 November. Clark *père* had been the first to try this (in 1905), but was unaware of the first ascent by McLaren and the Shadbolt's in 1906, so that the party was dismayed to find a cairn at the gully exit (see Raeburn's article *SMCJ*, 12/70 (1913), 209–14). The Gully got its name from the suggestion that an elephant could pass behind the upper chockstone, Raeburn remarking that 'a 70 foot whale would have no difficulty due to waist measurement'. No conclusions should be drawn either from the existence of a contemporary photograph of an Elephant in Glen Croe in the Club Collection, or from William P. Ker's reference to the woolly elephants roaming Coiregrogan in his splendid poem 'Ben Vane' (*SMCJ*, 12/67 (1912), 46).

While the Club was achieving little in the stormy Alps, others were storming the unclimbed parts of the Cuillin. In early August the Irish climbers Conor O'Brien and Ernest Julian made the first climbs on the Coruisk flanks of Sgùrr Dearg and Sgùrr MhicCoinnich. Their *North-East Gully* on the latter peak was probably the most difficult climb on the island to date, and their routes were not repeated until Mike Dixon and Dan Stewart's ascents on 7 September 1951 (see Stuart Pedlar's unpublished *Across Unmeasured Space*, Volume 2, 2009). O'Brien climbed these routes in bare feet, his habitual practice. However, it is not known whether it was O'Brien that Raeburn had in mind when making the remark quoted in the paragraph above. Later in the month came the extraordinary visit to Skye of Siegfried Herford and John Laycock (see article in this issue by Noel Williams), which culminated in the exploration of the gullies of unknown Coire nan Laogh. At the same time Everard Steeple and Guy Barlow climbed *West Gully* on the Ghrunnda face of Sgùrr Alasdair (the first route on that face), and the *Direct Route* on the Eastern Buttress of Sròn na Cìche, possibly the best route of its standard in the Cuillin. They also added their *Chimney Route* on the same buttress, and the monstrous *Girdle Traverse* of Sròn na Cìche. Steeple & Barlow eventually became members, but not until 1921, just before publication of their wonderful Skye Guidebook.

Highlights of the Journal for the year were, besides those articles mentioned in this or last year's report, a series of rather misplaced antiquarian articles about 'The Islands of Loch Awe' by Mr & Mrs Wm. Douglas, German member Henry Hoek's bewildered encounter with the worst of our weather 'A Wet Day on Garbh Bheinn of Ardgour', 12/68 (1912), 104–6, in the company of Team MacRobert, Wm. Inglis Clark's review of 'Aonach Eagach', 12/69 (1912), 146–50, J.H. Bell's review of 'Ardgour', 12/69 (1912), 153–63, and Naismith's history of 'Bidein Druim nan Ramh', 12/69 (1912), 173–6.

The whole of Volume 12 may be downloaded in PDF or Kindle format from Google's <http://www.archive.org>.

Robin N Campbell

SCOTTISH SNOW PATCHES 2011

'The winter 2010/2011 was the third consecutive cold and snowy one but, much like the previous two, few patches survived.' This is the main conclusion of the annual survey of snow patches carried out in 2011. The two patches which survived were in Observatory Gully on Ben Nevis, and in the hollow below Sphinx Ridge, Garbh Choire Mòr, Braeriach. But for the heavy snow which fell in mid-October these patches would probably not have survived the mild weather in November 2011. Six small patches had survived the previous winter.

The report was authored by Iain Cameron, Adam Watson & David Duncan and was published by the Royal Meteorological Society ['Two Scottish snow patches survive until winter 2011/2012', *Weather*, 67/6 (2012)].

Information about winter snow conditions and many other useful winter links can be found at <www.winterhighland.info>.

50 YEARS AGO

This year marks the 50th anniversary of the accident in the Pamirs that robbed us of Robin Smith and Wilf Noyce.

Robin Smith in Creag Meagaidh.

Photo: Jimmy Marshall.

SCOTTISH MOUNTAINEERING TRUST - 2011
Scottish Charity SCO09117

The Trustees met on 3 June and 7 October 2011. During the course of these meetings support was given to Colwyn Jones – Iridium Satellite Phone, John Muir Trust – Quinag Footpath, Mountain Aid – Mountain Safety Day, R Crawford – Dundee Mountain Film Festival, Ochils Mountaineering Club – Inverardran Cottage, Jonathan Conville Mountaineering Trust – Scottish Winter Courses 2012, Mountaineering Council of Scotland – Access and Conservation, John Muir Trust – Wild Footpath Project and Mountaineering Council of Scotland – Visually Impaired Course.

The Trustees until December 2011 were Des Rubens (Chairman) (ex officio as immediate past President of the SMC), R Aitken, J T H Allen, R Anderson (ex officio as Convenor of the Publications Sub-Committee), W H Duncan, B S Findlay, A S Nisbet (ex officio as President of the SMC), C R Ravey, D N Williams (ex officio as Editor of the SMC Journal) and D Whalley. J Morton Shaw is the Trust Treasurer and James D Hotchkis is the Trust Secretary.

The present Directors of the Publications Company are R K Bott (Chairman), K Crocket, M G D Shaw, C M Huntley, C R Ravey and T Prentice (Publications Manager). C R Ravey (both a Director of Publications Company and Trustee) provides valuable liaison between the Publications Company and the Trust as does Rab Anderson in his capacity as Convenor of the Publications Sub-Committee.

The following grants have been committed by the Trustees during 2011:–

Cowlyn Jones – Iridium Satellite Phone	£400 grant
John Muir Trust – Quinag Footpath	£4,000 grant
Mountain Aid – Mountain Safety Day	£500 grant
R Crawford – Dundee Mountain Film Festival	£1,500 grant
Ochils Mountaineering Club – Inverardran Cottage	£5,000 grant and £5,000 loan
Jonathan Conville Mountaineering Trust – Scottish Winter Courses 2012	£1,508 grant
Mountaineering Council of Scotland – Access and Conservation	£12,600 per annum for the the next three years
John Muir Trust – Wild Footpath Project	£10,000 per annum for the next three years
Mountaineering Council of Scotland – Visually Impaired Course	£2,310 grant

The Trustees record their gratitude to John Allen (who retired by rotation) for his services to the Trust.

J. D. Hotchkis
Secretary

MUNRO MATTERS

By Dave Broadhead (Clerk of the List)

ANOTHER YEAR and another file bulging with fascinating letters and lists to review before passing them on to the National Library. This is the first report to cover the calendar year 1 January to 31 December (2011). As ever the five columns below give number, name, and year of Compleation of Munros, Tops and Furths as appropriate. *SMC member **LSCC member.

4711	David Blair	2011		
4712	Chris Green	2010		
4713	Sheila M. Russell	2010		
4714	Tom Ferguson	2010		
4715	Miles Goff	2010		
4716	Ken Roxburgh	2010		
4717	Alison Mason	2010		
4718	William S. Burr	2010		
4719	Colin Ward	2009		
4720	Ian McMenemin	2002		
4721	Colin Cadden	2011		
4722	Roger Eastwood	2003		
4723	Mike Jones	2003		
4724	Douglas Smart	2010		
4725	Graham P. Sadler	2011		
4726	*Brian Dullea	2010		
4727	Doug Brown	2011		
4728	Stephen Peatfield	2011		
4729	Mark Longley	2011		
4730	Bart Doornbosch	2011		
4731	Willem Vermeulen	2011		
4732	Ian Elliot	2011		
4733	A.S. Digby Harris	2011		
4734	Sheila Snowden	2011	2011	2009
4735	Chas Newstead	2011		
4736	John Pearson	2011		
4737	Frank Coyle	2011		
4738	T. Roy Kenniston	2011		
4739	Fiona Stewart	2011		
4740	Eric Davies	2011		
4741	Jane Anderson	2011		
4742	Jim Watson	2011		
4743	Ian C. Buchanan	2011		
4744	Adam M. Gouldsworthy	2011		
4745	Roland Ingram	2010		
4746	Tim Hawkes	2011		
4747	Stuart Penny	2011		
4748	Chantal E.N. Elson	2011		
4749	Paul H. Kidner	2011		
4750	Christopher Paul Thorpe	2011		
4751	Iain Cope	2011		
4752	Brian W. Keighley	2011		
4753	John Whitfield	2011		
4754	Peter Atkinson	2011		
4755	Anja Bruske	2011		
4756	Jean Gaskell	2011		
4757	Derek Caborn	2011		
4758	Mark Dutton	2009		
4759	Gayle S. Martin	2011		
4760	*Di Gilbert	2011		
4761	John Harris	2010		
4762	Alasdair T.M. Cairns	2011		
4763	Sylvia Woodford	2011		
4764	*Cliff Smith	2011		
4765	Andrew Steel	2011		
4766	Susan Davison	2011		
4767	Chris Murray	2011		
4768	Roger H. Webber	2011		
4769	Mel Smith	2011		
4770	Andrew Armitage	2011		
4771	Alan Wright	2011		
4772	Margaret Jones	2011		
4773	Colin Jones	2011		
4774	Pippa Manson	2011		
4775	Alexandra Macleod	2011		
4776	Stuart W. Cummings	2011		
4777	Richard Dixon	2011		
4778	Wang Liston	2011		
4779	Lorna M. Bell	2011		
4780	Pam Long	2011		
4781	John Ibbetson	2011		
4782	Geoff Butcher	2011		
4783	Helen Claire Boothman	2011		
4784	Michael Boothman	2011		
4785	Graham Roberts	2011		
4786	John Hall	1999		
4787	Brent Browning	2011		
4788	John Haddock	2001		
4789	Andrew Heathcock	2011		
4790	David Geere	2011	2011	
4791	Margaret Sweet	2011		
4792	Alan D. Gilroy	2011		
4793	Tony Carlyle	2011	2011	2009
4794	Stanley D. Morris	1991		
4795	Ronald A. Morris	1992		
4796	Colin Bradley	2011		
4797	Richard Simmons	2011		
4798	Bob Garner	2011		
4799	Dave Johnson	2011		
4800	Ian J. Swann	2011		
4801	Anne Diack	2011		
4802	Aidan Joy	2011		
4803	Susan Low	2011		
4804	David Bethune	2011		

4805	Shona Jackson	2011		4864	Colin McBeath	2011	
4806	Fraser Jackson	2011		4865	Jacqueline Verth	2011	
4807	John H. Ramsden	2011		4866	John Verth	2011	
4808	Frank G. Joyce	2011		4867	Clare A. Rainbow	2011	
4809	Colin Patrick	2011		4868	Dolores Steen	2011	
4810	Malcolm Pounder	2011		4869	David A.Steen	2011	
4811	Robin E. Beard	2011	2011	4870	John Mulgrew	2011	
4812	Neil Clements	2011		4871	Ronnie Wade	2011	2011
4813	Pam Kinnaird	2009		4872	Douglas Robin	2011	
4814	Ian Lewis	2008		4873	Alex D. Russell	2011	
4815	John Butterick	2011		4874	Austin Dunn	2011	
4816	Bret H. Collins	2011		4875	Gordon Wylie	2005	
4817	Gordon Mackie	2011		4876	J. Elwyn Williams	2011	
4818	Susan Brown	2011		4877	Sheila Hobson	2011	
4819	John Brown	2011		4878	Phil Dover	2011	
4820	Ben Stobbs	2011		4879	Peter McGowan	2011	
4821	Denis M. Wilson	2011		4880	Anne Morrissey	2011	
4822	David Dowden	2004		4881	Terry Hoy	2011	
4823	Robert Davis	2011		4882	Linda Tomalin	2011	
4824	Sheona York	2008		4883	David Williamson	2011	
4825	John McGrath	2011		4884	Tom O'Connell	2011	
4826	Richard McGrath	2011		4885	Alex Robinson	2011	
4827	Dianne Pallett	2011		4886	John P. Rosie	2011	
4828	Ian Pallett	2011		4887	Stephen R. Lister	2011	
4829	Roger A. Smith	2011		4888	Charles Craig	2011	
4830	Patricia Thomson	2011		4889	Paul Milhench	2011	
4831	Cathy Meunier	2011		4890	Peter H. Grayson	2011	
4832	Phillip Dungate	2011		4891	Philip Newton	2011	
4833	Sandy G. Macdonald	2005		4892	David Parminter	2011	
4834	Steven Morrice	2011		4893	Rod Cook	2011	
4835	Margery Johnston	2011		4894	Valerie Springett	2011	
4836	Jean I. Young	2011		4895	Tom Clarke	2011	
4837	Peter Coupe	2011		4896	Martin Buchan	2011	
4838	Deborah Howard	2011		4897	Norma Bisset	2011	
4839	Malcolm Longair	2011		4898	Ron Bisset	2011	
4840	Ron Norman	2011		4899	Geoffrey H. Watkins	2011	
4841	Andrew Howie	2011		4900	Allan J. Reid	2011	
4842	Barrie Haworth	2011		4901	Richard Haydock	2011	
4843	Tony Hallard	2004	2011 2000	4902	Alistair Barnard	2011	
4844	*Paul Manson	2011		4903	Brian Watt	2011	
4845	Jeremy R. Purvis	2011		4904	Michael McAnenay	2011	
4846	Stewart Blagg	2011		4905	Alan Edwards	2011	
4847	Peter Westrick	2011		4906	Elaine J. Speirs	2011	
4848	Richard Collins	2011		4907	Cameron A. Speirs	2011	
4849	Douglas A. Doig	2011		4908	Philip Lightfoot	2011	
4850	Martine McIndoe	2011		4909	Donald McGill	2011	
4851	Ken McLeish	2011		4910	William J. Townsend	2011	
4852	Neil K. Cameron	2011		4911	Michael Smith	2011	
4853	Lynda Langlands	2011		4912	Hazel M. D. Gibbs	2011	
4854	Scott Langlands	2011		4913	Terence P. Heyward	2011	
4855	Tim Denvir	2011		4914	Steve Murray	2011	
4856	Jonathan Richards	2011		4915	Jamie Bankhead	2011	
4857	Gerry Webb	2011		4916	Jennifer Logan	2011	
4858	Tim Flisher	2011		4917	Gordon Lacey	2011	
4859	Jim Roche	2011		4918	Steve Beresford	2011	
4860	David Nicol2011			4919	Corrinna Paterson	2011	
4861	Catherine E. Mansfield	2011		4920	Richard Paterson	2011	
4862	Alan Puckrin	2011		4921	Bill Wickham	2010	
4863	Tom Turton	2011		4922	Oliver Bartrum	2011	

4923	Paul Keen	2011
4924	Derek M. Barnes	2001
4925	Alex Smith	2011
4926	Mick Bashford	2011
4927	Karine Butler	2011
4928	David Butler	2011
4929	Colm Smith	2011
4930	John C. Gay	2011
4931	Philippa Cockman	2011
4932	Declan Phelan	2011
4933	F. Adams	2011
4934	Kate Durkacz	2011
4935	Ian Durkacz	2011
4936	Alex Cook	2011
4937	Yvonne Abson	2008

4938	Derek Morley	2008	
4939	George Abson	2008	
4940	Neal Clark	2011	
4941	Mark Crawford	2011	
4942	*Andrew Fraser	2011	
4943	Christine Hill	2010	
4944	Keith Hill	2010	
4945	Madeleine Younger	2011	2011
4946	Kate Walshaw	2011	
4947	Alasdair Law	2011	
4948	Annette Hardman	2011	
4949	Duncan Buchanan	2011	
4950	Ronald Cameron	1998	
4951	George Walkingshaw	2011	
4952	Tony Davies	2011	

BEFORE delving into the highlights of the letters, a brief summary of some simple data to allow comparison with last year (shown in brackets): New Munroists 242 (217); comprising males 78% (78%); resident in Scotland 54% (59%); couples 16% (15%); average age 55 (53); size of Compleation party 11 (15); time taken 24 (22) years.

COMPOSING a song is sometimes part of the celebrations. Alison Mason (4717) 'included a song my husband wrote for my Compleation party – it has the name of every Munro in it!' *Ali's Munros* can be sung to the tune of *The Irish Washerwoman* and starts 'Your first, from Glen Nevis was Mullach nan Coirean/ And next day the Ben with its snow covered cairn/ That's what must have triggered the bug I suppose/ And for 42 years you've been climbing Munros.' This jolly ditty continues in similar style for a remarkable 25 verses.

DISTANCES feature in a number of letters. Richard Simmons (4797) counted up that 'it has taken eight years using the bulk of my holidays. My distance has added up to 1550 miles walked and 524,000ft climbed (including the ones that took several attempts).' Christopher Paul Thorpe (4750) calculated 'I have averaged about 2 to 3 Munros per round trip from Sheffield with each trip approx. 800 to 1000 miles. It has been well worth the driving!' Gerald McPartlin (1644) accomplished what he claims is 'the fastest Round by a pensioner (aged 66), with the help of a camper-van. I walked on 84 days, covered 1,191 miles and climbed 438,000 feet with 140 different companions.' Gerry raised a remarkable £50,000 for the 'David Gemmell Living Memorial Fund' – further details <http://dglmlf.wordpress.com>

EXPATRIATE Compleations confirm that once hooked on bagging there is only one possible outcome, whatever the distance involved. John Pearson (4736) justified his 46 year Round by mentioning 'that since 1973 I have lived abroad, in Brussels until 2001 and since then in France…so my Round may be one of the dearest and a probable factor in Ryanair's success.' Geoff Butcher (4782) accomplished his 14 year Round from bases in Kent (2 Munros), Aberdeen (190 Munros) and Texas (92 Munros). Aidan Joy (4802) 'emigrated to Australia with my family in 2004 with 53 Munros still to climb. I have been able to return to Scotland on eight occasions to climb them all. I am slowly working my way through the Corbetts too.' Putting these admirable efforts in the shade must be Frank G. Joyce (4808) who 'was challenged to complete a round of the Munros about a year after I moved permanently to the USA in 1996 from Chester, England. I have finally Compleated after 13 trips over 13 years.' He also e-mailed a photo of his Pennsylvania car registration plate BAGD 283.

FAVOURITE Munros include Lochnagar, nominated by Susan Davison (4766) 'on a fabulous winter day when we could see snowy peaks to the horizon in every direction.' Graham Roberts (4785) gave a top six: Sgùrr nan Ceathreamhnan; Beinn Fhionnlaidh; Beinn Fhada; Seana Bhraigh; Blà Bheinn and Ben Alder. Donald McGill (4909) nominated his 'best single day on the hills in Scotland? A summer traverse of the full Cuillin Ridge.' Annette Hardman (4948) also noted 'the highlight has to be the Cuillin Munros completed in my 50th year and in perfect weather.'

GOLDEN Munroists this year include Wang Liston (4778) (58 years), Margery Johnston (4835) (51 years), Peter Coupe (4837) (50 years), Phil Dover (4878) (51 years), Alex Cook (4936) (51 years) and Tony Davies (4952) (52 years).

HISTORICAL links are always interesting. Alan Puckrin (4862) 'did my final Munro with my uncle, Finlay McKenzie who was GP for Kirriemuir for many years and visited the Munro family home on a number of occasions during the course of his duties.' Veteran member, Miles Hutchinson (23) reported a Graham Compleation on Beinn a' Chearcaill. Among the party was Jill Dodgson, daughter of the late Colin Dodgson (16) who was also the first Grahamist. Miles notes that 'at 85 I find the Munros rather hard going but there are plenty of lower hills to be enjoyed before I hang up my boots!'

INSPIRATIONAL Munroists include John Ibbetson (4781) who 'met with some serious difficulties along the way because my kidneys started to fail in 2000 when I still had around 90 Munros left to do. I did as many as I could before they failed completely a couple of years later, leaving me with 33 to go. I spent nearly five years on dialysis. By the time I got a transplant in 2008 I had four Munros left to do. These four have taken me a while to get round to as they are all fairly remote and I took a long time to get fit again after multiple surgery.' Reporting her Donald Compleation, Hazel Strachan (3438) 'was looking forward to Compleating a fourth Munro Round. Unfortunately the physiotherapist treating my pelvis condition had other plans. From only managing half an hour walking uphill after weekly physio sessions for almost four months to walking a five hour day over rough hills, the Donalds have been ideal training ground.'

JOINING the queue to Compleat on the ever popular final summit of Ben More (Mull), Charlie Craig (4888) and his party of 12 arrived half an hour after John Mulgrew (4870). On the same summit Bill Wickham (4921) 'met a pair of Geordies who were also celebrating their Compleation. They'd forgotten their bottle & were good enough to share ours!'

KEEN young lads, Tom O'Connell (4884) and Alex Robinson (4885), both students at Exeter University, accomplished a continuous car-free Round. Starting on Ben More (Mull) on 1 August 2011 and finishing an amazing 48 days

6 hours and 56 minutes later on Ben Hope on 18 September, raising money for DecAid. More details on <www.decaidmunromission.blogspot.com>. Aged 21, Alex becomes the youngest self-propelled continuous Munroist. Another former 'Youngest Munroist' and still very keen, President Andy Nisbet belatedly reported a fourth Munro Round Compleation on Stob a' Choire Odhair on 29 December 2009. 'The original plan was to do a new route on Stob Gabhar and then finish on that, but there was deep snow and my companion refused to climb Stob a' Choire Odhar first (he'd done it before). So we did a new route each on Stob Gabhar (I called mine *Munrovin*) and I was left to bag the last in darkness and deteriorating weather and spindrift.'

LATE notifications are always welcome, on the basis of better late than never. Jonathan Richards (4856) Compleated in 1996, followed by Tops in 1998 but waited until he finished his Furths in 2011 before writing. He explained 'the gap between Tops and Furths was filled with Alpine 4000ers, a couple of Himalayan trips and a wife and children.' Another excuse was offered by Christine Hill (4943) who explained 'Keith (4944) proposed at the summit and the rest as they say is history. Part of the reason for not writing earlier was the chaos of organising a wedding!' Ronald Cameron (4950) Compleated in 1998 and admitted 'after due reflection I think I'd like my name added to the List.' He went on to explain 'my greatest current Munro obsession involves badgering the OS to correct sloppy Gaelic in the place names on its maps. I've lost count of the number of names I've persuaded them to change but they include a number of Munros. They were very reluctant to change Stob Diamh (Cruachan) to Stob Daimh but eventually gave in. Such carelessness should not be tolerated.'

MOTIVATION comes from many sources. Stuart Penny (4747) reported 'my employer encouraged me by offering to give £1,000 to a charity if I Compleated. The cash will go to the Children's Critical care Unit at Hull Royal Infirmary where my daughter is a nurse.' Tom Ferguson (4714) reported 'I had a good day on Ben Vrackie yesterday where I reckon females outnumbered males by 3 to 1.' Susan Low (4803) 'used my weekends climbing Munros as training for expeditions to the Alps, Nepal, Kilimanjaro and Aconcagua.' Sandy G. Macdonald (4833) hoped 'my name being on the list may inspire my sons and grandchildren to take to the hills!'

NO review would be complete without mention of the many and varied amendments received, 73 this year, compared with 66 last year. David I. Nixon (1150) finished his third Munro Round on Luinne Bheinn on the same day as his Corbetts, Compleated on Sgùrr a' Choire-bheithe. Lindsay Boyd (1801) finished his fifth Munro Round on Christmas Day, the same date as his Corbetts in 2004 and Grahams in 2009. Diana J. Harkins (539) and Frank Baillie (4691) joined the 'Full House' List which now stands at 22. Member Mike Dixon (959) reported a second Round of Furths, Compleated on Skiddaw 'arriving in the Lakes via Colonsay, the Trossachs, Arran and Ailsa Craig (the best half day outing in Scotland).' Anne Butler (3366) Compleated her third Munro Round within a year, despite the severe winter and having to be airlifted off Liathach because of the fire. Robert B. Gunn (954) wrote to complain that his Furths Compleation, reported in 2000 had still not been added. Sorry Robert, I am always happy to correct mistakes and omissions, however small!

AMENDMENTS

The eight columns give number, name and the year of each Compleation of Munros, Tops, Furths, Corbetts, Grahams and Donalds

Number	Name	Munros	Tops	Furths	Corbetts	Grahams	Donalds
1150	David I. Nixon	1993 1998 2010		1994	2010		
1801	Lindsay Boyd	1997 2000 2002 2008 2010	2002		2004	2009	2010
539	Diana J. Harkins	1986	2010	1989	2009	2009	2009
3863	Bob Garrett	2007		2004			
3680	Peter John Herman	2006	2011				
3497	Richard Knight	2005			2010		2011
3062	Manoj Patel	2003			2011		
4691	Frank Baillie	1997	1999		2009	2010	2008 2011
959	*Mike Dixon	1991 2009	2008 2011	2000	1996	2002	2005
1335	James P. Fish	1994		2007			
954	Robert B. Gunn	1991	1991	2000			
2658	**Julia Banks	2001	2010				
2390	Colin Scott	2000 2008		2010			
433	*Brian Shackleton	1985	2009		2005		
1806	Ross Gervais	1997			2010		2011
2551	Carole A. A. Scott	2001			2011		
2552	Alan P. Scott	2001			2011		
107	*Andrew Nisbet	1972 1984 1996 2009	1991	1991	2000		
4305	Michael Earnshaw	2009		2010	2011		2011
1479	Stephen Hartley	1994	1994	1969	2011		
3366	Anne Butler	2005 2010 2011			2010		
3789	Stewart Watson	2007		2011			
2125	James Henderson	1999 2011			2008		
1644	Gerald McPartlin	1996 2010		1996			
4151	Norman Wares	2008	2010	2011			
759	Alistair M. Beeley	1990	1990	1990	2003		
4088	David McSporran	2008			2011		
2943	Donald R. Sutherland	2003			2006		

No.	Name						
216	Jeremy Fenton	1980	1984	1982	2011		
		1995					
		2005					
319	Ken P. Whyte	1984	1987	1987	2000	2000	2000
		2010	2011	2011			
3493	Andrew Lawson	2005			2011		
2871	Peter Hamilton	1992		2002	1997		
		2002			2011		
		2008					
3987	Colin Lees	2004					
		2007					
		2011					
23	*Miles Hutchinson	1955	1955	1970	1992	2009	
		1992		1998			
		1998					
		2004					
1407	Jacqueline Cummings	1995			2011		
2346	David Allison	2000	2003	2002	2008		2011
2900	Richard Baker	2003	2011				
4691	Frank Baillie	1997	1999	2011	2009	2010	2008
							2011
3438	Hazel Strachan	2005					2011
		2008					
		2010					
3645	W. Alan Johnston	2006			2011		
3646	Susanne Johnston	2006			2011		
4572	John Spiers	2010		2011			
4037	Sue Lyth	2008	2011	2011			
2433	Alan Rowan	2000		2011	2009		
		2011					
3217	Ian K. Ratcliffe	2004					
		2011					
431	Mark McCann	1985		1990	2011		
		1998					
1265	Dorothy McCann	1993			2011		
1148	Colin Wilson	1993		2005	2000	2005	
		2011					
1266	Joan Wilson	1993		2005	2000	2005	
		2011					
1572	David Eccles	1996	2011				
		2011					
1173	Bernhard Lapp	1993	2011				
1238	Raymond J. Anderson	1993	2011	2003			
1222	Gilmour Strang	1992	1992	2008			
		2011					
3263	Eddie Wilkinson	2004			2009	2011	
3264	Jeanie Clabbie	2004			2009	2011	
375	Robert H. Macdonald	1984	2008	1989			
		1987					
		1990					

No.	Name						
375	Robert H. Macdonald (continued)						
		1992					
		1995					
		2002					
		2007					
		2011					
1067	Frank Malloy	1992			2011		
		2002					
2567	Graham Ingram	2001			2011		
1711	Stewart Newman	1997	1998	1998	2006	2011	
604	Nev Wiseman	1988			1999		
605	Mal Newlyn	1988			1999		
606	Ian Holland	1988			1999		
3593	Ambrose Gillham	1992	2011	2011			
335	Graeme Carracher	1984	2011	2011			
		2011					
3885	David S. Batty	1994	2011				
		2011					
3044	Brian McWilliam	2003					
		2011					
1879	*Peter Stewart	1997	1997				
2241	Mary Abercrombie	1999			2011		
2242	Colin Abercrombie	1999			2011		
3943	John R.G. Rogerson	2006		2011			
3964	Brian Fraser	2007		2011			
1331	John Mackay	1994	1994	1997	2002	2006	2002
		2011	2011				2011

OVERSEAS Compleations never cease to amaze! Dutch activity continued with Bart Doornbosch (4730) and Willem Vermeulen (4731) Compleating on Ben More (Mull), accompanied by three other Dutch Compleaters among their 26 friends and family. Bart wrote 'life after Compleation will exist of doing the most beautiful ones once again' while Willem promised 'finishing the Munros won't stop me going to Scotland!' Chantal E. N. Elson (4748) became the second Dutch woman to Compleat, though now living in Cheshire. She climbed her last 150 in 18 months, raising £25 per summit for the charity 'World Peace Flame', the cost of a cataract operation in India. These enthusiasts keep in touch on a website <www.buitensport-schotland.nl>. Anne Morrissey (4880) counted up 'it has taken me 13 years and 27 trips to Scotland' from her native Ireland. She wonders 'how many Irish people have Compleated the Munros?' Sorry not to have been counting, as there must be quite a few by now. Writing from Austria, Anja Bruske (4755) 'has followed the Munros only during my annual holidays (usually 3 weeks in spring) because I had not the privilege of living in the UK. But the long journeys were well worth it.' Bernhard Lapp (1173) became the first overseas Munroist to Compleat the Tops, noting 'since 1993 I have reclimbed 70 Munros in 5 holidays (from Germany) to Compleat the Tops.' The SMCJ Editor also tipped me off about <www.bgmb.de> a blog by 'bloody German Munro baggers'.

POSTHUMOUS Compleations are occasionally received. Stanley D. Morris (4794) was notified by his brother Ronald A. Morris (4795). They both Compleated in the early 1990s but it was not until after Stanley's tragic death from cancer in June 2011 that Ronald decided to register. He explained 'I had climbed most of my Munros with my brother and have renewed my interest in hillwalking and find that is where I can best reconnect with Stan recalling very fond memories of our times on the hills.' Jean Gaskell (4756) recounts 'In July 2005 my beautiful 17 year old daughter died in a car crash. How was I to carry on? I went in search of help to Scotland and made friends who suggested we climb the Munros. In August 2005 I climbed Bidean nam Bian and knew that this was to be my greatest support through a time of great anguish. They have not failed me.'

QUIRKY Compleations include Jeremy R. Purvis (4845) who started on his 40th birthday and Compleated on his 50th. Colin McBeath (4864) 'enjoyed many gastronomic delights on the Munros, including smoked eel on Sgùrr a' Chaorachain, various malts and fine dark chocolate and a particularly tasty Arbroath Smokie on Ben Chonzie!' Phil Dover (4878) was able to enjoy a 'birthday/Munro cake cooked by my wife and iced by my daughter' as Compleation 'coincided almost with my 70th birthday.' Robert H. MacDonald (375) Compleated his eighth Munro Round on Beinn Fhionnlaidh, 'the sixth time that I finished a Round on this hill…for nothing other than a bit of British eccentricity.'

REACHING a balance between Munro bagging and other commitments presents its challenges. Mick Bashford (4926) worked part-time and 'was able to fly up to Scotland on a Wednesday evening, walk Thursday, Friday and Saturday, then fly home Saturday evening and have Sunday with my other half several times a year.' Alasdair Law (4947) reported 'my first summit was way back in 1986 with my then (nearly) 6 year old son for company. I am delighted to report he was with me on Bynack Mor, my final summit.' Tony Davies (4952) seems to have got it right too and Compleated on Beinn nan Aighenan with his wife, 'three daughters, two son in laws and three grandchildren.'

SKIS get an occasional mention. Member Brian Dullea (4726) 'Completed on Sgòr an Lochain Uaine on 26 November 2010, solo, on Nordic skis, from Achlean car park in Glen Feshie.' Roland Ingram (4745) reported 'my Round includes nearly 30 ski Munros.'

THE MUNRO SOCIETY have been up to more shenanigans as their 'Heighting Campaign' continued and I was very sad to hear of the demise of Beinn a' Chlaidheimh, the worthy start (or finish) of the 'Fisherfield Six'. My impression is that most Munroists find these changes to the List a bit confusing and unsettling, especially now they are becoming more frequent.

UNUSUAL stories sometimes emerge. Stuart W. Cummings (4776) recalled 'my first Munro was way back in 1975 while a student at Strathclyde University. With a number of fellow students and lecturers we left Rowardennan car park at midnight to begin our ascent of Ben Lomond where a few hours later together with some 200–300 other walkers we watched the sunrise. The walk was memorable for the fact that during the ascent, two of our party, a fellow Mexican student and his German girlfriend invited us to their wedding. A few hundred yards later we learned this was to be at 9 a.m. at the Glasgow Registry Office. After some very early morning coffee at the Buchanan Arms Hotel in Drymen we duly made our way there and celebrated the wedding by sharing a couple of bottles of champagne before heading to our respective beds.' John Harris (4761) recalled climbing his first Munro, Ben Lomond 'in June 1970. I had to get a bus from Faifley to Clydebank, then the train to Balloch and finally the Maid of the Loch to Rowardennan. We had to complete the climb for the return of the Maid of the Loch or we'd have been stranded in Rowardennan.' Alexandra Macleod (4775) announced most alarming future plans – 'to give my knees and ankles a break!'

VOCATIONAL details are not required to register, though some correspondents are keen to disclose. Mark Longley (4729) described himself as 'a Train Driver, living and working in London.' Deborah Howard (4838) and Malcolm Longair (4839) gave details of their web-pages which revealed them to be Cambridge Professors of Architectural History and Natural Philosophy respectively. Malcolm is also a former Astronomer Royal of Scotland. Given away by his headed notepaper, Ron Norman (4840) is actually Sir Ron, OBE, DL and author of 'Odd Man Out in the Alps'. John Mulgrew (4870) described himself as 'PGA Master Professional' and may be the first such to Compleat. To celebrate, John 'hit a few drives off the top of Ben More (Mull), even though I could hardly stand.' Jamie Bankhead (4915) 'is the Centre Manager at the Ice Factor in Kinlochleven.'

WEATHER of course features in many reports, particularly those who had the misfortune to choose a poor day for Compleation. Gordon Mackie (4817) was a bit more objective, accumulating a record 'over 48 years, in all 4 seasons, with 285 data points.

View from the Top	61%
Good day out but no view from the Top.	24%
Wet and miserable with little visibility.	15%

I have always found this evolving trend surprising in that I have had a view from the Top. It is not what is generally thought to be the case in the Scottish hills.' Denis M. Wilson (4821) achieved a remarkable Round, starting on Cairngorm in 1949, 'during which I had a view from every one (I believe there is a name for this?) and did not count an ascent without a view.' Sheona York (4824) reported 'only 35 in truly awful weather, only struck by lightning once.' Sheona also documented her Round in 'a serious diary with photos , which now amounts to a small book' and kindly sent a copy on CD, to add to the ever growing archive of fascinating material held for posterity in the National Library. Tim Flisher (4858) reported 'notwithstanding Scotland's dreadful reputation, I have reached the majority of summits in clear weather. I was caught in thunder storms on three different Munros in 2007 but not any other time.'

XTRA-TERRESTRIAL is the only explanation I can think of for Derek M. Barnes (4924). Writing to report a bumper Compleation of Munros (in 2001), Corbetts, Grahams and Donalds he claimed 'I had not appreciated that Compleater Lists existed!'

YEAR long career break was the opportunity for Elaine J. Spiers (4906) and Cameron A. Speirs (4907) to achieve a lifelong ambition. Starting on Sgùrr nan Coireachan on 6 November 2010 they finished on Braeriach on 1 October 2011. Clocking up 174,252 metres of ascent and walking 2,794 kilometres they also raised over £1000 for Cancer Research UK. More details on <www.scotlandinview.com>.

ZEBRAS have never featured in any correspondence, though I saw plenty on my summer holiday in Tanzania, returning to a pile of 45 letters to work through. No rest for the Clerk of the List who is always happy to register a Compleation or amendment. Please write to Dave Broadhead, Cul Mor, Drynie Park North, Muir of Ord, IV6 7RP. For a Munro or Corbett Compleation certificate, please enclose an A4 sae (with the correct postage please). Once you have received a number, a Compleation photo can be e-mailed or posted to the Webmaster for the popular photo-galleries at <www.smc.org.uk/Munros/MunroistsCompleatists.php?T=5>

Enjoy your hills

Dave Broadhead
Clerk of the List

*Elaine &
Cameron Speirs
celebrate
completion on
the summit of
Braeriach,
1 October 2011.*

THE MOUNTAIN RESCUE COMMITTEE OF SCOTLAND

Annual Statistics Report 2011

The Mountain Rescue Committee of Scotland Incident Statistics and the information in this report may be reproduced free of charge in any format or medium for research, private study or for internal circulation within an organisation. This is subject to the information being reproduced accurately and not used in a misleading context. The material must be acknowledged as Mountain Rescue Committee of Scotland copyright, and the title of the publication specified.

All enquires about the content of this report or any other matter associated with Incident Reporting should be directed to the Association of Chief Police Officers Scotland (ACPOS) on whose behalf the MR statistical data is held.

Introduction

The data reported here has been collated by the MRCofS Incident Reporting System, which was initiated in 2010. Every attempt has been taken to ensure the accuracy and completeness of the information given in this report. All teams have been given the opportunity to examine the summary data that is contained in this document.

Since the production of the 2010 report the ownership of the data relating to Mountain Rescue Incidents has been clarified. The MRCofS Statistician receives the data from the Scottish teams, and produces the report on behalf of Association of Chief Police Officers Scotland (ACPOS). The incident reports and their contents are the property of the eight police forces in Scotland. It is intended that a fully electronic system run by the police, using a Scotland-wide database will be introduced in the next year. Once this is in place, the role of the MRCofS statistician will change to that of interpreting the data generated and the production of future versions of this report. This will be a very welcome reduction in the workload of the statistican, who like his predecessors, and indeed every Scottish Mountain Rescue team member provides his time on a voluntary basis.

The information given in this report should be taken as a summary of the work of the Scottish Mountain Rescue Teams over 2011. No attempt has been made to analyse the information in detail. Factual data with no analysis other than the noting of historical trends is presented. The intention is to let the statistics themselves demonstrate the value and service that the voluntary teams have provided, in terms of assistance to the mountaineering community and the wider population, within their remit for land based search and rescue in Scotland.

Executive Summary

There were a total of 573 incidents in 2011 during which the combined resources of all MRTs, the SCRO and the two SARDA teams expended around 24,000 team member hours. The number of incidents and time expended varies considerably between teams, Police authorities and areas within Scotland. Following a decrease in the number of incidents in 2010, 2011 shows an increase in the number of incidents to which teams were called out. This is the continuance of a general trend over the last 10 years.

A total of 693 people were assisted of which 270 were injured and 52 died. These, are all slightly increased from the 2010 figures.

The number of non-mountaineering incidents decreased to 158 compared to 194 in 2010. This is equivalent to 27% of all incidents as opposed to 36% recorded in 2010. Mountaineering incidents are those where the activity undertaken was hillwalking, rock scrambling or climbing in either summer or winter. Nonmountaineering incidents include Snow and Water sports, Mountain Biking, missing persons and walkers in lowland, rural and urban areas. The percentage of non-mountaineering call-outs for each team varies considerably, but broadly reflects trends in previous years.

45% of all non-mountaineering incidents were searches either for people reported missing including despondants (individuals who may self-harm).

Helicopters from the RAF, RN or the MCA assisted in 34% of all incidents. There was also a small but significant contribution from police helicopters assisting in searches, and Scottish Ambulance Service Aircraft evacuating casualties.

SARDA dog teams assisted in almost 26% of all incidents. This includes 20 occasions when SARDA was called out directly by the Police, where no other MRT was required. Of these 1.5% involved both SARDA Scotland and SARDA South Scotland.

Continuing the trends of previous years, summer hillwalking is the activity which results in by far the highest number of incidents. Mobile phones remain the most common method of asking the emergency services for assistance, though for approximately 10% of incidents the method of contacting was not recorded by the team.

The number of rock climbing incidents (13 for 2011) is a marked increase on 2010 when there were only six. However, it still remains a small proportion of the total number of incidents and a single year's high figure may not be a major change in the frequency of climbing accidents in the longer term.

The small number of incidents involving avalanches and cornice remains very low. There were no incidents involving cornices reported in 2011, in spite of the long winter.

19% of all incidents resulted from a slip or trip. People who were lost, overdue or reported missing were cited in 12-15% of reports.

Leg injuries were by far the most common in incidents. This follows the pattern observed over many years.

Finally it should be noted that in 2011 an additional team joined the MRCofS – Hebrides Search and Rescue (HEBSAR). Their incident reports have been included in this report.

Overall Statistics
The summary data for years 2001–2011 is shown in Table 1 below.

Table 1: Summary Data from 2001–2011

Year	Mountaineering	Non-mountaineering	Total
2001	347	65	412
2002	258	81	339
2003	289	101	390
2004	308	90	398
2005	321	137	458
2006	315	119	434
2007	333	145	478
2008	387	188	575
2009	402	172	574
2010	340	194	534
2011	415	158	573

There has been a general increase in incidents over the last ten years. From year to year numbers vary up and down considerably, so it is the longer term trend that is more revealing.

Generally, teams are busier than they were in 2010.

Types of Incidents

Incidents have for a number of years been separated into two broad categories. Mountaineering incidents represent those which the teams were originally created to respond to. Mountaineering Incidents are defined as those involving Hillwalking in Summer or Winter, Scrambling, Rock Climbing and Snow/Ice Climbing. They still represent the majority of incidents that teams are called out to, however as a percentage of the total number of incidents they are decreasing over the longer term. The 2011 results show an increase in the percentage of mountaineering incidents; future years will show whether this is a one-off results or a reversal of the longer term pattern.

Table 2: Mountaineering and Non-Mountaineering figures for 2011 (Figures for 2010 shown in brackets)

Type of Incident	Incidents	Fatalities	Injured	People Assisted
Mountaineering	415 (340)	21 (16)	210 (198)	553 (488)
Non-Mountaineering	158 (194)	31 (29)	60 (57)	140 (171)
TOTAL	573 (534)	52 (45)	270 (255)	693 (659)

The proportion of non-mountaineering incidents has been steadily increasing over time as a proportion of the total number of incidents. In 2011 this trend has reversed with 27 % of the total number of incidents falling into the nonmountaineering category a fall from 2010's figure of 36%. There is a huge variation in the percentage of non-mountaineering incidents from team to team, varying from zero to 90%. For 2011 Glencoe MRT did not provide data on mountaineering vs non mountaineering incidents, so all their call-outs have been placed in the mountaineering category.

[Non-mountaineering incidents described in the report are not included here.]

Table 3: Number of Incidents in each Mountaineering Activity Category

Activity	Number of incidents
Hillwalking Summer	242
Hillwalking Winter	61
Rock Climbing	13
Snow/Ice Climbing	33
Scrambling	4
Mountain Rescue	2
Others	6
Total defined	**361**

The table above does not include 54 incidents, for which no details were provided, hence the total is 361 rather than 415.

Summer Hillwalking dominates the activities for which teams were called out. The small number of rock climbing incidents is also a continuing trend though the number of incidents has doubled in 2011 from the previous year.

Two incidents involved injury to team members during training sessions. The 'Others' category spans both mountain and non-mountaineering activities and includes false alarms, animal rescue (such as cragfast sheep), crime-related events or medical evacuations.

Incidents by SMC Region

Traditionally, MRCofS Incident reports are published annually in the Journal of the Scottish Mountaineering Club (SMC). In this, incidents are divided into the regions as defined by the SMC District Guides. Table 4 provides details of the incidents by SMC area and the type of incident that occurred. The incidents for Glencoe MRT have all been assigned to the area of that name.

Table 4: Incident information for each SMC region

	Mountaineering	Non- Mountaineering
Northern Highlands	22	6
Western Highlands	31	0
Ben Nevis	94	1
Glencoe	59	1
Other Central Highlands	10	9
Cairngorms	71	21
Southern Highlands	71	50
Skye	15	1
Islands other than Skye	20	12
Southern Uplands	22	56
Total	**415**	**158**

Method by which Alarm was raised

The overwhelming majority of incidents (63%) were initiated by calls from mobile phones. This is similar to previous years. Landlines were the next most common method of the alarm being raised. One interesting new statistic is the use of personal locator beacons which were legalised for use in Scotland in 2011, where four incidents were initiated from these devices. It should be noted that these report initially to a facility in Denver, USA, who then inform the Aeronautical Rescue Coordination Centre (ARCC) at RAF Kinloss, Moray. ARCC then inform the Police or the MCA dependant upon whether the location is over sea or land..

In the context of Table 5 below, 'Not recorded' simply means that the mountain rescue team was not aware of the means by which the alarm was raised to the Police initially. 'Other' includes word of mouth, witnessed by a team member or while the team were out training.

Regrettably in 2011, this category includes two incidents that occurred where team members were injured during training exercises as recorded in Table 3.

Table 5: Method by which Alarm was raised

Method	Number
Mobile Phone	366
Landline	90
Personal Beacon*	4
Email	0
Not Recorded	66
Other	47

Reasons for Mountain Rescue Call Outs

It is often difficult to assign a simple cause or causes to an incident. A slip where a walker injures their leg and needs to be carried off is has an obvious cause. Their location means an MRT is needed to bring them down to the nearest road where they can be handed on to the Scottish Ambulance Service. In other cases, the answer is not straightforward. If a walker's body is located after they have fallen a considerable distance, the direct cause of the fall may not be obvious, and may involve a number of factors, weather, skill level, equipment failure, none of which may be obvious to the mountain rescue team when they arrive at the scene. It is thus quite difficult to define exactly what caused the incident, and issues such as the ability of the casualty are very subjective.

The individual incident forms provided by the teams do allow the identification of a few factors relevant to the cause of the incident. Where these are not judgmental, i.e. do not include subjective issues such as ability and experience, or adequacy of footwear, clothing or equipment carried, it is possible to provide some objective data. These are shown in Table 6 below.

Where multiple causes were provided these are included, hence the total numbers below add up to more than the total number of incidents, even though for some incidents no cause was recorded. Percentages have also been calculated.

The figures show that following the trend of previous year, accidents are dominated by simple slips and trips. There are similar percentages for those reported lost, overdue and reported missing.

One in twelve causes involved a person in whom illness was a factor in the teams being called out. Small number of incidents involved people becoming cragfast (stuck and unable to move up or down) on steep ground and where poor weather was a factor.

Very small numbers of incidents (all less than 1%) listed rockfalls, avalanches or cornice-related incidents, and failures of belays.

~1% of reports listed a work related accident, i.e. shepherding, stalking, forestry accidents where the teams were called out to assist.

Table 6: Main Causes associated with Incidents

Cause	No	%	Cause	No	%
Slip	116	19	Belay Failure	4	<1
Fell	77	12	River or Water based	19	3
Lost/Navigation error	86	14	Reported Missing	97	15
Overdue	75	12	Weather	21	3
Benighted	19	3	Avalanche Natural	4	<1
Illness	49	8	Avalanche Triggered	4	<1
Cragfast	27	4	Fell through cornice	1	<1
Rockfall	5	<1	Cornice collapse	0	0
Work Accident	9	1			

Injuries or Illnesses of Casualties

Table 7 shows the injury profile for those injured in mountaineering incidents in 2011. This details the main injury to a casualty. As in previous years, injuries to the leg and foot dominate the figures, with 39% of all injuries. Multiple injuries were recorded where the casualty had, for example, head and leg injuries, both of which were serious. Cuts and bruises were the next highest.

For people who became ill and were rescued by the teams, the main problem reported was hypothermia, with exhaustion reported as the next most common cause. Additionally five individuals suffered heart failure of whom three unfortunately died. Asphyxia includes some suicides.

Table 7: Types of Injury or Illness

Injury or Illness	Number
Arm/Hand	10
Leg/Ankle/Foot	105
Chest/Shoulder	4
Pelvis	3
Cuts and bruising	19
Lacerations	1
Hypothermia	26
Hyperthermia	0
Back/Spine	16
Head Face	12
Multiple injuries	22
Heart Failure	5
Asphyxia	6
Other Illnesses	26
Exhaustion	15
Total	270

Method of Casualty Evacuation

Lost, stuck or injured people may be evacuated or helped to safety in a number of ways once they have been located and made safe or their condition stabilized. The table below shows the evacuation method for each of the 564 incidents that occurred in 2011. Helicopter evacuation proved the most common, proving the value of this service to the teams and to the casualties.

Walking off (assisted by the team) was the next most numerous. These do not include 'talk-downs' which form part of the total under 'Found own way back'. A talk-down is where the team is able to speak to the lost person by mobile phone, establish their location and provide directions for a safe route off the hill.

The traditional stretcher evacuation was the next most frequently required. Smaller numbers were picked up in rescue vehicles (this includes boats), and a few were located by the police, i.e. were not on the hills. In 4% of incidents the individuals were able to 'Self-rescue' i.e. make their own way off, after the team had been informed of their situation.

Table 8: Method of Evacuation

Method	Number
Not Evacuated/Evacuation not needed	146
Helicopter	157
Stretcher	65
Walked off by team(s)	71
Vehicle	32
Combination of methods	1
Found own way back	25
Located by police	9
Other	5
Not recorded	62

Usage of Helicopters

With the current contract for the Future UK Search and Rescue Helicopters at the bidding stage, the usage of the existing RAF/RN/MCA capacity in Scotland may be of interest. The number of times each asset assisted with an incident involving Scottish Mountain Rescue teams is given below. Assistance from Police and Scottish Ambulance is also recorded.

Table 9: Usage of helicopters

Aircraft	Call Sign	Times assisted
RN Gannet	Rescue 177/8	60
RAF Lossiemouth	Rescue 137/8	90
RAF Boulmer (Northumberland)	Rescue131/2	7
MCA Stornoway	Rescue 100/1	40
MCA Shetland	Rescue 102/3	0
Police	Various	19
Scottish Ambulance Service	Heli-med	9
Private Aircraft		0

IN MEMORIAM

WILLIAM DIXON BROOKER j. 1957
Honorary President 1996–2011

BILL BROOKER died on 27 November 2011, aged 79.

Tall, genial and courteous, a popular geography teacher and lecturer, he served the Club as an attentive member of Committee, a diplomatic President and an assiduous Editor of the Journal. These qualities, together with his earlier major role in the post-war revival of Scottish mountaineering, made him a natural successor to Bill Murray as Honorary President in 1996, the same year in which he received an honorary degree from his Alma Mater, Aberdeen University, recognising his great contribution to mountaineering in Scotland and to education in Aberdeen and the North East.

Bill was born in 1931 in Calcutta where his father was an engineer. At the age of six he returned to his mother's home in Aberdeen where he attended the Grammar School. He was an intrepid boy who took part in daring street sledging, hands-off competitive cycling and probing underground city waterways. He found further scope for adventure when he joined the 1st Aberdeen Scout Troop which offered camping and exploration on Deeside. He made an ascent of Mount Keen from a camp at Aboyne at the age of 12. He soon formed a splinter adventure group which gradually displaced school rugby in his sporting interests. When 14 he cycled to Skye with a fellow scout. After an immediate ascent of Sgùrr Alasdair he overheard climbers discussing the Inaccessible Pinnacle. He asked the warden at Glenbrittle Hostel if it was truly 'inaccessible'. He was advised that it was so 'for the likes of you'. The next day he climbed it solo.

Bill was undoubtedly influenced by his elder brother who was a member of a small group of senior medical students who were very active Cairngorm climbers, but he was more attracted to the body of ex-servicemen, led by Mac Smith, who were pursuing their new freedom in climbing the Deeside hills and their crags every weekend. After overcoming the problems of remoteness they camped, made howffs and used the many estate bothies, especially in Glen Muick and at Luibeg on Mar estate, as their climbing bases. They built up a tough, carefree and fun-loving culture which included an intense feeling for the natural and social history of the Cairngorms. No small influence on them all was the figure of keeper Bob Scott of the Derry, an ex-serviceman himself and witty dispenser of hill wisdom and lore.

Into this scene strode the young schoolboy Brooker. Along with trainee architect Johnny Morgan and young engineer Doug Sutherland he proceeded, in the years 1949–50, to astound the Aberdeen climbing world with over a dozen climbs including: Ben Macdui, Coire Sputan Dearg: *Crystal Ridge* (w), *Anchor Route* (w), *Snake Ridge*. Creagan a' Choire Etchachan: *Winter Route* (w), *Flanking Ribs*. Braeriach, Coire Bhrochain: *Pyramus* (w). Lochnagar: Black Spout Pinnacle – *Route 1*, the third ascent (free from aid) of *Eagle Ridge*, *Giant's Head Chimney* (w), *Shadow Buttress A* (w), *West Rib* (w). Skye, Sgùrr Alasdair: *Abraham's Climb* (w).

By the time he left school he had developed a huge interest in the natural world

Bill Brooker at Corrour Bothy, April 1950.
Photo: Mac Smith.

and the pursuit of adventure which led him to study for a BSc in Geography at Aberdeen University. There he encountered a band of keen climbers in the medical faculty – Patey, Leslie, Taylor and, later, Grassick and Nicol. This led to an outburst of hard exploratory climbing in the three years of his university career pushing up standards to match the best in Britain especially in Winter using the tools of the thirties, long ice-axes and Tricouni nails.

Among his new climbs were Lochnagar: *Eagle Ridge* (w) (a Scottish jewel to this day), *Gargoyle Chimney* (w), *The Stack*. Creag an Dubh Loch: *Labyrinth Edge*. Beinn a' Bhuird: *Mitre Ridge* (w). Ben Macdui, Creagan a' Choire Etchachan: *Red Scar Route*. In Skye, with Mike Dixon from Leeds, in 1950 and 1951 he opened up the Coireachan Ruadh face of Sgùrr MhicCoinnich with *Fluted Buttress* and *Crack of Dawn*.

On motor bikes with his medic friends he visited Nevis, Glen Coe, Ardgour and opened exploration in Applecross with *Cioch North Wall* on Sgùrr a' Chaorachain.

On the hill Bill was easily recognised by his loping gait, his black army beret, brown muffler, ex-army anorak and trousers. His urban variant of subfusc jacket and flannels failed to conceal his charisma. His arrival in coffee shop or student bar instantly enlivened his group of friends with enthusiastic observations, the latest climbing gossip and plans for fresh adventures. He participated in student affairs, including the obligatory midnight ascent of the Mitchell Tower's spire during Charities Week. His motor bike was a well-restored and meticulously-maintained vintage 1929 600cc BSA Sloper…a social asset as well as ideal transport to the hills. Bill's skills on the rocks were matched by those in the student dance hall. He was widely popular, never bearing a grudge or rancour. He merely dismissed all poseurs and all Yahoos like he did scary pitches with a confidential grin and his usual catch phrase, 'What a laugh, man!'

When the Aberdeen party set off for the Alps in 1952 Bill scorned train tickets and laborious hitch-hiking but covered the journey to Chamonix in short order on the Sloper, pausing only somewhere north of London to seek a part to fettle his valve gear. At Chamonix he had a very good time on the classic Aiguilles with Johnny Morgan. At the end of the brief holiday they crossed the Col du Géant accompanying another Aberdeen rope. After a night in the Entrèves woods they all climbed the Brouillard Glacier to bivouac on Pic Eccles at the tragic scene of destruction of the small cabin in a rockfall a few days earlier. They crossed Mont Blanc by the beautiful Innominata face and a fine high summit walk in perfect conditions to descend to the ancient Grands Mulets hut. There they awoke to a terrible storm which chased them to the valley, glad they were a day ahead.

Bill followed graduation in 1953 with two years National Service commissioned in the Royal Engineers stationed in the South of England. This was immediately followed by three months prospecting in East Greenland for a Danish mining company…a great experience in those days. His working life continued with a year-long stint as a site investigation engineer with the central laboratory of George Wimpey. The lure of academic life and love of the open spaces called him back to Aberdeen for his honours BSc degree. He followed that with a year of teacher training at Aberdeen College of Education. He had kept in touch with Aberdeen during these times by modern motorcycles often in long wet runs in the dark.

During this period in the late fifties he had good times climbing. He notably took part in the breakthrough on Central Gully Wall of Creag an Dubh Loch with *Waterkelpie Wall*, *Theseus Grooves* and *Caterpillar Crack*. On Creagan a' Choire Etchachan he did *The Talisman* and on Lochnagar *The Link*. His Winter efforts on Lochnagar produced *Eagle Buttress*, *Parallel Buttress* and *Black Spout Pinnacle*, and on Creag an Dubh Loch *Labyrinth Edge*, *North-West Gully* and *Bower Buttress*. On Nevis he did *Hadrian's Wall* (w) and *Raeburn's Buttress* (w).

In 1959 he married Margaret Parkinson a fellow student with a love of the outdoors. He started his career as a geography teacher at Aberlour High School. The new year of 1960 saw him as principal teacher of Geography at Keith Grammar School. After two years he was seconded to the Institute of Army Education which took him to King Richard School, Cyprus as principal teacher of Geography. This suited his adventurous spirit. Apart from the enjoyable work and company he was able to climb, keep a boat and take up bold snorkelling and spear fishing. It was also an ideal base for him to pursue his interest in ancient civilisations and there were trips to Egypt, Petra, Crete and mainland Greece where he climbed Mount Olympus. It was from friendships there that he got his UN blue beret which was his chosen hill wear on return to Scotland.

Bill and Margaret returned with their two small children in 1965 to Keith where his post had been retained for him. He was shortly appointed to a post as Tutor-Organiser in Extra-Mural Studies at Aberdeen University. This involved lecturing in geography and current affairs across North East Scotland and organising Summer courses for, amongst others, the American Institute for Foreign Studies. He was director of the department when he retired in 1992.

Although the most intense of his climbing days were over he remained heavily involved in mountain activities much of it through the Club. He and Margaret pursued their Munros in a steady fashion in all seasons. There were adventurous family holidays, an example being two weeks exploring the inner Hebrides with a powerful inflatable and a tent. Loch Scavaig, Eigg and Rum were reached in high seas and climbing was enjoyed. When in Spain Bill and his son Iain climbed two splendid summits in the Picos de Europa on sight…no guide books required. Bill had taken up modern gear and techniques and it gave him great pleasure when in due course Iain led him up *Eagle Ridge* and became in 1986 a member of the SMC.

With the family grown Bill and Margaret visited relatives in USA and Canada. Opportunities were seized to pass a night under the stars on top of Half-Dome and to hike in the Rockies, carefully avoiding grizzlies. Much later when Iain and his wife were working as doctors in New Zealand they met them there and enjoyed a two-day crossing of the Copland Pass from Mount Cook Village to Fox Glacier.

Following active Committee work (1966–70) he became Vice-President (1970–72) and followed George Roger as President (1972–74) where he very ably represented the Club in UK climbing circles. In 1975 he followed a line of great Editors of the Journal – Bell, Dutton and Campbell – whose high standards he maintained for eleven years. During this time he promoted many of the excellent Club publications and edited *A Century of Scottish Mountaineering* (published in 1988). Around this time the SMC had the task of keeping the records of Munro 'Compleaters'. The job had fallen to the Editor but when Bill stepped down from that post he continued to keep the log and remained Clerk of the List until 1992. It was a task he particularly enjoyed as large numbers of people wrote to him about their achievements.

Bill was an honorary member of the ancient Cairngorm Club and an enthusiastic member of the revived Etchachan Club, home of the new Aberdeen hard men. He was involved in the North-East Mountain Trust and the Mountaineering Council of Scotland and contributed to mountain leadership training.

With Margaret he was a keen piste skier in Scotland and the Alps. He took up ski mountaineering, in Nordic and Alpine modes. In 1973 he traversed the four highest Cairngorms from Aberdeen and back in a day. He completed the Haute Route in 1977 and a crossing of the Vanoise massif in 1980 with SMC parties.

In 1990 Bill went to Kenya in a party of four Club members. After enjoying the Maasai Mara they climbed to Top Hut and then Peak Lenana. It was on this ascent that the medical man in the group noticed the first flicker of muscular incoordination in Bill's little stumbles on overgrown sections of the path. The following day Bill started up Nelion with Donald Bennet but had to call retreat due to difficulty in coping with footholds. When skiing with Iain later that Winter on A' Chailleach he found new langlauf gear just 'failed to work'. These incidents led to investigations into the degeneration of his motor nervous system which progressively crippled him and which caused his death 20 years later.

A great pleasure in later times was conducting with friends Margaret's completion of her Munros. With old Aberdeen friends he frequently visited the great Deeside estates with the assistance of wardens and gamekeepers in Landrovers. There he would discourse on botany and birds, photography and student ghillying and bothy days. Escorted, he frequented the West Coast, especially relishing first occupancy status of the new Naismith Hut and a visit to Cape Wrath from a camp at Scourie…hard work but a lot of laughs. During these physically demanding times he cruised from Vancouver to Alaska supported by Margaret and Iain. This was of great pleasure due to Bill's great interest in the Yukon and Alaska. One is reminded of Bill's love of the work of Robert Service (and his dramatic rendering of 'Dangerous Dan Magrew' at the end of a social evening)

He enjoyed the Centenary Yacht Meet on board the Steam Yacht 'Carola'. He was accorded the pleasure of observing a supply lift to the CIC hut from the helicopter cockpit. He attended Presidents' lunches and Club Dinners as long as he could, usually retiring to bed long after his table companions, so engrossed in conversation would he be with younger members.

He remained a hugely sociable character enjoying Probus, monthly meetings with old Aberdeen friends, a world-wide correspondence and a continuing lively interest in others' adventures and in the progress of the Club. He was a warm host to visiting old comrades.

Unfailingly supported by Margaret he showed no self-pity, thinking he had been fortunate, not least in his family. He remained at home until the last few months when bedfast and requiring admission to a nursing home where he died peacefully.

He is survived by Margaret, his son Iain and daughter Fiona to whom we offer our great sympathy.

JMT

GORDON LINDSAY JOY j. 1973

GORDON JOY WAS born on the 24 September 1925, in St Andrews, Fife and brought up in Market Street where he attended the Fisher School, then from Glebe Road to the Burgh School. The family moved to Dundee in 1937 in the hope that Gordon's father might find work there, so Gordon attended Dens Road school before gaining a bursary to then attend Morgan Academy. As a schoolboy he claimed he was inspired into a life of outdoor investigation and exploration by reading Treasure Island and attaining his Wayfarer's Badge in the Boy's Brigade.

On completion of his education at the Morgan, aged fifteen, Gordon was employed as an office boy at the Dundee Royal Infirmary, which he did not really enjoy at all. He was more interested in drawing and artwork which resulted in him joining the employment of Valentines of Dundee where he completed his apprenticeship as a Lithographic Artist.

When called up for National Service during WW2, he followed his father into the Black Watch, when, on completion of his basic training, he became a tank radio operator before joining the Reconnaissance Corps. At this stage he was selected as a candidate for a commission, but after discussing the offer he turned it down because his parents were concerned he would not be able to pay his officer's mess bills! That was the legacy of his father's experiences during the First World War.

In the run up to what became the Battle at Arnhem, Gordon volunteered to train as a glider pilot in the Airborne Division, and although he sat on the runway awaiting take-off with a glider full of troops and equipment they never actually took off. He celebrated his nineteenth birthday during the week that the battle raged, and possibly that was a continuation of a Joy trait. Having fought at the Battle of the Somme, Gordon's father returned home and was reunited with all seven of his brothers who had survived active service in the First World War. Gordon completed his National Service with the Airborne Reconnaissance in Norway, tracking down collaborators and Germans at the end of the war. Whilst preparing for demob, he returned to his artistic aspirations and completed an art training programme to complement his Lithography before rejoining Valentines in Dundee. In the early 1950s, Gordon left Valentines and joined D. C. Thomson and Co. Ltd., printers and publishers, Dundee in the Art Department. Although this work career started with lettering rather than drawing or painting, this did broaden out and he was promoted, initially, to the position of 'Head of Lady Artists' in the Meadowside Office, then Head Artist at the Bank Street offices, a job he continued in until his retirement in 1990.

The earlier interest in the great outdoors was re-awakened in Gordon when he became a member of the Scottish Youth Hostels Association. He soon established strong friendships with other members and became very actively involved in the running of the Association's affairs, participating in work parties and even took on the responsibilities of warden of the new Garth Hostel in Glen Lyon. Such was his ardour he started exploring the Scottish hills and mountains with the Youth Hostel groups. In his quest to seek out places farther afield at that time, Gordon joined the Càrn Dearg Mountaineering Club. Although not a founder he was one of the very early members of the club and upheld his membership all of his life.

He started to develop rock climbing and winter mountaineering skills initially in the Glen Clova and Glen Doll areas, and by regular attendance on the club

week-end meets, travelling by bus, was soon gaining further experience in the major climbing areas of Lochnagar, Cairngorms, Glen Coe, Creag Meagaidh, Ben Nevis, Torridon, the Arrochar Alps and Skye.

I first made the acquaintance of Gordon on a Càrn Dearg meet to Glen Coe in May 1957, whilst camping beside the River Coupall, opposite Jacksonville. A party of the members were heading up onto Buachaille Etive Mòr via Curved Ridge and I was invited to join them. Gordon and I hit it off right away and from that day onwards we remained lifelong friends in both climbing and socialising. We teamed up as climbing partners from that time onwards. Never being ones to climb beyond our capabilities, nor to seek out new routes we were quite content to visit all of the major climbing areas as previously mentioned in Scotland, selecting and ascending the early pioneered classic routes on faces, buttresses and in gullies. These routes were climbed in summer and winter conditions, extending over quite a number of years – years that were interspersed with the ascent of numerous Munros, high camps and long hill treks.

Early in the 1970s, Gordon and I were in the company of the late Doug Lang, Neil Quinn and the late Quintin Crichton, all with whom we had both climbed at some time prior to this particular meeting. Doug, forever the diplomat, ventured to suggest that both of us had the proper credentials to become members of the Scottish Mountaineering Club. Not only that, the three of them were prepared to propose and sponsor us. Thereafter the necessary information was appended to the Club's membership application forms and sent off.

In October 1973, 'Gordon was over the moon' when the applications were successful and we were accepted as members to the Club. He claimed it was an honour to join such a prestigious Club and its elite band of mountaineers. Gordon served on the SMC Committee from 1980 to 1983 and also gave of his time by participating with the members on hut maintenance work parties.

Gordon and his wife Elma, whom he married in 1956, were both keen and expert skiers starting on nursery slopes of Tullybaccart, north of Dundee and Glen Isla before progressing on to Glen Shee. When their sons, Ian and David were born and old enough, they too learned from Gordon to become proficient young skiers but more into the Tiger Runs' scenario than general downhill skiing on the pistes. In the days of perfect winters, with an abundance of snow, Gordon drove to Glen Shee virtually every Saturday between Christmas and Easter where there were memorable times spent on the slopes and at the Dundee Ski Club's Gulabin Lodge at the Spittal. Then horizons broadened to the Cairngorms and later on to Europe.

Gordon and Elma spent numerous package skiing trips with their many like-minded friends in various ski resorts throughout Europe. Besides spending a holiday in his early years at the skiing resorts of Geilo and Myrdal in Norway, Gordon's favourite areas were Chamonix, La Playne and La Praz in France, Borgata in Italy and Cron Montana in Switzerland.

Gordon was still active in mountaineering pursuits until his mid 70s but as his ability to sustain his fitness waned he concentrated more on his other life passion, painting, especially in water colours. During his life-time he regularly exhibited in local art shows, was a member of the Dundee Art Society, a founder member of the Broughty Ferry Art Society and was a benefactor of the McManus Gallery in Dundee. He was also a man of many other parts, well read, informative with detail, meticulous about safety when climbing, always caring about one's welfare and an interesting companion just to be with on the hill. One other keen interest he had was his garden. He just loved pottering about among the borders and beds tending plants and flowers in his spare time.

Sadly, Gordon spent the latter years of his life in nursing care and passed away after a mild stroke in Balhousie Care Home in Perth on the 13 December 2011, aged 86. From all who knew Gordon, our sincere sympathies go out to Elma, his wife, Ian, Laura and family, David, Deirdre and family and his sister, Ena Strachan. For many fond memories of happy camping, classic climbs and numerous halcyon days on long horizons, Gordon – thanks buddy!

Brian A Clark

Since receiving this tribute we were saddened to learn that Gordon's wife, Elma, died peacefully in April 2012. A ceremony to remember her life took place in Broughty Ferry, Dundee on 11 May 2012. We extend our deepest sympathy to all of the family.

FERGUS STANLEY JAMES MACCALLUM j. 2001

Fergus died on the 8 January 2012 after a period of illness. He was just 35 years old. At his funeral his close school friend Magnus Holbourn shared the following words:

I first met Fergus when he enrolled as a pupil at Rannoch School in 1989. As 12-year-old boys we found that we had a lot in common. We were both from Scotland, our fathers both worked with sheep, we loved adventure and outdoors and our names sounded kind of similar, which is as good a reason as any for two 12-year-old boys to become friends.

Fergus was a natural athlete, and from the day he arrived at the school, he was instantly signed up to compete in every type of sporting event on offer. I can still see the look of shock on the athletics coach's face on the first day of the season, when Fergus broke the school long jump record after only his third attempt ever at the event. In fact he pretty much was the athletics team that year, competing in almost every event, from shot put to 1500m. As a rugby player he was tenacious and committed, as a runner he was relentless, on the hockey field his shinty background made him somewhat terrifying. But it was his love of the wilderness that was to characterise him most.

Off the sports field Fergus was a gentle and quiet guy and one always felt that the spectacle of competition was somehow beneath him. Had he wanted Fergus could have no doubt gone far in almost any athletic pursuit, but being better than someone else at something was not what Fergus was about. Fergus was the kind of guy who would finish a race by your side, even thought he could have easily won, just so you wouldn't feel bad about loosing by a mile.

A kinder more generous guy you could not have hoped to meet.

So it was a different type of competition in which we saw Fergus thrive. Competing with oneself in the wilderness, where the prize was the thrill of being alive. That is where the guy we all know as Fergus shone like a star. The rain could be pouring, the track, if there was one, could be knee deep in mud, your belly empty, your tent with a massive hole in it where you set fire to it the previous night, 50 miles to go and only half a mars bar in your pocket, and Fergus would be there grinning from ear to ear, absolutely loving it; and that side of him never changed. Over the next six years we went on countless expeditions together, climbed more rock faces than I can remember and Fergus was happy on every single occasion. His enthusiasm was infectious and he quickly became the centre of the close-knit band of like-minded friends. Together we all shared some fantastic times. If I think back to those days I know how lucky we all were as teenagers to find something so real to embrace in our lives. And after school when we all went our separate ways and subsequently met up to lament about good old days, Fergus was there and was still living the dream and still smiling and still happy.

Rest in peace my friend.

Following school, Fergus finally settled on a career in Rope Access. After gaining extensive experience at home and abroad he found work in the oil industry. Latterly, this enabled him to work for short concentrated periods of time giving him the opportunity to travel extensively in pursuit of his various sporting activities.

Fergus topping out on Ben Nevis.   Photo: Dave Ritchie

He excelled in mountaineering, rock and ice climbing, skiing and snowboarding, mountain biking, and latterly kite surfing, following the seasons round the world.

Despite being abroad for long periods of time, Fergus loved being at home in Taynuilt, and from there climbed with many Club members at home in Scotland.

His enthusiasm, incredible kindness and consideration for others and his wonderful smile will never be forgotten.

His friend Nicholas Zvegintgov gave the following tribute at Fergus's funeral:

Over the years you might have asked
Where Fergus on his travels tasted
The answer to be unspecific, across the Atlantic and Pacific
Brazil and Thailand, Greece, Australia, Morocco, France or Venezuela
Switzerland and Costa Rica, Spanish main to fair Venicia
US, Norway, Canada and other places twice as fair
Orkney, Shetland, Hebrides, he travelled round them with ease
He wasn't just being lazy, not for him, relaxed
Sight-seeing but what, you ask, did he do there
This caring daring pioneer?
With skiing, climbing (we are hearing)
Go surfing, kiting, mountaineering or miles and

Miles of moorland hiking
In his van with skis and pack and sometimes
With his doodle sack – off he'd drive on
Ventures new or novel sports to find and do
Now what of him you may well ask? To list
His travels is quite a task – A nicer man is
Hard to find and here's a few which spring to mind
A caring friend, a loving son,
A man who packed his life with fun,
Polite and smiling, seldom down, ne'era
Frown, Considerate beyond belief
Right to the last he hid his grief
A better friend I doubt you'd find
We'll hold him in our hearts and mind.

DR

PROCEEDINGS OF THE CLUB

The following mountaineers were admitted to the Club in 2012.
We welcome:

NEIL GF ADAMS (30), Engineer, Glasgow.
ROBERT J ADIE (30), BMC Competitions Officer, Buxton, Derbyshire.
DAVID J COWAN (28), Designer, Aberdeen.
ANDREW D INGLIS (31), Chemical Engineer, Westhill, Aberdeenshire.
RONALD J KENYON (61), Accountant (retd.), Penrith, Cumbria.
GORDON LENNOX (40), Mechanical Engineer, Newmachar, Aberdeenshire.
BRUCE C MACROSSON (41), Depute Procurator Fiscal, Edinburgh.
JANE L MURDOCH (54), Depute Head Teacher, Dunfermline, Fife.
GRAHAM STEIN (37), Helicopter Pilot, Loanhead, Midlothian.

The One-Hundred-and-Twenty-Third AGM and Dinner

At the 2010 Dinner, the Club Secretary was pleased to announce that it looked like the Club had a new venue for the AGM and Dinner. After a break of many years he'd found a venue in Speyside. However late in September John was taken aback to be told that the hotel could not honour our booking as it had decided to close for the winter. Fortunately the Ben Nevis at Fort William had kept our 'backup' booking and it was another long drive for the Aberdonians.

The afternoon talk was by Graeme Tough who took us through a summer trip to Greenland. Nothing went to plan for them (a bit like Dinner booking) but they survived. After a short break at the end of the talk members moved onto the Annual AGM. More discussion took place over the renovation of the CIC and in particular the style of windows. The Club was informed that our lease of the Ling Hut continues to be short. Although there are not signs that the estate are wanting to reclaim the building it seems prudent to not commit time and money to long term renovation projects. The Journal Editor reported on the quandary of where the Journal should be printed. Should we support the home market or go abroad? A vote was taken which concluded he should be allowed to choose.

Numbers seating at the Dinner were slightly down on recent years but we still filled the hotel dining room. The food was well received and during the speeches our President, Andy Nisbet, highlighted the rapid rise in climbing standards during the winter season. Many top end routes were put up by club members. He also recorded the deaths of two very prominent members of the club. Bill Brooker died a short while before the Dinner after a long illness and Doug Lang was sadly swept away by an avalanche in Glen Clova at the tail end of the previous winter. The invited evening entertainment was a 'one man show' based on diaries of the Alistair Crowley, former SMC and AC member. I think this might have the first time the Dinner attendees had been expected to provide audience participation.

The following morning most members and guests dispersed across the hills and few joined the President for a walk up to the CIC. No climbing gear was taken although although we all enjoyed cake and coffee in the hut.

Next year we are due back at the Ben Nevis Hotel while the Club Secretary continues his quest for an alternative Highland venue that can take about 140 –50 diners on the first Saturday of December the following year.

Chris Huntley

The CIC Hut Meets, Ben Nevis

The damage to the roof in January and the mild winter resulted in less use of the CIC Hut this winter.

Dave Ritchie helps repair the damage to the CIC Hut roof, May 2012. Photo: Brian Shackleton.

20–21 January: One member and guest turned up. There were also four from another club. An attempt on Number 2 Gully Buttress on the Saturday was abandoned due to high winds and the team went down at lunchtime.

10–12 February: The attendance was 14 and conditions were poor below around 1000m. Even higher routes were often thin or non-existent. Members and guests made ascents including Comb Gully, Number 3 Gully Buttress, Number 2 Gully Buttress, Tower Scoop, The Gift, Smith's Route and Caledonia. One enthusiastic team made a day trip from Dunblane for Smith's Route returning later to relieve the baby-sitter, via tea in the Hut. An inversion occurred on Sunday.

2–4 March: The attendance was seven, which included three American guests. 'We have heard about Point Five, Zero and Orion Direct for 30 years and at last we get here to find they have gone.' Routes were even less numerous than in

February but teams completed North-East Buttress, Tower Ridge, Ledge Route and Raeburn's Easy Route. Fresh snow over Saturday night marginally improved the appearance of the Ben.

30 March–1 April: Some members with hut responsibilities made a site visit. The meet was well attended with three members and two guests. On Saturday ascents of North-East Buttress and Observatory Ridge were completed under summer conditions. The team on Observatory had such a splendid time that they did not arrive back at the hut until 11 p.m. On Sunday everyone headed home early.

Nigel M Suess

Ski Mountaineering Meet, The Cluanie Inn, Glen Sheil
18–19 February 2012

The 12 members and 17 guests (the meet had been organised jointly with the Eagle Ski Club) gradually accumulated by the fireside at the Cluanie Inn on the Friday evening. As in the previous year the weather forecast meant that travel was undertaken more in hope than expectation!

A team of four had been into Glen Affric staying at Strawberry Cottage for the two preceding days enduring high winds and temperatures. The Munros Sgùrr nan Ceathreamhnan (1143m), Mullach na Dheireagain and Sgùrr Mhaoraich, plus the Corbetts Sgùrr Gaorsaic (839m) and Càrn a'Choire Ghairbh (863m) had been ticked.

Saturday teasingly dawned with a dusting of fresh snow down to the hotel. It was windy as forecast and the snow showers continued intermittently all day. But the substantial full Scottish breakfast allowed time for everyone to deliberate on the best approach to the sparse conditions.

The Vice President went in a party of five (Ann, Amie, Graeme T & Wendell) direct from the hotel across the A87 to the summit of A' Chràlaig (1120m – the basket or creel). They touched the impressive cairn, quite close to the cornice; those without goggles swiftly donned them and they returned directly to the hotel. Conditions were described as somewhat windy, although no one admitted to having been blown over. A small lee slope windslab avalanche was triggered on the descent. The crown wall full thickness (20cm) went down to a base of older frozen snow on grass.

Bob B, Dave C, Dave H, Ewan and Graham D, headed south to the north-east spur of Aonach air Chrith (1021m). Strong gusty snowy squalls cut short the original plan of an extended ridge walk. The descent into a north-east facing corrie east of the summit contained plenty of deep soft snow and gave the feeling of a mini 'Lost Valley'. They returned to the hotel for a piece of Colwyn's birthday cake, which was approximately the size of a manhole cover; that's the whole cake, not the individual portion!

First time at this ski meet and Murray had an excellent time getting blown about on the ridge between Mullach Fraoch Coire and A' Chràlaig with Anthony, Chris R, Bob R, Ian and his father John! All but one decided not to take crampons so – all but one – were turned back by iced slabs 400m horizontally and 100m vertically from the top of Mullach Fraoch Coire. They then battled south over a wee top and on to A' Chràlaig. A bit slippery near the top and the wind got up so they near enough had to crawl, but all of them made it and they had a lovely run down.

Deciding there was too much wind for the higher tops, Brian and Anne headed down to Dornie and along Loch Long to Beinn Conachra. Despite its modest 453m height, it is an excellent viewpoint with fine views up Loch Long to the Corbetts at the head of the loch and the Mullardoch Munros beyond.

Many took advantage of the proximity of Am Bathach (798m) to the hotel. A group of seven split into two distinct teams as three opted to drive the 1km to the closest parking area; John K, Diane and Mark. The second half walked along the short stretch of the A87. The two groups met part way up the hill and continued onto the summit, stopping briefly before descending down to the bealach. John K, Diane, John and Victor headed back down to the road, whilst the others continued on to Ciste Dhubh. A short while later the weather closed in, and with thunder and lighting all around, they too headed back. A third group, consisting of Angus, Bill S and Alan followed the second group up the hill before coming off the north ridge in gusting winds. Pushing on hopefully before finally turning round before the final summit cone due to gusting winds of 60mph plus. A sound mountaineering decision.

Paul & Chris O went back down Glen Quoich for a windy traverse of Spidean Mialach and Gleouraich. The initial shoulder at the end of the stalkers path was a bit blowy but with the wind at their backs the remainder wasn't too bad.

So plenty of hills climbed but not one on skis!

Sunday dawned bright, fresh and with 8cm of fresh snow at the hotel (210m). The bright early sunrise inspired talk of great deeds!

To their surprise Ewan, Graham D, Dave C, Dave H and Bob B found that they were able to put skins on by the car and keep them on all the way to the summit of Sgùrr nan Conbhairean (1110m). Then to ski all the way from the summit to within five minutes of the road. They found excellent powder on the descent into Coire Lair but a fair bit of heather 'combat skiing' lower down. Dave H broke a binding 10 minutes in and did the entire trip held together with string and cable ties. Gold medal for the most spectacular dismount went to budding senior gymnast Dave C.

Anthony, John P and Murray skinned up the east flank of Maoile an t-Searraich on to Sgùrr an Doire Leathain (South Cluanie Ridge) and had a great ski back down on dreamy new snow, with enough snow on the grass at lower levels to allow skiing all the way back to the road.

Colwyn, Ann, Chris R, Graeme and Amie walked the ridge between Mullach Fraoch Coire and A' Chràlaig with crampons this time and they were all successful in reaching the top of Mullach Fraoch Coire. Colwyn returned over the top to A' Chràlaig, thereby climbing it twice in 2 days while the others returned to the glen for an easier descent. They did regret not taking skis for the descent.

Bob R and Ian joined up with five Eagles (Alan, Angus, Bill, Stuart and Sonia) to ski up A' Ghlas-bheinn. They skied along the forest track from the Strath Croe carpark at virtually sea level, and most of the party were on skis all the way up to the summit and down again (although Ian, being a rubbish skier and timorous to boot, went by foot up and down the steep initial slope of the WNW ridge). A delightful mountain – and a great weekend; including the visit to the bedroom window early on Sunday morning by a red deer hind and her two sons. A nice touch.

Victor and Charlotte went downhill skiing at Glencoe. Wendel went downhill skiing at Nevis Range which also allowed a view of a helicopter rescue on the Ben. Di and Mark went up Geal Chàrn on skis from Balsporran at Drumochter. Paul and Chris O had a long way to drive so headed home.

Another successful SMC ski meet, and with some skiing for a change!

Members present: Bob Barton, Ewan Clark, Ian Crofton, Graham Dudley, Colwyn Jones, Ann MacDonald, John Peden, Chris Ravey, Bob Reid, Brian Shackleton, Graeme Tough, Anthony Walker.

Guests: Angus Armstrong, Mark & Di Cassidy, Paul Cook, Dave Coustick, Amie Goodill, Dave Howard, Stuart Johnston, Victor Kakebeeke, John Kentish, Wendell Martin, Anne Morrison, Chris Ottley, Sonja Panchen, Murray Peden, Alan Sloan, Bill Stephens and Charlotte Whitmore.

Colwyn Jones

Easter Meet, Shieldaig Lodge Hotel, Gairloch
12–15 April 2012

This year's Meet was housed in a quixotic Victorian lodge at the edge of the loch where evenings were enlivened by sightings of porpoises and seals splashing around the anchored boats. The weather was bright and accompanied by a keen sharp wind with snow flurries on the summits.

The close proximity of sunny Raven's Crag lured out several parties on to the good rock. Climbing also took place on Càrn Goraig by the Gruinard River, Tollaidh Crags and Loch Tollaidh Crags at Poolewe, Sàil Mhòr of Beinn Eighe and at Diabeg.

The following hills were ascended in various combinations of parties: Ruadh-stac Mòr and Spidean Coire nan Clach (Beinn Eighe), Meall an Doirein, Sgùrr Dubh, Beinn a' Chlaidheimh, Sgùrr Bàn, Mullach Coire Mhic Fhearchair, Beinn Tarsuinn, Ruadh-stac Beag, Baosbheinn, Beinn a' Chaisgein Beag, Beinn a' Chearcaill, Lurg Mòr, Bidean a' Choire Sheasgaich and An Ruadh Meallan.

One member's attempt at the Fisherfield six (or is it now five?) became the Fisherfield four when he realised the scale of the task having started late. A return in darkness all the way from Shenaval and a locked hotel door at 3.30 a.m. meant a night in the car. All members owning a geologist's hammer are under suspicion. We all enjoyed a pleasant dinner on the Saturday evening.

Members present: Bob Aitken, Paul V Brian, David Broadhead, Robin N Campbell, Steve Chadwick, Robin DG Chalmers, Geoff Cohen, Helen GS Forde, Campbell Forrest, John RR Fowler, John YL Hay, Andy M James, Peter F Macdonald, Bill McKerrow, Gordon Macnair, Roger JC Robb, Des Rubens, Iain HM Smart, Colin Stead, David Stone, Nigel M Suess, Noel Williams and John Wood.
Guests: Calum Anton and Maureen Suess.

EASTER MEET 2012   Front (L to R): John Fowler, Nigel Suess, Robin Campbell, Helen Forde, Maureen Suess (guest), Dave Broadhead, John Wood, Noel Williams, Roger Robb.
Back: Peter Macdonald, Gordon Macnair, Calum Anton (guest), Iain Smart, Andrew James, Des Rubens, Raymond Simpson, Colin Stead, Geoff Cohen, Steve Chadwick, Paul Brian and Bob Aitken.
Photo: David Stone.

Our thanks go to the Hon Secretary, John Fowler for his successful organisation of the Meet.

Helen GS Forde

Skye Meet, Allt Dearg Cottage, Sligachan
5–12 May 2012

Our timing was out again this year. We were just too early for one of the best spells of weather on the island for many years. We had a cold week of blustery weather with drizzle and snow flurries, but a fortnight later people were skinny dipping in the Fairy Pools.

However, parties snatched routes on the sea-cliffs and much exploring was done. Tom Prentice and Peter Wilson managed an ascent of Pinnacle Ridge on Sgùrr nan Gillean in poor weather. John Temple snooped about on the east face of Marsco.

On the worst day of the week a party of six, including member and local resident Simon Fraser, ventured into Coire nan Laogh in the Cuillin. It was the centenary year of the pioneering visit by Herford and Laycock. An ascent of

SKYE MEET 2012 – Allt Dearg Cottage, 8 May 2012.
(L to R) John Fowler, Helen Forde, Eve Austin (guest), John Mackenzie, John Temple, Peter Wilson,
Willie Jeffrey (guest) and Tom Prentice.
Photo: Noel Williams.

Central Gully proved quite interesting in the conditions and later helped sort out the true whereabouts of the various routes in the corrie.

Members present: Paul Brian, Robin Campbell, Helen Forde, John Fowler, Peter Macdonald, John Mackenzie, Tom Prentice, John Temple, Noel Williams and Peter Wilson.
Guests: Eve Austin and Willie Jeffrey.

Noel Williams

Aspirants' Meet 1, Naismith Hut, Elphin
25–27 May 2012

This was the first of two trial meets to invite aspirants to meet and climb with established members. The events were modest in scale but were judged a success and our thanks are due to Ross Jones and Andy Nisbet for leading the events. The aspirants were all most enthusiastic and it is hoped to repeat the meets next year.

From the Naismith Hut, Ross Jones (meet leader), Andy Nisbet, Pat Ingram and Alan Walker climbed on the first day with aspirants Carlos las Heras, Andy Long and Roy Plenderleith on Quinag and Sgùrr an Fhidleir. The second day saw activity on Stac Pollaidh (Vlad the Impaler, Wingless Warlock, Release the Bats, and November Groove) plus a walking team.

Alpine Meet, Orco Valley and Gran Paradiso National Park
20 July–1 August 2012

This was, we were told, the first Alpine meet of the SMC for quite a number of years – and an enormous success it was. Eschewing the scary glaciated terrain of the high snowy dollops, and following the prophetically pointing finger of John Temple, the party of a dozen or so members plus sundry guests headed for the sun-kissed granite and gneiss of the Orco Valley (Valle dell'Orca), and the fine rock peaks of the adjacent Gran Paradiso National Park. Such were the pleasures to be found in this demi-paradise that it was deemed that the letter S in SMC should stand, temporarily at least, for 'Sybaritic'.

John Temple had been to the area every year for a decade, and had long sung its praises. His enthusiasm for, and knowledge of, the area was shared by our guest, Richard Nadin of the Alpine Club, and between them John and Richard shared their expertise with the greenhorns, pointing us at suitable routes and warning us of the vagaries of the local grading (in which *Francese* 5a appears to mean anything from 4b in UK money to, well, 5a).

For the first two days our valley base was the campsite at the unspoilt village of Locana. At first the campsite appeared to lack much in the way of amenity, catering more for campervans than campers. But once we had all foregathered and formed our tents into a *laager scozzese*, the site mutated into a place of fun and laughter. Wizard-like, John and Richard wrought their transformational magic, barbequing local trout stuffed with fresh-plucked thyme, sploshing out

292 SCOTTISH MOUNTAINEERING CLUB JOURNAL

over-generous measures of Primitivo and Nebbiola. As the sun set, Italian families of all ages tumbled out of their campervans to tango with enviable élan to the music of the accordion deep into the neon-lit night. We Scots, hovering on the edge of the open-air dance floor, were like kids pressing our noses against a sweetie shop window. Thus the place began to cast its *glamourie* over the gradually relaxing mortals from the gloomy North.

Our welcome was enhanced on the Saturday evening by the ebullient Mayor of Locana, who generously hosted a reception for the SMC (whom he mistook for the Alpine Club, but never mind). The occasion was marked by speeches in a variety of languages, copious quantities of food and drink, and the presentation to the Mayor of Greg Strange's *The Cairngorms – 100 Years of Mountaineering*.

Oh yes, we also did some climbs those two days in the valley: the 3-pitch *Fessura Per P.A.* (4b) on the Pyramid; various well-bolted crimpy slab routes (mostly single pitch) on the Cavalieri Perdenti, all imaginatively called *No Name*, and all about 5c (French); and the magnificent trad 5-pitch Kosterlitz route on the Torre di Aimonia, called *Pesce d'Aprile* ('April Fool'; 170m, 5c, which turned out to be about HVS 5a). Apparently on the first ascent in 1973 Mike Kosterlitz had amazed his Italian companions by producing, one by one, strange objects called 'nuts' from his rucksack and popping them into the crack at the back of the great crux corner. At various other times, parties had successes on *Nautilus* (270m, 6a) on the Sergent, and on the *Legolas Variant* (130m, 6b) on the Pyramid.

Our main base for the holiday was not the Orco Valley, but the Rifugio Pontese, at 2200m in the Vallone di Piantonetto, a high valley that cuts deep into the little-frequented southern side of the Gran Paradiso National Park, a home for ibex, chamois and marmots, together with a wonderful array of alpine plants. A steep and heart-stoppingly hairpinned road takes you up to the dam of the Lago Teleccio, where (and this is where the 'Sybaritic' bit really kicks in) a little wire-borne aerial trolley takes your heavy gear up to the hut, leaving you to amble comfortably among the wild flowers for 40 minutes or so, until you arrive at the yellow-roofed Rifugio. Here you are greeted into a new world by *la padrona*, Her Utter Wonderfulness, Ms Mara Lacchia.

Casa Mara is unquestionably the most welcoming, laughter-filled, four-course-belly-filling hut in all the Alps, and La Mara is supported in her mission to make her guests sublimely happy by a clutch of charming young assistants. John Temple, a veritable Falstaff-Without-the-Fatness, spoke – quite moved – of Mistress Quickly, and Doll Tearsheet, then babbled of green fields and routes done and routes still to do ...

Prior to the arrival of the masses, the advance guard of Anthony Walker and Chris Ravey had bagged the classic line of the cirque, the *Via Malvassora* (240m, D, 4c) on the Becco Meridionale della Tribulazione (3360m) – a mountain whose name translates as the 'Southern Beak of Tribulation' (although, intriguingly, *becco* can also mean 'billy-goat' or 'cuckold'). The Tribulazione is a glorious wedge, jagging into the sky like a piece of parmesan and as photogenic as the Matterhorn; and the *Malvassora* takes the great golden-red pillar in the centre of the awesome East Face. Where others, later in the week, followed their footsteps in sun and smugness, Chris and Anthony had to deal with tough Scottish conditions of wind and snow and pulling over-trousers over harnesses and not enjoying themselves to unseemly excess.

The weather thereafter was warmer and kinder. Punta Mara (2803m) – a peak named in honour of *la padrona* – proved a popular training ground, with a number of parties getting their acclimatization in on the delightful gendarmed ridges on the mountain's western side, namely *Cresta Julia* and *Bikini Top*. (John and Richard had been responsible, on a previous visit, for both the climbs and the names – whereby, allegedly, there hangs a tale not fit to print.) Later visits to this peak saw further ascents of these routes, plus ascents of *Julia's Bikini* and two new, even shorter routes (by Mark Hudson and Ian Crofton) on the northernmost pillar nearest the Bochetta di Valsoera, namely *Torre Arancia* ('The Orange Tower', 80m UK VS 4c) and *Sweet Lorena* (90m, UK HVS 5a), the latter named after one of La Mara's kindly helpers.

Similar-sized routes nearer to the hut were also climbed by many of the party on off-days, on the bolted slabs of 'Falesia Rock Paradise' (up to *Francese* 6a or so) and on the two-pitch unbolted buttresses of 'Nuova Kernow' ('New Cornwall'). Various parties repeated routes on the latter first pioneered by John, Richard and Hugh Alexander, an expatriate Fifer and member of the AC who also joined us this year. Notable among these routes were *Butterfly Buttress* (to which each party allocated a different grade, with an average of about VS), *Citizen's Arête* (VS) and *Fruits of the Sea* (HVS 5a). John, Richard and Hugh put up a new route named *Wicked Aisling* (HVS 5a), in honour of another of Mara's not-so-little helpers (a former Italian woman's rugby international), while Mark and Ian ungallantly snatched one of John's projects to produce the delightful *Oggetti Smarriti* ('Stolen Property', VS 4c). They are, they hope, forgiven.

Oh, but it was not all crag-ratting within spitting distance of the hut. The Cuckold of Tribulation saw visits from Alan Smith and Pete Wilson, who climbed the *Malvassora*, and from Richard, Ian and Pat Ingram, who started up *Via Machetto* (250m, TD-, 5b) then dodged the final 6c headwall by slanting up left to join the *Malvassora*. There is a straightforward, equipped abseil descent back down the face.

Only Pat and Ian felt the lure of the Becco Di Valsoera (3369m), across the cirque from the Tribulazione. They had a long day on the mountain's massive Southwest Face climbing the straightforward but loooong *Leonessa-Tron* (650m, D-, 4c). As they neared the summit the mists wisped up from the valley, and Pat suggested to Ian that those rumbles the latter had been trying to convince himself were distant aeroplanes were anything but. Pat was right. Luckily the gods were in a benevolent mood, and held back from unleashing the storm until the duo had crossed the summit and found an overhanging boulder to shelter under on the far side. Having deposited all their metal gear at the end of the ledge they counted the storm in, then counted it out again, successfully remaining not only dry, but unfried. (Alan and Pete and others descending the Punta Mara that day were not so lucky, and received a battering from the hail and a soaking from the rain.) Once the storm passed, the descent resumed, with an abseil into a foul, rotten couloir, followed by a nasty, brutish and thankfully short ascent to a col, and then more – much more – foul, rotten couloir to descend on the far side. Ian began to kick steps in his trainers down a snow patch, using a nut-key as an ice-dagger. Pat quickly saw the folly of his companion's ways and rigged up an abseil. Thereafter the descent continued without incident, apart from Ian performing a spectacular prat-fall when an unattached boulder ran away from under his feet. Luckily, no more damage than bruised pride and a dead leg. The pair eventually made it back to the hut in the dusk, after fourteen and a half hours on the hill.

Thank heavens it rained all next day and we didn't have to go out and play.

ALPINE MEET 2012

Instead, the company indulged in one of Mara's four-course lunches, while three old blokes (or 'even-older-than-us' blokes) serenaded each other accompanied by an accordion and a rich repertoire of cod histrionics. Not a bald head was left unkissed by the oldest of the three, an Antonio Carluccio lookalike with sweetness in his voice and mischief in his eyes.

That was just lunch. A mere warm-up for The Party that came in the evening, the excuse for which was the ceremonial handover from the SMC to the Pontese Section of the CAI of *Ben Nevis – Britain's Highest Mountain*. The formalities out of the way, the wine flowed even more copiously than usual, while Richard's friend Pierre pulled out his flute and began to improvise with two local guitarists in a unique species of folk-jazz fusion. By this time, Ruth Love and Graeme Tough had arrived hotfoot from their triumph on Monte Rosa, and Ms Love was to be seen dancing on a table with an imaginary rose between her teeth. Just to show that us Northerners are not as buttoned-up as you might suppose.

But (in true Scots fashion) after the pleasure came the penance. Sunday saw the bulk of the party transfer over the Bocchetta di Valsoera to the remote Val Soera, and the rigours of the Bivouaco Pocchiola Meneghello. 'Rigours' might be pushing it a bit – Spartan, indeed, compared to the Rifugio Pontese, but decadently flesh-potty in comparison to (say) the rotting bothy at Geldie Lodge. And if you were cunning and got your timing right you could nip down the hill to the workers' hut by the dam and sneak a hot shower ...

In the Val Soera we were joined not only by Wicked Aisling but also by Shy, Retiring Costantina, partner of a local guide who was teaching some young kids how to climb back at the Pontese. The big tick hereabouts is the beautiful West Face of Monte Destrera (2596m), and several parties made ascents of the classic *Locatelli* route (330m, TD-, 5c), with its superb corner cleaving the face at half height. John followed Costantina's irresistible fluffy yellow chalk bag up the *Frachey* route on the Southwest Spur (AD, 300m, AD, 4b), while Richard and Pierre climbed the impressive *Directa* on the West Face (280m, TD+, 6c) – nae bad fer a pair o' gran'paws.

As the meet drew to a close, the participants shambled in their varied ways back across the Bocchetta di Valsoera (some of them inadvertently collecting an additional col en route). There was one last memorable night at Casa Mara, where the wine was followed by the grapa and the grapa by something greenish in an unlabelled bottle. Over which memory draws a veil.

But the memories of the whole trip that survive are of great happiness, much laughter, entertaining company, beautiful rock, elegant peaks, and Southern hospitality of unsurpassed warmth.

We will be back.

Members present: David Buchanan, Ian Crofton, Mark Hudson, Pat Ingram, Ruth Love, Chris Ravey, Alan Smith, John Temple (meet convener), Graeme Tough, Anthony Walker and Pete Wilson.
Guests: Hugh Alexander (AC), Pat Buchanan (JMCS), Richard Nadin (AC) and Jan Walker.

Special guest appearances: Aisling, Costantina and Pierre.

Ian Crofton

Aspirants' Meet 2, Raeburn Hut, Laggan
31 August–2 September 2012

This was attended by SMC members Andy Nisbet, John Lyall, Heike Puchan and Brian Whitworth, together with aspirants Bob Allen, Alison Coull, Steve Perry and Colin Rowe.

On day one it was wet at Creag Dubh, even wet at Huntly's Cave, so all went to Cummingston where, apart from an hour's rain mid-day, we climbed. The best leading routes were done by all up to HVS, including the well known trio of Left, Right and Centre. Heike had prepared a great evening meal for all.

On day two Creag Dubh was wet again and the forecast not great but the teams decided to go to Coire an t-Sneachda and climb something in the mountains, even if wet. But it remained dry, although cold and windy. John Lyall & Steve Perry climbed Just a Spot o' Sightseeing, with the rest making a sociable group on Pot of Gold.

Lake District Meet, Robertson Lamb Hut, Langdale
7–9 September 2012

Once again the comfortable and conveniently situated Robertson Lamb Hut in Langdale was the venue for the annual Lake District Meet. Although the weather gods were rolling their dice again, this year the outcome was more benign than in 2011. Various doings were reported on the Friday before the party foregathered, including ascents of Blencathra, and of 'the curiously denoted route *No Name*' on Castle Rock.

Members driving south on Saturday morning reported torrential rain, whereas in Langdale there was just a short spell of drizzle – although this was enough to make morning ascents of *Slip Knot* (MVS) and *Gordian Knot* (VS) on White Ghyll 'scarily greasy'; others had similar 'moments' on *Middlefell Buttress Left Hand*, *Subsidiary Ridge* (VDiff) on East Raven and *Damascus* via the first pitch of *Hollywood Babylon* (VS) on Far East Raven. But in the afternoon the sun came out, the rock dried, and those on White Ghyll enjoyed ascents of *Forget Me Not* (E1), *White Ghyll Wall* (MVS), *Haste Not* (VS) and *Laugh Not* (HVS). Elsewhere that day, there were ascents of the Old Man of Coniston and Wetherlam via Low Water Beck and Brim Fell, and of the Langdale Pikes. The day was crowned by a splendid feast laid on by Dick Allen and his various talented assistants, and the conviviality continued late into the night.

Sunday dawned glorious, and remained fine until mid-afternoon, when black clouds began to roll in from the west – although the deluge did not commence until most parties were well on their way home. There were ascents of High Raise via Jack's Rake (returning by Stake Pass); of *Cub's Groove* (VDiff) on Lower Scout Crag; of *Route 1* (VDiff) and *Route 2* (direct var. S) on Upper Scout Crag; of *Revelation* (HS), *Centipede* (S), *Holly Tree Direct* (HVS), *Nadir* (VS) and *Muscle Crack* (E1) on Raven Crag; of *Damascus* (VS 'yer granny', as the leader reported of the testing first groove) on Far East Raven; and of *Mamba* (S) and *Ophidia* (VS) on East Raven.

LAKES MEET 2012

Behind (L to R): Ian Crofton, Simon Fraser, Bob Reid, John Temple, Ian Gray, Peter Sterling, Laetitia Sterling, Jane Murdoch, Stuart Murdoch (and a Brown phantom!).
Front: Derek Buckle, Noel Williams, Maureen Suess, Nigel Suess, Peter Bettess, David Stone, Dick Allen, Pippa Cocker, Geoff Cohen, John Wood, Mike Cocker.

Lakes Meet 2012
Derek Buckle leads the second pitch of Gordian Knot (VS), White Ghyll.
Pippa and Mike Cocker are on the stance. Photo: Dick Allen.

Members present: Dick Allen (meet convenor), Hamish Brown, Derek Buckle, Mike Cocker, Geoff Cohen, Ian Crofton, Brian Davison, Simon Fraser, Jane Murdoch, Stuart Murdoch, Bob Reid, David Stone, Nigel Suess, John Temple, Noel Williams and John Wood

Guests: Pete Bettess, Pippa Cocker (AC), Ian Gray (CC), Laetitia Sterling (CC), Peter Sterling (CC) and Maureen Suess.

A big thank you to Dick Allen for organizing the weekend, and to the Wayfarers' Club for letting us use their premises.

IDC

JMCS REPORTS

Edinburgh Section: Regular readers of this annual report (if any) will notice that it is becoming something of a commentary on the Scottish weather insofar as it affects climbing. Last year I remarked upon the early finish to the winter and the poor summer that followed. This year the winter was curtailed by an even earlier thaw – the theatre curtain coming down with apparent finality just when one was looking forward to the final act – and was, by and large, followed by another wet summer. Between times there was a spell in April when the final act of winter did resume its course, but not all of the players could be bothered getting into costume again, having stashed their crampons at the back of the garage and moved on to other pursuits.

Fickle weather is not conducive to big attendances on weekend Club meets. If flexibility in choice of destination and activity is key to a good weekend, folk are reluctant to commit in advance to a journey north in the dark of a post-work Friday evening and tend to make last minute arrangements to suit themselves. This throws more emphasis on climbing at indoor walls to maintain cohesion among Club members. Fortunately this modus operandi has not adversely affected the level of our membership, nor their enthusiasm for getting out and doing whatever might be available to do.

Looking back on a mainly poor season of weather, the good times stand out more emphatically. For me the highlight was a Club meet in Glen Brittle in May. It was too cold for most people to rope up for multi-pitch routes high up in the Cuillin (the north faces were bedecked with icicles) but scrambling in the dry sunny weather was a delight and the new guidebook's coverage of the lower crags came in very useful.

Before signing off for another year, I would like to pay tribute to our Hut Custodians, Ali Borthwick and Helen Forde. They face a never ending list of things to be done, with limited thanks from the outside world for tasks completed, but anxious enquiry from all and sundry about whatever remains undone. I do not know why Ali and Helen have stuck to their roles for the many years that they have, but we depend on them to an extent that is not often brought to mind and they do not let us down.

We always welcome new faces. Please come along to our Monday or Wednesday night activities and meet and climb with some of the existing members. It is probably best to contact Terry Lansdown, the Membership Secretary, beforehand to make sure there has been no last minute change of venue. We go to Ratho on winter Wednesdays and Alien Rock on winter Mondays. During the summer we tend to climb outside on local outcrops on both days; you can see where we are going by looking at our website which also lists our forthcoming weekend meets. Just Google 'Edinburgh JMCS'.

Our huts are available for booking by kindred Clubs; please contact the Custodians whose names are shown below. We have 'The Cabin' in Balgowan, between Laggan and Newtonmore, and 'The Smiddy' at Dundonnell in the North West.

The present committee is; *Honorary President*: John Fowler; *Honorary Vice-*

President: Euan Scott; *President*: Chris Eilbeck; *Vice President* and *Smiddy Custodian*: Helen Forde (30 Reid Terrace, Edinburgh EH3 5JH, 0131 332 0071); *Secretary*: David Small (5 Afton Place, Edinburgh, EH5 3RB, <secretary@ edinburghjmcs.org.uk>); *Treasurer*: Bryan Rynne; *The Cabin Custodian*: Ali Borthwick (01383 732 232, before 9 p.m. please); *Membership Secretary*: Terry Lansdown (<t.lansdown@hw.ac.uk>); *Meets Secretary*: James Dalgarno.

David Small, Secretary

Glasgow Section: The Glasgow JMCS continues to thrive with well attended meets throughout the year throughout Scotland and a fortnightly wall-then-coffee (or when weather allows) crag-then-pub evening midweek. A total of 26 weekend meets were planned through 2011, all were in Scotland except for a late Summer foray to the Lakes. Typically the meets are very well attended from Autumn through to Spring with a quieter lull in the midsummer.

The Burns meet at Milehouse was as usual fully attended with as many squeezed in as the hut would allow for the communal meal, though this meant some members not being able to leave their seats for lack of space to move when the tables were set up. Whilst the Cairngorm winds were very strong on the Saturday, teams got out both days – *Pateys Route* one day and then ventured in to Loch Avon basin on the Sunday for *Salamander*. The wind had cleared any loose snow and an abundance of ice was found.

A few weeks later the first CIC meet took place, rain early on and then heavy snow meant for an overall disappointing meet with the only the *Clanger*, *Joyful Chimneys* (both V,5) and *Ledge Route* being climbed before a retreat down the hill. At other meets and in between the fantastic ice/snow was enjoyed by the winter climbers in the club with forays to Creag Meagaidh, Creagan a' Choire Etchachan, Braeriach, Beinn Eighe, Liathach, Ben a' Bhuird, Sheltestone, Ben Ledi and Hells Lum.

The club had a mixed downhill/ski mountaineering meet to Pointe de Voraiz in March, individual members made other summer trips to the Alps, Meteora (Greece) and the Julian Alps.

The honorary member of the section, Alan Thrippleton, celebrated his 100th birthday. Alan has a long association with the section and was one of the driving forces that established the club hut at Coruisk, he was also its first custodian from 1959–65. The hut is still going strong and the new roof has made for light work for the yearly work meet which enjoyed fantastic weather and not much work…

Member Colwyn Jones completed the Corbetts with a large turnout on Creag nan Gabhar, near Braemar and later in the year Charlie Craig completed the Munros with a wild day on Ben More.

As always the year ended well with the annual Christmas meet at Lagangarbh for the mince pies and a chance to show-off one's annual activities in the annual slide show. Fortuitously the meet coincided with a cold snap resulting in early season routes being climbed in an otherwise rather poor early winter.

The membership stands at 100, with 3 new members in 2011.

Officers for 2012: *President*: Matt Munro; *Secretary*: Tomoko Iwata; *Treasurer*: Justine Carter; *Coruisk Hut Bookings*: Iain Sneddon.

For more information on meets and other events see our website <www. glasgowjmcs.org.uk>. The club operates a members and non-members e-mail list which you can join at the above address for details of meets etc.

Matt Dent

Perth Section (Perth Mountaineering Club): The section continues to thrive, maintaining a reasonably stable membership and engaging in a full programme over the year, with regular monthly weekend meets and intervening day meets. The rock climbers have had a restricted summer on account of the weather, with few of them able to have the opportunity of getting up to the north-west where the sun shone almost continually. The hill-walkers have had a surprising number of good days, especially on the day meets – a glorious day in the Cairngorms comes to mind, when the weather confounded the MWIS forecast and gave an outstanding day, much to the chagrin of the climbers, who had abandoned any hope of decent conditions; a reminder, perhaps, that the best policy is often to get out and have a look.

A warm sunny day in Glen Coe gave an opportunity for the Aonach Eagach and another that improved as time wore on provided a fitting ambience for the second round 'compleation' of the Munros by Ron Payne on Beinn a' Ghlo. Earlier, Grahame Nicoll 'compleated' his third round on the Laggan hills in atrocious conditions and the celebration swim in Loch na Earba was put on hold for a while, and Jeff and Julia Banks finished their Corbett rounds in July on Beinn Damph and Fuar Tholl, respectively. Meets have been held at the SMC huts of Elphin and Lagangarbh and the section is always grateful to the parent club for the use of these splendidly situated huts.

More members than in previous years have expanded their horizons to include trips to the Alps, with Chamonix and Saas Fee being the favoured venues, with one group missing the fatal avalanche on Mont Maudit by a distance of ten miles or so. The Pyrenees has also been a popular destination and one member combined a thirteen week holiday with trips to both the Pyrenees and Chamonix – oh to be retired and still active!

Information about the activities of the club can be found on the Club website <www.perthmountaineering-club.co.uk/>. To contact the club secretary e-mail <secretary@perthmountaineering-club.co.uk>.

Des Bassett

SMC AND JMCS ABROAD

EUROPEAN ALPS

Des Rubens had an enjoyable visit to the Alps in 2011 with Geoff Cohen. The above photograph of Mont Collon (3637m) was taken from Arolla on 29 July 2011. The left skyline is the impressive NNE arête, first ascended by Naismith 1895. Photo: Des Rubens.

CHAMONIX RE-VISITED
By Jamie Thin

OK last time I was in Chamonix, I was camping at Snell's field and the friendly Polish climbers next door were teaching us a few tricks of the trade which mostly included how to fire-breath with spare paraffin fuel, while not burning down the tent!

Back in 1988 it was camping in the field with a few mates from Uni, the Bonatti Pillar and the American Direct were the big ticks, but there was no rush they would still be there next year.

Now in 2011, I was back in Chamonix but in a chalet with a hot tub, and half of the Dru had fallen down. The Bonatti Pillar no longer existed, it was a pile of shattered rocks at the bottom of the mountain. I had missed my chance.

There's not the same incentive to set-off up the hills on a dark night in the rain, when its warm in the chalet and banter is good. OK the wind and rain was familiar and reminded me of Chamonix, sheltering under the rocks below the Enver slabs, waiting for the slabs to dry out.

But no excuses, I might be too old for hard Alpine routes (and too young for the golf course), so I was here as one of the self-styled 'Random Scottish Punters' to do the UTMB – Ultra-Trail du Mont-Blanc – a 100-mile race round most of the Chamonix Alps.

(Not that I should mention the golf word – which is more like a four-letter world to most SMC climbers…but even ex-SMC President Bill Wallace used to have a regular game of golf with my Dad, and long past getting their free bus pass, they still set a benchmark for dogged toughness, playing in all weather when the youngsters wouldn't venture out!)

It is 11.30 p.m. on a Friday night. The locals are in the bars finishing off their beers. It is pouring with rain and I am now standing in a square with 2,300 other crazy folk, about to start running round a mountain walking route that takes ten days and the cut-off for the race is 46 hours.

I've traded in the big boots and big sack for light-weight trail shoes and sack.

There is some warmth from the other runners but no shelter.

The race organiser is dancing to 'singing in the rain' and loud-speakers are blasting out music.

The UTMB course.

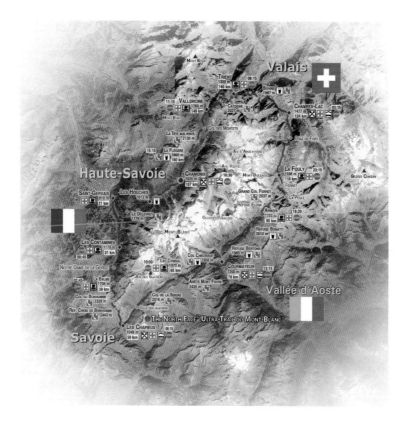

And then we are off…it is like a river of humanity clad in lightweight waterproofs.

I'm getting reflective now, but when does it change? You dream of climbing the American Direct on the Dru or the Bonatti Pillar, and then 20 years later, time has moved on – I don't want to do the same routes any more – I am probably as climbing fit as I have ever been – I still meet my mates for a cup of tea and a boulder at Alien Rock on a Tuesday evening through the winter – but the drive to do the long lonely leads has gone. I know my limit these days, and today that is more likely leading the kids up a Severe at Ben A'an, rather than the Dru.

My mind has stopped drifting, and I am back running out from the packed square in Chamonix town centre, past Bar Nat, and the climbing shops.

I am in my long shorts with compression socks up to my knees! (When in Rome…or Chamonix…and all that.) I'm just glad it is dark and I'm not running down Princes Street.

I blend into the mass of continental-types – gnarly looking French, Spanish, German and Italian runners, with a few random Scots, Irish, Americans, Canadians and Japanese. I'm running beside a familiar figure Ritchie Bell (from rival running club Carnethy in Edinburgh). HBT and Carnethy might be arch rivals in Edinburgh, but we are all pals abroad. There is lots of cheering and 'Bravos' as we run through the streets of Chamonix, out onto the muddy trail through the trees, with at last some temporary shelter from the still lashing rain.

It is a great feeling to be off and away – half the battle is getting to the start line. At least this is what I tell myself, it makes me feel better – this is the easy bit now! It does help that the race starts with 10km of gentle downhill running along the valley floor.

And at least, it feels like home. It's the summer monsoon season back in Scotland too – and now, the last weekend in August, here in France the forecast is more rain with snow on the high passes.

The race was cancelled last year due to storms and mud-slides, so this year the race organisers have been watching the weather, and they push the start back by five hours to avoid the worst of the weather which has been lashing the mountains all afternoon.

The first hill, I'm still with Ritchie…and I feel good…I should probably be worrying that I am racing up the first hill but it is hard not to get carried along with the flow of energy and in the dark I don't have a clue where I am in the pack. (As it turns out I go through the first 20km in about 250th place out of 2,300 – being in the top 10 or 20% in a race in Scotland is probably OK, but what I forget is that everyone who lined up at the start has already done their local equivalent of the West Highland Way as a qualifier, so I am the punter racing against some of the best ultra-runners from around the world.)

The path coming off the first hill is a torrent of mud. Up till now we had been on road and forest trails; now it is more-like an East District XC league race at Livingston or Broxburn. I edge ahead of Ritchie and plunge down through the trees to the first pit stop in St Gervais.

I keep the pace up and, after another couple of hours, I realise it is still the middle of the first night and I am definitely going too fast and beginning to feeling tired already!

Most of my training had been on Arthur's Seat on Monday lunchtimes…so I have already been running for eight times longer than my usual weekly sprint round the Hunters Bog, and only another 150km to go.

At least there is no shortage of company. I chat to a French runner from Paris, this is his third attempt on the UTMB and his target is to get under 30 hours. After some fast running along a gently rising valley floor, we are back climbing steeply and, as I've already gone all continental with the long socks, it's now time to get out my light-weight running poles! They snap together like tent poles, and in fact bend like tent-poles, but I'm surprised how helpful they are on the climbs, especially in the dark they lull you into a gentle rhythm. The top runners don't use them, and they are probably right – if you are Killian Jornet or Lizzy Hawker, poles will slow you down – but for the rest of us punters poles keep us alive and moving…when all you want to do is sleep.

My mind begins to wander and the poles bring me back to St Peters Primary in Edinburgh. I'm dropping my daughter off to school on the tandem bike (best way to fight through the Edinburgh rush-hour traffic) and I bump into another cycling parent doing the school run. It's Olly Stephenson and – while the other Mums and Dads are fussing over the kids – he shows me his latest purchase… lightweight racing poles perfect for the next adventure. He snaps them together and happily trips up a passing 6-year old on their way to school.

That brings me back to the dark and the rain…why exactly am I here, running through the night? I'm on holiday, I could be back in the chalet in the hot tub. I blame Olly – I find it always helps to blame someone else once you have committed yourself to some crazy outing.

We had just got round the last of our 24-hour rounds…Bob Graham, Ramsay and lastly the Paddy Buckley round down in North Wales…and I was thinking of more golf next year. But Olly's not a golfer…we now have enough qualifying points for the Ultra-Trail du Mont-Blanc…it would be rude not to.

So January 2011 – it has all the excitement of the national lottery – we send in our entries and nervously wait for the results from the ballot. Every year about 5,000 ultra-runners apply for the 2,300 spaces – so in a surprisingly un-French democratic way – they pick numbers out of a hat. I got my email – I was in! I was delighted for a moment, until my French work colleague Franck reminded me, that all I had won was the dubious privilege of running a two-day race round a long-distance mountain walking route that normally takes ten days.

But while I had slipped through the ballot, Olly hadn't. So that killed off any plans of running together. Olly, never one to be put off, quickly found another classic 100-mile ultra race on the same day over different mountains – the Grandes Raid de Pyrenees – so while not racing together we would at least both be racing the same weekend, and could train together and swap texts on race day.

While my mind was wandering, the lights of another pit stop brings me back to Mont Blanc.

The other person I could blame was another Carnethy runner Murdo McEwan – he had done the race twice before and he loved it. The magic had rubbed off on me and here I was – but at least Murdo had redeemed himself having fixed me up with a berth in the Chalet in Chamonix (via his pal Richie Cunningham of West Highland Way fame – Richie having won the WHW again, as his warm up for the UTMB).

I begin dreaming of the hot tub and sleep.

By now I am feeling pretty wasted and my stomach isn't too good – but the locals have a roaring bonfire going and I slurp down some hot soup while gently roasting by the blaze.

It is tempting to linger for a bit longer, but I am still in race-mode (soon it will be in survival shuffle-mode but I don't know this yet), and as other runners stream past me, I join the back of the train. The pace on the climbs is relentless, I know I am with guys far fitter than myself and probably more used to the altitude, but – what the hell – I might only do this race once, so I might as well give it my best shot and keep going till I fall over.

Cresting the top of the first high mountain pass – Croix du Bonhomme (2479m) – feels great. I'm catching the first light of dawn and there is fresh snow everywhere. Ice in places but mostly soft fresh snow which makes the flanks of Mont Blanc look fantastic with all the rocky ridges plastered in the white stuff.

The legs are feeling it on the big descent – I can see the path zigzagging and snaking down to the next valley floor, there is the whirr of a helicopter overhead and next I see another familiar figure run by – it is another random Scottish punter – Mark Leggett from Aberdeen direction.

We had only met the day before in Richie Cunningham's chalet – OK that sounds grand and it did have a hot tub – but Richie being a UTMB regular had kindly booked a big chalet in Chamonix and it was quickly filled with an unlikely bunch of West Highland Way veterans and random others (including me). Mark was a vet (animal kind) and had entertained us the day before with tales of operating on the same dog several times to remove various items (mostly rocks which it had a penchant for swallowing).

We were out the back of the Chalet – Flip Owen was in the hot tub – the rest of us were taking in a bit of sun before the forecast bad weather rolled in. While Mark had tales of mad dogs, and I had few tales of cycling round the Alps in my youth – it was Bob Allison who stole the show with the unlikeliest life-history of an ultra-runner. Bob's from Fife and that probably says it all. Folk will know him from multiple West Highland way races – but what you might not know is that he shattered his lower leg when his motorcycle came off the road and hit a wall. His leg was pieced together again with pins and plates and his doctor said at best he would be able to walk with a limp and a squint leg. But there was no stopping Bob. He hopped up a Munro on his one good leg, went back for more bone grafts, got his leg straightened in another op, and after the West Highland Way and more broken ribs – here he was doing the UTMB (when any other old codger from Fife would be back by the fire at home).

I chat to Mark for a bit and perk up. We get onto a wee path down grassy slopes – this is more like Arthur's Seat again!

We grab some bread and soup at Les Chapieux, and then it is back onto the road along a desolate valley floor – it is still cold, early morning and no sun with steep mountains on all sides.

Mark is going well, I keep up with him for a few miles but I am struggling and when we reach the next big climb up to Col de la Seigne (2516m) which is the gateway to Italy and Courmayeur. He surges on ahead.

I am back in my own wee world now, and shuffling more slowly, the poles are out again and I am back above the snow-line in a temporary white-out as a flurry of snow showers are blown across the col. I'm glad I'm not high up on the Brenva Face or on the Dru, nor facing a treacherous abseil back down thousands of feet of rock with dodgy belay anchors.

I also know why I'm here.

This is part holiday, part race, but more than that it is a chance to remember an old friend.

The chalet with the hot tub was round the corner from Chamonix hospital.

The leading group on the ascent to the Bonatti Refuge. Photo: © Tom Humpage.

The amazing Lizzy Hawker in the Aosta Valley. Photo: © Tom Humpage.

Nineteen years ago, a mountain rescue helicopter had flown in with a young British climber. He had fallen on abseil from the Aiguille du Dru, was still alive when help reached him, but dead on arrival at Chamonix hospital. He was my running and climbing pal Roger Lawson from Yorkshire. I hadn't been back to Chamonix since then and it still felt uncomfortable to be back.

We had progressed from rock climbing in Northumberland, winter routes on the Ben, our first mountain marathon in Galloway, to climbing in the Alps and Karakoram.

My memories aren't of the rock routes and winter gullies or the weary miles of the mountain marathons, they are of the camping and bivvying in bad weather – who could outlast the other before making the brew –living off the cheapest food we could find in Grindelwald only to find we were eating Swiss dog biscuits!

OK, I remember the swollen rivers and driving rain in the Galloway KIMM of 1986 – but most of all I remember trying to find my pal in an age before mobile phones…tricky when you arrive at the Friday night campsite at Loch Rannoch (KIMM 1990) way after midnight after a long hitch from North Wales, with no rendezvous plan and Roger has the tent. Only problem is – there are dozens of identical lightweight tents dotted around the many hundreds in the campsite.

He would have laughed at me now shuffling along and pretending to run – I'm sure he would have walked round here faster than my attempt at running. (Roger was a quiet, tough Yorkshireman from Thirsk in North Yorkshire. He might have been one of the strongest climbers of his generation – soloing all the routes on the Brenva Face of Mont Blanc, and climbing the Central Pillar of Freney. But his teenage years were spent roaming the North York moors on long-distance walking events with the scouts.)

By the time I get into Italy the sun comes out – it gets hotter – and my mood lifts with the weather. I am still tired but I am smiling as I remember my pals who would love to be here.

I'm taking a rest at a ski station above Courmayeur, when Ritchie Bell comes into view – great to see a familiar face again.

I'm not racing anymore now, I am just enjoying being on two feet, with some stunning views of the Alps. I'm winding my way down to Courmayeur with a chatty Irish runner and a gesticulating Hungarian.

Ritchie stops for some food, so I am still ahead of him – but he will catch me soon.

I stop in the big smoke of Courmayeur. It is like being back in Chamonix, but I'm not even half-way round. I'm in a bit of a daze but get some food, change shoes and clothes and look out for Ritchie – then press on.

By now it is mid-afternoon – the footpath to the Bonatti Refuge is majestic – contouring round a wooded hill-side with stunning views to the shining snows of the Brenva Face of Mont Blanc, and the Grandes Jorasses.

I've stopped eating now and I'm surviving on cups of tea – for some reason I can't get any food down. It's amazing how far you can get on one cup of tea.

At Arnuva, I don't even stop just fill up my water bottle with hot tea and keep going as I want to get over the Grand Col Ferret (2537m) and into Switzerland before dark and the second night.

Suddenly up ahead is Ritchie again – it is great to have company as its beginning to get cold and dark – he must have passed me in the medley at Courmayeur, and now I have caught him up again. We trudge up the steep slopes ahead, I stop thinking of Switzerland or even Chamonix – but just one step at a time, the next rock, the brow of the hill.

It is night-time again and the sleep tugs at my eyes – I follow Ritchie's steps then he follows mine – other runners join us and we stick together in the dark.

The dark goes on for hours – it is a blur – the odd pit stop, a pool of light in the dark with voices and more hot tea and coffee

About 3 a.m. Sunday morning, Ritchie starts to worry about catching his flight home in 12 hours time – Sunday afternoon seemed plenty of time for the return flight when sitting in Edinburgh!

We discuss binning it and making sure we can get home…but why keep going for 30 hours and then stop. Graeme Reid and Bob Allison catch us up. Bloody hell if Bob can do this with only one good leg – what excuse have I got. I keep going.

Bob and Graeme get ahead of us – me and Ritchie finally give into the sleep and have a 20-minutes cat nap at Champex-Lac (though Ritchie later owns up that he kicked me awake after only 15mins…he must have been taking his tips from Ernest Shackelton)

The faint light of dawn and we are heading down into the vineyards around Martigny in Switzerland – a friendly local offers us a breakfast swig of whisky and fresh grapes off the vine.

Ritchie is now stronger than me and moves into the distance. My mind is wandering again – we have to carry a mobile for safety cover so I text home to say hello and pick up a message from Olly. He has finished his race in the Pyrenees already. OK, he did start at 5 a.m. on Friday morning, rather than Friday night – but it only took him 28 hours! He must have had a stormer – meanwhile I am still plodding on after 32 hours with probably another eight to go.

But Olly's message fires me up – it is as if he has just run past my shoulder – bloody hell, I'm going to chase him down!

I kick myself wide awake, lean forward and stride out. And I plug into my emergency rations – my daughter's tiny MP3 player with loads of teenage dance tunes. First I have to catch Ritchie, then Bob and Graeme.

I am suddenly enjoying the race again and picking up speed – my feet are blistered and bruised but the legs still work and adrenaline floods my veins.

I catch Ritchie, we run together again, then slog up another climb back over to France. On the way to Vallorcine, we see Bob slumped at the side of the track half-asleep – we kick him awake, give him a few gels but don't expect to see him again. Twenty minutes later Bob races past us on the rocky path into Vallorcine. Now the race is on. We get a drink and some food. 20km to go to Chamonix – we are going to make it.

Ritchie and I set off again – for some reason I am convinced that Bob is ahead of us (in fact he is still getting a drink in the tent behind me). It is a flat path by the river – I urge Ritchie on – I don't want to get beat by Bob the Fifer. Ritchie is not so sure – so I head off alone and spur Ritchie on to pick up the pace.

It turns into a headlong rush for the finish, after hours of being passed – the tables are now turned and I am passing the same runners again – we exchange greetings – we all know we are close to the finish. I am now running faster than I have run for the past two days, I've tapped into another reserve and feel great, until I catch a toe on a rock and go flying – spread-eagled like Superman on the rocky path. My fellow runners wince. I dust myself down – no broken bones but a few more scars and lots of blood from my arm. I dip myself in a stream – and get going again but more carefully now.

Graeme Reid (frae Glasgow) comes into view – lack of sleep is finally catching up with him but he is going to make it – I shout a few words of encouragement. But I still think Bob is ahead of me – have you seen Bob? He must be going like the wind.

Through Argentière village – the marshals want to patch up my arm but the bleeding has stopped so I keep going – where's Bob?

One last climb in the woods above Chamonix, then a plunge down to the town.

There are plenty of crowds at the finish line and after 41 hours I am finally back in Chamonix – and in my bleary-eyed state of exhaustion, I am still convinced Bob the Fifer has beaten me!

Mark and Helen Leggett are there at the finish. Mark had a storming run to finish in 36 hours, Richie Cunningham led home the Scots in 29 hours 30 minutes and a top 50 finish.

Ritchie Bell, Bob Allison and Graeme Reid follow me in.

Then Ian King (Carnethy), Malcolm Hughes (Linlithgow), John Malcolm (Livingston) in 44 hours and Derek Morley (Glasgow) in 45 hours

There is time for food and drink and a trip to the first-aid post to get the cut cleaned out and bandaged up.

I'm walking round in a daze – there is a plan for a big session in the pub. I go back to the chalet, have a shower, fall asleep and that's it.

No pub, no hot tub – I wake up the next morning. Some holiday!

But it has been good to be back in familiar mountains – OK I didn't bag any

On the steep ascent to the Bertone Refuge. Photo: © Tom Humpage.

The finish.

tops but I was out for two nights and two sunrises, and saw the mountains from all angles in all shades of light and dark.

Not the same as climbing, but nice not to be carrying a big sack for once, and I made a few new friends and we all came back safe and sound, but with a few less toe-nails.

Stats:

170km and about 9,750m of climbing…a bit like running the West Highland Way plus running up and down the height of Ben Nevis every 25km.

Results:

Men

   1 Killian Jornet (ESP) 20hrs 36mins
   2 Iker Karrera (ESP) 20hrs 45mins
   3 Sebastien Chaigneau (FRA) 20hrs 55mins

Ladies

   13 Liz Hawker (UK) 25hrs 02mins (top UK finisher, beating all the UK men)
   25 Nere Martinez 27hrs 55mins
   31 Darcy Piceu 28hrs 30mins

Random Scottish Punters

   47 Richie Cunningham 29:30
   238 Mark Leggett 36:47
   540 Jamie Thin 41:05
   575 Ritchie Bell 41:22
   614 Bob Allison 41:49
   701 Graeme Reid 42:35
   989 Ian King 44:25
   999 Malcolm Hughes 44:30
   1006 John Malcolm 44:33
   1103 Derek Morley 45:12

DNFs

   Helen Johnson
   Karen Donoghue
   George Reid
   Phil Owen
   Tommy Hepburn

Post-script:

We all went back to Geneva Airport and I ended up sitting on the front step sharing some of Derek's malt whisky – which he had to finish before he could get through security!

Not everyone made it round this year – with 2,300 starters , there were 1,133 finishers, but everyone had their story to tell.

The same for the Random Scottish Punters – Karen Donoghue, Helen Johnson, Flip Owen, Tommy Hepburn, George Reid all DNFed (even last years winner Jez Bragg) – some were carrying old injuries, or had picked up coughs and chest infections during the week or just had bad luck when they were timed out at some of the early checkpoints.

It had been a long haul from training on wee hills in Scotland…and great to make some new friends

Everyone was great company – there was good craic from George Reid with his tales of trying to do the WHW twice back to back – some fated crazy escapade of starting in Fort William and running to Glasgow in time to start the WHW race and then run back to Fort William with the rest of the field (only they got their timing a bit off!) – that sounded like me – as the one time I did the WHW race, I missed the start and had a lonely stretch to catch the back markers!

But when it comes down to it – you don't do it just for the racing – you do it for the company and you have to enjoy the training.

More than once when I was out training on my own from home, I bumped into other UTMB hopefuls doing Double-Pentland-skylines or some other long run – and I spent one memorable Saturday running with John Malcolm and Malcolm Hughes over the Pentlands, through thunder and lighting and hail and torrential rain – which proved better training than we realised!

NORTH AMERICA
Kenai Mountains, Alaska – June/July 2012

After a successful expedition in 2010, Jas Hepburn, Graham McDonald and Niall Ritchie returned to the Kenai Mountains of South Central Alaska with a group of eight senior students from Banchory Academy. The party was made up of two girls and six boys aged 16–18.

Arriving in Anchorage to temperatures in the 70s was a promising start and a good omen for things to come. With provisions purchased and gear packed the group headed the 130 miles down Seward highway to the Kenai Fjords National Park. A look at the long term forecast for the area did not make good reading and after the grim weather in 2010 the worst was anticipated. This in an area that sees the Harding Ice field exceed 100ft of snowfall in a season. The forecast thankfully proved incorrect and a settled spell of beautiful weather was enjoyed. Travelling across the largest ice field solely in the United States in dreamy conditions was a complete wilderness experience to rival anything.

The area has over thirty glaciers flowing outward from the ice field and has numerous nunataks protruding through the ice, thousands of feet thick. We again climbed one of these at just under the 5000ft contour and had the most stunning of panoramas seen by any of us. Our tents appeared a mere speck in the sea of ice below. Although we spent several days on the ice setting up three camps we barely scratched the surface in this big area in the vastest of states.

The first known crossing of the Harding Ice field which covers 700 square miles was first completed in 1940. It is rarely done but would make for a magnificent and demanding undertaking on ski. A local guide we met described the way off as 'gnarly' with some rappels!

We descended in time to make the 4th of July festivities in Seward and witness the annual Mount Marathon race, the second oldest hill run in the USA. This can be left for another visit. Aye right!

The flight adds a less strenuous dimension with great views of Greenland on the way over and a setting sun on the melting ice pack of Hudson Bay on the return.

The group on the Harding Icefield – having descended from the nunatak, on the return to camp.

The expedition members back at the starting point at the Exit Glacier Nature Centre.
Photos: Niall Ritchie.

A truly memorable time was had by all and thanks go to the SMT for some financial assistance which is much appreciated.

NR

CHINA
Ma Long Feng – a Chinese 4000er

I recently spent five years living in China's SW province of Yunnan (bordering Tibet, Burma and Laos) and managed to squeeze a small amount of trekking and low-grade mountaineering into family holiday trips. The mountains here are the southern expression of the tectonic ruckle that is the Himalayas before they founder into the forested hills and muddy river valleys of southern Yunnan. The area doesn't seem to be as popular with foreign groups as neighbouring Sichuan, despite some impressive 6000m peaks in the far north around Deqin. The reason for this is probably the relatively limited number of high mountains and proximity of the Tibetan border which means that the most attractive summits are off-limits due to their cultural and religious significance. The jewel in the crown is beautiful Miyetzimu (Miancimu) 6054m, though Kawakarpo (Kawagebo) 6740m is the highest. Both are unclimbed.

My goals however lay at a somewhat lower altitude, and I scoured the maps for something hassle-free and accessible that I could get up partner-less and quickly. In the process I managed to become mildly fixated on getting to the top of the highest 4000m peak in the Cang Shan above the famous tourist town of Dali. Could that cross on the map be the furthest south 4000er in the Himalayan range? It seemed like a decent challenge. Dali is a relaxing backpacker retreat and a node on the Ancient Teahorse Trail, a southern Asian 'Silk Route' along which tea bricks were once transported from China to Tibet, Burma and beyond. These days it attracts increasing numbers of domestic tourists as well as laptop-wielding Western travellers gorging themselves on banana pancakes.

Ma Long Feng (4122m) is the highest peak in the Cang Shan mountains and a worthy highpoint, a rocky top at the end of a pinnacled ridge leading westwards from the main N-S ridge axis. The other main peaks are Yu Ju Feng (4097m), adjacent on the main ridge, and Zhong He Feng (4092m) to the north. The latter two hills can be easily ascended by walkers on reasonable paths, but Ma Long Feng presents some difficulties: exposure, route-finding, greater remoteness and a less-travelled path. In Scotland it would be regarded as an easy scramble. There's no permanent snow up here but a daytrip to these summits is always going to be physically demanding, with well over 2000m of ascent from Dali, and the effects of altitude to consider. One overnight possibility on the mountain is the Higherland Inn, a small guesthouse at 2680m, just above an interesting Taoist temple, but this is really too low and it's only an hour above Dali. A better option would be to camp (or bivvy) at a flat meadow (3700m) in the hanging corrie just below the tiny Wash Horse Pool and spend a few days up there. A traverse northwards along the main ridge of the Cang Shan would be possible.

Previous failure is always a good incentive to build on obsession, and so it was with my Ma Long Feng saga. Numerous visits over three years of attempts involved (separately and in no particular order): climbing the wrong mountain (no map); persistent low cloud (a common problem in the summer rainy season months); deep snow cover down to 2500m (in January – no progress beyond the

Higherland Inn, but good snowman-building potential for the kids); high winds on the upper ridge (another January failure). It should be pointed out to readers that this long litany of defeat in no way reflects the difficulty of the mountain, merely a dearth of published information combined with my own ineptitude.

With all that build-up, the triumphal ascent was always going to be a bit of an anticlimax. Eventual success was achieved in an efficiently executed daytrip in February 2009 (following a period of high-altitude tourist activity up at the monasteries of Deqin and Zhongdian). A 5.45 a.m. start from the guesthouse in Dali meant I avoided paying the 'Entry Tax' to the mountain and enjoyed dawn over Er Hai Lake from well above the Higherland Inn. The Cang Shan are justifiably renowned as a botanical paradise. The climb up from the rice plains of Dali passes through a number of distinct vegetation zones: eucalyptus trees, pine forest, bamboo, and finally, beyond the tree line at 3800m, azaleas (and a wonderful selection of alpine flowers). This microclimate gradation was one of the attractions for Western plant hunters in the 19th and early-20th Century, in addition to the general remoteness and the fact that the great trenches of the Salween, Mekong and Yangtze rivers carve out uniquely separate ecological niches.

Five hours steady climb up from Dali and I was taking a rest at the familiar meadow under Wash Horse Pool. Here on a previous visit I'd encountered a Base Camp of fully kitted-up Chinese mountaineers who press-ganged me into a photo-session. I couldn't help but contrast my scruffy appearance and lack of axe, crampons, and Gore-tex with these cheerful, friendly (and rather over-equipped) characters.

Another half an hour took me to the summit of Yu Ju Feng (scene of the 'wrong mountain' incident mentioned above). The pinnacled ridge leading out to Ma Long Feng (which appears the same height from here) looked intimidating, much like a vegetated Cuillin Ridge, but a faint path skirted round the overhanging bits and the snow on the northern flanks, which was knee-deep in places, didn't cause any problems (the trusty pine bough ice-axe I'd picked up in the forest wasn't needed). In fact the only difficulty was caused by snapping azalea branch handholds in the crux groove. The solitude, and the exploratory nature of the mountaineering in this part of the range, more than compensated for the lack of technical spice.

It felt good to have finally made the summit. The blue swathe of Erhai Lake looked a long way down, and to the north I could make out a white smudge marking Yu Long Xue Shan (Jade Dragon Snow Mountain, 5596m, first climbed in the 1980s) above Lijiang. Behind that, beyond the Tiger Leaping Gorge (a good trek), is Haba Xue Shan (5396m) a fairly popular and easy snow peak. It would be a good add-on to the TLG trek.

That was 2009. In 2011 the rumour is that there are plans for a hotel development at Wash Hose Pool serviced by a tourist cable car from Dali. Such is the way in China as it ploughs on relentlessly into the 21st Century.

Alastair Matthewson

Miyetzimu (6054m) – also known as Miancimu – viewed from Feilai Si, near Deqin.
Photo: Alastair Matthewson.

Alastair Matthewson notes this peerless unclimbed peak straddles the Yunnan-Tibet border and is revered by the local Tibetans.

The botanist Joseph Rock better described the view in 1923: 'Miyetzimu is the most glorious peak my eyes were ever privileged to see; no wonder the Tibetans stand in awe and worship it. It is like a castle of a dream, an ice palace of a fairy tale ... a majestic dome of ice tapering into an ethereal spire merging into a pale-blue sky.'

Some summits are maybe better left untouched by human footsteps...

REVIEWS

Blencathra : portrait of a mountain: Ronald Turnbull. (London: Francis Lincoln, 2010, hbk, 176pp, ISBN 978-0-7112-2986-0, £25.)

I have been on Blencathra/Saddleback more than once, and on one or two of the lesser hills in its hinterland, but I cannot in any way claim to know the mountain, and in consequence feel rather less than qualified as a reviewer, in the face of Ronald Turnbull's extensive knowledge and deep love of Blencathra, which are evident on every page of this impressive and rather expensive book.

There are a lot of pictures in the book, but it is more than a coffee-table picture book. Most of Turnbull's pictures are excellent, some of them breathtaking. The shape and location of Blencathra, rising steeply from the Vale of Keswick with St John's Vale beyond, lend themselves to views with a mountain foreground and a long vista of farmland beyond (or the reverse), and he gives us plenty of these; and the number of times 'dawn' or 'sunrise' appears in the captions is evidence of his dedication in pursuit of the picture he wants.

The book is divided into an introduction and ten sections, one for each of the various areas or aspects of Blencathra and its northern neighbours, with the two kilometre summit ridge getting the final section to itself. The same clear and attractive map of the whole area appears on both end papers, but the book would have been improved by the inclusion of more detailed maps to accompany the individual sections. Text and pictures are closely intermixed, to the extent that the text is sometimes interrupted by a page of pictures in the middle of a paragraph.

The text itself is a rich and varied mixture. There are descriptions of routes and views, both the author's own and those of a range of historical figures including Wordsworth and Coleridge, John Stuart Mill, Charles Dickens and Wilkie Collins, as well as lesser-known locals and Victorian guide-book writers. There is discussion of the eighteenth century notions of 'picturesque beauty' and the Sublime, as applied to mountain scenery, earnestly enquired into by Edmund Burke and ridiculed by Jane Austen. There are accounts of the formation of the Lake District and the detailed geology of Blencathra, and of the history of mining on Carrock Fell and elsewhere. What seems to be a curious love-hate relationship with Wainwright is revealed in numerous references to his account of Blencathra in The Northern Fells. Turnbull explains his inclusion of a chapter on what he calls 'the bad ways up Blencathra?' (the ravines between the five front ridges) as resulting from 'the strong desire to go up there to see if it's really so bad as he says'. Wainwright is also the prompt for a rather overplayed account, by way of comparison with other uninteresting Lakeland humps, of the extreme uninterestingness of Mungrisdale Common. This is one of a number of attempts by Turnbull to lighten the tone of his text with humour which do not really succeed.

As he says in his conclusion, a 200-page book about a single hill must to a large extent be a book about the people who have walked on it and written about it, and he succeeds admirably in blending the historical accounts with his description of the mountain today. But what impresses at least as much as the extent of his knowledge of Blencathra and its history, is the evident strength of his enthusiasm for and love of the mountain. Whether or not to do so is to know the whole world, as Turnbull claims, his book will have succeeded if it makes his readers, as I am sure in most cases it will, want themselves 'to simply see, and be on, Blencathra'.

Peter Moffatt

Echoes of a Dream : a crag rats tale: Alan 'Richard' McHardy. (Monkey Goes to Heaven, 2011, pbk, 248pp, ill., ISBN 978-0-9570563-0-5, £12 + £3 p&p from: <www echoesofadream.co.uk>.)

The 1960s were a bit indistinct in terms of British rock climbing. It was an era wedged between the higher profile 1950s, with the feats of Joe Brown and Don Whillans, and the 1970s, when real fitness and training came into focus, spearheaded by Pete Livesey. It was also a time when climbs started to become bolder as they moved away from the security of crack-lines and onto the open faces. However there seemed to be few top-drawer climbers to take over the mantle from Brown and Whillans. In Scotland, Robin Smith was the leading light and would have gone on to great things had he not sadly been killed at an early age. Climbing was healthy though and there were a number of determined, very brave climbers operating, of whom one of the most enthusiastic and probably the boldest of them all was Richard McHardy.

Echoes of a Dream is essentially an autobiography and has been written in Richard's own unique style. It is unorthodox, brutally honest and laced with a subtle sense of humour. It is engaging, and although the literary fraternity may find it difficult to look past the unusual style and grammar, it is well worth reading on. The book is written in the manner that Richard would tell his story if you were in conversation with him. At times, (especially if you don't know Richard), you would wish him to go into a bit more detail in some of the passages as they truncate rather quickly. However, if he did expand on the material in this book, it would fill ten volumes. The pictures go hand in hand with the script and some are of superb quality.

Being born and brought up in the war, in a working class environment in Manchester, is the backdrop to this incredible story of an individual who has lived his life to the full. Almost every chapter is bursting with both adventure and misadventure. Passages detailing the leaving of his dead friend on an Alpine face, and the onset of epilepsy after 'breaking his head' as a result of a big fall in Llanberis pass, are moving and saddening. Richard moved to Scotland in the 1970s to start a family but he continued to push the boundaries of bravery. His soloing was legendary; soloing routes such as *Carnivore* and *Apparition* in Glen Coe at a time when the top standard routes of the day were only a notch or two harder, (*Titan's Wall* and *Cougar* come to mind), was a staggering achievement and really gives the true measure of this man who lives to climb.

This was a story that needed to be told, not just for the nostalgia, for his mates to read and reminisce over, but for the younger generation of climbers – those who boulder and those who only visit the climbing wall – so that they can see the bigger picture and look through the porthole to find out what the life of an audacious 1960's crag rat was like, warts and all.

Now at the age of 71, Richard's story continues. In marked contrast to his earlier days, he has now embraced the safer concept of Sport Climbing. The pure love of climbing still burns strongly within him and he is planning further adventurous climbing holidays with his wife Barbara.

Rather unusually, Richard's name has been omitted from the cover of the book, but for an honest, entertaining and at times hard-hitting read this unique book is worth every penny.

Julian Lines

Triumph and Tragedy: The Life of Edward Whymper: Emil Henry. (Leicester: Matador, 2011, hbk, xxxii, 428pp, ill., maps, ISBN 978-1848765-788, £17.99.)

Emil Henry is an American, inspired by his own guided ascent of the Matterhorn in 1984, who has written a sympathetic biography of Whymper. As well as tracing Whymper's achievements in the Alps, Greenland, the Andes and the Canadian Rockies, he attempts, with some success, to understand the personality of the man who became the public face of mountaineering in Victorian and Edwardian Britain. Contrasting his own biography with that of F.S. Smythe (1940), he draws a more humane picture of the great mountaineer.

Drawing on 'Scrambles in the Alps' and other sources, he reminds us of the awe in which the Matterhorn was held prior to its first ascent, and the assumption of many that the mountain would never be climbed. The story of the years of the 1860s which lead up to the first ascent and its tragic aftermath, including descriptions of leading Alpinists and guides displaying heroism, generosity, opportunism or downright deception, is an enthralling read.

The months spent in Ecuador on Chimborazo, the first mountain summit climbed of over 20,000 feet, and Cotopaxi is informative. The frustrations and successes of his two seasons in Greenland are also documented.

One is left with a sense of the great exploratory accomplishments of Whymper. Additionally, the respect in which he was held by his contemporaries, such as Leslie Stephen, was due not only to his qualities as a mountaineer, author and engraver but also to his honesty and sensitivity in dealing with the aftermath of the tragedy which publicly defined him. Henry draws these qualities out well.

There are drawbacks. Some of the maps are unreadable, though perhaps they were just included for historical interest. The style of the prose is rather over clichéd for this reviewer's taste; and Henry draws some general assumptions about Whymper and about mountains which I found irritating. Possibly an author with a mountaineering background would have made a more acceptable job. However, the book does provide a comprehensive and well researched overview of Whymper's life and a reminder of the importance he has as a figure in the history of our sport.

Des Rubens

A Zoologist on Baffin Island, 1953: four months of Arctic adventure: Adam Watson. (Paragon Publishing, 2011, pbk, 240pp, ill., ISBN 978-1-907611-70-4, £32.99.)

During the summer of 1953, 23-year-old zoologist, Adam Watson, took part in the trip of a lifetime when he joined a scientific expedition to explore the mountainous interior of Baffin Island's Cumberland Peninsula. The four month long expedition had been organised by Pat Baird, then Director of the Arctic

Institution of North America, and sponsored jointly by that institution and the Swiss Foundation for Alpine Research. Baird had previously lead an expedition to the Barnes ice cap further north and believed the higher Penny Ice Cap in the Cumberland range would provide further valuable research into the glaciology of the area. Among the 13-strong team of scientists and general assistants were four experienced Swiss alpinists who, when not involved with research, made first ascents and named several prominent peaks including the spectacular twin-towered Mount Asgard.

The expedition arrived at the Inuit settlement of Pangnirtung in early May and with the help of a Norseman ski-plane set up a base camp at Summit Lake in Pangnirtung Pass, as well as two glacier camps to the north, on the Penny ice cap. A cache was also left beside a frozen lake in upper June Valley, which was to be used by Adam to set up a biological camp at the north end of Pangnirtung Pass.

On 20 May, Adam and Don Kid, a Canadian geologist, were flown from Pangnirtung to Padloping on the north coast. From here they travelled by dog-sledge with an Inuit hunter across sea ice around coastal islands, spending some time at the impressive headland of Cape Searle with its large fulmar population. Eventually they reached the head of Padle Fiord before parting company with Samo the hunter. Carrying heavy loads and travelling independently, Adam and Don then walked west in deep snow via the cache in June Valley to the proposed site of the biological camp. This, they established with help from Ben Battle on 9 June, on the east bank of the wide braided river flowing north into North Pangnirtung Fiord. Opposite the camp, on the west side of the river, the view was dominated by two massive granite buttresses estimated to be over 3000 feet in height.

'Bio' camp was to be Adam's home for the next two and a half months. He spent the long arctic summer days in this wonderful, very remote place, studying animals, mostly birds and mammals, often alone, but from time to time with other expedition members, in particular, the Swiss botanist, Fritz Schwarzenbach. A significant part of Adam's research was his study of nesting snowy owls (it was a bumper year for lemmings) and he named the braided river Snowy Owl River (shortened to Owl River by the Canadian Board of Geographical Names). The big cliff across Owl River was named Ozymandias by a Cambridge mountaineering party when in the area eight years later.

In the months following the expedition, Adam contributed to a note on zoology in a summary report by Baird and other members of the team. He also wrote six technical papers published in international scientific journals in Canada and Britain. Over the years he had always had a hankering to write his own account of the expedition and in 2010 at 80 years of age, when only one of four members still living, he concluded 'It is time for this book.'

And, what a splendid book it is too. Large in format, it is packed with superb original colour photographs, many full page, depicting the magnificent scenery, wildlife, flora, the Inuit people, dog sledging, camping and expedition members at work and play. The bulk of the book is a detailed daily diary of the full four months using Adam's own field notes taken at the time, supplemented by his own recall and information from other colleagues. Later chapters include specific sections on his zoology work and individual appreciations of Baird, Schwarzenbach and geomorphologist, Ben Battle, a good friend, who sadly drowned on the expedition when he fell through ice near Base Camp. In a final short chapter Adam compares the Baffin Island of 1953 with that of today, conceding that although he is glad he saw Pangnirtung Pass in the 1950s, before it became a National Park with wardens, huts, signposts etc, he does not begrudge the resourceful Inuit his adoption of a more modern way of life and freedom to improve his lot by self government.

You do not have to be a trained scientist to appreciate this book. Anyone who enjoys exploring new terrain, whether wide open valleys or steep rock walls, will have no problem empathising with Adam's great enthusiasm for the Arctic wilderness of Baffin Island.

Greg Strange

The Sound of Gravity: Joe Simpson. (Jonathan Cape, 2011, hbk, 234pp, ISBN 978-0224072649, £16.99.)

Joe Simpson's reputation in mountain literature is forever assured through his first book *Touching the Void*. This is his second work of fiction. It opens dramatically on an alpine north face in winter, at a bivvy site sandwiched between a lower ice band and an upper rock buttress. Due to a careless miscalculation, Patrick's wife slips and he fails to arrest her fall. Part one of the book charts his harrowing escape route off the face and the frostbitten descent down an easier ridge to the glacier. In desperation he locates the likely crevasse she disappeared down. The tension and mental torment that Patrick experiences are depicted in superb detail. Simpson himself has famously endured many epics and his descriptions of the character's sensory experiences of being in a tight situation are visceral and compelling. The portrayal of mountains as places of wonder and beauty is successfully realised as Patrick becomes marooned in a savage arena contemplating the unfathomable.

Part two begins 25 years later when Patrick is the unofficial warden in a basic hut at the foot of the mountain on which the initial tragedy took place. A death occurs to a terminally ill mountaineer on the same mountain, the body of whom is evacuated by a rescue team as far as the hut in a developing storm. At the same time another couple descend the peak with the exhausted woman Cassie, in the throws of hypothermia. While everyone else heads down, Cassie and Patrick survive the worsening conditions which literally break the hut apart. Patrick's care brings Cassie back from near death, brought on by her dangerously low body temperature. Upon recovery she pierces his hard shell and he shares the story of his life since his wife's death. It brings them together emotionally and the book ends with Cassie repaying his compassion by seeking out his own troubled self on the glacier below the face where the original tragedy occurred.

My main problem with the second part is that I just didn't buy that for 25 years Patrick had been so trapped in his grief as to want to spend large periods of time in a place which holds so many negative memories. The relationship between Patrick and Cassie is thoughtfully handled but I predicted where the novel would end up from quite early in part one. The blurb on the back did nothing to keep this a secret.

Part one could have worked well on its own as a novella if supplied with a more surprising ending. Some might feel Patrick's introspections are overdone in comparison to the at times gripping action sequences. It is a claustrophobic story: same hut, mountain, glacier but this accords nicely with the idea that Patrick is trapped in his own past.

A lot of mountain literature is concerned with strife, soul searching, earnestness and the type of material that goes down well when survivors are invited to speak at corporate presentations to inspire desk job employees. I'd like to see more anarchic stories which lampoon the joyful ridiculousness of the glorious activity that is mountaineering. It's been a long time since Rum Doodle and something new in this genre would be most welcome. Or perhaps the world in general is just a more serious place? Modern Pateys or PG Wodehouses seem thin on the ground. The latter would have needed no more than half an hour at an SMC dinner or AGM to come up with a satirical gem.

Despite the misgivings I wouldn't hesitate in recommending this novel.

Mike Dixon

To Ride the Mountain Winds: a history of aerial mountaineering and rescue: Leslie Symons. (Sandstone Press, 2011, hbk, xxxii, 304pp, ISBN 978-1-905207-60-2, £15.99.)

The book is a history of aviation associated with flying in the mountains and to a lesser extent mountaineering. The content is essentially a series of abstracts from extensive reference sources (222 references) on events dating from the earliest balloon and gliding flights over mountains to ultimately landing a helicopter on the top of Mount Everest.

The aviation history covers the full gambit of flying activities from ballooning, gliding, airship, fixed wing, rotary, seaplanes, ski planes, parachute, hang gliding and paragliding through to base jumping in the mountain environment. The use of 'flying machines' in exploration both for mapping and reconnoitering unknown terrain is extensively discussed.

A large part of the book is devoted to the evolution of flying for rescue purposes in the mountains starting with parachuting rescue teams and equipment into accident sites and more recently high altitude evacuations from High Himalayan and other Peaks. The European Alps also feature extensively with Swiss and French mountain accident reports.

For those technically minded the book contains a large amount of data on flying machines and flying limits of these machines together with weather conditions/limitations. Evolution of training for mountain flying in Switzerland was particularly interesting.

The book is probably best read in small doses due to the huge amount of information contained therein and will be a useful reference source for those interested in aviation and mountain rescue. To a lesser extent the book discusses the use of aviation to access remote locations for the purposes of mountaineering.

W. Forbes

Prelude to Everest: Alexander Kellas, Himalayan Mountaineer: Ian R Mitchell & George W Rodway. (Luath Press, 2011, hbk, 288pp, ISBN 978-1-906817-74-9, £20.00.)

Alexander Kellas was a pioneering Himalayan climber, and a pioneer in the field of high altitude physiology too. While his Himalayan exploits before and after the Great War were not entirely forgotten, his scientific work largely was, and the stimulus for this book came from the revival of interest in his high-altitude work initiated by the Australian scientist John B. West (now at San Diego) in the 1980s. The book is most appropriately dedicated to West.

Here there is an interesting parallel with another mountaineer-physiologist Thomas Graham Brown: Brown's work on interneurons was of Nobel-winning quality, but his *magnum opus* appeared in a German Journal during the Great War, and passed into oblivion until discovered and publicized by the Swedish neuroscientist Anders Lundberg in the late 1960s. Members might enjoy the very entertaining account of Brown and his chaotic life by J. Gareth Jones and others in *Journal of the History of the Neurosciences*, 20 (2011), 188–209.

West passed the Kellas baton on to a younger physiologist George Rodway, who was also an enthusiastic mountaineer. Rodway published a few articles about Kellas (one in our own Journal, 39/196 (2005), 13–20) and when Ian Mitchell offered to fill in the Scottish end of the Kellas story, the Kellas biography became a going concern.

The heart of the book is the story of Kellas's explorations in the Indian Himalaya (Garhwal and Sikkim) from 1907–14, and 1920–21. With very little mountaineering background, and very often with no European companion, he made numerous lengthy and successful expeditions to the lesser peaks of the Kanchenjunga group, and to the Kamet group. The authors discovered that in ascending Pauhunri (7125m) east of Kangchenjunga, he had achieved the world summit record, not displaced until 1930 when Jongsong Peak (7462m) in the Kanchenjunga group (also attempted by Kellas) was climbed by Hörlin and Schneider. This interesting record was not recognized by Kellas or his contemporaries, however, since Pauhunri had been under-measured, and Longstaff's ascent of Trisul (7120m, Garhwal) in 1907 was generally regarded as the summit record. This discussion sets to one side (as do Mitchell & Rodway) the possibility that William Graham's ascent of Kabru (7338m) in 1883 was an accurate report of what he climbed.

This section of the book makes fascinating reading, revealing Kellas as a true pioneer: in his approach to Himalayan climbing, his use of Sherpas as porters and climbing companions, his interest in acclimatization, the value of high camps, and the possibilities of oxygen supplementation. It also reveals Kellas as the architect of the A.C./R.G.S. strategy for Everest put in place in the 1921 Reconnaissance, and followed thereafter. Kellas enjoyed the confidence and support of the difficult Arthur Hinks of the R.G.S., perhaps because he presented himself as more of a geographer/explorer than as an alpinist/mountaineer. At any rate, Hinks was always ready to listen to Kellas, and the authors make a reasonable case for the notion that Kellas might have led the Reconnaissance, had it not been for the unreasonable objections from Percy Farrar at the A.C.

The initial sections of the biography deal with Kellas's Aberdeen background, scientific training, research work at William Ramsay's Laboratory at University College London, and teaching at the Middlesex Hospital. While this is interesting in its way, there is not much in the way of Kellas writing or correspondence to work with, and the account necessarily wanders off the highway into the byways of Aberdeen sociography, the Cairngorm Club and our Club, the roles of Collie and Travers in the discovery of the inert gases, and so forth.

The final section deals with Kellas's sad death from heart failure following severe dysentery on the approach to Everest in 1921, and finishes with a summation of his career and achievements. A useful Appendix supplies a Chronology and an English version of Kellas's long article 'A Consideration of the Possibility of Ascending Mount Everest', originally obscurely published in French in 1921.

The book employs an excellent historical apparatus throughout, with each chapter liberally footnoted, and is well illustrated by maps and photographs. There is a Bibliography as well (though some of the footnoted material doesn't find its way there), and an adequate Index.

Mitchell and Rodway have provided a first-class biography that not only describes Kellas's life, but also tells a large part of the story of early Himalayan exploration. There is, however, one conclusion drawn about Kellas that seems to me to be inadequately supported: namely, their judgment that he suffered from mental illness, even 'severe psychosis' (p. 27).

This diagnosis seems to rest on three observations: that he left school at age 16 and does not re-appear in the educational process for a few years; that he heard voices during adult life, if not earlier; that he left his post at the Middlesex Hospital in 1919 – resigning in early 1920 – due to ill-health, and subsequently consulted an Aberdeen psychiatrist. None of these observations is adequate support for the view that Kellas suffered from mental illness. There could be many reasons for his leaving school at 16, and no evidence is adduced here that he left because of any sort of illness, mental or otherwise. Many people hear voices while awake (estimates lie between 10% and 15%) but only a tiny fraction of these suffer from mental illness. But since a sizeable proportion of people diagnosed with schizophrenia hear voices, the process of stigmatization is apt to turn this relationship around, and I fear that this is what has happened here. 'Hearing voices' when unaccompanied by other psychiatric symptoms such as delusion, is simply auditory hallucination – troublesome perhaps (Kellas described it as a disability in a letter to Hinks), but not any sort of clear sign of mental illness. As for resigning his post, he would have had to do so in any event since he was about to take off for Kamet in the spring of 1920, 'ill health' notwithstanding, and the Aberdeen psychiatrist was just one of several that he had consulted about his auditory troubles.

Kellas was perfectly open about his hallucinations, and mentioned them to Hinks in 1919 and again in February 1920 shortly before leaving for India to attempt Kamet (and carry out experiments there) with Morshead (p. 157). But he added that 'I have consulted several specialists both in London and here who can find nothing wrong whatever, physically or mentally.' Although Hinks was plainly quick to stigmatize, and fired off inquisitive letters to Henry Kellas and Norman Collie (pp. 155–6), these were met with firm assurances of Kellas's health. In the months that followed, Kellas performed admirably on Kamet. It is surprising to me that the authors reached these conclusions about Kellas's mental health, knowing as they must do what it takes in the way of mental and physical fitness to keep going strongly above 20,000 feet, as Kellas undoubtedly did in 1920.

Robin N Campbell

A Snow Book, Northern Scotland: Adam Watson. (Paragon Publishing, 2011, pbk, 137pp, ISBN 978-1-908341-12-9, £24.99.)

You have got to like snow before you collate information on cover and patches over 64 years. Well, the author certainly loves the white stuff and this book is a testimony to that fact. The first two chapters give a hint of the extremely onerous task the author set himself. Here is a record of how much snow has lain on the Ben Macdhui plateau after 1 June every year since 1947. Next is data on fresh falling snow on the Cairngorms, 1944–2010.

A fascinating section is the review of Scottish snow-bed survival, 1900–2010. The author writes: 'I used the terms survived and survival to mean old snow that remained until the first lasting snowfall for the next winter (not the first snowfall, which was often ephemeral).' Information on snow patches has been collated from many sources – journals of the Cairngorm Club and the SMC, and most publications pertaining to Scottish snow. Mention must be made of his team of hardy helpers who climb hills likely to have late snow patches in various parts of the country and report back to the author.

For the technically minded there are three graphs and 14 tables giving details of all trends of snow conditions in Scotland over the past 110 years. To accompany the text there are 80 coloured illustrations – some are great photos with the Cairngorms at their best, while others show the use of snow by hill birds and mammals.

The work involved here is phenomenal – a product of a scientific mind. Given the choice this reviewer would consider re-writing the Bible an easier option.

Derek Pyper

Into The Silence : The Great War, Mallory and the conquest of Everest: Wade Davis. (London: Bodley Head, 2011, hbk, xiv, 655pp, ISBN 978-1-847921840, £25.)

Not yet another book about Mallory/Everest, one might think. However, this one also proposes that a generation of British climbers 'grown up in the age of civilised peace' – as G.W. Young wrote – but inured to death and its consequences by the slaughter of the Great War, carried this do-or-die legacy on their expeditions and consequently accepted a previously unimaginable degree of risk on the mountains – an interesting suggestion but one that I regard with several degrees of scepticism. The author is a Canadian anthropologist/ethnobotanist and Explorer-in-Residence – whatever that oxymoron means – at the National Geographic Society but would not appear to be a mountaineer. If this is the case then it is significant, as a more general approach to the subject is a refreshing change to the somewhat tunnel-visioned 'we went to climb' emphasis of some mountaineering writers. This presentation works, especially if you haven't got the time or inclination to read over 600 source works. It's a compelling subject and Davis recounts the story with lucidity, adding his choice of tailoring to an already well-fleshed skeleton but the validity of his selection of clothing and material is open to question and I don't feel that he really understands the climber's psyche.

Thus, the main strength of this book is also its major weakness; the author succeeds in drawing together an array of opinions from the works of a multitude of other writers but in so-doing, perhaps inevitably in such a comprehensive overview, is compromised by the generalisations and interpretations of a layman. A good example is to be found on page 77 where a history of the dangers of climbing to increasing altitude is presented. The author claims that *pure nitrogen is highly toxic* which, if true, would be the death of us all given that some 80% of the air that we breathe is nitrogen, an inert gas rather than a poisonous one. Another such mistake occurs in the description of Shackleton's 1914–16 Antarctic expedition when the author states that the epic voyage from Elephant Island to South Georgia was made *in an open dory* (p.129). In fact, the 'James Caird' was decked over with timber and canvas prior to the journey and had a substantial keel rather than the flat bottom of a dory. How did errors such as this – and there are plenty of others – slip through the publishing net?

I was exasperated at the outset by the lack of specific references for the many quotations used in the text. Source material is thus not accurately identified, an unforgivable omission in a supposedly all-seeing work such as this. Then, early in the book, I came across such an example of unenlightened misrepresentation and downright error that I subsequently looked upon all of the author's findings with suspicion – but more of this later. The book opens on Great Gable in the Lake District as some eighty people assembled in the rain to dedicate a bronze plaque to the memory of those FRCC members who had sacrificed their lives in the Great War. It was 8 June 1924 and, poignantly, the very day that George Mallory and Sandy Irvine made their Everest summit attempt. Thus are drawn together the three strands of the hawser – the War, the people who loved the hills and the British quest for the Everest grail – that runs through the first two decades of the twentieth century and through this book. The appalling facts of World War 1 are described with feeling and craft; there is no letup in the shocking bombardment of horror and the roles played in the various campaigns by survivors such as Geoffrey Winthrop Young, Arthur Wakefield and Howard Somervell. It's an engrossing backdrop and the annotated bibliography at the end of the book provides more interesting information and source material. The three Everest expeditions of the 1920s involved 26 men and, as each is introduced, his wartime experiences are detailed with similar precision. It's fascinating stuff, as is the comprehensive history of the British interest in climbing Everest which grew out of the Great Trigonometric Survey of India; from the machinations of the Empire builders to the surveyors, diplomats and early Himalayan explorers. All too often do expedition accounts give just cursory mention to the culture, religions and politics of the country; not in this book where such background is fully detailed. Negotiation with the Tibetan authorities, wary of British expansionist intentions, about access to Everest from the north, hung on a knife-edge. Then, in 1919, a Charles Howard-Bury volunteered to travel to India and Tibet with the intention of obtaining permission to approach Everest at a time when his own estate in Ireland *at the time convulsed in upheaval and revolution* (p. 108) was threatened. The author gives a very full and fair account of this man when he might have been tempted to assume that he was just another over-privileged upper-class toff but was, in fact, *the recipient of every medal of valour save the Victoria Cross* (p. 101). Similarly, Davis has been entirely fair to Alexander Kellas, fully outlining his outstanding scientific and Himalayan record.

The efforts of Howard-Bury paid off and he was invited by the Mount Everest Committee to lead the 1921 Reconnaissance Expedition, which included Kellas, and of which the SMC's Harold Raeburn was selected as the climbing leader, a choice which Davis describes (p.130) as *the deeply flawed selection of an irascible Scot*. He states that Raeburn was:

> a keen birder and at fifty-six he was, as Mallory would describe him, a 'crabbed and crusty old man' well past his prime. A serious fall on a Scottish face had robbed him of courage and nerve. He suffered constant abdominal pain, most likely from an undiagnosed gastric or duodenal ulcer. His temperament was dictatorial and defensive, utterly bereft of humour, incapable of calm. In the end he would survive the first Everest expedition but the effort would drive him mad. A broken man, certain in his delusions that he had been a murderer responsible for the fate of Kellas. Raeburn would himself fade into delirium and pass away at the age of 61 in 1926.

Most of this is absolutely without foundation or is exaggerated misinterpretation of half-truths. Raeburn, whilst a keen ornithologist in his youth was a well-educated Edinburgh brewer by trade and it seems rather offhand to describe him as a 'birder'. It is true that he had a serious accident in 1910 but an examination of his subsequent climbing record, for example his outstanding first winter ascent of *Observatory Ridge* on Ben Nevis in 1920, reveals a man with abundant courage and nerve and clearly capable of calm. His medical records make no mention of constant abdominal pain and how the medically unqualified Davis can suggest his diagnosis is ridiculous. Significantly, Davis has failed to study any SMC Journals (he similarly failed to locate Howard-Bury's Everest diary) in which he would have found Raeburn's own articles and where he would have discovered his subject most certainly to have had a sense of humour. This first expedition was only ever intended as a reconnaissance and Raeburn was chosen, despite his age, for his great experience and route-finding expertise. His failure to knit with the other team members was largely due to a clash of cultures, up-bringing and the fact that he had not been a serving member of the military. I take great exception to the concept of 'a broken man … driven mad'. Upon his return from Everest and greatly disappointed by the turn of personal events Raeburn suffered from severe delusional depression – something that could conceivably affect any one of us – and one might expect a token of enlightened sympathy from Davis, who claims (p. 582) that his *goal from the start was to learn as much as possible about the lives of all twenty-six men who went to Everest*. Well, he undoubtedly failed with Harold Raeburn even going so far as to make the claim that he *had been diagnosed as clinically mad* (p. 398) when no such psychiatric diagnosis was ever made nor ever would be. Davis appears to have similar issues with John Buchan, another SMC member, who had headed the Department of Information during the war and whose role was, basically, to manipulate propaganda in the press. But to claim (p. 109) that *one senses the hand of John Buchan at work, spinning the story … toward the embrace of a climbing expedition that would become the ultimate gesture of imperial redemption* is entirely the author's unfounded speculation.

Such inconsistency must surely be due to the sheer scale of the task that Davis has set himself, just like those tough pioneers attempting Everest from the north. After the 1921 expedition, perhaps in some respects the most interesting one to read about, we are on more familiar ground with the actual mountaineering attempts of 1922 and 1924 and the inevitable speculation about Mallory and Irvine. Could Odell possibly have sighted them surmounting the Third Step?

And has Davis succeeded in his attempt? In my opinion it's a good read but he's fallen short.

Mike Jacob

Skye Scrambles: D. Noel Williams. (SMT, 2nd Ed, 2011, 400pp, ISBN 978-0-907521-99-0, £25.)

This already excellent book, first published in 2000, has now been expanded and updated in a handsome new edition in keeping with our current series of climbing guides. Its full title is 'Scrambles, Easy Climbs and Walks on the Isle of Skye' and it includes rock-climbs of up to Very Difficult standard and, at the other end of the scale, a number of straightforward but interesting walks. In between is the main subject-matter, the real scrambles where hill-walking and rock-climbing merge to become mountaineering, for which Skye offers such unlimited scope. As the author freely admits, these are not easily classified but a logical, three-tier grading system is used for the scrambling routes, while a three-star system for quality is applied to all the outings.

Immediately obvious is the increased bulk of the book, although it is still a convenient size and not unreasonably heavy. It is a mine of information put together from the author's outstanding knowledge of the island, both within and outwith the Cuillin. The number of routes selected has been increased by about a third and the description of the Main Ridge traverse has been expanded. The other striking improvement is in the diagrams, which are now colour-shaded for added clarity with very pleasing results, as well as being more numerous.

There are informative sections on geology, history and wildlife, some of which have been re-written and the plant illustrations have also been brought to life with the addition of colour. The photographs, most of which are by the author, are inspirational and well selected to convey the character and variety of the expeditions described. I have never been too keen on the practice of adding the name of the climber – or in this case the scrambler or walker – to the captions in what are after all guide-books, not journals, especially where the figure is just a dot in the distance; but it does add a bit of human interest.

For days when the hills are shrouded, or just for a change from the Black Cuillin, there are plenty of worthwhile outings in other parts of Skye including some fine coastal walks. There is something here for everyone and for all weathers except the worst, when one can still take pleasure in browsing through the pages and dreaming of better days. This is quite simply one of the best guide-books the SMC have produced and no-one heading for Skye should be without it.

Peter MacDonald

Skye: The Cuillin: Mike Lates. (SMT, 2011, 324pp, IBSN 978-1-907233-13-5, £25.)

The new climbing guide to the Cuillin, though long-awaited, does not disappoint. Local mountain guide and Cuillin guru, Mike Lates, has blended modernity and tradition to appealing effect in a text which provides mouth-watering descriptions of newer climbs with appropriate celebration and some re-grading of grand old classics. The Main Ridge Traverse gets a detailed description at the end of the guide. The SMC's integrated colour format gives splendid reproduction of many maps, diagrams and new photographs.

Despite having climbed on Skye for 25 years myself, I read this guide and become sorely aware of my lack of knowledge of the Cuillin's myriad nooks and crannies. This book gives numerous ideas for excursions with my clients to beautiful venues at modest grades and beckons new adventures on the higher echelons of rock when we get those precious heatwaves on the island. Happily, this guide reveals as much of what is still left undone as of past achievements.

One must speculate whether Mike's guidebook will get the intensive usage it deserves. Together with many colleagues I am aware that the Cuillin are discernibly less popular than they were 20 years ago. Changing fashion and styles have by-passed these mountains. The campsites are no longer thronged at Bank Holiday weekends as once they were. True, there are still dozens of Munro-baggers and Main Ridge traversers to be seen out in fine weather, but as a rock climbing destination the Cuillin now languish as an esoteric realm. Take away the Cioch and its supporting slabs and I would guess there are rarely ever more than a handful of rock climbers out on these cliffs on a fine weekend. The growing aversion to adventure climbing counts against the Cuillin. Here you can still get spanked on old school VSs. Unprotected off-width struggles on *Petronella* (VS, 4b) recently had me more stretched than a neatly-wired E3 over in Wester Ross. Above all, the weather is the eternal deterrent. There may be more bare rock here than anywhere in the country, but what use if it is habitually wet or slimy.

Mike Lates is making worthy efforts to promote the Cuillin as a winter climbing destination. The new guide promotes Gillean's *Pinnacle Ridge* to grade IV. Much as I suspect upgrading tendencies this is a sensible call. As many of my groups have failed as have succeeded. The quality and rapid-conditioning of many Cuillin mixed climbs deserves far greater recognition. The continuing exclusion of Skye from the SMC selected Winter Climbs guide is a criminal negligence to be laid at the door of the SMC's turf-wedded erstwhile President! The routes high on Gillean and Am Basteir can be instantly rimed in a nor-wester and concede nought in quality to honeypot venues. As for that elusive winter traverse of the Main Ridge I continue to dream as old-age beckons. With this and other fond Cuillin ambitions, Mike Lates's guide will be both a beacon of hope and a consolatory companion.

Martin Moran

Skye Sea-Cliffs & Outcrops: Mark Hudson. (SMT, 2012, 336pp, ISBN 978-1-907233-14-2, £25.)

On our first trip to Skye during the school holidays we climbed in damp misty hills but also on the sea cliffs at Talisker; it was obvious there was no good climbing on the sea–cliffs of Skye.

Thanks to climbers like Noel Williams and Ed Grindley, this view has changed somewhat and Skye sea–cliffs now have a new guide. Skye gives some superb climbing away from the gabbro classics, and not just when the hill routes are unpleasant! Numerous venues have been included from the large number of dolerite cliffs to sandstone at Elgol, gneiss on neighbouring Raasay and a few granite climbs.

This guide is encyclopoedic: as well as the crag climbing and a few deep water solos, it also includes ice-climbs and lists of bouldering routes and sea stacks. It appears that even *Waterstein Arete* was repeated.

Sunny topos encourage people to get out on the cliffs, and there are plenty in this guide. I didn't know Skye was so sunny, even dank Staffin Slip is bathed in sunlight! The clean gneiss walls of Raasay also look inviting. These topos show numerous cliffs, from the lesser known crags at Neist and the mighty Rubha Hunish to some previously unpublished crags.

Like sunny topos, good action photos encourage climbers to get out, and there is a good selection, though not as sunny as the topos. I always think large photos have the biggest impact. Karen Latter's photo of *Mother's Pride* is stunning (even with the usual Elgol greenery). *Young Pretender* is another big photo that works well even though the climber doesn't seem to be climbing.

There are two styles of maps. The small scale maps are full of colour. At first glance the large scale maps appear old fashioned and lacking in colour, but they have every detail a climber needs to locate the routes, from fences to belay blocks. These should make locating routes much easier than before. Gully Walls at Bornesketaig are in the wrong place, but that is not going to ruin anyone's day.

The history section is different from the previous guides. It concentrates on routes put up by different climbers rather than working through the years. It's nice to see a new approach to history, but it would only work in areas that have a limited number of activists. Personally I would have liked to have seen how key routes were first climbed in relation to others in this guide as is usually done in the history section of guide books.

Enthusiasm shows through in this volume, but I think the star ratings have been a little generous in places compared to other parts of Scotland. People starting up three and four star routes do not expect sections of loose rock and vegetation. As a result Rubha Hunish is rapidly gaining a reputation as an overrated crag. The first pitch of *Willey's Last Stramash* (an E5 which is given three stars) used to have the line 'concentration on the limitations of the rock must be maintained throughout'; I think it is odd that this warning has been removed. Climbers intending to do the two star *Glorious Five Year Plan* at Staffin Slip will find that the ivy that was to the right of the route is now growing up it; I suspect that route has not been climbed for several years.

This is an impressive guide which many of us have been waiting for, especially impressive from an author who lives in London. I look forward to many fine days using it.

Colin Moody

Norway the Outdoor Paradise : a ski and kayak odyssey in Europe's great wilderness: James Baxter. (Scandinavian Publishing, 2012, hbk, 448pp, ISBN 978-0-9550497-1-2, £29.95.)

This is the story of James Baxter's remarkable eight and a half month journey, in which he skied the length of Norway from south to north (Norge på langs) and then kayaked back round the coastline to finish in Oslo, clocking a total distance of 6213 kilometres. Whilst many Norwegians have done the ski trip and a few have kayaked the north to south coast route, no one is known to have done the two expeditions consecutively without any break. Undoubtedly, this is one of the finest achievements by a British traveller since the days of Empire. For James this great journey was the consummation of a lifelong love affair with Norway's wilderness and her people. The expedition also had a charitable purpose in raising funds for schools in the remote Limi valley of North-West Nepal, another area which James knows and loves.

James had already produced an attractive guidebook to the 2000 metre peaks of the Hurrungane massif in the Jotunheimen under his own publishing imprint, which I regard as one of the most informative and inspiring guides I have ever used. The account of the ski-kayak journey employs similar layout, graphics and typeface, but is an altogether weightier volume, recording in detail every day of the 249 that he was on the move.

The diary narrative encourages the reader to become immersed in the vastness of the terrain. The early weeks are an exciting struggle for survival as James fights a lonely battle against huge snowfalls and maritime tempests across the southern plateaux. Once he quits the Jotunheimen massif and heads into the interior the pace and interest of the narrative flags. One senses the easy rhythm but also the tedium of a hundred days spent traversing forests and tundra plateaux, each ending in the twilit search for lodgings in remote cabins. James's freedom to travel is to be envied, but the text makes such repetition of minor problems, observations and encounters that at times you feel that you are wading with him in the snow. Yet this reflects the reality of wilderness as much as any romantic evocation. Scandinavian landscape doesn't pander to our taste for variety and excitement, and is barren, unending and oppressive as well as it is beautiful.

Throughout the journey James is helped by countless kind Norwegian folk, who provide lodgings, meals and social comfort wherever he pitches at nightfall. His narrative pauses to describe many notable events in Norway's history from the disastrous invasion of the Swedish Karoliners in the 18th century to the Nazi occupation of the Second World War. James also diverts from his daily routine to tell us a great deal about the country's geology and culture.

In the straight-laced tradition of pre-war expedition writing James is noticeably reserved about himself. There are few moments of doubt, no introspective interludes, and no hints of homesickness. His ability to delegate his business and disappear for nine months remains unexplained. How we would love to know how to pull off that trick! We only find out that he was once married to a Norwegian when his ex-mother-in-law offers accommodation near the end of the trip. This is all rather frustrating. Apart from occasional mild self-deprecation, he never adopts the detached satirical view of himself that might have been revealing, and so we end the journey little wiser about James the man.

The kayaking half of the book is distinctly more scenic, colourful and adventurous than the ski journey. Going round Nordkapp you share the commitment of crossing 20km of choppy open water of death-inducing temperature. The island paradise from Tromsø down to Trondheim is splendidly described and his travails dodging surf and skerries round the Skagerrak coast make for a gripping finale to the adventure.

The book has hundreds of photographs, many of them so beautiful that they deserved full page reproduction. There are 35 large scale maps to help the reader plot the journey's progress.

By the end you will be with James in heart and soul, and fulsome in admiration of the passion and patience which enabled him to achieve this wonderful odyssey.

We might wish that the book was a hundred pages shorter and that diary discipline had occasionally been relaxed in favour of reflective narrative, but no reader could be left unmoved by what he achieved with such modesty and willpower. Most importantly, many will be inspired to get out into the Scandinavian wilderness and explore themselves as a result of this book.

Martin Moran

Some days from a hill diary : Scotland, Iceland, Norway, 1943–50: Adam Watson. (Paragon Publishing, 2012, pbk, 131pp, ISBN 978-1-908341-48-8, £19.99.)

This is a collection of extracts from the author's diaries from 1943–50 when he was aged 12 to 20. Adam grew up in the north-east town of Turriff, and it shows how keen he was to continuously visit the hills and glens of Deeside – undaunted by the 40-mile train journey to Aberdeen and then on to Ballater or Braemar by train or bus.

The original writing has been kept, but Adam says: 'I omit great detail on wildlife. Also I leave out a few over-frequent youthful excesses such as "like the Himalaya" or "terrific" views.' You can just feel the thrill he got from his first meeting with Seton Gordon and his subsequent days on the hill with the great man.

There are interesting stories of his weekends spent at Luibeg Cottage with days out with legendary keeper, Bob Scott. It was at Luibeg that he first met SMC stalwarts Tom Weir and Allan McNicol who introduced him to the wonderful world of ski-mountaineering. The author immediately realised travelling on skis gave a whole new perspective to exploring the high tops. Also, his many hard winter days spent in the hills stood him in good stead when he later visited Iceland, Norway, Lapland and Lofoten.

What is apparent after reading this book is how much the wildlife has changed. Adam recalls seeing huge herds of deer grazing near Luibeg and Glen Derry. Nowadays, you will be lucky to see any. Entry for 30 December 1947: 'Stags grazed in Glen Lui, with lines of them on hillsides and black like ants on the glen floor, and some hinds and calves.'

The birdlife has changed also. This is a typical observation: 'On the way to the lodge we had a fine view of four golden eagles. They raised a cock capercaillie which flew over fast, and then one eagle – a big hen – flew close to us.' I don't think anyone would witness that today.

Considering that the illustrations in the book are around 60 years old they have reproduced very well. In this modern world of Gore-tex and fleeces it's interesting to look at the gear Adam and his companions are wearing – aye, in affa coorse days!

If you hanker back to the days when the hills were not a 'crammage of humanity', no Munro baggers and no mountain bikers then you will enjoy this work. But, if you are too young to have experienced the old days, you will certainly enjoy learning about them.

Derek Pyper

ERRATA

Several typos have been identified in last year's Journal.

Contents page:

Line 1. 'Stone Temple Pilots' was missing the final 's'.

Line 15. The author of 'Mike O'Hara & the Dragon of Carnmore' was
Dave Atkinson.

Page 409, photo caption:
The mountain should be 'A' Mhaighdean'.

Page 636:
The top line should read 'Office Bearers 2010–11'

Also, the article in 'SMC Abroad' on the Scottish-American Sikkim Expedition
was a repeat of the same article in the 2010 SMCJ, although this time with
pictures.

OFFICE BEARERS 20011–12

Honorary President: Iain H.M. Smart
Honorary Vice-Presidents: Neil Quinn and Bill Skidmore
President: Andrew D. Nisbet
Vice-Presidents: Colwyn M. Jones and Allen F. Fyffe

Honorary Secretary: John R.R. Fowler, 4 Doune Terrace, Edinburgh, EH3 6DY. **Honorary Treasurer:** John A. Wood, Spout Close, Millbeck, Keswick, CA12 4PS. **Honarary Membership Secretary:** Geoff Cohen, 198/1 Grange Loan, Edinburgh, EH9 2DZ. **Honorary Meets Secretary:** (Acting) John R.R. Fowler. **Honorary Editor of Journal:** D. Noel Williams, Solus Na Beinne, Happy Valley, Torlundy, Fort William, PH33 6SN. **Honorary Librarian & Honorary Archivist:** Robin N. Campbell, Glynside, Kippen Road, Fintry, Glasgow, G63 0LW. **Honorary Custodian of Slides:** David Stone, 30 Summerside Street, Edinburgh, EH6 4NU. **Honorary Reporter on Accounts:** Nigel M. Suess, 35 Woodhall Road, Edinburgh, EH13 0DT. **SMC Webmaster:** Tony Stone, 68 Avontoun Park, Linlithgow, West Lothian, EH49 6QG. **Convener of Publications Sub-Committee:** Rab Anderson, 24 Paties Road, Edinburgh, EH14 1EE. **Convener of Huts Sub-Committee:** Andrew M. James, 41 Urquhart Road, Dingwall, IV15 9PE. **Representative to the MCofS:** Brian R. Shackleton, 4A Campbell Road, Edinburgh, EH12 6DT. **Committee:** Susan L. Jensen, Neil McGougan, Heike Puchan, Bruce Kerr, John T. Orr, Robert Durran and James Edwards.

Journal Information

Editor:	Noel Williams, Solus Na Beinne, Happy Valley, Torlundy, Fort William, PH33 6SN. **e-mail** <journal@smc.org.uk>
New Routes Editor:	Andy Nisbet, 20 Craigie Avenue, Boat of Garten, PH24 3BL. **e-mail** <newroutes@smc.org.uk>
Photos Editor:	Andy Tibbs, Crown Cottage, 4 Crown Circus, Inverness, IV2 3NQ. **e-mail** <journal.photos@smc.org.uk>
Distribution:	Roger Robb, Blaven, Upper Knockbain Road, Dingwall, IV15 9NR. **e-mail** <journal.distribution@smc.org.uk>
Back Numbers:	Cliff Smith. **e-mail** <journal.archive@smc.org.uk>

INSTRUCTIONS TO CONTRIBUTORS

The Editor welcomes contributions from members and non-members alike. Priority will be given to articles relating to Scottish mountaineering. Articles should be submitted by 1 May if they are to be considered for inclusion in the Journal of the same year. Material is preferred in electronic form and should be sent by e-mail direct to the Editor. Most common file formats are acceptable – PDF, Open Document Format (odt), Rich Text Format (rtf), Plain Text (txt) or MS Word (doc/docx).

LibreOffice is an open-source, multi-platform productivity suite which is free for individuals to download from <www.libreoffice.org/download/>.

Those without access to e-mail can send hard copy (typewritten and double-spaced) by post to the Editor's home address. Illustrations not relating to an article should be sent to the Photos Editor.